NATIONALISM AND PRIVATE LAW IN EUROPE

While the internationalisation of society has stimulated the emergence of common legal frameworks to coordinate transnational social relations, private law itself is firmly rooted in national law. European integration processes have altered this state of affairs to a limited degree with a few, albeit groundbreaking, interventions that have tended to engender resistance from various actors within European nation-states.

Against that background, this book takes as its point of departure the need to understand the process of legal denationalisation within broader political frameworks. In particular it seeks to make sense of opposition to Europeanisation at this point in the evolution of European law when, despite growing nationalist attitudes, great efforts have been made to produce comprehensive legal instruments to synthesise general contract law—an area that has traditionally been solely within the ambit of nation-states.

Combining insights from the disciplines of law, history and political science, the book investigates the conceptual and cultural associations between law and the nation-state, examines the impact of nationalist ideas in modern legal thought and reveals the nationalist underpinnings of some of the arguments employed against and, somewhat paradoxically, even in support of legal Europeanisation.

Volume 45 in the series Modern Studies in European Law

Modern Studies in European Law
Recent titles in this series:

Children and the European Union: Rights, Welfare and Accountability
Helen Stalford

Federalism in the European Union
Edited by Elke Cloots, Geert De Baere and Stefan Sottiaux

Toward a Prosecutor for the European Union Volume 1: A Comparative Analysis
Edited by Katalin Ligeti

Empowerment and Disempowerment of the European Citizen
Edited by Michael Dougan, Niamh Nic Shuibhne and Eleanor Spaventa

Legal Reasoning and the European Court of Justice
Gunnar Beck

Lawyering Europe: European Law as a Transnational Social Field
Edited by Antoine Vauchez and Bruno de Witte

Services and the EU Citizen
Edited by Frank S Benyon

The Accession of the European Union to the European Convention on Human Rights
Paul Gragl

Normative Patterns and Legal Developments in the Social Dimension of the EU
Edited by Ann Numhauser-Henning and Mia Rönnmar

The European Neighbourhood Policy and the Democratic Values
of the EU: A Legal Analysis
Nariné Ghazaryan

EU Security and Justice Law: After Lisbon and Stockholm
Edited by Diego Acosta Arcarazo and Cian C Murphy

EU Environmental Law, Governance and Decision-Making
Maria Lee

Shaping the Single European Market in the Field of Foreign Direct Investment
Philip Strik

For the complete list of titles in this series, see
'Modern Studies in European Law' link at
www.hartpub.co.uk/books/series.asp

Nationalism and Private Law in Europe

Guido Comparato

•HART•
PUBLISHING
OXFORD AND PORTLAND, OREGON
2016

Published in the United Kingdom by Hart Publishing Ltd
16C Worcester Place, Oxford, OX1 2JW
Telephone: +44 (0)1865 517530
Fax: +44 (0)1865 510710
E-mail: mail@hartpub.co.uk
Website: http://www.hartpub.co.uk

Published in North America (US and Canada) by
Hart Publishing
c/o International Specialized Book Services
920 NE 58th Avenue, Suite 300
Portland, OR 97213-3786
USA
Tel: +1 503 287 3093 or toll-free: (1) 800 944 6190
Fax: +1 503 280 8832
E-mail: orders@isbs.com
Website: http://www.isbs.com

First published in hardback 2014
Paperback edition, 2016

Hart Publishing is an imprint of Bloomsbury Publishing plc.

British Library Cataloguing in Publication Data
Data Available

ISBN HB: 978-1-84946-587-8
ISBN PB: 978-1-50990-741-0

Typeset by Compuscript Ltd, Shannon
Printed and bound in Great Britain by
Lightning Source UK Ltd

Acknowledgements

This book was written in the Netherlands, Italy and Germany. More precisely, it was developed at the Centre for the Study of European Contract Law of the University of Amsterdam in the framework of a broader research project sponsored by the Hague Institute for the Internationalisation of Law and carried out by the University of Amsterdam and the University of Maastricht. It has further benefited from the inspiring environment of the Ius Commune Research School, from the research facilities of the Max Planck Institute for Comparative and International Private Law of Hamburg, as well as from useful discussions at the European University Institute of Florence.

A sincere thanks goes to all the people who contributed to this outcome with their ideas, support and observations who have accompanied me during my time in the Netherlands, ed in modo speciale alla mia famiglia.

Sicily, August 2013

Table of Contents

Table of Cases

Italy

United States of America

Table of Legislation

Hungary

Italy

Latvia

Luxembourg

Malta

Netherlands

Poland

Portugal

Prussia

Slovenia

Spain

United States of America

International

Introduction

THE DISCIPLINE REFERRED to as law, which in many countries even bears the demanding title of 'science', is for the most part ancient, renowned and widespread. Nonetheless, even in an increasingly globalised world, it remains firmly anchored in a limited territorial unit, quite often a small one on the world map; such a territorial unit is most often referred to as 'the nation'.[1] This book describes the relation between private law and the concept of the nation, portraying the scenario in which the actual situation characterised by a coincidence of private law and nation originated and describes how and in what measure this picture is undergoing a complicated modification specifically in the European context, in which plans for the Europeanisation of law are confronted with instances of resistance from different actors within the Member States. The narration of this story specifically focuses on one fundamental protagonist in this development: the ideology of nationalism.

It was the influence of nationalism—the political principle sustaining the necessity of a coincidence of nation and state[2]—that led to the nationalisation of private law—the branch of the legal system governing the relations between citizens. Furthermore, it is exactly when the political strength of nationalism was at its weakest that considerable steps were taken in the direction of de-nationalisation and, in the specific context of Europe, a Europeanisation of law. All the same, new forms of distrust toward supranational institutions and a general revival of nationalist feelings have altered the picture and our approaches to reaching an understanding of the relation between law and the nation. It has been said that the last centuries in the history of mankind would be incomprehensible without some knowledge of the idea of the nation[3] and in this sense nationalism can also contribute to shedding light on the development and perhaps possible evolution of modern legal systems. But what is, therefore, the influence of nationalism on private law? What are the implications of this relation for the further development of a private law for Europe?

[1] *See* R Zimmermann, 'Roman Law and the Harmonisation of Private Law in Europe', in A Hartkamp, MW Hesselink, EW Hondius, C Mak and E du Perron (eds), *Towards a European Civil Code. Fourth and Expanded Edition* (The Hague, Kluwer Law International, 2011) 27 ff.

[2] E Gellner, *Nations and Nationalism* (Oxford, Blackwell, 1983) 1.

[3] EJ Hobsbawm, *Nations and Nationalism since 1780* (Cambridge, Cambridge University Press, 1990) 1.

While the trends of globalisation and Europeanisation seem to alter the traditional configuration of national private law, a considerable degree of resistance to change[4] to this modification can be detected. Even an observer not familiar with the technicalities of law can easily note a tension, which had already become particularly manifest in the past with regard to various institutional issues. Indicative in this sense is the well-known history of the proposed European Constitution, as well as the never-ending arm-wrestling that opposes the Court of Justice of the European Union on the one side and the constitutional and highest courts of several Member States on the other. Away from the spotlight, the development of a European private law has also run into certain resistance. So for example, the comparatively new history of European private law has already experienced several abandoned proposals for directives and regulations that did not survive the incurable contrasts between national interests, rules issued at the European level that got 'renationalised' when Member States implemented them, and even more clearly, many a legal scholar has expressed numerous arguments to halt the process of Europeanisation. The dimension of the nation continues to dominate legal discourse and even the very debate on European private law, which one would expect to be transnational in nature, has become increasingly nationalised over the years, with several authors showing little propensity to refer to the work of foreign colleagues.[5] At the same time, law students 'are marked by a nationalism which is unknown in other sectors of higher education',[6] while legal scholars take an internal perspective[7] that contributes to making legal studies inherently national. If all this were not sufficient, in a context characterised by growing competition between legal systems, national legislators find incentives for promoting the use and 'export' of their own national rules—every so often pretentiously presented as part of a national tradition—while even the projects of Europeanisation occasionally seem to be more or less knowingly steered in a direction more in line with the national traditions of those states that managed to express the strongest influence on the decision making process, generating distrust and disillusionment among the other nations. Resistance to Europeanisation may indeed take place not only to oppose the influence of Europe on national law but also, and probably more effectively, to exercise a higher influence on European law. A non-European observer, in this sense, has received the impression of a growing rhetoric of the specificities of the national legal tradition

[4] O Lando, 'The Principles of European Contract Law and the Lex Mercatoria', in J Basedow (ed), *Private Law in the International Arena/Privatrecht in der internationalen Arena. Liber Amicorum Kurt Siehr* (The Hague, TMC Asser Press, 2000) 395.

[5] MW Hesselink, 'The New European Legal Culture—Ten Years On' (2011) *Centre for the Study of European Contract Law Working Paper*, 3; L Vacca, 'Cultura giuridica e armonizzazione del diritto europeo', in O Troiano, G Rizzielli and MN Miletti (eds), *Harmonisation Involves History? Il diritto privato europeo al vaglio della comparazione e della storia* (Milano, Giuffrè, 2004) 43.

[6] J Basedow, 'The Case for a European Contract Law', in S Grundmann and J Stuyk (eds), *An Academic Green Paper on European Contract Law* (The Hague, Kluwer Law, International, 2002) 153.

[7] MW Hesselink, *The New European Legal Culture* (Deventer, Kluwer, 2001) 14.

among European countries, which can be promoted as playing up 'the idea of a European legal tradition in order to constitute a transnational space within which, working as cosmopolitans, they have a chance of exercising more influence than would be possible in a world of dispersed national systems'.[8] On the other hand, advocates of Europeanisation may easily give in to the temptation of accusing their opponents of merely being conservative and scared of anything new or plainly nationalistic, of course implying that such nationalism is an inherently negative intellectual attitude. The significance of considering nationalism as an element possibly relevant to the processes of the internationalisation of private law emerges clearly at this point. But precisely because of the dramatic weight of that ideology in history and in contemporary societies, particular care in the use of the term is required. If one intended to use the term 'nationalist' for any argument aimed at opposing an attribution of competences at a non-national level, for sure, applying the term would amount to a truism and academic disputes could turn into a series of more or less veiled reciprocal personal attacks, and this book could come to an end now. It is, on the contrary, opportune to adopt a more objective standpoint, verifying the normative contents of the nationalist political principle and looking for its influences in legal discourse. This is indeed the aim of this book, which takes nationalism as a neutral political category, suggesting that this intensely, although not always easily noticeably, inspires the legal discourse in Europe, often taking the form of methodological nationalism.

In order to describe the development of private law in Europe and, in a way, the private law of Europe, this book looks at both the past and the present from a broader perspective. A perspective which looks at a positive legal order from the outside, instead of describing it from the inside of its more or less coherent structure, means, of course, to lose sight of the technical aspects and the mechanisms through which a jurisdiction works, but at the same time it appears the only capable means of making the political and ideological dimension of positive law come to the fore. The book therefore aims to contribute to a better understanding of the political dimension of private law and to introduce a new perspective on the on-going debate in European private law. Given the multidisciplinary nature of a study that aims to integrate the insights of political science as well as European private law within a coherent narration, clarifications will be indispensable. It is necessary to set the scene in order to address in what sense nationalism can still represent a significant ideology capable of influencing the institutional development of Europe and, thus, the evolution of a private law for Europe. A few introductory remarks on the process of Europeanisation of private law are opportune at this point.

[8] D Kennedy, 'Thoughts on Coherence, Social Values and National Tradition in Private Law', in MW Hesselink (ed), *The Politics of a European Civil Code* (The Hague, Kluwer, 2006) 30.

1.1 NATIONALISM

Although nationalism can be seen as a recent historical phenomenon, a 'doctrine invented in Europe at the beginning of the nineteenth century',[9] it has had enormous relevance in the evolution of political institutions over the past two centuries, contributing to the formation of the contemporary political consciousness and already undergoing several important transformations in that period. In general terms and provisionally, it is useful to distinguish different phases in the evolution of the phenomenon. During its first phase, from the eighteenth to the beginning of the twentieth century, nationalism was mainly a progressive movement aimed at the formation of independent and primarily democratic nation-states. This was a liberal phenomenon, which could even coexist with European ambitions,[10] while the natural division of people among different nations was considered to be essential for maintaining international peace.[11] Subsequently, once the aim of forming nation-states was achieved in most European countries, the ideology took on a conservative and occasionally aggressive connotation, inspired by the intention to promote exclusively the national interest and safeguard national homogeneity, often intended in ethnic terms. This shift very soon led to the bloody events of world conflicts. In light of those events, nationalism is mainly associated even today with chauvinism, if not directly with fascism, in the common vernacular, although those who underline the liberal aspects of that ideology correctly reject this reductive and inaccurate interpretation in particular. The role played by world conflicts—and in particular the Second World War—in the development of nationalism is, however, of pivotal importance as the world scenario has changed profoundly.

1.1.1 From Nationalism to Supranationalism

Immediately following the end of the Second World War, the awareness of the dangers inherent to nationalist ideology considerably increased. In order to reduce the likelihood of a reoccurrence of the disasters associated with this war, a limitation of the omnipotence of the nation-state was identified as a possible solution. Already from a Hegelian perspective,[12] war appears as the only way—though a particularly painful one—to settle conflicts between states when every attempt to reach an agreement has failed in a scenario characterised by the inefficiency of international sanctions. Consequently, the edification of an institutional scenario

[9] E Kedourie, *Nationalism* (New York, Frederick A Praeger Publisher, 1962) 9.

[10] The link between nationalism and Europeanism will be deepened in Chapter 4.

[11] T Schieder, *Staatensystem als Vormacht der Welt. 1848–1918* (Frankfurt am Main, Propyläen, 1977) 81.

[12] GWF Hegel, *Elements of the Philosophy of Right*, edited by A Wood and HB Nisbet (Cambridge, Cambridge University Press, 1991) 369.

in which states are legally obliged to negotiate instead of resorting to violence should chase away the eventuality of a war, creating the conditions of a Kantian perpetual peace.

It is against this background that the United Nations was created and in Europe six states initiated a whirling integration process, while the new constitutions of several European states that had just experienced the horrors of war explicitly accepted that under strict conditions, national sovereignty could be limited in favour of international organisations. In a strict positivistic perspective, these provisions did not signify the end of the idea of state sovereignty—as the limitation of powers is only possible if the state itself agrees to it—but in a broader sense they marked a considerable switch from the traditional Bodinian view of a sovereign who cannot tie his own hands. Even philosophers of law now dismantled the dogma of the omnipotence of the state by downplaying the importance of the legal notion of independence and sovereignty, a political formula unable to grasp the complexity of an international order where every state depends upon others for numerous factual reasons.[13] In more recent years, the possibility for certain international institutions to adopt a measure on the basis of a mere majority of votes instead of unanimity dealt the classical conception of sovereignty another blow, so that in the European context, Member States in the end seem to share a 'pooled sovereignty'.[14] The realist conception of international relations lost significance in favour of a new functionalist approach that underlined the growing interdependence between states—as an optimistic condition to reduce the risk of military conflicts[15]—as well as the emergence of the civil society as a distinct actor in the international arena beside the states. The revolutionary capacity of the European institutions to adopt acts that directly bind the citizens is evidence of such a trend. A theoretical cosmopolitanism and a practical internationalism seemed to have finally cured the world of its 'infantile sickness', as Albert Einstein famously characterised nationalism.[16]

But this is too partial and too sweetened a narration. Yet, today, while the institutional architecture of supranational organisations starts to show its limits, nationalism seems to have made a spectacular comeback in the international arena and in the consciousness of people.

[13] HLA Hart, *The Concept of Law* (Oxford, Clarendon Press, 1961) 215–21.

[14] RO Keohane, 'Ironies of Sovereignty: The European Union and the United States', in JHH Weiler, I Begg and J Peterson (eds), *Integration in an Expanding European Union. Reassessing the Fundamentals* (Oxford, Blackwell, 2003) 312: 'Sovereignty is pooled, in the sense that, in many areas, states' legal authority over internal and external affairs is transferred to the Community as a whole, authorizing action through procedures not involving state vetoes.'

[15] J Goodman, *Nationalism and Transnationalism. The National Conflict in Ireland and European Union Integration* (Aldershot, Avebury Press, 1996) 42.

[16] H Dukas and B Hoffman, *Albert Einstein: The Human Side* (Princeton, Princeton University Press, 1979) 38.

1.1.2 The Persistence of Nationalism

Paradoxically, although nationalism acquired a bad name after 1945, it became all the same the dominant political attitude that the 'whole of mankind has accepted'.[17] The most evident clue of such a return to nationalism is provided by a simple empirical datum: although the imminence of 'the end of the nation-state' has become a suspiciously abused *leitmotif* in the field of political science and political discourse, reality proves otherwise and the number of nation-states in the world has increased instead of diminished in the second half of the twentieth century. Even against the recurrent rhetoric on globalisation and the fading away of nations, the role of the state still continues to be central also in the global economy.[18] Particularly important in this perspective are the events linked to the Cold War.

The collapse of the Soviet Union—one of the great ideological and military world powers—determined the dissolution of one of the constrictions on an international world order whose balance had been kept frozen for years during the Cold War. Before the fall of the Soviet Union, the contrast between the two superpowers made it, on the one hand, hard for nationalist groups to claim political independence without altering the geopolitical balances and without their claims being absorbed and exploited, militarily repressed or culturally denied by one of the superpowers.[19] On the other hand, the contrast between a liberal West and a socialist East divided the world on the basis of a political criterion, overshadowing other possible distinctions not of an ideological nature and to which nationalist movements normally refer in order to build a collective identity. As soon as one of those blocks collapsed, independence movements were able to raise their voices. The disbanding of the Soviet Union indeed represented not only the decline of an ideological model but also the end of a typically multinational state, replaced by an outburst of national and regional claims. The clearest example of these dynamics is nonetheless the gory disintegration of Yugoslavia, whose history should always be kept in mind as a warning against the risks and the costs that nationalism can demand in passing from theory to practice. Aside from those macroscopic examples—together with the less dramatic case of the split of Czechoslovakia—Europe is still crossed by old and new movements, which can be considered nationalist and that normally prefer to claim a higher degree of autonomy instead of the more drastic (and often economically untenable)

[17] H Kohn, *Nationalism: Its Meaning and History* (Princeton, Van Nostrand, 1965) 89.

[18] R Gilpin, *Global Political Economy. Understanding the International Economic Order* (Princeton, Princeton University Press, 2001) 15.

[19] As retrospective introduction to a paper presented at a conference held in Bulgaria in September 1970, W Connor, *Ethnonationalism. The Quest for Understanding* (Princeton, Princeton University Press, 1994) 28 recalls that '[e]ven my very few, bland references to growing ethnic antagonisms within the Soviet Union were vehemently criticized' by the many academicians from socialist countries who were present.

solution of independence.[20] In this context, the nation-state appears once again as the most appreciated system of community organisation.

In a world scenario that has changed dramatically, even the international-oriented interpretation of national constitutions is criticised and, in order to solve the contrast between security and freedom giving more attention to the former, some claim that even constitutional rights have a merely domestic projection, so that the nation-state is bounded by its constitution only in its internal relations with its own citizens but not in international relations.[21] At the same time, from an external perspective, American commentators have exposed the alleged rhetorical character of European references to internationalism, critically pointing out that 'Europeans obey international law when it advances their interests and discard it when it does not'.[22]

Already in its formative years, the European Union was proceeding toward a federal form in its legal perspective while in the political realm it strayed progressively from that institutional model.[23] Upon closer analysis, sovereignty has not been given up but merely and partially transferred to a different level where it continues to be exercised by the nation-state in accordance with other Member States on the basis of a voluntary act. Thus the notion of pooled sovereignty 'seems to miss important features of the EU as a multi-level system of governance, namely that sovereignty resides at various levels including the supranational level', and indeed 'it makes a difference whether states transfer legal authority to the supranational level, and thus accept the jurisdiction of an external authority in their internal order, or whether they jointly exercise sovereignty accepting that they may be overruled by majority decisions'.[24] In the end, nation-states remain the 'masters of the treaties',[25] even entitled to step out of those treaties if they wanted to.[26]

Nevertheless, the exercise of sovereignty at the European level is much more complicated than it is at the national level, since a compromise is required between different members who may exhibit diverging national interests. This situation brings about tensions within the European Union as well as between the European Union and the nation-states jealousy anchored to their national

[20] A Melucci and M Diani, *Nazioni senza stato. I movimenti etnico-nazionali in Occidente* (Milano, Feltrinelli, 1992) 120–21.

[21] *See* N Feldman, 'When Judges Make Foreign Policy', *The New York Times*, 25 September 2008.

[22] J Goldsmith and E Posner, 'Does Europe Believe in International Law?', *The Wall Street Journal*, 25 November 2008.

[23] JHH Weiler, 'The Transformation of Europe' (1991) 100 *The Yale Law Journal* 2403–83, 2410.

[24] T Risse, 'Sovereignty Puzzles: A Comment on Keohane', in JHH Weiler, I Begg and J Peterson (eds), *Integration in an Expanding European Union. Reassessing the Fundamentals* (Oxford, Blackwell, 2003) 335–36.

[25] German Constitutional Court, Maastricht [1993] BVerfGE 89, 155.

[26] The Treaty of Lisbon, just like the proposed European Constitution, explicitly contains an 'exit clause', probably adopted in order to break some resistance from the Member States, although a right to abandon the Union already existed.

competences.[27] In a broader perspective, such tension could even be linked to the more general contrast between the trends of globalisation on the one hand and the growing national consciousness of modern communities that, put into contact with different economic and social organisational models, rediscover (or re-invent) their own institutions, values and traditions on the other hand. These dynamics are inexorably patent in times of economic and political crisis. The cracks in the European building—often initially created by those who feared the making of a building much more imposing than the 'edifice' of the nation-states—become more evident, leaving margins for new forms of interstate cooperation to develop outside the supranational institutions and feeding a sense of disbelief among populations who, as a result, cling to their revitalised national identities.

Against this background, many decades after the presumed historical defeat of nationalism, these observations lead us to reconsider that ideology in order to understand better the dynamics of the process of Europeanisation. As discouraging as it can be, the starting point should be that the European Union, at least in practice, does not appear as a simple and reassuring expression of post-nationalism, but '[r]ather it is a context, or theatre for another form of nationalism, or, advancing national interests by other means, filtered through and enacted by political, diplomatic and bureaucratic representatives of national populations in multilateral arrangements'.[28]

1.2 PRIVATE LAW IN EUROPE

The establishment of the European Communities, followed by the European Union, has been of pivotal importance for the development of private law in Europe. As a matter of fact, some of the most important innovations in the legal systems of European countries have been adopted under supranational obligations. In this sense, although the current state of private law remains primarily national, there are trends that point to a gradual alteration of this situation in Europe. A considerable and highly important corpus of private law rules has been created at a non-national level and the European institutions continue elaborating new projects for legal harmonisation. Over the years, an extensive series of regulations and directives in the field of private law have been enacted with the declared aim of removing the major obstacles to the establishment of a well-functioning common market. This corpus of rules—usually referred to by the French expression *acquis communautaire*—has contributed to the edification of a branch of the legal order that was new for numerous Member States, consumer law, and the establishment of a new field of investigation in academia, European private law.

[27] J Schwarz, *Der Aufbau Europas. Pläne und Dokumente 1945–1980* (Bonn, Osang, 1980) 39.

[28] S Wood, *Germany, Europe and the Persistence of Nations. Transformation, Interests and Identity, 1989–1996* (Aldershot, Ashgate, 1998) 2.

1.2.1 The *Acquis Communautaire*

Despite the heterogeneous nature of regulated topics, European directives have certain common characteristics, such as their 'pointillistic'[29] nature. Since the regulatory competences of the Union are limited to a number of areas as to which powers have been conferred by the Member States, directives only address some specific issues which can represent a relevant hindrance—as later specified by the Court of Justice[30]—for the proper functioning of the common market, surrendering to a systematically incoherent regulation. Directives are characterised therefore by an economic functionalist approach: their fundamental aim is the establishment of the common market and other objectives appear as subordinate to the former. The policy aim of consumer protection, for instance, has long been considered only as an instrument necessary to the market, so that the consumer has been chiefly intended just as an economic actor. Over the years through a series of new treaties, the European communities have moved toward a political unit which has resulted in the extension of their competence, but despite these institutional developments the approach of the directives has remained chiefly functionalist, which has once again led to fierce criticism from those more interested in the consideration of further dimensions in contract law such as social justice.[31]

The imprecise and sketchy nature of the first directives led to several interpretative problems, while their spare content, interwoven with the characteristics of the single Member States, resulted in new diversities in contrast to the original aim of bringing about convergence in those areas.[32] The nature of the directives has therefore undergone a gradual but evident change over the years. Both the number and the length have notably increased ever since the first directives were published in the eighties, while the later examples, adopted under a majority rule, have become more and more detailed and accurate. The consequence of this development is that the Member States' leeway—that are still requested to implement the directive and 'translate' it into their legal orders—is diminished. At the same time, while scholars complained about the unsystematic approach of EU private law directives, the European institutions kept producing a highly significant number of directives and regulations in particular sectorial fields. Even without the primary aim of harmonising private law, these have had, on the contrary, a strong impact on the regulation of economic relations between citizens, contributing to the edification of an autonomous European private law to a much

[29] H Kötz, 'Rechtsvereinheitlichung—Nutzen, Kosten, Methoden, Ziele' (1986) 50 *Rabels Zeitschrift für ausländisches und internationales Privatrecht 1–7*, 5; WH Roth, 'Transposing "Pointilist" EC Guidelines into Systematic National Codes—Problems and Consequences' (2002) 6 *European Review of Private Law* 761–76.

[30] Court of Justice, Tobacco, C-380/03.

[31] Study Group on Social Justice in European Private Law, 'Social Justice in European Contract Law: A Manifesto' (2004) 10 *European Law Journal*, 653–74.

[32] G Teubner, 'Legal Irritants: Good Faith in British Law or How Unifying Law Ends up in New Divergences' (1998) 61 *The Modern Law Review* 11–32.

larger extent than a first look at the differences between the traditional systems of private law as embodied in civil codes and common law typically reveals.[33]

1.2.2 Plans for Further Europeanisation

Several solutions have been envisaged by the European institutions to foster an economic integration, which at times appears to be jeopardised by legal diversity as well as coping with the technical problems linked to the pointillist approach to harmonisation. Intuitively, the more logical solution in this sense would be to move from a simple harmonisation to a more radical unification of private law in Europe, perhaps by means of a mandatory instrument like a code. The European Parliament first proposed the idea in two resolutions in 1989 and 1994. The European Commission had initially been at least willing to discuss this possibility. In order to investigate the needs and opinions of stakeholders, the European Commission started up a series of consultations to determine the best way to cope with the problems posed by the fragmented harmonisation of contract law in 2001. In a famous communication[34] the Commission presented four options to the stakeholders. The first option consisted of a simple inactivity of the European institutions: the market would have taken care to solve possible problems automatically. In the second place, the elaboration of common contract law principles that would have in the end led to a convergence of legislation could have been promoted. The third option consisted in an improvement of the quality of the *acquis communautaire*, while the last and most controversial option presented consisted in the elaboration of a new European instrument containing both general and specific rules on contracts that could have been adopted as a mandatory or an optional instrument. It emerged from the responses that, while the laissez-faire option gained little support, particular interest existed in support of the second and the third option. The need for a new instrument—in particular a mandatory one—was not felt to be particularly compelling by the respondents.

On the basis of these results, the Commission outlined an action plan for improving the 'coherence of European contract law' in a new communication of 2003, in which the instrument that would achieve the objectives laid down in options three and four of the previous communication was chiefly identified in a 'Common Frame of Reference' (CFR). Such an instrument, with its aim of 'establishing common principles and terminology in the area of European contract law',[35] would have different functions. It could serve as a 'tool-box' for the European legislator, that could refer to the principles and terminology of that

[33] *See* H-W Micklitz, 'The Visible Hand of European Regulatory Private Law. The Transformation of European Private Law from Autonomy to Functionalism in Competition and Regulation' (2009) 28 *Yearbook of European Law* 3–60.

[34] COM(2001) 398 final.

[35] COM(2003) 68 final, 59.

instrument to achieve a higher coherence while improving the *acquis*, but it could also be employed by national legislators to revise their own legislations, so that in the end, a convergence between the different systems would be facilitated and, again, be used by the European Commission as a base for 'reflections' on the convenience of elaborating a new optional instrument.[36] The nature and objectives of the CFR were then deepened in a further communication of 2004, in which it was clearly stated that 'The CFR will provide clear definitions of legal terms, fundamental principles and coherent model rules of contract law, drawing on the EC *acquis* and on best solutions found in Member States' legal orders'.[37] In that communication, the Commission furthermore continued to express its own interest in the possibility of developing an optional instrument in the future[38] and even sketched a possible structure for the CFR, which already resembles one of a code.[39]

In 2006, another Green Paper[40] initiated a new consultation amongst stakeholders. The Commission drew new directions for the development of consumer law from the new consultations focusing more on the harmonisation of specific aspects of contract law that could represent a barrier to trade and favourably considering the possibility of 'full harmonisation'; in other words, issuing rules Member States could not derogate from even in order to increase the level of protection acknowledged to consumers. The troubled work on a new directive on consumer rights was the first result of this new course. Against this background, the hypothesis of a European civil code to be elaborated starting from the CFR faded out, as the Commission also later clarified.[41]

In the meantime, the academic lawyers in charge of the preparation of a draft CFR, associated with the Study Group on a European Civil Code and the Research Group on EC Private Law, completed their activities and published their results—the Draft Common Frame of Reference (DCFR)—together with comments on the drafted model rules in a definitive edition that appeared in 2009.[42] The work does not represent a creation *ex nihilo* but draws on the legal traditions of the Member States represented in study groups and, what is more, is clearly based on the previous works performed by the Commission on European Contract Law, best known as the Lando Commission after the name of its chairman Professor Ole Lando, established in 1982 with the aim of drafting a set of principle of contract law common to all European Member States (PECL).[43] That initiative—financed

[36] COM(2003) 68 final, 62.

[37] COM(2004) 651 final, 2.1.1.

[38] COM(2004) 651 final, 2.3.

[39] COM(2004) 651 final, Annex I.

[40] COM(2006) 744 final.

[41] COM(2007) 447 final, 11.

[42] C Von Bar, E Clive, H Schulte-Nölke et al (eds), *Principles, Definitions and Model rules of European Private Law. Draft Common Frame of Reference* (DCFR) (Munich, Sellier, 2009).

[43] O Lando and H Beale, *Principles of European Contract Law. Pt I and II. Combined and Revised* (The Hague, Kluwer Law International, 2000); O Lando and H Beale, *Principles of European Contract Law. Pt III. Combined and Revised* (The Hague, Kluwer Law International, 2003).

by the European institutions but born as a spontaneous academic endeavour—had also the aim of providing a set of model rules of *lex mercatoria* that could be used by contractual parties in their international agreements.

The year after the final edition of the DCFR was published, the European Commission created a new Expert Group of European contract lawyers with the aim 'to assist the Commission in the preparation of a proposal for a Common Frame of Reference in the area of European contract law, including consumer and business contract law'[44] as well as 'restructuring, revising and supplementing the selected contents of the Draft Common Frame of Reference, taking also into consideration other research work conducted in this area as well as the Union *acquis*'.[45] In other terms, this should have opened the transition process from the academic to the political Common Frame of Reference.

Later that year, the Commission published a new Green paper 'to launch a public consultation to gather orientations and views from relevant stakeholders regarding possible policy options in the field of European Contract Law'[46] and in which new possible strategies for the harmonisation of contract laws were outlined. Once again, the Commission presented and left several options open: the work of the Expert Group could simply be published and informally serve as a source of inspiration for legislators or as a compendium useful to promoting the knowledge of contract law, something that, again, could produce a spontaneous convergence in the long run. As a more incisive option based on the results of that study, the European institutions could issue an 'instrument of European Contract Law', the scope and purposes of which remain quite unclear, while various options are presented. For instance, a recommendation of the Commission to the Member States could be issued whereby the adoption of the 'instrument' is suggested in addition or even as a replacement of national laws. This would signify the voluntary adoption of an optional or mandatory European civil code in some Member States, while the Commission also alluded to the possibility of issuing such a code as an optional instrument that contractual parties would be free to adopt both in cross-border and domestic transactions. Again, the options presented became more audacious and the possibility of a unification by means of a regulation covering general contract law or even a European civil code covering 'not only contract law, including specific types of contracts, but also tort law, unjustified enrichment and the benevolent intervention in another's affairs'[47] is explicitly envisaged by the Commission.[48] Nonetheless, it is the idea of an optional instrument of sales law that later gained momentum, so that the Commission presented a proposal for a regulation that would allow not only consumers but also small

[44] Commission Decision of 26 April 2010 setting up the Expert Group on a Common Frame of Reference in the area of European Contract Law, 2010/233/EU, art 2.

[45] Commission Decision of 26 April 2010 setting up the Expert Group on a Common Frame of Reference in the area of European Contract Law, 2010/233/EU, art 2(b).

[46] COM(2010) 348 final, 5.

[47] COM(2010) 348 final, 4.3.4.

[48] COM(2010) 348 final, 4.1.

businesses to opt for a fully European set of rules to govern their transborder economic transactions.[49] The process of Europeanisation of private law, in other terms, is still underway and arguably still far from its conclusion.

1.3 METHODOLOGY

1.3.1 Descriptive Character

This book aims to highlight the theoretical relation between private law and the phenomenon of nationalism and, consequently, one aspect of the ideological and political dimension of the European private law. In doing so, it is only concerned with a description—or at least an interpretation of—an existing situation, without any intention of evaluating it in light of particular normative standards or recommending modalities in which the process of Europeanisation should be continued or arrested. In other words, the analysis performed here is of a descriptive rather than normative nature. Admittedly, that descriptive–normative distinction which can be formulated in clear-cut terms in the rational world of theory eventually tends to fade away when applied to the complexity of reality, and this holds particularly true for this book, in which descriptive and normative elements could easily merge, given the political nature of the processes investigated. This makes some preliminary remarks on certain particular aspects even more compelling.

As already mentioned, since the end of the world wars, the term 'nationalism' has assumed a negative connotation which is even more perceivable in certain languages than in others[50] and has come to be intended as a reactionary idea linked to militarism and xenophobia. If one starts from this understanding, speaking of nationalism in European private law could immediately sound confrontational and implicitly normative. If it were claimed that nationalist elements can be found in the European private law discourse, the soundest logical conclusion that one could draw is that these elements should be eliminated, and if nationalism were to be found as one of the reasons justifying resistance to Europeanisation, an implicit counter-argument in favour of Europeanisation would naturally follow. This is not the point made in this book.

In the first place, the very idea that nationalism is a negative theory per se can be disputed: in recent years many attempts have been made to view it as a politically neutral category to be employed in the analysis of historical and political events. In this sense, this book too accepts nationalism as a legitimate political model. The whole first chapter is therefore dedicated to the deepening of the

[49] COM(2011) 636 final.

[50] It is bound to a particularly negative and 'militaristic' understanding in particular in some Slavic languages, M Hroch, *Das Europa der Nationen. Die moderne Nationsbildung im europäischen Vergleich* (Göttingen, Vandenhoeck & Ruprecht, 2005) 13.

tricky concept of nationalism mainly as a political principle. It can already be said that the coincidence of nationalism and militarism or racial intolerance can be rejected at least in theory. Nationalism turns out to be a legitimate political set of ideas that cannot be simplistically and unfairly equated *tout court* with some of its dramatic historical manifestations, whose link and coherence with the ideology cannot however be ignored. Consequently, even the affirmation that arguments employed in the discourse on European private law show contiguity with nationalist ideas should not be considered per se evidence of the insufficiency and censurability of those argumentations. Those might be unconvincing, disputable or incoherent, but in any case they cannot be deemed *wrong*. It goes without saying the reader is more than able to make up his or her own mind, judging how persuasive those arguments are—reproving or accepting them—but such a conclusion is a further step that the author of this book has deliberately chosen not to take.

The reader could however get the impression that, at several moments, the book he or she is reading tends to abandon a neutral standpoint, putting more emphasis on the limits of nationalism and the fallacies of the argumentations that are presented as connected to that ideology. These are indeed presented in a critical manner with various objections proposed, particularly in the first and third chapters. This operation is not aimed at throwing discredit on the nationalist political principle, neither at surreptitiously suggesting that supranationalism or cosmopolitanism are necessarily preferable models, but is necessary as only through this methodological process can the peculiarities of the nationalist arguments, as opposed to those of other political theories, emerge. Only towards the end does the book utilise some of the results of the previous parts to assess possible evolutions of the process of the Europeanisation of private law.

1.3.2 European Union as Multinational and Multi-level System

A large part of this book, and more specifically of the third chapter, is dedicated to an analysis of some of the arguments that have been employed by legal scholars to object to the process of (or at least, a particular kind of) Europeanisation of national private laws in light of the theories developed in the political and economic science concerning the role of nationality in political institutions. These arguments have been developed and employed in very different social sciences and at a first sight they seem to be functionally very different from one another, so that such an association can be methodologically challenging. For this reason, it seems opportune to address this issue in this chapter.

As an example, take the arguments employed in the economic theory of federalism and later in law and economics, sustaining that the decisional power in a multi-layer system should be allocated at the lowest possible governance level.[51] These serve to determine whether a certain competence should be assigned at the

[51] This will be discussed further in Chapter 3.

federal or at the local level of the governance system, but in any case, within an already formed and functioning federal state, regardless of whether this is also a nation or a multinational state. In this sense, those arguments are different from a structurally similar argument made by liberal nationalists to advocate a world order in which a state corresponds to each nation. Also, liberal nationalists claim that the closer the regulatory power is to the citizen, the more democratic and efficient will be the regulation, but from their perspective the point only serves the purpose of demonstrating that a smaller homogeneous nation-state is a better form of political organisation than a larger multinational state. The perspective of liberal nationalists is therefore broader, since instead of inquiring what the perfect division of competences among the institutions of a given nation-state is, they devote themselves to the preliminary question as to why these competences have to be acknowledged to a nation-state instead of a multinational state in the first place. Is it therefore methodologically correct to affirm that both law and economics scholars and liberal nationalists base their assumptions on the same argument?

Despite these differences, there is nonetheless a link between these two approaches that emerges if one considers that, among the various theories of federalism, it has been suggested that one of the necessary elements for different states to give rise to a political federation is that a 'community of outlook based on race, religion, language or culture'[52] exists. In other words, even the federal state can only function if it is also, somehow, a nation. This view has gained momentum and is now commonly supported by public law scholars, who point out how some kind of 'cultural similarity' among citizens is needed in order for a federation to properly function.[53] Yet, this is still insufficient to affirm that a federalist theory necessarily presupposes a nationalist organisation of the state. It should be noticed that although political scientists have enumerated a long list of essential conditions in order to speak of a political federation, it is commonly agreed that none of these conditions is really indispensable or of universal application, as a simple empirical analysis of the existing federalist states can reveal.[54] What is more, federal structures could also be imagined as political compromises with the aim of making state unity possible in the presence of particular ethno-nationalistic groups advancing autonomy or independence claims, thus

[52] RL Watts, *New Federations: Experiments in the Commonwealth* (Oxford, Oxford University Press, 1966) 42.

[53] E McWhinney, 'Re-thinking Federal Constitutional Law Theory: The Contemporary Limits of Classical, Juridical Federalism', in *Toward Comparative Law in the 21st Century. The 50th Anniversary of the Institute of Comparative Law in Japan* (Tokyo, Chuo University Press, 1998) 495: 'The classical federal system based on a juridical equality of the constituent units of the federal system without regard to their political–social differences in terms of population, territory and resources, adapts with extreme difficulty to any society characterised by fundamental cultural, linguistic religious or other similar divisions. The classical federal system seems most viable, as a paradigm or model, for culturally more or less homogeneous societies where the differences referred to can be more easily accommodated through the basic federal institutions and processes'.

[54] D McKay, *Federalism and the European Union* (Oxford, Oxford University Press, 1999) 24.

already in a multinational state.[55] However, the picture is made unclear by the vagueness implicit in a definition of nation; while some political proponents of federalist reforms tend to emphasise the lack of national homogeneity of their states, others underline that even apparently very inhomogeneous federalist states—like those where two or three languages are spoken—nonetheless share some common traits which permit those institutions to qualify as nation-states.

The two approaches come to an even clearer convergence in the context of the European Union. It is widely held that the European Union presents both traits of a state and of an international organisation. Such a hybrid nature makes possible that many of the arguments used in a federal perspective can also be employed in a nationalist one. Although the European Union can be better described as a supranational[56] rather than a federal form of organisation, the peculiarity that competences can be allocated at two different levels justifies a functional comparison with an ordinary federal organisation. Being normally less formalistic than legal scholars, political scientists can simplify the discussion: 'although, after the implementation of Maastricht, the EU remains an unusual and still evolving political entity, it also qualifies as a species of federal state'.[57]

In this sense, both the arguments developed with regard to the distribution of competences within a federal state and the arguments employed by nationalists to defend the nationalistic principle can be related and are both employable in the European scenario.

1.3.3 Considered Countries

The title of this book calls for a preliminary clarification. Since each European country has one (and often more than one) private law system that would deserve a specific account, it is unclear what 'private law in Europe' stands for. If this were not sufficient, not only private laws diverge in Europe, but also even the historical developments associated with both the creation of the nation-state and the organisation of the legal system are rather diverse. Even slight differences in the connotation of the word 'nation' in different languages reveal different historical paths. In this sense, clarification is needed as to which specific national context we refer to when speaking of nationalism.

The most accurate way to deal with these differences would consist in treating each European country separately, following its historical development, analysing its legal order with particular regard to its interactions with the law of the European Union, and, of course, looking at the academic debate in the leading

[55] On this aspect, *see* MG Forsyth (ed), *Federalism and Nationalism* (Leicester, Leicester University Press, 1985).

[56] R Keohane and S Hoffman, 'Ironies of Sovereignty: The European Union and the United States' (n14), 12 ff.

[57] D McKay, *Federalism and the European Union* (n 54), 21.

legal journals of the country. Performing such highly demanding research is well beyond the possibilities and the aims of this book;[58] more modestly—but at the same time probably more ambitiously—the aim here is rather to sketch general trends in the European context. In this sense, this analysis does not deal with the private laws of Europe, but rather with private law in Europe. Thus, the book adopts a broad approach which is more typical of an intellectual history focussing on the diffusion of a certain idea rather than a monographic study providing an exclusive account of a given country or jurisdiction. It therefore offers a more comprehensive account of the developments that took and take place in Europe, whose specific manifestations usually differ in various national contexts but still appear as interrelated components of a more general narration involving Europe. This does not mean that the discourse remains on an ideal and abstract 'nowhere' dimension; quite on the contrary, the book systematically refers to the laws of a number of European countries, chosen on the basis of the significance of their legal experience and the availability of information.

As a final but essential clarification, it is also opportune to warn the reader that all considerations contained in this book refer to the European experience and cannot therefore be extended straightforwardly to other social and political contexts that can show differences under several points of view.

1.4 STRUCTURE AND TOPICS

The chronicle of the transformation of private law under nationalism and through Europeanisation evolves through different stages. One chapter is focused on each of these changes. The first chapter introduces and offers a theoretical portrayal of the individuated main 'protagonist' of this narration, the nationalist ideology. There, the phenomenon will be defined, contextualised in its empirical manifestations and analysed in its theoretical foundations as they have been described in that branch of the political science known as nationalism studies. In the same chapter, the fundamental assumptions and political claims of that ideology are presented, discussed, and, at the same time, some of the recurring criticisms of them are also introduced, in order to provide the analytical tools necessary to detect and discuss the core elements of nationalism even in the field of law in a later moment, chiefly in the third chapter. Only in a purely historical

[58] Furthermore, some studies addressing the (in a broad sense) nationalist tendencies of legal scholarship in certain countries already exist: *see* R Sefton-Green, 'DCFR, the Avant-projet Catala and French Legal Scholars: A Story of Cat and Mouse?' (2008) 12 *Edinburgh Law Review* 351–73; C Amodio, 'Nell'occhio del ciclone. La Francia alla prova dei processi di denazionalizzazione del diritto' (2009) 40 *Politica del diritto* 605–38. More specifically, *see* the contributions in the special issue of the *European Review of Contract Law* vol 8 of 2012, in particular R Michaels, 'Code vs Code. Nationalist and Internationalist Images of the Code Civil in the French Reistance to a European Codification' (2012) 8 *European Review of Contract Law* 277–95; R Sefton-Green, 'French and English Crypto-nationalism and European Private Law. An Exercise in Sentiment and Reason' (2012) 8 *European Review of Contract Law* 260–76.

description could nationalism be discussed alone, without reference to different and conflicting political principles, but in a theoretical account such juxtaposition is required. The chapter therefore broadly deals with the simple and pivotal question: *what is nationalism?*

Moving from a theoretical to a more concrete dimension, one can see that the rise of nationalism in Europe coincided with a particularly important stage in the history of private law as well. It is in this phase that the 'nationalisation of private law'[59] took place or, more correctly, was completed. Ever since that moment, political nationalism has shaped the law, shaping in a path-dependent institutional evolution the methodological nationalism that characterises even contemporary law. The narration and analysis of that particularly important moment in European legal and political history is set in the second chapter, which, instead of offering a new historical account of certain events, rather aims at reading known legal historical developments through the lenses offered by nationalism studies. The book intends to deal with nationalism and private law in Europe not from the viewpoint of legal history but rather from the viewpoint of the political theory of private law. A theoretical account of the function of private law as an instrument of nationalisation of societies is also provided. Progressively shifting the focus from the past to the present, the chapter addresses more recent developments of denationalisation and renationalisation of private law. In several ways, the process of denationalisation challenges the nationalist idea of law inherently linked to the nation, and it has already manifested itself in the specific form of Europeanisation. This, nonetheless, has not led to a medieval-like state of private law, and a certain resistance to this process is given by several actors at the level of the Member States, determining in practice a sort of 'renationalisation' of European law. The question addressed in this chapter is broadly summarised as *why and how is private law related to nationalism?*

The third and longest chapter investigates the reasons behind such resistance, looking in particular at the discourses of legal scholars. In investigating contemporary instances of methodological nationalism in the debate on European private law, the chapter will have to adopt an even more strongly analytical approach. Obviously, the impact of nationalism on legal orders can be investigated in a large number of institutions and actors, including legislators, courts, economic actors and so forth, but it is precisely in the scholarly debates that the link between nationalism and law becomes more clearly identifiable, and it is at those debates that the chapter will look in order to further elucidate the link between private law and nationalism as a political principle and *not* as an historical movement. The process of Europeanisation has in fact given rise to a wide and multi-disciplinary debate among lawyers, in which several critical positions have been advanced, based on different arguments. The chapter looks in particular at three of these: the

[59] H Coing, *Europäisches Privatrecht. Bd II 19. Jahrhundert: Überblick über die Entwicklung des Privatrechts in den ehemals gemeinrechtlichen Ländern* (München, Beck sche Verlagsbuchhandlung, 1989) 1–2.

economic, the social, and the cultural arguments. This choice is not arbitrary, as these are the arguments which are most frequently met in the literature any time that the possibilities of legal Europeanisation are discussed. At the same time, the chapter will highlight that these are not just 'legal' arguments but rather have direct equivalents in analogous opinions uttered in the more general political discourse. The question dealt with in this chapter is therefore *what is the influence of nationalism in the European private law discourse?*

But nationalism could also influence the evolution of private law in Europe in a very different way. It is, indeed, imaginable that this multi-faceted and unstable political principle can develop in Europe as a pan-nationalist form too, in other terms, as Euronationalism. Typically nationalist arguments can then be used not only to oppose, but also to sustain, the need to unify the laws of the European nations. The fourth chapter is dedicated to this scenario, and it deals with the question *can nationalism serve legal Europeanisation?*

A brief final chapter draws on and summarises the main points developed in the previous chapters, formulating final remarks that are conclusive within the general framework of this book but, hopefully, introductory to further reflections, remarks, and criticisms by the reader.

Chapter 1

Nationalism

THE NATURE AND content of nationalist ideology is the focus of this chapter, followed by an analysis of the impact of nationalism on the processes of nationalisation and the Europeanisation of private law. Provisionally, nationalism can be understood as the ideology, which aims 'to give the state a national foundation'.[1]

The general introduction proffered views as to how nationalism can be considered to be a very topical ideology with assumptions that exercise an influence on the development of political and legal systems, while the primary aim of this chapter is to understand what the theoretical and normative foundations of nationalism as a political principle are and to provide the analytical tools necessary to investigate further the phenomenon, rather than to expose the evolution of the nationalist phenomenon. It is therefore opportune to make clear now that the approach chosen here, as well as in the rest of the book, is theoretical, or at the most slightly historiographical, rather than historical. The vagueness and flexibility of that concept make it necessary to delimit the field of examination, by first providing a definition of nationalism.

The chapter is organised as follows: the first part deals with methodological problems with regard to the study of nationalism and pays particular attention to the juxtaposition between two analytical approaches widespread amongst members of the political science community. The second part takes a definition of nationalism as its starting point and analyses its constitutive elements, putting particular emphasis on the central concept of 'nation'. The last part specifically analyses the theoretical and normative foundations of the nationalist political principle introducing the main arguments that are employed by advocates of nationalism, mainly referring to the work of *liberal nationalist* authors, as well as the recurring criticisms of those.

1.1 APPROACHING NATIONALISM

The study of nationalism presents difficulties that have been debated by political scientists for decades. The first of these difficulties derives from the fact that

[1] J Leerssen, *National Thought in Europe: A Cultural History* (Amsterdam, Amsterdam University Press, 2006) 169.

nationalism has historically emerged in very different forms so that doubt can arise as to whether it is really possible to speak in general terms of nationalism as an ideology that covers such diverse manifestations. The second methodological tricky aspect consists of the presence of two main 'schools of thought', which can be distinguished in a study of nationalism, whose basic assumptions appear to be opposite, and to some extent, even irreconcilable. They offer different answers to the fundamental questions as to how, when and why nation-states developed. As a result of these alternatives, it is clear that the choice for one or the other of these approaches may strongly condition the way in which nationalism is intended. In the following pages the main differences and convergences between these positions will be expounded upon, since such scrutiny is necessary to examine critically some of the assumptions, and sometimes contradictions, of the nationalist theory.

1.1.1 How Many Nationalisms are There?

Nationalism is one of the most discussed concepts in the field of political science and one of the most complex and many-sided doctrines of the last decades. As Hans Kohn pointed out,

> Nationalism has been one of the determining forces in modern history [...] but [it] is not the same in all countries and at all times. It is a historical phenomenon and thus determined by the political ideas and the social structure of the various lands where it takes root.[2]

But exactly such a multiplicity of nationalist forms represents an obstacle if the ideology were to be sketched in its entirety, for 'although it may be correct to talk of *a* general theory of nationalism, nationalisms on the ground are quite different from each other'.[3] Should the aim of coming up with a general definition of nationalism be abandoned? This problem is well known to political scientists,[4] who are still wavering between two opposite solutions to the problem. If one admits that it is only possible to discuss single types of nationalism (*nationalisms* in the plural), since 'no single, universal theory of nationalism is possible',[5] it will be necessary to distinguish and focus on each of them, putting emphasis on the difference and perhaps building a bipolar system of contrasts. A discontinuity will emerge between different nationalist manifestations and the impossibility of tracing them back to a general structure. For example, if one discusses

[2] H Kohn, *Nationalism: Its Meaning and History* (Princeton, Van Nostrand, 1965) 4.

[3] TH Eriksen, *Ethnicity and Nationalism: Anthropological Perspectives* (London, Pluto Press, 2002) 115.

[4] O Dann, 'Der moderne Nationalismus als Problem historischer Entwicklungsforschung', in O Dann (ed), *Nationalismus und sozialer Wandel* (Hamburg, Hoffmann und Campe, 1978) 9.

[5] JA Hall, 'Nationalisms: Classified and Explained', in S Periwa (ed), *Notions of Nationalism* (Oxford, Oxford University Press, 1995) 8.

the German historical experience, it will be impossible to consider Nazism and German Romanticism as equal expressions of nationalism, as two sides of the same coin, since the former was a destructive *political* movement which aimed at the subjugation of other nations, whereas the latter was just a fertile *cultural* movement which occasionally contributed to the spread of a sentiment of unity in the German nation. The other approach, on the contrary, urges a focus on the common aspects of different experiences in order to find a guiding principle. One could then underline a certain continuity between Romanticism and Nazism almost as completely different manifestations of the same phenomenon,[6] stressing, for instance, the telling and frequent references to *Blut und Boden* in the speeches of both Herder and Hitler.

The choice for one of these approaches could also be influenced by ideology; in particular when it is politically convenient for a nationalist movement to distance itself from unfavourable historical antecedents, even in the substantial identity of the employed arguments or the pursued aims. Closer analysis shows that even the numerous forms of nationalism described in the literature are not always different phenomena but rather the same one considered from different macro- or micro-perspectives and sometimes seen through lenses coloured by ideology or economic considerations. Such confusion increases because, to cite the words Haas uses to refer to Anderson,[7] Gellner,[8] Seers[9] and Smith,[10] 'Authors fail to make any serious effort to acknowledge or use, leave alone integrate, the plethora of existing work on the subject'.[11] If one accepts this premise, one can more easily support the view that 'while nationalism changes with the time, place and culture, it does have characteristics that can be identified'.[12] It seems opportune to focus on those common characteristics, looking first and foremost at theory but considering the practice, without which one would not be able any more to grasp the necessary differences between nationalist manifestations and, enraptured by the systematic order of theory, lose of sight reality, because 'Fichte or Gandhi are not Bismarck; Bismarck or De Gaulle are not Hitler' and '[w]e have no right whatever to equate the nationalism of the dominant with that of the dominated, the nationalism of liberation with the nationalism of conquest'.[13]

[6] T Nairn, *Forces of Nationalism: Janus Revisited* (London, Verso, 1997).

[7] B Anderson, *Imagined Communities: Reflection on the Origin and Spread of Nationalism* [1983] (London, Verso, 2006).

[8] E Gellner, *Nations and Nationalism* (Oxford, Blackwell, 1983).

[9] D Seers, *The Political Economy of Nationalism* (Oxford, Oxford University Press, 1983).

[10] AD Smith, *Nationalism in the Twentieth Century* (New York, New York University Press, 1979).

[11] EB Haas, 'What is Nationalism and Why Should We Study It?' (1986) 40 *International Organization* 707, 714. Also M Hroch, *Das Europa der Nationen. Die moderne Nationsbildung im europäischen Vergleich* (Göttingen, Vandenhoeck & Ruprecht, 2005) 7 remarks that, 'Jeder Autor, der mehr als seine bloße Beschreibung oder Narration vorzulegen beansprucht, ist um Originalität bemüht, die jedoch meist darauf hinausläuft, dass er einen Aspekt des Problems aus dem Kontext reißt und aufbauscht oder längst geläufige Erkenntnisse auf neue Weise kombiniert'.

[12] BC Shafer, *Faces of Nationalism: New Realities and Old Myths* (New York, Harcourt Brace Jovanovich, 1972) 11.

[13] ER Balibar and IM Wallerstein, *Race, Nation, Class: Ambiguous Identities* (London, Verso, 1991) 45.

In order not to confuse different types of nationalism and avoid a situation in which the characteristics of a particular historical type are extended to the whole phenomenon,[14] another distinction should be considered. As Gellner put it, nationalism can be seen as a *sentiment* and as a *movement*[15] as well as a political principle (it could also be said, an *ideology*). In this sense, the mere fact that a particular historical form of nationalism has appeared in an authoritarian and violent way should not be considered a sufficient reason to sustain that the ideology, by which the movements are inspired, is violent in the same way. Nationalism should therefore be primarily understood as an ideology, while references to nationalist movements in this book will be made only in order to clarify some aspects of the ideologies. Adopting this view it becomes clear that, although nationalism stimulated a multiplicity of historical movements, the essential assumptions on which its ideology is based basically remain the same. In this sense, it becomes possible to speak of *a* general theory of nationalism—even at the cost of resorting eventually to a long series of further indispensable specifications and distinctions.

1.1.2 Interpreting Nationalism

Contemporary studies of nationalism have been characterised by the juxtaposition of two analytical approaches:[16] the classic 'primordialist'—which sustains an ancient nature of the nations—and the 'modernist'—which more critically believes the nation to be a modern phenomenon somehow constructed by the nationalist ideology. To simplify the juxtaposition between the two schools of thought—which in political science are also occasionally identified with different denominations[17]—one could say that the primordialist posits that nations preexist nationalism, whereas the modernist claims the opposite notion: nationalism makes nations. While the primordialist approach takes the existence of nations as an almost 'natural' reality, the modernist approach considers the nation as an artificial fact and more problematically lets further questions arise, in particular what the means of and the reasons for such an 'invention' are.

This juxtaposition can be collocated in a specific historical context: the primordialist understanding of nations which underlines the 'positive' nature of nationalism was widely spread, in particular in the era of the formation of the

[14] EB Haas, 'What is Nationalism and Why Should We Study It?' (n 11), 716 criticizes AD Smith's *Nationalism in the Twentieth Century* for '[i]t is impossible to tell whether nationalism refers to an "ideal," the actual modal beliefs of a "movement," a typical historical pattern of development, or an inescapable state of affairs, because the author uses all these meanings interchangeably'.

[15] E Gellner, *Nations and Nationalism* (n 8), 11.

[16] U Özkırımlı, *Theories of Nationalism: A Critical Introduction* (New York, Saint Martin's Press, 2000) 12 ff; J Hearn, *Rethinking Nationalism: A Critical Introduction* (London, Palgrave Macmillan, 2006) 7 ff.

[17] For example, essentialists and constructivists, and so on, *see* Hroch, *Das Europa der Nationen* (n 11), 8. In this book, the most recurring denomination primordialism and modernism is adopted.

first nation-states, and inspired the drawing of state boundaries in Europe. We can therefore find strong primordialist rhetoric in the discourses of the eighteenth- and nineteenth-century patriots who strove for national unity. Johann Gottfried Herder provided a notable example. Modernist theories have, on the contrary, spread in academic circles, in particular after the Second World War, the historical event that most clearly showed the world the destructive potential of nationalism and that contributed to giving nationalism the bad name that the common language links to the word, usually replaced by functional synonyms like patriotism[18] or blurred 'politically correct' specifications.[19]

The heyday for critical studies on nationalism dates back to 1983,[20] when the important works of Gellner,[21] Anderson[22] and Hobsbawm and Ranger[23] were published. Nonetheless, 'modernist' positions are much older in the scientific debate.[24] Their basic assumption that nations are pure artefacts can be seen in the light of the state of the cultural studies of the period, which moved 'from the representation to the construction';[25] new constructivist theories adopted a critical approach to reality and led to extreme consequences: the consideration that it is human observation that determines the observed object.[26] In the same way in which reality is determined by the observer, nations are created through the imagination of people. Several modernist authors adopted a social and economic approach, a consequence of their Marxist intellectual background, which widened the perspective on the phenomenon, providing new theoretical instruments that could be used to comprehend the historical events.

Since then, modernist positions have become predominant in the historiographical debate and could be said to represent the dominant trend in the study of nationalism. It is, nonetheless, necessary to note that outside restricted academic circles, 'popular discussions in the media often seem to uncritically invoke primordialist assumptions'.[27] Political discussions are, of course, no exception. The doubt seems then justified, that even in other scientific areas—like legal studies—nations are still intended more in primordialist than modernist terms. Modernist positions have more often come to be criticised while neo-primordialist positions have been at least in part assumed by several scholars, a situation that is more

[18] Beside rhetorical nuances, it seems that nationalism and patriotism have the same focus. *See* S Wood, *Germany, Europe and the Persistence of Nations. Transformation, Interests and Identity, 1989–1996* (Aldershot, Ashgate, 1998) 41.

[19] Wouter Bos, then leader of the Dutch Labour Party, spoke of the necessity of developing a 'beschaafde vorm van nationalisme' (civilised form of nationalism), in NRC Handelsblad, 30 January 2009.

[20] HU Wehler, *Nationalismus. Geschichte, Formen, Folgen* (München, Beck, 2001) 8.

[21] E Gellner, *Nations and Nationalism* (n 8).

[22] B Anderson, *Imagined Communities* (n 7).

[23] EJ Hobsbawm and T Ranger (eds), *The Invention of Tradition* (Cambridge, Cambridge University Press, 1983).

[24] M Hroch, *Das Europa der Nationen* (n 11), 201.

[25] P Burke, *What is Cultural History?* (Cambridge, Polity Press, 2008) 85 ff.

[26] Ibid, 85 ff.

[27] J Hearn, *Rethinking Nationalism* (n 16), XIII.

in step with the nationalist revival of recent years. In this context, in particular the perspective of so-called *ethno-symbolists*[28] has to be mentioned, in which the importance of both ethnic and cultural–symbolic elements of the nation are underlined, while at least some modernist points are rejected.[29]

Yet, one should not get the impression that these approaches are ideologically biased per se, concluding that nationalism seems 'good' to primordialists and 'bad' to modernists. In fact, the aim of modernist authors is not to disqualify the nationalist ideology *tout court*, with the intent of showing its radical irreconcilability with democratic, socialist or liberal principles. Looking at some of the writers whose names are commonly associated with modernism, we discover that Plamenatz could not see anything non-liberal in cultural nationalism,[30] whereas Anderson later clarified that he does not think of nationalism as an 'ugly' ideology and even referred to its positive aspects.[31] By the same token, primordialists cannot be considered all-dedicated nationalists considering the identity with their co-nationals as something self-evident.[32] Both approaches aim to explain the reasons and dynamics of the development of nations, adopting two diametrically opposed analytical perspectives, and cannot be reductively considered as the theory 'in favour' and the theory 'against' nationalism. Furthermore, there is no essential incompatibility between the two approaches, as will be explained.

1.1.3 The Awakening of the Nation: Primordialism

According to the primordialist view, the nation is a natural phenomenon and its origins have to be investigated through a historical analysis that dates back to ancient history. Nationalism 'awakened' an already existing national awareness, thanks to cultural elites that stimulated a sleeping national consciousness drawing on an already existing repertoire of ethnic symbols, myths and memories.[33] Such

[28] AD Smith, *Nationalism and Modernism* (London, Routledge, 1998) 170 ff.

[29] *See* J Hearn, *Rethinking Nationalism* (n 16), 172 ff. AD Smith, 'A Europe of Nations. Or the Nation of Europe?' (1993) 30 *Journal of Peace Research*, 129–35, 130, for instance affirms that 'Historically, the nation is a subvariety and development of the ethnie, though we are not dealing with some evolutionary law of progression, nor with some necessary or irreversible sequence. While the ethnie is an historical culture–community, the nation is a community of mass, public culture, historic territory and legal rights. In other words, the nation shifts the emphasis of community away from kinship and cultural dimensions to territorial, educational and legal aspects, while retaining links with older cultural myths and memories of the ethnie'.

[30] J Plamenatz, 'Two Types of Nationalism', in E Kamenka (ed), *Nationalism: The Nature and Evolution of an Idea* (Canberra, Australian National University Press, 1976) 27.

[31] In an interview in 2005, to the question whether he was a little nationalistic despite the 'revealing books' he wrote on the subject, Anderson answered: 'Yes, absolutely. I must be the only one writing about nationalism who doesn't think it ugly. If you think about researchers such as Gellner and Hobsbawm, they have quite a hostile attitude to nationalism. I actually think that nationalism can be an attractive ideology. I like its Utopian elements', Benedict Anderson: 'I like nationalism's utopian elements' interview by L Khazaleh, www.culcom.uio.no/english/news/2005/anderson.html.

[32] J Hearn, *Rethinking Nationalism* (n 16), 21.

[33] AD Smith, *Nationalism: Theory, Ideology, History* (Cambridge, Polity Press, 2001) 77.

an understanding of the nation, that many modern day scholars might consider rhetorical, was the predominant approach in both the eighteenth and nineteenth centuries.

The 'natural' character of the nation claimed by primordialists[34] is highlighted by describing nations as a kind of 'fully extended family'[35] where 'members are brothers and sisters, or at least cousins, differentiated by family ties from outsiders,'[36] who respond to the innate human need of staying together with their fellow men. Considered almost as a collective organism, the nation undergoes a process of anthropomorphisation, almost an autonomous biological organism[37] with its own date of birth, history and qualities that are even innate. Nationalities are compared to animals or plants, with an autonomous life and spirit—the *Nationalgeist.*[38] Belonging to a nation is therefore a natural and 'objective' matter and not an issue of free choice of the individual: choosing one's own nationality would be as foolish as thinking of being able to choose one's own parents. If the nation has these characteristics, it can only be ancient: the roots of modern nationalism can be already found in ancient Greece, and around the year 1000 it was already possible to perceive the existence of French, German and English nations in Europe.[39] From this perspective, it was just a matter of time before a 'spring of nations' would have given nations a political representation. Consequently, from a primordialist perspective, any serious study of nationalism should start at least from the Middle Ages,[40] analysing the evolution of nations over *la longue durée.*

In contrast to the modernist approach, authors close to primordialist positions insist on the irrational character of the sense of belonging to a nation, which leaves economic and other utilitarian arguments out of consideration. The way in which mechanisms of collective identification work remains at a deeper and more inscrutable level, and as a consequence, there is a tendency to neglect the study of economic factors in the formation of nation-states. It is argued that a merely economic approach is not viable in comprehending many aspects of the nationalist phenomenon, since it still leaves important questions unanswered. For example, 'if ethnonational competition is fundamentally economic in causation, then *substantial* changes over time in the economic relationship should come to be reflected in the ethnonational relationship', but since comparative empirical data does not support this assumption, we should conclude that the proposition is false

[34] Also F Engels, in K Marx and F Engels, *Werke*, vol 13 (Berlin, Karl Dietz Verlag, 1971) 267, defines 'real and natural' the frontiers determined by 'language and sympathies'.

[35] W Connor, *Ethnonationalism. The Quest for Understanding* (Princeton, Princeton University Press, 1994) 202.

[36] AD Smith, *National Identity* (London, Penguin, 1991) 12.

[37] I Berlin, 'Nationalism: Past Neglected and Present Power', in I Berlin, *Against the Current: Essays in the History of Ideas* (London, Hogarth Press, 1979) 341.

[38] RR Ergang, *Herder and the Foundations of German Nationalism* (New York, Columbia University Press, 1931) 82 ff.

[39] M Bloch, *Feudal Society*, vol 2 (Chicago, Chicago University Press, 1964) 436 and 432.

[40] More references can be found in W Connor, *Ethnonationalism* (n 35), 211.

and that ethno-national conflicts are independent of economic considerations.[41] These points remain nonetheless controversial. Quite curiously, for instance, the mere fact that people are ready to die for their country—with no consideration of their personal interest with regard to the maximisation of welfare—does not even demonstrate the irrationality of that nationalist behaviour but instead can be interpreted as a quite bizarre economically rational action itself, asserting, for instance, that national martyrs seek to increase their own 'symbolic utility'.[42]

1.1.4 The Invention of the Nation: Modernism

Modernist studies underline the nature of political artefact of modern nations. Nationalism is the ideology that led to the creation of them,[43] while the traditional primordialist perspective has been completely overturned. Modernist argumentations start from a deep criticism of primordialist assumptions. In the first place, modernists openly reject as a simple supposition unsupported by facts the idea that nations are ancient because a national consciousness was already embryonic even before it found expression in a political organisation. It is almost impossible to be sure whether people in a certain period of the Middle Ages felt they were a part of some kind of nation, and the problem persists when we focus on more recent years, since the political and literary documents developing the idea of nation were produced by restricted elites. The main problem lies in the fact that, reasonably, '[w]hat Herder thought about the *Volk* cannot be used as evidence for the thoughts of the Westphalian peasantry'.[44] What is more, we could even reach the opposite conclusion that in some contexts characterised by a strong political fragmentation, a national consciousness—even a dormant one—was totally nonexistent.[45] For sure, national rhetoric tends to present the history of the birth of the nation and the movements towards unification as a popular movement normally directed against some foreign power, but this interpretation neglects the strong political, social and economic tensions—which occasionally led to violence—that characterised those processes in several countries.

[41] Ibid, 149.

[42] U Pagano, 'Can Economics Explain Nationalism?', in A Breton, G Galeotti and R Wintrobe (eds), *Nationalism and Rationality* (Cambridge, Cambridge University Press, 1995) 190.

[43] E Gellner, *Thought and Change* (London, Weidenfeld & Nicolson, 1964) 169: 'Nationalism is not the awakening of nations to self-consciousness: it invents nations where they do not exist'.

[44] EJ Hobsbawm, *Nations and Nationalism since 1780: Programme, Myth, Reality* (Cambridge, Cambridge University Press, 1990) 48.

[45] CM Wieland wrote in 1793: 'There are doubtless patriots of Brandenburg, Saxony, Bavaria, Württemberg, Hamburg, Nuremberg, Frankfort, etc., but German patriots who love the whole German empire as their fatherland, love it above anything else, and are willing to make considerable sacrifices not only for its preservation and protection against a common enemy, but also, after the danger has passed, for its prosperity, for the strengthening of its weakness, for its outward respect—where are they? Who will show them to me or at least name them?', *Sämmtliche Werken*, vol 31 (Leipzig, Göschen, 1858) 247, quoted by RR Ergang, *Herder and the Foundations of German Nationalism* (n 38), 30.

Even acknowledging that forms of national consciousness already existed before nationalism, it is still hard to believe that people imagined that they were part of a community whose borders basically coincided with those of modern states. It is not disputed that people felt commitment to some kind of social organisation, but to sustain that this organisation should coincide with the modern idea of nation bears the risk of engaging in theoretical retrospection. The primordialist approach, in other words, seems to be characterised by a certain 'methodological nationalism',[46] whereby old phenomena are seen as steps toward the present state of affairs. In the primordialist approach the bias toward continuity typically associated with the social sciences is then evident.

The analysis of Hobsbawm put particular emphasis on the linguistic element to highlight the impossibility of a 'natural' national consciousness as supposed by primordialist nationalists. According to this view, it was impossible for a national consciousness to develop on the basis of a common language, since a common national idiom simply did not exist yet at the historical moment in which most nation-states were created.[47] By the same token:

> There is no evidence whatever that the Balkan Slavs had ever considered themselves parts of the same nation, but the nationalist ideologues who emerged in the first half of the century thought in terms of an 'Illyria' hardly more real than Shakespeare's, a 'Yugoslav' state which was to unite Serbs, Croats, Slovenes, Bosnians, Macedonians and others who to this day demonstrate that their Yugoslav nationalism is, to put it mildly, in conflict with their sentiments as Croats, Slovenes, etc.[48]

Today's reader cannot avoid noting that, while Hobsbawm wrote these considerations on the Yugoslav state in 1975, the subsequent tragic breakup of that state proved that even the most audacious nation-building projects are often inadequate in suppressing the nationalist sentiments of smaller groups.

How then do linguistic factors relate to the formation of nation-building? In Europe, on the one hand, there are numerous cases of nations that were built without taking linguistic factors into consideration, while the fact that the same language or mutually intelligible languages were spoken in different communities did not lead to national unity and did not prevent nationalisms from arising based on other criteria.[49] On the other hand, national languages were more often promoted, drawing on ancient languages or by extension of a particular dialect, only *after* the formation of the nation-state: 'Languages multiply with states; not the other way round'.[50] Linguistic politics of this kind, though not particularly widespread at the time of the creation of the first nation-states, became more common afterwards and in the twentieth century there have been

[46] U Beck, *Der kosmopolitische Blick. Oder: Krieg ist Frieden* (Frankfurt am Main, Suhrkamp Verlag, 2004) 40.

[47] EJ Hobsbawm, *The Age of Capital. 1848–1875* (London, Weidenfeld and Nicolson, 1975) 89.

[48] Ibid, 86.

[49] Ibid, 86–8; EJ Hobsbawm, *Nations and Nationalism since 1780* (n 44), 51 ff.

[50] Ibid, 63.

no nationalistic governments in Europe that did not pursue a cultural policy of linguistic unification; often manifestly prohibiting the use of local languages. Since the beginning of nationalist experiences, the linguistic factor has been used to solve the contrast between different nationalisms—in a way, an almost paradoxical contrast between 'nationalism' and the movement for the creation of nation-states.[51] As soon as the 'spring of nations' let the voices of several aspiring nations arise, the first nation-states in the making disregarded the claims of several other groups aspiring to build a nation of their own, degrading that nationalism to a mere 'regionalism' and considering their languages just different 'dialects'.[52] Surpassing such political use of the distinction between languages and dialects, modernist theorists—accordingly to modern linguistics—reject the contrast between languages and dialects, highlighting that the distinction has a political rather than linguistic fundament. Quoting a Yiddish saying[53] well known to linguists, 'a language is a dialect with an army and navy'.

As it delves into the very roots of the nation, modernism therefore opts for a different period of time, which coincides with the beginning of the industrial age. It recognises that some kind of political associations on a national basis already existed in the Middle Ages, but it considers these associations to be mere forms of 'proto-nationalism',[54] founded on criteria and interests that are very different from those of modern nation-states.

1.1.4.1 Techniques of Nation-building

'Nation-building' is an expression that has become particularly popular in academic circles, and refers to all the techniques which are used by the 'state' to build the 'nation'. Assuming that nations are—borrowing the famous expression of Anderson—*imagined communities*, these techniques aim to let people think that a certain community that can be defined as a nation exists. According to Anderson, a nation will necessarily be an imagined community, as it is practically impossible for all people in a country to know one another, so that one can only 'imagine' being part of a community with given characteristics that distinguish it from others. In this sense, communities only differ in 'the style in which they are imagined'.[55]

According to the constructivist perspective, of course, people can be deliberately led to imagine nations in a particular way, often opposing it to others. While classic primordialist nationalism has insisted on the ethnic and cultural differentiation of nations, modern scholars of comparative literature highlight 'a systematically diversified and particularised assignation of characters to specific ethnic

[51] EJ Hobsbawm, *The Age of Capital* (n 47), 88.
[52] Ibid, 86–7.
[53] M Weinreich, 'Der YIVO un di problemen fun undzer tsayt' (1945) 25 *YIVO Bletter 1945* 3–18.
[54] EJ Hobsbawm, *Nations and Nationalism since 1780* (n 44), 46 ff.
[55] B Anderson, *Imagined Communities* (n 7), 6.

groups [...] appears in European written culture only during the early modern period, whereby character traits and psychological dispositions were distributed in a fixed division among various "nations"'.[56] Such a national characterisation was the first step to identifying nations while later, national characters acquired a normative content, evolving at first in a *Geist* and then in pure stereotypes to be used even to ridicule other national groups.[57]

However, the building of a nation also requires a shared past as well as a cultural homogeneity. In order to suggest that a nation 'shares a common past and future', the process of 'invention of tradition' is particularly important. According to Hobsbawm,[58] traditions that are thought to be ancient are in reality more often very recent and deliberately invented to serve particular aims. To further this aim, arts and literature have often been used in order to create or consolidate the idea of a common national origin.[59] Even the diffusion of the newspapers became a fundamental element of nation-building, since every citizen could now read in an intelligible and standardised common language[60] about events taking place in every corner of the country: *print-capitalism*—ie 'the convergence of capitalism and print technologies'[61]—contributed to the development of national consciousness in diverse countries.

These techniques did not operate at a particular moment in history, subsequently exhausting their function, but are continuous; so, for instance, newspapers still focus primarily on the events which occur in their nation, school programmes are still chiefly focused on national history and so on. After having invented the nation, nationalism must preserve it: 'the ideology operates to make people forget that their world has been historically constructed'.[62] Flags, anthems, statues are merely techniques to make people aware that the nation exists. This is a form of nationalism which is much less patent than the one dramatically revealing itself on the occasion of military conflicts, but which is often more effective, though merely 'banal', using the famous expression of Billig. Once the nationalist

[56] J Leerssen, 'The Rhetoric of National Character: A Programmatic Survey' (2000) 21 *Poetics Today* 267–92, 272.

[57] Ibid, 274.

[58] EJ Hobsbawm, 'Introduction: Inventing Traditions', in EJ Hobsbawm and T Ranger (eds), *The Invention of Tradition* (Cambridge, Cambridge University Press, 1983) 1 ff. The idea that national traditions could simply and deliberately be invented is anyway older, *see* for instance JB Halsted, *Romanticism* (New York, Harper & Row, 1969) 35, who clearly affirms: 'where a national heritage of greatness did not clearly exist, it might be invented'.

[59] A recurring element is the accent upon the heroic actions of the forefathers of the nation: in the years between the eighteenth and nineteenth centuries, Europe discovered a huge number of contemporary national 'Homers' whose feats only then came to light after the discovery of some dusty old manuscript, A-M Thiesse, *La création des identités nationales: Europe XVIIIe-XXe siècle* (Paris, Éditions du Seuil, 1999) 107. Such emphasis on the folk heritage has indeed always been the first stage of 'national revival', EJ Hobsbawm, *The Age of Capital* (n 47), 85.

[60] B Anderson, *Imagined Communities* (n 7), 44.

[61] Ibid, 46.

[62] M Billig, *Banal Nationalism* (London, Sage, 1995) 37.

sentiment has been built, the nationalist doctrine can be seen as 'the deliberate exploitation of national and/or ethnic sentiment for political ends'.[63]

1.1.4.2 Reasons for Nation-building

From a *political* perspective, nationalists never considered the multinational state as an appropriate model of political and social organisation. It is easier to ensure social peace and to maintain—in Weberian terms—the monopoly of the use of the force in a state of homogeneity rather than in a society where different social formations are present;[64] that is also one of the reasons why nationalist regimes contrasted or reluctantly accepted *corps intermédiaires* on their territory. It is then clear why modern states—that, as it is commonly agreed, appeared as states on the world scene in 1648—rapidly evolved as *nation*-states.

The main modernist argument is, however, of an *economic* nature. In the perspective of, among others, Gellner, it was industrialisation that led to the formation of nation-states. In a legal historical perspective, that moment coincided with the highest point of the slow and long historical shift from *status* to *contract*, to use the expression of Sumner Maine.[65] Nationalism itself is a product of modernisation, so these two phenomena do not occur in the same period out of pure coincidence (*chronological* modernism) but because of their necessary interrelation (*structural* modernism).[66] As Hobsbawm suspected, the nation-state that had to be at least moderately large was 'in fact the 'natural' unit of the development of the modern, liberal, progressive and *de facto* bourgeois society'.[67] Whereas in particular socialist thinkers like Kautsky[68] have articulated the idea that the rise of nationalist movements coincided with 'the victory of capitalism over feudalism',[69] non-Marxist authors too later agreed on the fact that, at least initially, nationalism was essentially a bourgeois phenomenon.[70] The nation-state represented the most advanced form of political organisation in order to pursue the aims of an industrial economy that called for a certain type of division of labour.[71] Even '[t]he risks associated with specialisation in modern dynamic economies can be greatly reduced if the individuals happen to share a general common culture'.[72] A higher

63 J Mayall, *Nationalism and International Society* (Cambridge, Cambridge University Press, 1990) 43.

64 A Giddens *The Nation State and Violence* (Cambridge, Polity Press, 1985), 120; W Kymlicka, *Contemporary Political Philosophy: An Introduction* (Oxford, Oxford University Press, 2002) 329.

65 HS Maine, *Ancient Law: Its Connection with the Early History of Society, and Its Relation to Modern Ideas* (New York, Charles Scribner & Co, 1867) 165.

66 *See* AD Smith, 'The Poverty of Anti-nationalist Modernism' (2003) 9 *Nations and Nationalism* 357–70, 358.

67 EJ Hobsbawm, *The Age of Capital* (n 47), 86.

68 K Kautsky (2009) 'Nationality and Internationality' 37 *Critique. Journal of Socialist Theory* 371–89.

69 VI Lenin, *Collected Works*, vol 20 (Moscow, Progress Publishers, 1972) 394.

70 LL Snyder, *The New Nationalism* (Ithaca, NY, Cornell University Press, 1968) 32.

71 E Gellner, *Nations and Nationalism* (n 8), 24.

72 U Pagano, 'Can Economics Explain Nationalism?' (n 42), 178.

degree of mobility among workers, which would have been restricted within a state composed of different groups, became a necessity. It has been argued that the only real nationalists in German society were the merchants and bankers, whereas the aristocracy and proletariat did not feel the need for nationalism.[73] But again, from a different point of view, nationalism was, on the contrary, a valuable idea for the poorer echelons in society who made the move from rural agricultural to urban and industrial societies, since the new ideology provided a model of identification that replaced the old social ties and local identities, lost on the way toward the city.[74] It was indeed necessary to create new bonds between citizens. Whereas in a *Gemeinschaft* (community) everyone knows their fellow citizens, in a large modern *Gesellschaft* (society) this becomes impossible, and the necessity arises for creating new social bonds. In this context, nationalism became, in Hroch's words, the 'substitute for factors of integration in a disintegrating society'.[75] This author has nonetheless also challenged Gellner's idea of nationalism as inherently linked to industrialisation, noting that most of the national movements in Europe 'emerged well before the arrival of modern industry', and even more 'before they had any contact with it—many of them, indeed, in overwhelmingly agrarian conditions'.[76] Moreover, Gellner's theory suggests 'in the style of classic nineteenth-century unilinear evolutionism, that there is some predetermined path that all societies must follow'.[77] With regard to this point, one should recognise that modernist authors more than primordialists pay the price for trying to develop a more general and comprehensive theory of nationalism, which therefore appears to some extent vague and open to criticism for not taking into account all the differences among various historical manifestations.

1.1.5 Primordialism vs Modernism?

Although some of the basic assumptions of primordialist and modernist theories give the impression of existing in a state of insufferable contraction, they are less radical and do not seem necessarily mutually exclusive in their original formulation. The differences between different conceptions of nationalism are in fact less considerable than normally suggested.[78] So for example, Hobsbawm claims in a very moderate and almost conservative fashion[79] that what he wants to discuss

[73] T Hamerow, *The Social Foundations of German Unification, 1858–1871* (Princeton, Princeton University Press, 1972) 295 ff.

[74] BC Shafer, *Faces of Nationalism* (n 12), 220.

[75] M Hroch, *Nationale Bewegungen früher und heute. Ein europäischer Vergleich*, 14, in EJ Hobsbawm, *Nations and Nationalism since 1780* (n 44), 173.

[76] M Hroch, 'From National Movement to the Fully-formed Nation' (1993) 198 *New Left Review* 3–20, 10.

[77] J Hearn, *Rethinking Nationalism* (n 16), 106.

[78] M Hroch, *Das Europa der Nationen* (n 11), 7.

[79] P Burke, *What is Cultural History?* (n 25), 86.

in his study is true for 'most' of historical experiences.[80] Gellner too, using the metaphor of the navel to symbolise the perennial nature of nations, explicitly affirms that 'some nations possess genuine ancient navels, some have navels invented for them by their own nationalist propaganda, and some are altogether navel-less', nonetheless insisting on the fact that the second category is 'by far the largest'.[81] Furthermore, these authors do not seem to suggest that nations can be simply created *ex nihilo* in any particular historical moment, but they choose to investigate the objective conditions—in particular of an economic nature—that led to nationalism developing,[82] which for sure is not incompatible with a primordialist-like idea that national consciousness already existed, simply waiting to be awakened when political contingencies would have allowed it. It would admittedly be very naïve to sustain that something like a nation could be created overnight by some political power, rather than being the result of social dynamics with more ancient roots. On the other hand, even primordialists do not deny that some distinctions between nationalities might be artificially constructed; Fichte complained that 'the distinction between the Prussians and the other Germans is artificial, founded on institutions established arbitrarily or by chance. The distinction between the Germans and other European nationalities is founded on nature',[83] therefore with the purpose of sustaining the nationalist assumption that institutional lines should be drawn along 'natural' national lines. Moreover, modern authors adhering to ethno-symbolism do not deny the importance of cultural practices for the definition of nationality, but also put emphasis on the necessity of ethnic substrata.

Although modernist theories have probably been represented as more extreme than they are, in particular by later theorists, it is a sign of their historiographical success the fact that today even liberal nationalists—those who explicitly advocate the nationalist political principle—have adopted some of the basic assumptions of modernists and embraced in particular Anderson's theory of imagined communities.[84] This was possible since, as already said, primordialism and modernism cannot be simplistically considered respectively as the theory sympathetic to nationalism and the theory antagonistic to it. It should finally be underlined that none of these theories can provide a single 'right' answer to a universal question. The historical events which led to the formation of the modern nation-states are complex and heterogeneous, and what primordialists in particular suggest seems true—that events have to be investigated in the *longue durée*. Neither can it be inferred that what has happened in a particular social context and in a given historical period may be valid also in very different environments and moments.

[80] EJ Hobsbawm 'Introduction: Inventing Traditions' (n 58), 1 ff.

[81] E Gellner, *Nationalism* (London, Weidenfeld & Nicolson, 1997) 96.

[82] M Hroch, *Das Europa der Nationen* (n 11), 23–4.

[83] JG Fichte, Nachgelassene Werke, vol 3 (Bonn, A Marcus, 1835) 232, in RR Ergang, *Herder and the Foundations of German Nationalism* (n 38), 249.

[84] Y Tamir, *Liberal Nationalism* (Princeton, Princeton University Press, 1993) 8.

Both approaches can therefore be employed for the analysis of different nationalist experiences, keeping in mind that even if we accept the concept of 'nationalism' as a political principle that emerged after the eighteenth century, we cannot ignore the existence of a less developed earlier 'proto-nationalism'.

1.2 IDEAS OF THE NATION-STATE

Many different definitions have been given for nationalism; to sum up all of them would be a tedious and misleading exercise since, surveying a number of them, one soon discovers that most definitions do not really diverge. Gellner—who is perfectly aware of the difference between nationalist movements and ideologies—provides a definition that is particularly useful for our purposes;[85] at the very beginning of his fundamental work of 1983, he affirms that 'Nationalism is primarily a political principle, which holds that the political and the national unit should be congruent.'[86]

Such is the contemporary understanding of nationalism, free from the sedimentation of particular historical experiences and that was known until the second half of the nineteenth century simply as 'principle of nationality'.[87] In the following pages, the constitutive elements of this definition—political unit, national unit, their congruence—will be dealt with, although the analysis will primarily focus on the fundamental concept of 'nation', whose different conceptualisations led historically to the development of specific nationalist forms.

Although the scientific debate on nationalism has often put strong emphasis on the differences between those manifestations, a sharp distinction is not useful. Although the definition of nation is central to the nationalist ideology, the criteria which can be used to define it are to some extent interchangeable and depend on historical circumstances.[88] Particular attention will be paid to the criterion of culture, which is most frequently employed by modern nationalists. It is also worth noting that the basic assumption of all nationalist forms is the necessity of the congruence of political and national units (where the political is not only an expression of the national but also acts in the interests of the latter), whereas further aims—whether of a racist, socialist, or liberal nature—are not per se nationalist aims. Nationalism in its different historical manifestations has usually taken on aspects of other ideologies and theories (racism, socialism, liberalism)

[85] Gellner has later been criticised for having described only 'statist' nationalism, neglecting the peculiarities of 'cultural' nationalism. *See* C Gans, *The Limits of Nationalism* (Cambridge, Cambridge University Press, 2003) 23–4.

[86] E Gellner, *Nations and Nationalism* (n 8), 1.

[87] EJ Hobsbawm, *The Age of Capital* (n 47), 82.

[88] For an historical example concerning Denmark *see* L Hansen, 'Sustaining Sovereignty. The Danish Approach to Europe', in L Hansen and O Wæver (eds), *European Integration and National Identity: The Challenge of the Nordic States* (New York, Routledge, 2002) 54.

that have nonetheless little or nothing to do with nationalism as such, creating a remarkable cause for confusion.[89]

1.2.1 The Political and the National Unit

When we speak of a political unit we mainly refer to the concept of state. 'State' is understood through Max Weber's definition as 'a human community that (successfully) claims the monopoly of the legitimate use of physical force within a given territory'.[90] Nevertheless, this is not the only form of political unit we can think of. 'Political unit' is indeed a much wider expression that covers any unit where decisions concerning a particular group of persons are taken; in a democratic system, for example, by representatives of the group itself. In this sense, the political unit is where the decision making power is located. Nationalism can therefore also be considered as the principle that aims at the maintenance or the transfer of decision-making power from one certain political unit to another where it is easier for the nation to exercise the decisional power and pursue its own particular 'national interest'.

While the definition of state has been relatively straightforward, the definition of the nation is much more intricate. The definition of the concept of nation is central to any nationalist theory. It would be impossible to establish who has the right to create a state without a clear idea of what is covered by that concept. This is a problem which is shared both by nationalism and democracy; the very basic principle 'let the people decide' is 'in fact ridiculous', as long as nobody determines who the people are.[91] Nationalism provides an answer to this question: the nation. In this sense, it is easily understandable how the nation can be intended as an instrument of democracy. However, this solution is not really satisfactory and only rephrases the initial problem, since once we have identified the people with the nation, it becomes immediately necessary to understand what a nation is.

The question as to what constitutes the nation cannot be eluded. If we imagine nationalism in Gellnerian terms, to define the nation is fundamental in order to determine who is entitled to exercise the decision making power as well as who will be affected by the decisions taken by the political unit. What is more, a clear idea of what constitutes a nation is necessary in order to distinguish different nationalist manifestations. There is no other criterion to distinguish, for instance, the nationalism of liberation or resistance from the nationalism of conquest than the 'nationhood'.[92] To find an answer to the question as to what

[89] P Spencer and H Wollman, *Nationalism: A Critical Introduction* (London, Sage, 2002) 95.

[90] M Weber, 'Politik als Beruf', in M Weber, *Wissenschaft als Beruf, 1917/1919; Politik als Beruf, 1919* (Tübingen, Mohr Siebeck, 1994) 36.

[91] WI Jennings, *The Approach to Self-Government* (Cambridge, Cambridge University Press, 1956) 56.

[92] In this sense, from the perspective of the Kingdom of Naples, the movement of Risorgimento represented a form of aggressive nationalism, and while the newborn Italian state considered rebels in the southern regions as outlaws and notoriously repressed them accordingly, in the end a clear

a nation is, *objective* and *subjective* criteria of nationhood can be employed. The former refer to particular circumstances that cannot be changed by the individual, whereas the latter involve the willingness of a subject and can therefore be also defined as voluntaristic. Objective criteria tend to be static, whereas subjective criteria are dynamic and permit inclusive citizenship policies more easily: one can change one's mind, but not one's blood. None of these sole criteria is sufficient to define nationality. Opinions vary as to which criteria are more important and take precedence in defining nationality. In this regard, different theories may be distinguished.

1.2.2 Ethnic Nationalism

The nationalist ideology that supports objective criteria of nationhood such as bloodline and tradition can be defined as *ethnic* nationalism. According to this concept, 'the nation can trace its roots to an imputed common ancestry and [...] therefore its members are brothers and sisters, differentiated by family ties from outsiders'.[93] Assuming such a common biological origin, it is also easier to posit that the same emotional bonds that exist between the members of a family also work in relation to co-nationals. Ethnic ties are able to surpass ideological distinctions and, in a constructivist perspective, are more effective as means of social control, for it is more likely that the level of unrest in the societies would be minor if people consider one another as relatives. In other words, ethnic nationalism provides the theoretical justification to the partiality of nationalism considering fellow countrymen as members of the same family. This particular form of nationalism is usually associated with Germany as well as with Herder's theories; he was probably the first intellectual to develop a philosophy of nationalism.[94] According to another view, ethnic nationalism developed in that particular context because German society was 'split between a feudal aristocracy and a rural proletariat'[95] and, given this condition, the nationalist phenomenon could not originate as a social movement, as it seemingly did in France, but only as a cultural movement,[96] which preferred the past over the present.[97]

Ethnic nationalism conceives nations 'primordially' as a natural organic reality. If this is true, belonging to the nation becomes almost a matter of biology. In the same way in which the zoologist and botanist Carl Linnaeus had systematised

difference between these and the patriots in other nations was already difficult for foreign observers of that period to distinguish; *see Cronaca degli avvenimenti di Sicilia da aprile 1860 a marzo 1861: estratta da documenti* (Italy, 1863) 373.

[93] A Smith, *National Identity* (n 36), 12.

[94] RR Ergang, *Herder and the Foundations of German Nationalism* (n 38), 50.

[95] H Kohn, *Nationalism: Its Meaning and History* (n 2), 30.

[96] Ibid, 30.

[97] H Kohn, *The Idea of Nationalism: A Study in Its Origins and Background* (New York, Macmillan, 1967) 330.

animal and vegetable species, nationalities could be scientifically distinguished mostly 'on the basis of ethnotypes reconfigured into what comes to be called 'national temperaments' or 'national characters''.[98] A certain mix of ethnic and cultural criteria has therefore characterised objective interpretations of the nation. Biological criteria have been used several times in the history of nationalism: many local groups advancing autonomy or independence claims have insisted on their alleged descent from some particular ethnic group. The objective criteria of bloodline and soil represent the 'natural elements' from which the sense of community develops into nationalism.[99]

It is undeniably true that identification with ancestors represents an important strategy for nation building in the history of nationalism,[100] and the very concept of 'nation' originally contains a reference to 'birth' and an ethnic element.[101] Nevertheless, biological criteria of nationhood are contradicted by modern genetic science.[102] From a scientific point of view, a criterion of nationhood based on the *ethnos* can hardly be defended—there are no populations or ethnic groups that are completely apart from others (though some are less so than others). Moreover, modern studies of individuality and society show how the identification of the individual with the community is chiefly a psychological and cultural process, which usually does not consider biological criteria, so that 'no serious scholar today believes that hereditary characteristics explain cultural variations'.[103] As it has been summed up sagaciously, '[m]easurements of skulls and classifications of blood types tell us little about men except about their skulls and blood types'.[104]

In conclusion, although ethnic nationalism provides a clear answer to the question as to what is a nation, that answer is nonetheless difficult to demonstrate in reality and encompasses several dangers. The problem consists in the fact that, whereas every criterion of distinction can easily degenerate into an argument of superiority, the criterion of bloodline has a logical tendency to degenerate into forms of racism, especially ever since it was started to be thought that a different genetic heritage determined not only different somatic characteristics but even moral and spiritual ones.[105]

[98] J Leerssen, *National Thought in Europe* (n1), 56.

[99] BM Telders, 'Nationalisme en internationalisme', in BM Telders, *Verzamelde geschriften V* ('s-Gravenhage, Nijhoff, 1949) 68.

[100] This strategy has been employed not only by Nazi Germany and Fascist Italy, but also by the French and notably the Norwegians, whose independence claims were perfectly sustained by the patriotic theory that Norwegians stem from an ancient population coming to the south from the north, whereas Danes and Swedes were descendants of different Gothic populations which walked the opposite way. A-M Thiesse, La création des identités nationales, 74.

[101] It also can be noted that in the Greek language ethnos translates as 'nation'.

[102] AR Templeton, 'Human Races: A Genetic and Evolutionary Perspective' (1999) 100 *American Anthropologist* 632–50.

[103] T Eriksen, *Ethnicity and Nationalism* (n 3), 5.

[104] BC Shafer, *Faces of Nationalism* (n 12), 326.

[105] Ibid, 323.

1.2.3 Civic Nationalism

If classical objective criteria spread in particular in Germany, due to Romantic thought and eventually, National Socialism, the traditional location of subjective criteria has been France, where a different understanding of nationality arose inspired by the Enlightenment and the theory of social contract. Herder and Rousseau's ideas were indeed authentically antithetic in several respects[106] and consequently at least partially different nationalist forms grew out of their ideas. Unlike in Germany, in France a 'civic' form of nationalism spread, so called 'because it envisages the nation as a community of equal, rights bearing citizens, united in patriotic attachment to a shared set of political practices and values'.[107] The spontaneous acceptance of the rights and duties arising from the 'social contract' and of the values underlying a community is the condition for being a member of it.

The manifesto of civic nationalism was codified in a famous speech given much later by Ernest Renan, with the title '*Qu'est-ce qu'une nation?*'. Rather than focusing on a common ethnic heritage from ancient Roman or Gallic populations, Renan preferred to speak of the French nation as a plebiscite of every day ('*un plébiscite de tous les jours*').[108] The speech draws freely on revolutionary theories of the social contract[109] identifying the foundation of the state in the will of the citizen rather than in an old God-given right of the king; the association of free citizens and their ideal signature on the social contract gives rise and legitimacy to the political unit and in a contract what matters is the will of the parties, not their ethnicity.

The word 'nation' itself was barely used in France before the revolutionary period,[110] indeed 'the Crown, the State and the Nation were but three words for the same thing'.[111] From this perspective, the deeper meaning of Louis XIV's famous expression, '*l'État, c'est moi*' becomes completely understandable. The function of the revolutionary concept of nation was just that of contending the king's power, so that revolutionaries could have replied to the egocentric affirmation of Louis XIV: the state is not the king any more; it is the nation—that is, the Third Estate. The nation became people[112] and the word 'nation' acquired a new

[106] RR Ergang, *Herder and the Foundations of German Nationalism* (n 38), 95.

[107] M Ignatieff, *Blood and Belonging: Journeys into the New Nationalism* (London, Vintage, 1994) 3–4.

[108] E Renan, *Qu'est-ce qu'une nation?: Conférence faite en Sorbonne, le 11 mars 1882* (Paris, Calmann Lévy, 1882) 27.

[109] J-J Rousseau, *Du Contrat Social ou Principes du Droit politique* [1762] (Paris, Ernest Flammarion éditeur, 1910).

[110] CI Keitner, *The Paradoxes of Nationalism. The French Revolution and Its Meaning for Contemporary Nation Building* (Albany, University of New York Press, 2007) 24 ff.

[111] K Martin, *French Liberal Thought in the Eighteenth Century* (London, Phoenix House, 1962) 26.

[112] B Shafer, *Faces of Nationalism* (n 12), 56 ff.

meaning,[113] now becoming the source of the state's sovereignty.[114] This change is of pivotal relevance: this was not the first time that people in France rebelled against their sovereign but it was the first time they rejected the legitimacy of that power.[115] However, Renan's speech was delivered only in 1882, thus a very long time after the events that led to the French Revolution. It therefore contains also elements that seem closer to those Romantic ideas which spread all over Europe, inflaming the continent just a few years earlier.

1.2.4 From Civic Nationalism to Constitutional Patriotism

A recent development of the spontaneous acceptance criterion that fosters integration rather than exclusion is the theory of constitutional patriotism developed in Germany by Jürgen Habermas[116] built upon an expression of Dolf Sternberger,[117] and which notably influenced the contemporary political thought on nationalism. According to this idea, a set of civic and political values of a liberal nature, which in contemporary societies are often laid down in national constitutions, should represent the object of identification of people independent of ethnic or linguistic factors. This would make a form of 'solidarity among strangers'[118] possible, and could then be employed for the development of a civic society organized in a nation-state which, rejecting the homogeneity advocated by many nationalists, rather qualifies as a liberal 'heterogeneous nation-state' in which cultural pluralism is guaranteed.[119] At the core of the theory lies a dynamic understanding of the concept of identity: rather than something inherited, this is a political construct.[120]

The expression 'constitution' should not be understood in a narrow sense, as the basic norm of a legal system—let alone a written one—but rather as the set of liberal values and democratic procedures that shape the basic structure of a liberal society. Loyalty thus manifests itself more toward the *idea of* constitution

[113] J Leerssen, *National Thought in Europe* (n 1), 86 ff.

[114] J Habermas, 'Staatsbürgerschaft und nationale Identität' [1990] in J Habermas, *Faktizität und Geltung: Beiträge zur Diskurstheorie des Rechts und des demokratischen Rechtsstaats* (Frankfurt am Main, Suhrkamp, 1994) 635.

[115] F Rigaux, 'Nations et nationalismes au cours des deux derniers siècles', in H-P Mansel, T Pfeiffer, H Kronke, C Kohler, R Hausmann (eds), *Festschrift für Erik Jayme*, vol 2, (München, Sellier, 2004) 1209.

[116] J Habermas, 'Staatsbürgerschaft und nationale Identität' (n 114), 642–43.

[117] R Sternberger, *Verfassungspatriotismus* (Hannover, Niedersächische Landeszentrale für politische Bildung, 1982).

[118] J Habermas, 'Why Europe Needs a Constitution' (2001) 11 *New Left Review* 5–26, 16.

[119] R Dahrendorf, *The Modern Social Conflict. The Politics of Liberty* (New Brunswick, Transaction Publishers, 2008) 184.

[120] J Habermas, 'Historical Consciousness and Post-Traditional Identity', in J Habermas, *The New Conservatism: Cultural Criticism and the Historians' Debate* (Cambridge, Polity Press, 1989) 262.

rather than to its contents.[121] A complete commitment to the constitution as such would be a tough requirement from all citizens, since in a modern and evolved society, it is more than likely that contrasts with regard to the contents of the law will occur.[122] People's consensus is referred to the 'procedure for the legitimate enactment of laws and the legitimate exercise of power'.[123] In the end, thus, constitutional patriotism is 'the morally necessitated readiness of a country's people to accept disagreement over the *application* of core constitutional principles of respect for everyone as free and equal, without loss of confidence in the *univocal content* of the principles'.[124]

Such a 'revival' of the voluntaristic criteria of identification that, however, 'must be embedded in the context of a historically specific political culture'[125] and therefore does not appear as totally abstracted from the social context, has to be set against a specific historical and cultural background. The theory of constitutional patriotism developed and gained momentum in divided Germany, where the memory of the Nazi period made it politically complicated to foster identification on the basis of the classical objective criteria of the German tradition. The idea of identification with constitutional values has been one of the key concepts in the extended debate on 'German identity', which began already in the 1960s as soon as a new generation began to raise disturbing questions about the Nazi period in reaction to the society's *Verdrängung* of the memories of the past in the immediate post-war period.[126] That self-analysis culminated in the 1980s in the *Historikerstreit*, the dispute between historians—including Habermas—over the responsibilities of the German people and their 'national character' for the crimes that were committed in the Nazi era. In this context, constitutional patriotism could provide both an identification model based on non-nationalist or even anti-nationalist values[127] and the theoretical guideline for successful integration policies in a country exposed to a massive flow of extra-European immigration. For comparable reasons, the theory was subsequently revealed to be an important element for the theoretical elaboration of citizenship in the European Union.[128]

[121] F Michelmann, 'Morality, Identity and "Constitutional Patriotism"' (2001) 14 *Ratio Juris* 253–71, 265.

[122] J Habermas, 'Struggle for Recognition in the Democratic Constitutional State', in C Taylor and A Gutmann (eds), *Multiculturalism: Examining the Politics of Recognition* (Princeton, Princeton University Press, 1994) 135.

[123] Ibid, 135

[124] F Michelmann, 'Morality, Identity and 'Constitutional Patriotism" (n 121), 269.

[125] J Habermas, 'Struggle for Recognition in the Democratic Constitutional State' (n 122), 135

[126] B Parekh, *A New Politics of Identity: Political Principles for an Interdependent World* (Basingstoke, Palgrave Macmillan, 2008) 72.

[127] M Canovan, 'Patriotism Is Not Enough' (2000) 30 *British Journal of Political Science* 413–32, 417. 'The German discourse of Verfassungspatriotismus [...] should be seen as a way of managing tensions between traditional understandings of national loyalty and the post-war constitutional arrangements of the Federal Republic. As a rhetorical response to that situation it seems to have been quite successful, partly no doubt because its local resonances were decently clothed in the language of unpolitical generality', 432.

[128] *See* Chapter 4 on 'Euronationalism'.

Despite its success—or probably as a consequence of that success—the theory has been criticised from different perspectives, in particular for two reasons: on the one hand it allegedly provides too 'thin' a model of identification, which is unable to cope with fundamental issues like the determination of the boundaries of the state,[129] whereas objective criteria may prove more useful to promote integration.[130] On the other hand, in order to be easily shared by the greatest number of people living in the community, these constitutional values have to be so basic and 'thin' that it becomes quite difficult to base any 'strong' national identity exclusively on them. Moreover, if every community is based upon the same general values, what is the criterion to distinguish one community from another? In this sense, the same objections that are usually directed to Rawls and Dworkin's idea that common principles of liberal justice may be employed to constitute and distinguish ethical communities can be directed to Habermas; these principles are often shared not only *within* states but also *across* states.[131] It can be even more problematic to employ the model of constitutional patriotism with regard to social values that require a high degree of social solidarity and consensus. One criticism of this theory is indeed that it does not provide legitimacy to a model of an extensive welfare state.[132]

1.2.5 Cultural Nationalism

Renan had already spoken of the ancestral legacy in order to define the nation, a legacy that, of course, is of a cultural nature instead of a biological one, since it would be a mistake to confuse '*la race avec la nation*'.[133] But the importance of culture as an objective criterion of nationality emerged primarily under German Romanticism, when cultural and ethnic elements were often combined. For a long time, objective nationalism has been based on an indissoluble combination of *ethnos* and culture, so that different ethnic groups were considered also to have different cultures. Such a link between culture and *ethnos* has been broken only in recent times, after the criterion of bloodline was discredited following the defeat of ideologies based on racism. Since then, the idea of nations as ethnically homogeneous communities has faded away whilst the view considering the nation as a community of people sharing a common culture has gained the upper hand. National belonging is now more often than not expressed in cultural rather than ethnic terms and 'culture' has clearly become the favourite criterion of national identification for modern nationalists. Neither bloodline nor spontaneous

[129] D Miller, *On Nationality* (Oxford, Clarendon Press, 1995) 163.

[130] J Müller, 'A General Theory of Constitutional Patriotism' (2008) 6 *International Journal of Constitutional Law* 72–95, 93.

[131] W Kymlicka, *Contemporary Political Philosophy* (n 64), 255.

[132] J Müller, 'A General Theory of Constitutional Patriotism' (n 130), 87.

[133] E Renan, *Qu'est-ce qu'une nation?* (n 108), 2.

acceptance constitutes the criterion of nationhood any more; culture has taken their place, intended objectively: culture is something everybody is born with and cannot change even if they wanted to. In these terms, the nation becomes 'a union of similarly thinking and similarly speaking persons',[134] while the language is the most important feature of a national community, as already in Herder's view, this is 'the purest expression of the spiritual character of a national group'.[135] Unlike Fichte's understanding, according to which 'whenever a separate language is found, there a separate nationality exists which has the right to take independent charge of its affairs and to govern itself',[136] modern nationalism downplays the importance of the linguistic factor and considers language as just one of the many manifestations of culture, which is instead the crucial feature.

Nationalist theories underline the substantial homogeneity of culture at the national level and its difference from those of other nations. Even those liberals who aim to distance themselves from classical nationalist positions are aware that nations 'tend to attribute to themselves a greater degree of cultural homogeneity than their members actually display' nonetheless advocate that a set of basic 'beliefs, practices, sensibilities' still give form to clearly distinct national cultures.[137] Accepting the nationalist perspective, nonetheless, it then becomes necessary to establish at which level of approximation the specificity of a national culture should be recognised, understanding that—at some level—a cultural difference between nations must be found in order to make a distinction possible and discover a common 'identity' to be based on that culture.

It is indeed usual that identity be constructed through a process of differentiation: 'National identity is equated with difference, and there is a constant, even obsessive, concern to remain different from others lest one should lose one's identity'.[138] But the construction of identity through juxtaposition is quite an odd mechanism; it is like defining an object explaining what it is not rather than what it is. More logically, 'difference is derivative, and not the central defining feature of identity'.[139] The nationalist theory of identity seems thus to be based upon three cornerstones '(1) each nation [has] a unique character, and (2) members of each nation [are] born with or acquired national characteristics stemming from the national character, and (3) every citizen of a nation should have these characteristics.'[140] The reason why national characteristics are transmitted to all members of the nation is, of course, because personal identity is primarily a social identity, determined by the social context in which the subject is embedded.[141]

[134] R Springer, *The National Problem* (Moscow, Obshchestvennaya Polza Publishing House, 1909) 43.
[135] Quoted by RR Ergang, *Herder and the Foundations of German Nationalism* (n 38), 150.
[136] JG *Fichte, Werke*, vol 5 (Leipzig, Meiner, 1910) 564.
[137] D Miller, *On Nationality* (n 129), 85.
[138] B Parekh, *A New Politics of Identity* (n 126), 61.
[139] Ibid.
[140] BC Shafer, *Faces of Nationalism* (n 12), 249.
[141] A MacIntyre, *After Virtue: A Study in Moral Philosophy* (Notre Dame, University of Notre Dame Press, 1981) 220.

National stereotypes, often ideologically biased, are the clear result of this process of generalisation. But when moral evaluations are linked to these characteristics, potentially violent and aggressive forms of nationalism can arise. The externalisation of the evil appears as a decisive step in the shift from a non-aggressive to a violent form of nationalism.

Nevertheless, this idea has many drawbacks and is discussed critically in academia: the simple nationalist concept of identity would strongly collide with the complexity of human identities, which are constructed by many elements and are not a static reality.[142] The nationalist theory makes individual and social national identity overlap, whereas an individual's identity is more likely the product of the dialectic combination of different identities—for example, one personal, one (or usually several) social and one human.[143] Thus, human beings have multiple identities, sometimes even contrasting with each other, from which plural affiliations to particular groups derive,[144] while national identities are but one of these allegiances. Though nationalist ideologies aim at reducing this complexity to unity, '[t]he political conception of a person as a citizen of a nation—important as it is—cannot override all other conceptions and the behavioral consequences of other forms of group association'.[145]

1.2.6 Is There a Good and a Bad Nationalism?

Nationalism gives the impression of having undergone a transformation over the years, in particular 'over the course of the nineteenth century, a slow, inexorable shift from the left of the political spectrum towards the right'.[146] In pre-revolutionary France, nationalism was clearly inspired by the ideas of the Enlightenment and its main purpose was to create a liberal rational society,[147] in which an underlining cosmopolitan inspiration was present. A similar connotation was initially present even in Germany but it later developed in that context into a different phenomenon. In the scientific debate, thus, a strong contrast between civic and ethnic nationalism—often proposed even in geographical

[142] 'While it is plausible to say that a person's character and core commitments are partly shaped by their community, it is implausible to suggest that they are wholly determined by their community and that we cannot attain any critical distance', S Caney, 'Liberalism and Communitarianism: A Misconceived Debate' (1992) 40 *Political Studies* 273–89, 276.

[143] B Parekh, *A New Politics of Identity* (n 126), 8 ff.

[144] A Sen, 'Justice across Borders', in P De Greiff and C Cronin (eds), *Global Justice and Transnational Politics* (Cambridge MA, The MIT Press, 2002) 42 and 43.

[145] A Sen, 'Justice across Borders' (n 144), 43.

[146] J Leerssen, *National Thought in Europe* (n 1), 215. This shift is one of the characteristics which distinguished nationalism of 1880–1914 from the Mazzinian phase according to EJ Hobsbawm, *Nations and Nationalism since 1780* (n 44), 102.

[147] H Kohn, *Nationalism: Its Meaning and History* (n 2), 29.

terms[148]—has been made. This juxtaposition was already clear to some of the bright intellectual minds of the nineteenth century; for instance the German poet Heinrich Heine, who mixed elements of both Romanticism and Enlightenment in liberal patriotic fervor, noted that:

> Der Patriotismus des Franzosen besteht darin daß sein Herz erwärmt wird, durch diese Wärme sich ausdehnt, sich erweitert, daß es nicht mehr bloß die nächsten Angehörigen, sondern ganz Frankreich, das ganze Land der Zivilisation, mit seiner Liebe umfasst; der Patriotismus des Deutschen hingegen besteht darin daß sein Herz enger wird, daß es sich zusammenzieht wie Leder in der Kälte, daß er das Fremdländische hasst, daß er nicht mehr Weltbürger, nicht mehr Europäer, sondern nur ein enger Deutscher sein will.[149]

One could therefore be tempted to conclude that the focus on objective elements of identification leads to 'evil' forms of nationalism, while the focus on subjective aspects does not imply such an outcome. This conclusion would be very incorrect. In the first place, it must be made clear that the possibility of collocating civic nationalism in France and ethnic in Germany is doubtful, while even a structural difference between civic and ethnic versions of nationalism is not convincing. A sharp distinction indeed appears 'conceptually ambiguous, empirically misleading, and normatively problematic'.[150] The advocates of the civic French nationalism have themselves used an ethno-nationalist vocabulary and imagery to some extent,[151] and many elements of ethnic nationalism can be found in the civic version and vice versa.[152]

In theory it is possible and useful to conceive—even accepting some conceptual ambiguity—a difference between civic and ethnic forms of nationalism, but such a clear-cut distinction is less evident in practice. Not even the accent on a voluntaristic criterion prevented French nationalism from taking an illiberal form, as became evident in the period of the Terror. Very soon, between the end of the

[148] In particular H Kohn, *Nationalism* (n 2), and J Plamenatz, 'Two Types of Nationalism' (n 30), made use of the distinction. Surprisingly, whereas both authors agree that French nationalism can be intended as a Western phenomenon, the nature of the German one is less clear: Kohn believes it represents a form of Eastern nationalism, while Plamenatz places it on the same level as the French in the category of Western nationalism, considering the Slav and even the South American experiences examples of Eastern nationalism; the one—in the opinion of this author—typical of 'peoples recently drawn into civilisation hitherto alien to them', in J Plamenatz, 'Two Types of Nationalism' (n 30), 33.

[149] H Heine, *Sämmtliche Werke*, vol 5 (Hamburg, Hoffmann und Campe, 1861) 51: The patriotism of the Frenchman consists in this—that his heart warms, is stretched and grows wider by this warmth, so that it no longer embraces merely its nearest relations, but all France, the whole civilized earth, with its love. The patriotism of the German, on the contrary, consists in this –that his heart grows narrower, that it contracts, like leather in the cold; that he detests what is foreign; that he wishes to be no longer a citizen of the world, no longer a European, but merely a narrow German(from (1985) 53 *The Quarterly Review* 225).

[150] R Brubaker, *Ethnicity without Groups* (Cambridge, MA, Harvard University Press, 2004) 5.

[151] P Spencer and H Wollman, *Nationalism* (n 89), 102; M Silverman, *Deconstructing the Nation: Immigration, Racism and Citizenship in Modern France* (London, Routledge, 1992) 20.

[152] A Walicki, *The Enlightenment and the Birth of Modern Nationhood: Polish Political Thought from Noble Republicanism to Tadeusz Kosciuszko* (Notre Dame, University of Notre Dame Press, 1989) 5 ff. In the same sense, AD Smith, 'National Identity and the Idea of European Unity' (1992) 68 *International Affairs*, 55–76, 61.

eighteenth and the beginning of the nineteenth centuries, France, Germany and the United Kingdom competed in an impressive and fully nationalistic arms race that led Europe rapidly to war. Even taking the roots of modern nationalism in a period prior to the French Revolution into consideration, it can be noted that the nation-building process used the marginalisation of minority groups as a primary technique of homogenisation—a form of 'cohesion by exclusion' which has been brought about by making use in particular of religious criteria.[153] In this sense, anti-Semitism has been an important factor. While the phenomenon became evident in France only during the Dreyfuss affair at the end of the nineteenth century, the legal historian can detect that already at the beginning of that century 'legal anti-Semitism' was quite common in France.[154]

A degeneration of nationalism from a liberal to an aggressive ideology appears less self-evident and 'civic' and 'liberal' do not appear to be synonyms. In this regard, civic and ethnic nationalism do not diverge considerably, as they both make use of a technique based on the exaltation of internal national homogeneity and of the differences between nations, which appears to reveal itself as a typical characteristic of nationalism. The same can hold true for constitutional patriotism, notwithstanding its commitment to liberal values. From the perspective of the legal scholar, Weiler detects the role that constitutional values can have in this sense; constitutions indeed:

> are about restricting power, not enlarging it; they protect fundamental rights of the individual; and they define a collective identity which does not make us feel queasy the way some forms of ethnic identity might. Mobilizing in the name of sovereignty is *passé*; mobilizing to protect identity by insisting on constitutional specificity is *à la mode*.[155]

1.3 WHY A STATE SHOULD BE NATIONAL

Having noted that nationalism is the political principle which holds that national and political units should coincide, we must now investigate the theoretical justifications for that principle: *why* national and political units should coincide. Authors adhering to a view called 'liberal nationalism', whose main arguments will be introduced in the following paragraphs, have recently tried to give an answer to this only seemingly simple question. The recurring criticisms to those arguments will be highlighted as well, in order to emphasise by contrast which points are openly rejected by other schools of thought and thus represent exclusively nationalist arguments.

[153] AW Marx, *Faith in Nation: Exclusionary Origins of Nationalism* (Oxford, Oxford University Press, 2003) 143 ff.

[154] J-H Halpérin, *Entre nationalisme juridique et communauté de droit* (Paris, Presses Universitaires de France, 1999) 33.

[155] JHH Weiler, 'A Constitution for Europe? Some Hard Choices' (2004) 40 *Journal of Common Market Studies* 563–80, 569.

It can already be said that two fundamental types of criticism can be made with regard to liberal nationalist theories: on the one hand one can affirm that nationalist conclusions are based upon incorrect assumptions or, on the other hand that, although those premises can be agreed with, they do not necessarily have to lead to liberal nationalist inferences. The former objection is the strongest and is normally motivated from a cosmopolitan perspective; the latter can more easily be advocated by communitarians who, nonetheless, reject the equalisation of community and nation made by liberal nationalist authors.

1.3.1 Nationalism and Liberalism

Most studies of nationalism have investigated and offered interpretations of the origins and main manifestations of that ideology, but there have been fewer attempts to explain its philosophical and normative foundations. Modernist authors have already explained the reasons for nationalist ideologies and their political and economic agendas, while a similar attempt by those who advocate nationalist positions has been less systematic. Liberal nationalists, who have attempted to find a remedy for the alleged philosophical 'poverty' of nationalism, take an interesting position in this debate.[156]

These authors have attempted to demonstrate that nationalism is not necessarily a reprehensible phenomenon and that its true nature is visible in historical experiences like the Italian Risorgimento and German Romanticism instead of Fascism and Nazism, which, paradoxically, even contradict many nationalist principles.[157] Liberal nationalists can actually support their allegation drawing evidence from history. The claim that the state should coincide with the nation may work as a limitation and therefore hinder the constitution of some kind of multi-national empire, an aspect which was problematic in particular for fascist regimes. In this sense, already those fascists who were more familiar with political and legal theory rejected the principle of nationalities, viewed with suspicion as a limit[158] that would have crystallised the international status quo.[159] On the other hand, 'real' nationalism has been perceived as functional to liberalism for a long time; some liberals already saw the nation-state as the model which best suits the

[156] B Anderson, *Imagined Communities* (n 7), 5.

[157] AD Smith, *Theories of Nationalism* (London, Duckworth, 1983) 262 ff; Y Tamir, *Liberal Nationalism* (n 84), 93.

[158] Camillo Pellizzi sustained in 1927: 'si tratta di stabilire se il principio nazionale debba costituire uno dei principii ispiratori e motori del Fascismo. Io dico di no [ ] La mia tesi è che il principio nazionale si fonda su un mito o pseudo-concetto empirico, di valore occasionale [ ] Dal Fascismo in poi non più ci si deve muovere per la nazione, bensì dalla nazione verso l'ideale fascista di stato e d'impero,' in R De Felice, *Autobiografia del fascismo. Antologia di testi fascisti 1919–1945* (Torino, Einaudi, 2004) 300. On the figure of Camillo Pellizzi, *see* A James Gregor, *Mussolini's Intellectuals. Fascist Social and Political Thought* (Princeton, Princeton University Press, 2005) 165 ff.

[159] C Costamagna, 'Il diritto internazionale nell'ordine nuovo' (1941) *Lo Stato* 401–20.

interests of a liberal society,[160] and this was actually the deep conviction of most patriots in the nation-building period: 'A world of nations would, it was believed, be a liberal world, and a liberal world would consist of nations'.[161]

Is nationalism therefore an unlucky victim of a historical misunderstanding? In reality, the possibility of reconciling liberalism and nationalism remains more controversial and, despite the optimism of the eighteenth- and nineteenth-century patriots, '[t]he future was to show that the relationship between the two was not as simple as this'.[162] In fact, the two schools of thought often appear in radical contradiction to one another; one is inspired by universalistic ideals, whereas the other school takes its cue from particularistic ones.[163] No wonder that, in the aftermath of the Second World War, after the idea of a nationalist world order peacefully organised in independent nation-states had revealed its fallacies, some of the most influential liberals of that period expressed clearly anti-nationalist views.[164]

More recently, however, various contemporary political theorists sustained a type of liberal—ie non aggressive—nationalism which, of course, appears as 'the most acceptable form of nationalism'.[165] Having discarded any form of political authoritarianism, their interesting effort has been to prove the philosophical compatibility of nationalism and liberalism. Liberal nationalists like David Miller and Yael Tamir quite surprisingly seem to adhere to modernist views. They accept the idea that a nation is an 'imagined community' instead of something similar to a biological entity and that nations have been 'built' through the employment of techniques as those described by Anderson and Billig. Nonetheless, the beliefs that hold societies together 'cannot be transmitted except through cultural artefacts which are available to everyone who belongs [to the nation]'.[166] In the end, it remains true that 'nations really exist, ie they are not purely fictitious entities'.[167] Moderate modernist in the positive part of their theory, liberal nationalists defend the ideology in its normative assumptions. As already discussed, this position does not necessarily result in a contradiction, since even modernists are more concerned with a description of nationalism and its origins rather than with its philosophical justification. In the opinion of liberal nationalists, a moderate nationalism is still a useful political principle that can be employed to promote peaceful and noble ideals such as social justice—as with Miller—or peace between ethnic groups at

[160] JS Mill, *Considerations on Representative Government* [1861] (New York, Harper & Brothers Publishers, 1867) 310.

[161] EJ Hobsbawm, *The Age of Capital* (n 47), 97.

[162] Ibid, 97

[163] A MacIntyre, *Is Patriotism a Virtue?* (Lawrence, University Press of Kansas, 1984) 19.

[164] A Vincent, 'Liberal Nationalism: An Irresponsible Compound?' (1997) 45 *Political Studies* 275–95, 279.

[165] Ibid, 294.

[166] D Miller, *On Nationality* (n 129), 32.

[167] Ibid, 10.

war with each other—as with Tamir.[168] They therefore describe and analyse a pure ideal form of nationalism, whose only assumption is that national and political units should be congruent, excluding external elements such as racism.

1.3.2 Nation and Culture Coincide

Liberal nationalists are not exempted from the recurring problem of defining a nation, and admit that not every minority group can be entitled to self-determination.[169] Liberal thinkers already singled out useful criteria to determine which communities are entitled to self-determination, which can be summed up in a prior inclusion in the actual state and in the failure of the state to deal with the needs of that community.[170] On the contrary, liberal nationalists resort to the distinction between *nationality* and *ethnicity* to understand 'when a national community presently incorporated in a multinational state is justified in demanding secession'.[171] Accordingly, only nationalities should be entitled to secession, whereas mere ethnicities could at most aim at the reform of the state.[172] An ethnic group can be described as 'a set of people with a distinct set of cultural values and a shared language, who recognise their cultural kinship with one another, and engage in practices that set them apart from outsiders'.[173] Unfortunately, as Miller himself recognises, the distinction between these two terms is not very clear[174] and indeed it already presupposes a theory of nationality based upon the employment of one of the criteria of nationhood examined before.

Adhering to some extent to modernist views and picturing the nation as an imagined community, liberal nationalists reject a traditional understanding of the concept of nation, based in particular upon objective criteria of nationhood exemplified by ethnicity, so that multi-ethnic nations can exist in their perspective.[175] The characteristics of a nation are then defined by its cultural homogeneity rather than the biological or linguistic similarity among its members. These authors are completely aware of the fact that an exaggeration of the cultural similarities amongst members of a nation and differences between different nations could lead to the creation of stereotypes which can prove to be dangerous. Nonetheless, having rejected this extreme position of classical nationalist rhetoric, they still argue that some kind of cultural homogeneity can be found in some nations and

[168] The Israeli scholar Y Tamir, *Liberal Nationalism* (n 84), for example, sustains a moderate nationalist position assuming that the creation of two independent states—one day maybe parts of a confederation—could put an end to the bloody conflict between Israel and Palestine.

[169] Y Tamir, *Liberal Nationalism* (n 84), 76.

[170] AH Birch, 'Another Liberal Theory of Secession' (1984) 32 *Political Studies* 596–602. *See* also J Breuilly, *Nationalism and the State* (Manchester, Manchester University Press, 1985) 6.

[171] D Miller, *On Nationality* (n 129), 108.

[172] Ibid, 112.

[173] Ibid, 127.

[174] Ibid,112.

[175] Ibid, 21.

can be employed in order to distinguish that community from other national groups,[176] just like in Herder's 'organic-genetic'[177] conception of culture, according to which 'every nationality is one people, having its own national culture as well as its language'.[178] Whether one calls it 'homogeneity' or not, co-nationals share a set of basic information and *conventions*: different 'ways of doing things'.[179] These are 'inherently arbitrary human artifices' and as such they cannot 'aspire to any objective truth status'.[180]

Yet, liberal nationalists mistrust subjective criteria of identifications exemplified by the ones advocated by the theory of constitutional patriotism, seen as too thin.[181] Even their concept of culture is predominantly objective.[182] Furthermore, Miller claims that 'national identities invariably contain some ethnic ingredients'[183] and that '[c]entral to the idea of nationality is not individual *will*, but individual *identity*',[184] blaming Renan for having confused these concepts. For all these reasons, unless one rejects the objective criterion of culture,[185] liberal nationalism cannot be intended as a mere synonym of civic nationalism.

Culture provides the state with legitimacy, but in return it demands protection. In Tamir's view, nationalism's end is cultural in itself.[186] In order to protect culture—implying that culture is worthy of protection independent of the values it embodies—the nation-state stands out as the best form of political organisation. The liberal theory, according to which liberties and local customs can only be preserved within a multi-national state,[187] is expressly rejected for wrongly assuming national identities as 'exclusive in their nature'.[188] Within a nation-state, it is indeed possible to promote policies of protection of the national culture that would be impossible in a multi-national state. This argument seems quite circular: a state has to be culturally homogeneous because this allows it to adopt policies of cultural homogenisation. But still, according to the liberal nationalist's view, differences have to be safeguarded, because cultures are a relevant part of one's identity[189]—indeed, 'the framework within which [people's] plans and various

[176] Ibid, 85.

[177] RR Ergang, *Herder and the Foundations of German Nationalism* (n 38), 234.

[178] Quoted ibid, 88.

[179] RE Goodin, 'Conventions and Conversions, or, Why Is Nationalism Sometimes so Nasty?', in R McKim and J McMahan (eds), *The Morality of Nationalism* (Oxford, Oxford University Press, 1997) 92.

[180] Ibid, 95.

[181] D Miller, *On Nationality* (n 129), 163.

[182] Tamir's position tends more to voluntaristic nationalism: *see* Y Tamir, *Liberal Nationalism* (n 84), 57.

[183] D Miller, *On Nationality* (n 129), 122.

[184] Ibid, 37.

[185] *See* for example B Barry, 'Statism and Nationalism: A Cosmopolitan Critique', in I Shapiro and L Brilmayer (eds), *Global Justice* (New York, New York University Press, 1999) 53 ff.

[186] Y Tamir, *Liberal Nationalism* (n 84), p. XIII.

[187] JEED Acton, 'Nationality', in JEED Acton, *Essays on Freedom and Power* (New York, Meridian Books, 1955) 160.

[188] D Miller, *Citizenship and National Identity* (Cambridge, Polity Press, 2000) 34.

[189] Y Tamir, *Liberal Nationalism* (n 84), 73.

projects are realized and exist'.[190] Building upon communitarian arguments, liberal nationalists argue that the construction of one's identity is a complex process dependent on the social context(s) where it takes place. Thus, cultural circumstances in the society influence the cultural identity of the person who is a part of that community. If this is true, the respect toward national culture perfectly coincides with the respect for the person's identity.

Culture is the basis of the liberal nation-state and even the term has become synonymous with nation, so that to speak of multi-national states means to speak of multi-cultural states. The model of the multi-national state is distrusted by both classical and liberal nationalists. In their view, an efficient democracy can only work within the context of a homogeneous cultural state, so that the existence of a common culture becomes the major premise of a wide range of nationalist arguments.[191] There are different reasons for this assumption.

1.3.3 Information

In the liberal nationalist state, fellow citizens must be preferred over outsiders not because outsiders are of a culture, language, or race which is inferior—which is what racist nationalism would suggest—or even because they are only 'foreigners' to which no sense of commitment is ethically due. From this perspective the contrast between particularism and universalism could never be bridged. On the contrary, the partiality of liberal nationalism is morally and politically justified by the fact that the needs and exigencies of one group are better known and therefore dealt with most efficiently by people of that same group;[192] in this sense, the justification of the partiality is merely 'instrumental'.[193]

Starting from a universalistic standpoint, liberal nationalists claim that particularism is not a value in itself but can be seen as an efficient way to achieve universalistic principles. The tension between impartiality and partiality can be solved by developing a morality of partiality, intended as a means to achieve an end—that of of justice—which is of a universal nature: 'in order to realise the values that lie at the base of our ethical theory most effectively, it makes sense for each agent to pursue those values in relation to particular other agents rather than the whole universe of agents'.[194] If everyone's needs were to be taken care of by all individuals within the society, exigencies would not be dealt with properly. Thus, a model of assigned responsibility seems to be more efficient[195]—as opposed to one of shared responsibility—whereby a small number of people are instructed

[190] C Gans, *The Limits of Nationalism* (n 85), 170

[191] P Gilbert, *The Philosophy of Nationalism* (Boulder, CO, Westview Press, 1998) 138.

[192] D Miller, *On Nationality* (n 129), 52.

[193] A Miklós, 'Nationalist Criticisms of Cosmopolitan Justice' (2009) 1 *Public Reason* 105–24, 114.

[194] D Miller, *On Nationality* (n 129), 51.

[195] RE Goodin, 'What is So Special About our Fellow Countrymen?' (1988) 98 *Ethics* 663–86, 678.

to take care of the needs of a few subjects, for 'hospital patients are better cared for by being assigned to particular doctors rather than having all the hospital's doctors devote one *n*th of their time to each of the hospital's *n* patients'.[196] By the same token, the administration of a nation should only take care of the needs of its members and not of outsiders.

Starting from this assumption, one could then think that it is only a matter of efficiency in terms of regulation that necessitates adherence to particularism instead of universalism. The national group, thus, could take political decisions for a broader group, but there would be the risk that these decisions would not fit that group's needs. Nonetheless—Miller claims—arguing that assigning responsibility for the rights and welfare of the Swedes to other Swedes is convenient because of reasons of physical proximity and administrative ease would be a mistake.[197] Instead, according to his theory, there is a cultural similarity between co-nationals; as a consequence, they are 'better informed' than outsiders.[198] Nationalist theories, thus, assume that co-nationals will be presumably more competent than others since they have a 'cultural similarity'. According to the criterion of culture, actually, people sharing a culture also share a nationality. But here a tension between liberals and nationalists could arise, for the former can argue that decisions are to be made by those—usually the ones who are 'closer' to the citizens—who are more informed on particular circumstances;[199] whereas nationalists will claim that competences have necessarily to be exercised at the nation-state level, because outsiders are 'culturally' unable to cope properly with the exigencies of other people.

Liberal nationalists defend the idea that co-nationals have to take care only of the interests of their fellow countrymen by positing that a common national culture justifies a kind of presumption of competence in dealing with co-nationals' needs. This line of reasoning can be criticised nonetheless from several standpoints. In the first place, it is easy to see that it is not sure that co-nationals are more aware of one another's needs. This would probably be true in a simple society where information spreads freely and members of the community are well acquainted with one another (*Gemeinschaft*). In modern and complex societies, however, it would be quite formalistic to assume that all compatriots have the same knowledge or even culture: members of the society are never (and can never be) totally informed. Certain kinds of information are spread particularly among certain groups, but those groups only occasionally correspond to national constituencies. If legislation had to regulate a particular technical issue, would the cultural homogeneity of the nation be relevant in order to affirm that this group is the most advisable for taking an informed decision? This is part of a more

[196] Ibid, 681.
[197] D Miller, *On Nationality* (n 129), 63.
[198] Ibid, 63.
[199] FA von Hayek, 'The Use of Knowledge in Society' (1945) 35 *American Economic Review* 519–30, 524 ff.

general argument against liberal nationalism, which criticises how nationalists put emphasis on national identity and culture, forgetting several other identities and cultures which are transnational and on occasion more relevant. Furthermore, the mere fact that a problem crops up in or directly affects a particular community does not mean that the people belonging to that community will be aware of it or be more able to deal with the problem itself.

These criticisms of the liberal nationalist argument can be taken to the extreme, making the question arise whether it is reasonable, in an era characterised by the globalisation of economic, social and environmental problems, to consign the regulation of those problems to local institutions, not making an 'internationalisation of political decision-making' follow an 'internationalisation of the problems' and 'of the societies'.[200] Both the nationalist argument and the counter-argument, nonetheless, appear to be quite indifferent to important questions of democratic legitimacy, on which it is necessary to focus.

1.3.4 Democracy

Liberal nationalists identify a particular justification for the national organisation of a state as democracy. Already in Mill's opinion, even democratic institutions are impossible in a state that is not also a nation.[201] Homogeneity is seen as the precondition for a liberal state, while where the population is too diverse, it becomes problematic for institutions to deal with the needs and interests of all the people, so that eventually imperfect or unsatisfying political choices could be made. Indeed, different groups within the nation will presumably have different interests, possibly opposite to those of other groups, which will soon or later lead to a high degree of social tension that, in turn, could induce the government to take oppressive measures.[202] On the other hand, if these differences were too significant it would be impossible for minority groups to participate actively in normal democratic life and they would therefore be slowly marginalised—linguistic minorities who cannot understand the political debate going on in the mass media provides one example. Furthermore, a culturally heterogeneous population will give no guarantee that the state laws will find homogeneous application in society. As it is likely that cultural minorities will not participate in the law-making process, legislation will be the expression of the interests of only one cultural group. In this sense, legislation (but also more generally state administration) will necessarily be an imposition highly doomed to failure, since:

> Much state activity involves the furthering of goals which cannot be achieved without the voluntary co-operation of citizens. For this activity to be successful, the citizens must

[200] K Goldmann, *Transforming the European Nation-State: Dynamics of Internationalization* (London, Sage, 2001) 8 ff.

[201] JS Mill, *Considerations on Representative Government* (n 160), 310.

[202] *See* also FA von Hayek, *The Road to Serfdom* (London, Routledge, 2007) 228.

> trust the state, and they must trust one another to comply with what the state demands of them.[203]

Mill's concern that democratic institutions may only exist within nation-states is nonetheless probably excessive, although it highlights important aspects of the organisation of a liberal society.

From a theoretical perspective, the fact that there are groups that have different needs within the state is the usual situation that occurs in any democratic state, in which political decisions are the outcome of a dialectic juxtaposition of social and parliamentary groups. In this sense, a society is *always* heterogeneous, if not from a national perspective, at least from an ideological one.

From an empirical perspective, it is self-evident that numerous states that are multi-national are also democratic. Of course, nationalists who sustain Mill's opinion will argue that to consider those countries multi-national denotes too strong a reliance on the objective criterion of the (native) language, whereas even those countries could be intended as nation-states, since a national identity independent of linguistic diversity already exists or because in the end one culture tends to overwhelm the others.[204]

The debate on nationalism, in other words, still suffers from a lack of certainty and consent as to the answer to the fundamental question '*Qu'est-ce qu'une nation?*'. The risk is to overlook the distinction between nation and state, in a positivistic way arguing that multi-cultural states are in any case nations because they are also states. Otherwise, acknowledging that there is no single univocal criterion of nationhood, the consideration that the modern world boasts no single state that can be considered fully national, will collide with the fact that numerous states are nevertheless democratic.

Without a doubt, it can be problematic, especially for linguistic minorities to participate actively in the public life of their country. It would be easier for them to follow political events in countries that are more linguistically homogeneous than in their own, and this situation can incite often legitimate independence claims. In several democratic countries, nonetheless, the institutions take into account these circumstances, granting minorities particular benefits and mechanisms of representation. The democratic character of a country is evident also in the way in which it deals with minorities, allowing them to participate in the political debate, so that in this sense, multi-nationality becomes not only the best guarantee but also some kind of test of democracy.[205]

203 D Miller, *On Nationality* (n 129), 90–91.
204 D Miller, *On Nationality* (n 129), 94 and 95.
205 JEED Acton, *Nationality* (n 187), 160.

1.3.5 Solidarity

Nationalist and liberal nationalist authors argue that a nation is characterised by the existence of social bonds between its members. They thus agree on the definition of the nation as a 'community of people, whose members are bound together by a sense of solidarity, a common culture, a national consciousness'.[206] The root of such solidarity ties is represented by the fact that individuals tend to relate to other people with whom they share similar characteristics.

According to this perspective, since solidarity automatically follows identification, no identification and therefore no solidarity would be possible in a community where people are too different, as exemplified by a multi-national society. This assumption has important consequences for state policies. Indeed, as long as we consider humans as individual subjects detached from the community, if the government takes a portion of the individuals' income to share with the have-nots in society, this would be perceived as unjust—which is indeed the sense of the libertarians' criticism of Rawls's liberalism—but if a strong sense of community exists, a redistributive taxation would be accepted as just because the economic resources would remain within the community. On the contrary, redistribution across community borders would be perceived of as unjust.

Miller makes clear that this assumption—sustained in particular by communitarians—is based upon studies of social psychologists that prove that perceptions of similarity affect the boundaries of the moral community.[207] If this is true, a multi-national state will not be able to enact welfare policies, and a concept of distributive justice which exceeds the state's borders will not be possible, since co-nationals have to take care of their fellows' interests only:[208] 'The duties we owe to our fellow–nationals are different from, and more extensive than, the duties we owe to human beings as such'.[209] Solidarity among people will arise only if and when some kind of social ties are present. The clearest examples of this kind of social obligations are those which can be found within a family: a father should naturally feel a stronger commitment to his own child; by the same token we are 'far more disturbed by someone who neglects his own children than by someone who fails to support someone else's children'.[210] The reason is that between father and son there is a particular moral and biological obligation not comparable to the one generally binding a person to another person's children. The case of the father neglecting his child is therefore more immoral, since it contains the violation of a stronger moral and natural obligation. No one would deny that this

[206] H Seton-Watson, *Nations and States* (London, Methuen, 1977) 1. The solidarity element is also emphasised by B Russell, *Freedom and Organisation 1814–1914* (London, Allen & Unwin, 1934) 394: 'a geographical group possessed of a sentiment of solidarity'.

[207] D Miller, *Citizenship and National Identity* (n 188) , 157–58.

[208] T Hurka, *The Justification of National Partiality*, in R McKim and J McMahan (eds), *The Morality of Nationalism* (Oxford, Oxford University Press, 1997) 143.

[209] D Miller, *Citizenship and National Identity* (n 188), 27.

[210] Y Tamir, *Liberal Nationalism* (n 84), 99.

particular kind of relationship deserves specific and particular attention,[211] and also legal orders usually consider these ties in order to establish differentiated legal treatment. For the same reason, we are more negatively struck 'by a person who deserts a friend in need than by one who does not help a stranger', and, continuing to quote from Tamir, 'by individuals who are indifferent to starving members of their own community than by those who do not care for starving people in faraway countries'.[212]

Whereas Tamir's first two examples are obvious and express principles which are indeed already recognised in different forms by most contemporary legal orders,[213] the third example is nonetheless more debatable. Why should a person who does not care about starving children in his or her own country be more immoral than a person who does not care about children in the same conditions in remote territories? Unless one seriously believes that the adage 'out of sight, out of mind' can be employed as a philosophical justification, the underlying idea holds that the nation is a kind of 'enlarged family'. From this perspective, not caring about a starving child in one's vicinity is as despicable as ignoring a dying brother.[214] As already seen, this sets out the reason for traditional and primordialist interpretations of the nation, which put a particular emphasis on the objective element of the bloodline. From this perspective, if everyone shares the same ancestors, all co-nationals can be part of a common family, therefore sharing the same social, moral and biological obligations which exist within a family. This view implies the 'natural' character of the nation, the cornerstone of primordialist theories of nationalism, critically considered by the same modernist theories that have been nonetheless accepted also by advocates of liberal nationalism.

Yet, starting from even moderately modernist positions, one should come to the conclusion that there is no natural relation between an individual and starving children either at home or in faraway locations. The relation, of course, is purely

[211] *See* for instance M Nussbaum, 'Patriotism and Cosmopolitanism', in J Cohen (ed), *For Love of Country: Debating the Limits of Patriotism* (Boston, Beacon Press, 1996) 135.

[212] Y Tamir, *Liberal Nationalism* (n 84), 99.

[213] So for example, family law imposes on people particularly strong duties only towards their own children, criminal law considers as autonomous more serious crimes or aggravating circumstances the offences directed against family, procedural law generally relieves people from the duty to testify against their family and so on.

[214] Studies in neuroscience have proved that human beings tend to be more empathetic with individuals from their own ethnic background (as long as it is recognisable) and presumably more willing to help them than individuals from other ethnic groups; *see* Xiaojing Xu, Xiangyu Zuo, Xiaoying Wang and Shihui Han, 'Do You Feel My Pain? Racial Group Membership Modulates Empathic Neural Responses' (2009) 29 *The Journal of Neuroscience* 8525–29. Nonetheless, these kinds of studies can hardly be employed to justify nationalist arguments, since the empathy with co-ethnicals can easily be seen as an ethnic bias, thus a consequence of nationalist politics rather than their justification. On ethnic biases *see* JE Kilbride and M Yarczower, 'Ethnic Bias in the Recognition of Facial Expressions: A Cross-cultural Comparison between Zambia and the United States' (1983) 8 *Journal of Nonverbal Behavior* 27–41 In this sense, it would be necessary to conduct experiments in which subjects have not been exposed to social conditioning yet. (A similar study involving children has been made with regard to the capacity to recognise vocal emotions: R Markham and L Wang, 'Recognition of Emotion by Chinese and Australian Children' (1996) 27 *Journal of Cross-Cultural Psychology* 616–43.)

imagined. From the same perspective, the creation of such an imagined link by nationalist movements is essential to provide the nation with a degree of social homogeneity which is necessary to further the economic system from an agrarian to an industrial economy, or—from a legal historical perspective—to boost the shift from the status to the contract. The function of national ties is to make up for the loss of traditional identities, occurring when rural populations moved to the industrialised city.[215] But in this sense, if the relationship between members of the nation—unlike a family or even a restricted community—is purely imagined and imaginable, there is no *ethical* reason why co-nationals have to be preferred to outsiders. Given that relations of affinity are not a fixed thing but are continuously changing,[216] one could think that there is no reason why the same nation-building techniques which have been successfully employed by the nation-state in order to create homogeneity on the inside cannot be also used, for example, at a European level to extend the borders of social solidarity, hitherto limited to the nation-state.[217]

More fundamentally, even admitting that solidarity could only arise as a consequence of identification, it remains questionable why only national identification should matter in this regard. Why should someone feel a major commitment to someone with whom he or she shares nationality and not with someone else with whom he or she shares political opinions, religious beliefs and so on? What is more, why should human beings prefer and identify only with 'their own kind'?[218] Of course, one of the contents of nationalist ideology is putting emphasis on the national identity while playing down all other elements: 'Nationality is de facto the main source of such solidarity'.[219]

Furthermore, according to the liberal nationalist's theory, the 'imagined' social obligation plays more than a merely subsidiary role, some kind of presumption of similarity between people who do not know each other, but has its own autonomy. People could also distrust or even detest their own co-nationals, but that would not affect the social obligations they still would have toward each other as members of the same national community; solidarity ties stem not from sympathy but from connectedness.[220] But since a nation has been defined as a 'community of people, whose members are bound together by a sense of solidarity, a common culture, a national consciousness',[221] we end up in a vicious circle: the sense of solidarity is a constitutive element of the nation, but its roots are the national community itself. Co-nationals have social ties because they live in the same

215 BC Shafer, *Faces of Nationalism* (n 12), 220.

216 J Rawls, *The Law of People* (Cambridge MA, Harvard University Press, 1999) 113.

217 J Habermas, 'The European Nation-State and the Pressures of Globalization', in P De Greiff and C Cronin (eds), *Global Justice and Transnational Politics* (Cambridge MA, The MIT Press, 2002) 230–31.

218 B Parekh, *A New Politics of Identity* (n 126), 83.

219 D Miller, *On Nationality* (n 129), 32.

220 Y Tamir, *Liberal Nationalism* (n 84), 98.

221 H Seton-Watson, *Nations and States* (n 206), 1.

nation, which is such because its members have common social ties. In another perspective, the duties that keep a community united diverge in terms of structure and cannot be compared with the duties toward one's family, since they are political obligations that imply reciprocity.[222] What is more, these duties are not even due toward fellow nationals but rather to the nation itself, with consequent benefits for all its citizens.[223]

1.3.6 Justice

As communitarians sustain, the concept of justice is not a universal: justice is socially embedded. There is no single and univocal understanding of solidarity and justice: what is just for one person can be not for another one and so on. According to communitarians, a certain concept of justice arises only from the shared way of life in the community; in particular, a distribution can be just or not only in relation to the social meaning of the good, which, of course, can vary depending on the society.[224]

Liberal nationalist authors specify (restrictively or extensively) the community as a nation. If a nation is a community mainly characterised by a common culture—a *Kulturnation*—and social obligations between its members, it is possible to imagine that different nations present different kinds of social ties. But if a transnational standard of social justice does not exist, it is also impossible to impose solidarity obligations among non co-nationals, since justice logically demands a community. Where such a community—ie nation—does not exist, there can be no justice. In liberal nationalists' argumentation, this point becomes particularly strong inasmuch as it is interwoven with post-modernist concerns of the protection of minorities' cultural rights since the definition of an ideal of justice is a cultural process expression of the identity of a community. In this respect, a difference between 'aggressive' and liberal nationalism emerges. Whereas the former acknowledges as legitimate only its own culture, the latter recognises the value of every culture but agrees to protect only one of them.

Starting from the exposed communitarian point, two normative consequences—one nationalist and one libertarian—can be drawn. If one admits that social justice policies are important, it will be opportune for societies to be organised as independent nation-states where solidarity between people will open up the possibility of enacting welfare policies. The same concept of global justice will entail on the one hand a minimum liberal duty not to harm, and the nationalist right to self-determination in order to pursue distributive justice on the other hand.[225]

[222] J McMahan, 'The Limits of National Partiality', in R McKim and J McMahan (eds), *The Morality of Nationalism* (Oxford, Oxford University Press, 1997) 129.

[223] Ibid, 130.

[224] M Walzer, *Spheres of Justice* (Oxford, Martin Robertson, 1983) 8.

[225] D Miller, *Citizenship and National Identity* (n 188), 177.

Given this interpretation, no tension between global justice and nationality arises.[226] Otherwise, from a communitarian and anti-nationalist perspective—which nonetheless acknowledges that solidarity can only arise where people are similar—the state will necessarily have to be minimal. In this case, therefore, a communitarian theory can support libertarian economic choices dismissing the relevance of social justice, furthermore seen as a mere 'mirage'.[227] From this perspective, a contrast between nationalist and cosmopolitan theories will necessarily arise, since it is impossible to justify from a universalistic standpoint why people should identify only with co-nationals or indirectly discriminate against outsiders. The contrast between liberalism and nationalism thus is of a mainly ethical nature, while liberal nationalists strove for a difficult conciliation of these different and contrasting approaches.

Building upon communitarian assumptions, liberal nationalists suggest therefore that welfare policies are only possible within a nation-state, since addressing a standard of distributive justice on a supranational or even global dimension makes no sense: every community—or nation—understands justice in a different way. This view is adopted by Miller in particular who, assuming that legislation choices are conditioned by the social understanding of what is good, asks the question:

> If the citizens of one state decide to opt for an entirely public system of education, while their neighbours prefer a mixture of public and private provision, why should a transnational court adjudicate on citizens' rights (discovering, say, a right to private education and applying it to both states)?[228]

According to this view, of course, it would be 'a serious form of oppression' to force that community to comply 'with the dictates of some foreign power',[229] and this, it would seem, independently of the will of the nation-state to be bounded by the decision of the 'foreign power', which is what normally occurs in the case of supranational institutions such as the Court of Justice of the European Union. This argument, that could undermine the 'fairness' even of European law, can nonetheless be criticised from different angles.

Cosmopolitans, for instance, affirm that all human beings share, beside an undeniable human nature, a common set of values and beliefs from which a common notion of justice can be derived; there are a series of basic goods which are relevant to every human being with no distinctions of cultures or nationalities.[230] In this regard, it makes no sense to object that there exist different interpretations in different contexts—a 'sufficient consensus and shared understanding' already

[226] Ibid, 178.

[227] FA von Hayek, *Law, Legislation and Liberty. Vol 2. The Mirage of Social Justice* (London and Henley, Routledge & Kegan Paul, 1976) 88 ff.

[228] D Miller, *Citizenship and National Identity* (n 188), 93.

[229] Ibid, 162.

[230] M Nussbaum, *Women and Human Development. The Capabilities Approach* (Cambridge, Cambridge University Press, 2000).

exists.[231] This sort of justice appears as some sort of greatest common divisor. Unfortunately, in order to be common, these values must also be particularly basic and generic. If it is easy to reach a consensus on the fact that human life is a good which is valuable in every community, other goods can be much more problematic.[232] Liberal nationalists argue, indeed, that this criticism is pertinent only 'by thinking only of the most basic of goods—food, shelter and clothing', but not as far as goods such as 'money, work, honours, status and political power' are concerned.[233] The goods belonging to the first category are so basic that if the national community did not acknowledge them in favour of outsiders, even a breach of a *positive* duty not to harm might materialise. Other goods, on the contrary, are highly dependent on the evaluation of the society and their configurability as rights is less obvious.

The cosmopolitan argument is therefore partially insufficient to confute the view of liberal nationalists. A different criticism can be obtained starting from a communitarian perspective, which assumes that the idea of the good is socially—but not necessarily nationally—conditioned: since every community is different from the others, it is likely that even within the same nation-state different concepts exist. How could a unified legislation deal properly with the social needs of all co-nationals? Two consequences derive from this example: no unified social justice policies are possible, or the country should be divided into different smaller nation-states each with its own idea of justice. But once again, empirical evidence contradicts the first point: there are in fact several modern societies that are multi-national and nonetheless enact solidarity policies. With regard to the second point, it is impossible to acknowledge a right to secession to every local community, because this would give rise to a potentially never-ending process of disintegration of the country that can be defined as 'Balkanisation'.[234] The most important criticism, however, remains that different ideas and concepts of social justice are expressions of political and ideological differences rather than of national ones. This consideration leads to the necessity of looking at the problem from a different perspective.

None of the approaches examined give an adequate answer to Miller's question that has been cited before. In Miller's example, the 'intangibility' of the political decisions taken by one nation-state seems to derive from the cultural nature of the decision itself, so that giving the power to decide on this matter to another authority (an international court for example) would imply not respecting the cultural and national identity of a country. In this respect, the nationalist character of the theory is revealed by the assumption that a national homogeneous concept of the good exists. In this sense, the legislative choice for, for instance, a public system of

[231] K-C Tan, 'Liberal Nationalism and Cosmopolitan Justice' (2002) 5 *Ethical Theory and Moral Practice* 431–61, 451.

[232] M Walzer, *Spheres of Justice* (n 224), 8.

[233] D Miller, *Citizenship and National Identity* (n 188), 168.

[234] Ibid, 38.

education is presented not as the outcome of a democratic parliamentary process where presumably an opinion prevailed over the others (that would already mean that in that society there is no unambiguous understanding of the good), but rather as the obvious consequence of the national character. This happens because it is 'also the *character* of national identity that matters from the point of view of social justice'.[235]

In this sense, the relevance of politics—as well as economics—is minimised, while political decisions appear to be the logical outcome of the character of a community according to a strong cultural determinism. It is then evident that any political indication coming from a foreign or supranational institution—in the example of Miller, an international court—would disregard national character. In practice, no form of transfer of competences and sovereignty would be possible. As we will see later on, this argument is often used in the debate on the harmonisation of European private law systems, where a general tendency considers numerous matters of legislation as cultural, denying the competence of the European institutions to decide on them.

Nevertheless, if we consider the dynamics of the democratic and legislative processes, it emerges that the 'culture' underlying most of the political choices is not national; otherwise it would make no sense to speak of majorities and minorities within the same national parliament. Those processes rather reflect ideological differences that, although possibly locally conditioned, are normally transnational or interests that depend on economic conditions rather than cultural traits.

1.3.7 Do Nation and Culture Coincide?

Liberal nationalists, as well as classical nationalists, assume that nationality and culture coincide and represent the most important criterion for distinguishing peoples. 'The religion of nationalism [...] makes a fetish of culture'.[236] So in this sense, as discussed previously, welfare policies would only be possible in nation-states because we identify with people with whom we share nationality; legislation should be enacted at a national level because only co-nationals know our needs due to cultural similarity; that legislation itself can only work at the level of the nation-state because it would not fit the interests of outsiders and so on. This basic assumption is nonetheless disputable and it can be challenged both from a cosmopolitan and a communitarian perspective. As already seen from a cosmopolitan perspective, we could argue that a basic identity is common to all human beings, so that the nationality does not always matter; communitarians would argue that identities depend on the particular community where the individual is

[235] D Miller, *On Nationality* (n 129), 94.

[236] B Kapferer, *Legends of People, Myths of State: Violence, Intolerance, and Political in Sri Lanka and Australia* (Washington, Smithsonian, 1998) 97.

embedded, which do not necessarily coincide with the nation-state, in particular if the state has a considerable geographical size.

Despite these objections, one could still accept that co-nationals share a distinctive set of common beliefs and values that form national culture, but to base a shared identity on this element would then require that those beliefs differ from the beliefs held in other countries. 'The problem here is how we recognize the national identity and culture of Britain, Canada, Australia, Germany, America or Israel? Is there a central public culture or distinctive set of values acknowledged by all the citizens?'[237] More importantly, it is not certain whether all members of the community will share those values. Although the nation continues to be represented as a basically homogeneous unity, people can in fact have different conceptions of the goods and values depending on their political, religious, cultural, or economic status. A French liberal would probably agree (and maybe develop solidarity) more easily with a Polish liberal—if they find a common language to communicate in—than with a French conservative. This happens for the reason that individuals have multiple and often conflicting group allegiances.[238] The national identity is definitely one of these and, in the perspective of many, still the prominent one, but it still co-exists with a number of different loyalties that can occasionally conflict with it or sometimes even reinforce it.[239] To disregard such sub-national distinctions and emphasise national homogeneity would mean, to some extent, to hide the existence of political, social, economic and more general cultural conflicts within the society—those conflicts which in mature countries are resolved through democratic processes rather than through homogenisation.

Cases in which those sets of values and beliefs are hopelessly irreconcilable come to mind. These are the situations in which even advocates of constitutional patriotism justify exclusion—as there is a lack of acceptance of the constitutional–patriotic principles—and that also modern legal systems tend to avoid even derogating from a purely democratic principle. Not even a formally democratic process could validate a statute which infringes fundamental rights, even if this were the expression of some hypothetical national, social or economic culture. In the context of a transnational constitutional law which completely rejects nationalism, the intersection of normative orders which embrace different and possibly irreconcilable values poses particular problems which can hardly be solved in the

[237] A Vincent, 'Liberal Nationalism' (n 164), 291.

[238] Ibid, 285. In the same sense, already in 1907, K Kautsky, 'Internationality and Internationality' (n 68), 374, challenged the idea of the nation as a 'commonality of destiny and culture' for it 'does not form anything that strictly distinguishes one nation from another. Despite their different nationalities, the German and the French Swiss are connected by a much closer community of fate and culture than the German Swiss and those from Vienna or Holstein'. In Kautsky's thought, it is indeed possible that a group of people living for a long time under the same conditions develop a common identity; nonetheless it is hard to affirm that the same can apply to larger states like Germany (376) and the most important factor to determine nationality is assumed to be the language (379).

[239] AD Smith, 'National Identity and the Idea of European Unity' (n 152), 58–59.

absence of a hierarchical order and that can at most hope to be dealt with in the framework of a 'dialogue' between normative systems.[240]

Although there is not a sufficient consensus as to a definition of national culture, nationalists assume that national culture will bind people much better than any other more concrete type of culture and identity. That the national identity should count more than other allegiances is of course the normative point of classical nationalist theories, aiming at the production of standardised citizens with no extra-societal allegiances that could challenge their loyalty to the nation,[241] but it is still unclear whether national ties are really the most important ones for individuals. Some questions unavoidably crop up: 'why liberals or anyone else *should* see any virtue or importance in nations above other types of group loyalty? Why should there be a virtue in giving political expression to nations above other groups?'[242] In the end, 'The fatherland above everything'[243] remains more of a prescription than a statement of fact.

1.3.8 National versus Social Identities: Notes on Socialism

Regardless of the theoretical objections to the primacy of national allegiance, some empirical evidence validates this particular point of liberal nationalists, and an interesting case is offered by the history of socialism. Socialism initially set itself up as a non-nationalist ideology that appealed to the international community of workers. By heritage, left-wing parties maintained a very critical position on the idea of nation. Nevertheless, despite such a transnational vocation, these are the workers who eventually agreed to fight against their fellows dressed in the uniforms of a different country whenever military conflicts between these nations occurred. Still today, international crises tend to strengthen national allegiances and undermine cosmopolitan views. Nationalism proved to be stronger than class solidarity and internationalism.[244] Thus, a modernist with a Marxist background, sharing the traditional suspicion of Proudhon,[245] would argue that nationalism had the political function of tearing apart large social classes in order to avoid the formation of a dangerous transnational coalition. This already came to pass after the collapse of the great multi-national states, as the creation of nation-states based on ethnic criteria may have had the role of contrasting socialism in Europe, since 'what looked like mobilizing the masses in 1917–18 was social revolution

[240] *See* M Neves, *Transconstitutionalism* (Oxford, Hart Publishing, 2013).

[241] R Robertson, 'After Nostalgia? Willful Nostalgia and the Phases of Globalization', in BS Turner (ed), *Theories of Modernity and Postmodernity* (London, Sage, 1990) 49.

[242] A Vincent, 'Liberal Nationalism' (n 164), 288.

[243] WC Buthman, *The Rise of Integral Nationalism in France: With Special Reference to the Ideas and Activities of Charles Maurras* (New York, Columbia University Press, 1939) 29; BC Shafer, *Faces of Nationalism* (n 12), 257.

[244] H Mikkeli, *Europe as an Idea and an Identity* (Basingstoke, Palgrave Macmillan, 1998) 88.

[245] P-J Proudhon, *Oeuvres Choisies* (Paris, Gallimard, 1967) 207.

rather than national self-determination'.[246] According to this interpretation, thus, the 'anti-hierarchical'[247] element contained in modern nationalism, according to which differences between social classes are reduced or even eliminated by new egalitarian categories (patriot, citizen, conational etc.), was an instrument of control rather than of equalisation. The 'bourgeois principle of nationality' was therefore meant to replace the 'socialist principle of class struggle'.[248]

But if it is true that nationalism was essentially bourgeois,[249] the ease with which workers took hold of weapons to protect the nation-state is even more surprising. Is national identity, independent from nationalism's ideological connotations, really stronger than any other relationship? In reality, imaging the nation-state as the guardian of the exclusive interests of the middle-class would create a misleading conception due to an excess of historical materialism. On the contrary, nationalism has been capable of winning the loyalty of numerous citizens, including the workers' social class: 'In fear and hope, individuals, rich and poor, and of the upper, middle, and lower classes, became nationalists'.[250] Neither God nor a cosmopolitan ideology but instead nation-states by means of constitutions and unified legislations, 'became the chief instrument for achieving security for life and property, for establishing and safeguarding whatever liberties were won, for protection against foreigners, and increasingly for the fulfillment of the hopes of the citizens'.[251] Within a few years, even socialist countries had to adapt the internationalism upon which their ideology was based to the benefit of the nation-state. 'The fact is that workers did become nationally minded as they received concrete benefits in the present, not in some remote future':[252] in Stalin's rhetorical words 'as long as people believed in a "bright future", they fought side by side irrespective of nationality [...] But when doubt crept into people's hearts, they began to depart, each to his own national tent'.[253] Moreover, if it is true that the nation-state serves industrialisation and industrialisation is a pre-condition of the communist order, nationalism could serve the aims of socialism,[254] provided that nationalism is a transitory phenomenon since class solidarity must eventually prevail on national categories.[255]

246 EJ Hobsbawm, *Nations and Nationalism since 1780* (n 44), 131.

247 O Dann, 'Funktionen des Nationalismus in modernen Gesellschaften', in O Dann (ed), *Nationalismus und sozialer Wandel* (Hamburg, Hoffmann und Campe, 1978) 213.

248 JV Stalin, *Marxism and the National Question* [1913] (Moscow, Foreign Languages Publishing House, 1947) 50.

249 Ibid, 27 sustained that 'the national struggle under the conditions of rising capitalism is a struggle of the bourgeois classes among themselves. Sometimes the bourgeoisie succeeds in drawing the proletariat into the national movement, and then the national struggle externally assumes a "nation-wide" character. But this is so only externally. In its essence it is always a bourgeois struggle, one that is to the advantage and profit mainly of the bourgeoisie'.

250 BC Shafer, *Faces of Nationalism* (n 12), 158.

251 Ibid, 158.

252 Ibid, 193.

253 JV Stalin, *Marxism and the National Question* (n 248), 7.

254 J Schwarzmantel, *Socialism and the Idea of the Nation* (New York, Harvester Wheatsheaf, 1991) 60.

255 Ibid, 64.

In more recent years, quite paradoxically in particular in reunified Germany, 'the traditional nineteenth-century concept of "the nation" survived most strongly in the working class',[256] whereas the interest of the nation has been taken over as a means of resistance against extra-European immigration[257] and the European Union even by socialist and communist parties. In France, driven by the fear that the new European construction could be symptomatic of a new German militarism on the rise,[258] these parties argued that 'internationalist means precisely "among nations" and not the destruction of nations',[259] denying the existence of some kind of peculiar European identity and conforming to the views of several other French political parties of the 1950s.

The inexorable importance of nationalism was revealed on a global scale at the end of a Cold War that previously opposed ideologies rather than nations, when the former Soviet Union, a gigantic aggregation of very different national and ethnic groups (even the Russian word for nationality has a strong ethnic connotation), disintegrated in a series of states organised on a national basis. In other words, whereas the relationship between nationalism and socialism remains problematic in theory, in practice these ideologies have often been complementary.

1.4 THE CONVENIENCE OF NATIONALISM

Many explanations can be given for the success of nationalism; most of them are of a sociological or even psychological nature. It could be pointed out that patriotism became the civic religion of the new secular society, providing individuals with a sense of belonging to a larger and possibly immortal community, a feeling that is able to fire the crowds and produce huge social movements.[260] Even empirical research seems to confirm that a feeling of attachment to the national community can contribute to life satisfaction, in particular for those subjects and in those countries whose societal conditions are considered poorer.[261] Tamir has gracefully pointed out that:

> The respect for continuity inherent in national membership enables individuals to place themselves in a continuum of human life and creativity, connecting them to their ancestors as well as to future generations and lessening the solitude and alienation characteristic of modern life.[262]

256 EJ Hobsbawm, *Nations and Nationalism since 1780* (n 44), 190.

257 *See* the statements of the leader of the left party 'Die Linke' O Lafontaine concerning foreign workers taking the jobs of German family men and women and the reactions it provoked, in R Roßman, 'PDS über ihr Zugpferd Lafontaine verärgert', *Süddeutsche Zeitung*, 17 June 2005.

258 M Jachtenfuchs, *Die Konstruktion Europas. Verfassungsideen und institutionelle Entwicklung* (Baden-Baden, Nomos-Verlag, 2002) 95.

259 F. Billous in 1953, quoted by M Jachtenfuchs, *Die Konstruktion Europas* (n 258), 96.

260 BC Shafer, *Faces of Nationalism* (n 12), 257.

261 M Morrison, L Tay and E Diener, 'Subjective Well-Being and National Satisfaction: Findings From a Worldwide Survey' (2011) 22 *Pyschological Science*, 166–71.

262 Y Tamir, *Liberal Nationalism* (n 84), 86.

By becoming part of a perpetual higher entity, people gain the illusion of overcoming their own particular mortality, in the tragic attempt to escape the oblivion that, sooner or later, befalls every individual. Nationalism can reassure people about one of their most fundamental fears, occasionally employing this feeling for bellicose purposes.

However, since nationalism is foremost a political principle, political and theoretical reasons must lie behind its continuous success. On the one hand, it can be said that one of the reasons for the success of nationalism has been exactly its alleged philosophical poverty. As a political principle holding that political and national units should be congruent, nationalism still has quite an unclear ideology; its rhetoric and strategies are particularly flexible and can be employed with different aims gaining wide support.[263] Its very historical evolution proves that it initially presented itself as a revolutionary force, aiming at the reform or the creation of new political institutions, while it has now assumed a more conservative aspect, aimed at the maintenance of the social status quo, which of course includes the defense of the existing nation-state against excessive interference on the part of often poorly legitimised international institutions. On the other hand, putting emphasis on the cultural homogeneity of the community and the exclusive national interest, nationalism also acts as a limit against tendencies towards the disaggregation of the society. If, from a utilitarian perspective, life in society is necessary only because the advantages it brings to individuals outweigh the disadvantage of the loss of a part of individual liberty, it could be possible to change the social contract any time it might be perceived as more convenient for a small privileged group to declare its autonomy from others. This circumstance would clearly destabilise the society, while the concept of national interest puts a limit on this process of Balkanisation.

The concept of 'national interest' works both inwards and outwards, so that any project of political or social institutions at a supranational level will bear the burden of the proof to demonstrate that the national interest would be pursued better at that level than at the national one. Federations are created when the benefits outweigh the costs of the association and, once they are formed, they risk breakdown when this relationship is overturned.[264] But even if the benefits (also considering hypothetical symbolic utilities) outweigh the costs, there can still be good reasons why a nation-state should not give up its competences and enter into a federation. This, of course, is because where more subjects are involved in the democratic decision-making power process the weight of each single vote diminishes proportionally in relation to the number of voters. From a pure mathematical perspective, states are more democratic than international organisations, local communities than nations and so forth.

[263] EJ Hobsbawm, *Nations and Nationalism since 1780* (n 44), 176, notes that 'Its very vagueness and lack of programmatic content gives it a potentially universal support within its own community'.

[264] WH Riker, 'Federalism', in FI Greenstein and NW Polsby (eds), *The Handbook of Political Science. Vol. V. Government Institution and Processes* (Reading MA, Addison-Wesley, 1975) 93 ff.

The relationship between nationalism and democracy is indeed an intricate one. The democratic process necessarily presupposes a unit,[265] which nationalism identified with the nation, indeed formalising the democratic concept of people. From a descriptive perspective, the main reason for the success of this ideology in modern political thought lies in the fact that it provides an answer to the difficult question 'Who are the people?' although it consequently opened up an even more controversial one: 'What is a nation?', which can be answered in a different way and notably by resorting to the concept of national culture.

1.5 CONCLUSION

In light of what has been discussed, nationalism should be viewed as an ideology or political principle that holds that national and political units should overlap. This basic idea can be detected in all nationalist manifestations. As such, this appears as a meagre political principle and it becomes easy to see why, in its historical evolution, it often took on elements of different ideologies and ideas. Furthermore, because of its 'poverty' and malleability, nationalism can be employed for very different ends—to promote imperialism, racism, socialism, liberalism, protectionism and democracy. This also represents one reason for nationalism's enduring success and explains the striking contrast between its philosophical poverty and its historical strength.

Although it is unclear whether a purely liberal form of nationalism that does not degenerate into illiberal practices can exist for a considerable length of time, in its basic form nationalism does not necessarily represent a deleterious principle. While nationalism's philosophical poverty may lead us to think that a direct influence of this ideology on the process of Europeanisation of private law is improbable, the arguments which have been used by liberal nationalist authors to explain and justify nationalism are particularly concrete and can still play an important role in the process of European legal integration.

The liberal nationalist line of reasoning can be summarised as follows: since a model of assigned responsibility is preferable over a model of shared responsibility, a subdivision of the world into several political organisms each entitled to take care only of the needs of a small portion of the world population is ethically justifiable and even instrumental to the establishment of universal principles. This first argument is not nationalist per se and can be shared with liberal or even cosmopolitan perspectives. It nonetheless opens up the question as to what criteria would be used to select a population that would live under the law of a given political organism. Nationalist ideologies resort to the element of nationality (the way in which the nation is defined—or more precisely, envisaged—distinguishes various nationalist ideologies): state and nation have to be congruent (the way in

[265] RA Dahl, *Democracy and Its Critics* (New Haven, Yale University Press, 1989) 207.

which the coincidence of these elements is intended to be brought about founds the distinction between nationalist movements). Nationalist authors, in particular liberal nationalists, have given several reasons in support of this principle. These arguments are based upon the assumption that a fully democratic political process will be possible only within a homogeneous community, while homogeneity is construed in cultural terms. Culture is therefore mainly national and people sharing a nationality also share a culture whose importance overshadows all other personal and social identities: identity is mainly nationally constituted.[266] In even more concise terms, the nationalist principle can be synthesized as the idea that a functioning political community can be established only among people sharing a common characteristic that defines them as a nation. It has been already pointed out that, in the modern understanding of nationalism, that element is usually 'culture'.

In social studies this tendency is reflected in methodological nationalism, whereby the nation-state is treated as the starting point of every social analysis and the national dimensions of personal and social identities are overestimated. Ever since the emergence of the nation-state, this approach has become widespread enough to become common even among politically non-nationalist scientists,[267] and still persists in the era of Europeanisation.

[266] P Gilbert, *The Philosophy of Nationalism* (n 191), 88.
[267] U Beck, *Der kosmopolitische Blick* (n 46), 43.

Chapter 2

Nationalisation and Denationalisation

THE NATIONALIST POLITICAL principle requires national communities to organise themselves politically without the interference of foreign non-national subjects. In contemporary western societies, law mainly performs the function of organising the society. As such, law is required to become inherently national according to nationalist ideology. It would indeed be contradictory to assume that nations should organise themselves freely and at the same time to admit that one of the most important instruments to achieve this goal may be decided by non-nationals or at a supranational level. In this sense, the nationalisation of law represents a necessary step in the nationalisation of society.

Corollaries to this assumption are that the history of legal nationalisation more or less organically follows the more general history of nationalism and that, since a conceptual–historical link between nationalism and law exists, processes of legal denationalisation—as notably in the case of European law—are likely to meet with resistance from nationalist perspectives. In this chapter, therefore, legal historical developments leading up to recent events will be seen through the lenses offered by nationalism studies, while the main focus will stay on the theory of law and nationalism, rather than on legal history.

2.1 THE DEVELOPMENT OF NATIONAL LAW

As one of the most influential political principles in contemporary politics, nationalism has left a significant print on modern legal systems. Although still philosophically poor and theoretically disputable, nationalism's basic assumption that nation and state should be congruent has become an almost universally accepted principle, first in social consciousness and second in established international law.

The emergence of the principle of nationalities in the eighteenth and nineteenth centuries radically changed not only the geopolitical map of Europe but also even the theoretical foundations of international law. Until that point, this area of law was based upon the state-centred assumption that only states—instead of nations—were actors in the international arena;[1] it took the influence of French, Italian and German liberal nationalism for the concept of nation to

[1] N Berman, '"But the Alternative is Despair": European Nationalism and the Modernist Renewal of International Law' (1993) 106 *Harvard Law Review* 1792–903.

assume relevance in law. Influential scholars such as, most notably, the Italian Pasquale Stanislao Mancini, whose ideas can be considered more than those of Savigny as the cornerstones of modern private international law, initially introduced that concept into private international law.[2] But those legal theories were not invented from scratch; rather they can be collocated in a specific cultural context[3] characterised by the emergence of nationalism in Europe. In particular Mancini, famed lawyer and political protagonist of the *Risorgimento*, claimed that it was the nation and not the state that represented the basic unit for the international legal order[4] and on the basis of this assumption, after having rejected the 'classical' views of Grotius and Puffendorf[5]—he built his system of private international law as revolving around the fundamental principles of nationality, sovereignty and freedom.

In a few decades, this view took the upper hand in the international arena and was formalised in the public international law principle of self-determination, which indeed appears as the translation in legal terms of the nationalist idea that every nation should have the right to constitute an autonomous and independent state. Consequently and significantly, many of the theoretical objections and problematic aspects, which are intertwined with the political principle of nationalism, reverberated in the interpretation of that legal principle. According to this fundamental principle, 'all peoples have the right to self-determination. By virtue of that right they freely determine their political status and freely pursue their economic, social and cultural development'.[6] Once they are organised into independent nations, people have a right to determine their internal development freely: the principle does not prescribe any particular way in which this has to be achieved; *internal* self-determination does not require a certain type of constitutional parliamentary democracy,[7] nor does it dictate the content of the statutes that internal parliament has to adopt. In fact, it is not even clear whether it requires a parliament to be present in the state organisation, and the question

[2] E Jayme, *Pasquale Stanislao Mancini. Internationales Privatrecht zwischen Risorgimento und praktischer Jurisprudenz* (Ebelsbach, Verlag Rolf Gremer, 1980) at VII.

[3] On the cultural and political premises of Savigny's system of private international law: J-H Halpérin, *Entre nationalisme juridique et communauté de droit* (Paris, Presses Universitaires de France, 1999) 48–66, where emphasis is put on its internationalist (and anti-Semitic) character. In this respect, it is still possible to detect a link between Savigny's thought and the early Romantics, more focused on Europeanism than nationalism, in particular Novalis and his conception of a Christian Europe—expressed in a speech from 1799 later published with the title *Die Christenheit oder Europa*.

[4] PS Mancini, *Della nazionalità come fondamento del diritto delle genti* [1851] (Torino, Giappichelli, 1994) 48. The text is of 1851.

[5] E Jayme, *Pasquale Stanislao Mancini* (n 2), 20, with quotes.

[6] This principle is included in several international law instruments like the UN General Assembly resolution 1514 (XV) of 14 December 1960 ('Declaration on the granting of independence to colonial countries and peoples'), the International Covenant on Civil and Political Rights of 1966, the International Covenant on Economic, Social and Cultural Rights of 1966. It is also accepted as customary international law.

[7] R McCorquodale, 'Self-Determination: A Human Rights Approach' (1994) 43 *International and Comparative Law Quarterly*, 857–85, 865.

whether self-determination coincides with democracy remains a delicate and debatable one.[8] Apparently, the only condition that has to be met in order to be entitled to self-determination is to be a nation, the definition of which remains an open problem in political science.

Whereas the basic formulation of the principle of self-determination, as famously expressed (although not called by this name) by President Wilson in his famous 'Fourteen Points' is basically unrestricted, the exercise of the right could of course be subjected to further requirements; so for example, another political leader who too had a central role in contemporary history—Joseph Stalin—affirmed that although a nation has the right to arrange its life on autonomous lines 'this does not mean that it should do so under all circumstances, that autonomy, or separation, will everywhere and always be advantageous for a nation, ie, for its majority, ie, for the toiling strata'.[9] In this case, nationalism seems to be purely instrumental, for in some cases it will be more convenient to recognise the right to self-determination and in other cases not, a specification which easily paves the way to political oppression or the intromission in internal politics of other countries, as it was soon conceptualised in the Brezhnev Doctrine.

It is interesting to note that even more recent developments in international public law—that may have taken place in order to compensate for the practical difficulties of a pure nationalist approach on the politically controversial questions of self-determination—pose limitations to the exercise of the right to self-determination, mainly due to the need for protection of human rights.[10] This tendency found within the confines of recently developed humanitarian international law therefore seems to move away from more nationalist theories and to get closer to the liberal approaches to the problem of self-determination. Instead of making reference to distinctions between nationality (legitimising secession from the state) and ethnicity (legitimising reform of the state)—as clear in theory as impracticable in reality, in particular if we were to adhere to an ethnic definition of the nation—like nationalists do,[11] liberals more pragmatically affirm that it is the failure of the state to deal with the needs of the community claiming independence that legitimises a right to secede.[12]

[8] It can be said that in President Wilson's idea, 'self-determination' was substantially a 'right to democracy' and thus only in its 'internal' sense, coinciding with people's right to choose a particular form of government. Furthermore, it was in his opinion possible that, according to changes in social and political conditions, national boundaries could also be changed; it was in other words evident an understanding of 'nation' inclined toward subjectivist theories typical also of the American experience; J Castellino, *International Law and Self-determination* (The Hague, Kluwer Law International, 2000) 13 ff.

[9] JV Stalin, *Marxism and the National Question* [1913] (Moscow, Foreign Languages Publishing House, 1947) 31.

[10] R McCorquodale, 'Self-Determination: A Human Rights Approach' (n 7), 876 ff.

[11] D Miller, *On Nationality* (Oxford, Clarendon Press, 1995) 112.

[12] AH Birch, 'Another Liberal Theory of Secession' (1984) 32 *Political Studies* 596–602. *See* also J Breuilly, *Nationalism and the State* (Manchester, Manchester University Press, 1985) 6.

This viewpoint helps clarify how nationalism may be linked to very different political ideologies: once the congruence of nation and state has been brought about, the policies enacted by the nation-state could be liberal, libertarian, socialist, communist and so on. All this is covered by the principle of internal self-determination. An inquiry into the influence of nationalism on private law, therefore, must note that nationalism is as such incapable of shaping the contents of private law in a distinctive way: the fundamental aspect in a nationalistic perspective is that any nation can organise itself and therefore also have a private law of its own, but there are no specific requirements as to the political choices contained in such a body of rules: just the persuasion that those contents will in any case reflect the needs and the 'spirit' of the nation.

2.1.1 From a Common to a National Private Law

The idea that private law is mainly a national phenomenon is a modern one. Looking at the legal experience of the Middle Ages and the early Modern Age, for example, one notes a very different state of affairs. The appearance of the 'medieval legal order'[13] is well known in the literature; here it suffices to note that private law was of a mixed universalistic and particularistic nature, being based both on local customs and on the 'science' of Roman law, but did not have a national dimension. The reason for this circumstance is remarkably obvious, but still telling: nation-states did not exist yet. In that context, rather, private law did not considerably differ from one end of Europe to the other and, as soon as universities were created, a flow of students and professors started travelling that geographical area spreading the same knowledge. Regardless of this apparently cosmopolitan situation, often romanticised today, one should not think that law was somehow 'unified' in the whole of Europe, at least in the modern terms in which we conceive legal unification today. The mixed universalistic–particularistic nature of the medieval *ius commune* is clearly explained by Zimmermann:

> Many individual legal problems were solved differently by different lawyers at different times and in different parts of Europe. But these differences, by and large, were variations of a common theme, because the development of the law occurred within an established framework of sources and methods, of concepts, rules and arguments. It was a tradition marked as much by a considerable diversity as by a fundamental intellectual unity.[14]

Such a fundamental intellectual unity, however, began to waiver as soon as the national idea emerged. In particular two important historical and cultural events stand out from the slow and continuous process that led to the nationalisation of

[13] P Grossi, *L'ordine giuridico medievale* (Bari, Laterza, 2006).

[14] R Zimmermann, 'Ius Commune and the Principles of European Contract Law: Contemporary Renewal of an Old Idea', in HL MacQueen and R Zimmermann (eds), *European Contract Law: Scots and South African Perspectives* (Edinburgh, Edinburgh University Press, 2006) 10.

private law, and lie at the roots of our present-day systems: the creation of the first modern states after the treaties of Westphalia[15] and the emergence of nationalist thought.

It is now commonly agreed that the Treaties of Westphalia mark the birth of the modern idea of sovereign state, though previous political organisations, which had characteristics similar to the state, already existed.[16] The conceptual elaboration of private law was already influenced by the political events in this era. Already in the period between the sixteenth and the eighteenth centuries an important transformation occurred and the idea that a positive law had to govern the relationships between nations developed.[17] The creation of modern nation-states did not automatically lead to the abandonment of the particularistic–universal nature of private law and its substitution with inherently national systems—though some legal scholars started to envisage this option from the Reformation[18] on, when the first seeds of the principle of nationalities began to germinate—so that the traditional *ius commune* continued existing normally in its local variations for decades. Newly formed states did not feel any need to become involved in private law yet, and several new independent states, such as the Netherlands, remained firmly bound to their system of laws.[19] The non-national character of private law never represented an issue, just like 'the differences in language and culture among the various regions had not been looked upon as problematic, at least not until the seventeenth century'.[20] The creation of the state was just the start of a process that rapidly evolved.

It is indeed true that since then, the modern state started expanding its competences by regulating more and more aspects of the life of its population. In order to obtain this result, fields that today are often considered to be part of the area of public law such as criminal, administrative and procedural law, became the first sectors in which the new state showed an interest, as instruments of organisation of the society. In contrast, while states administered private law through a massive system of courts, they did not pretend to create it as of yet and legislators

[15] More precisely, this event concluded a fundamental phase in European history that saw its beginnings in the Protestant Reformation of 1517, a subject that cannot be dealt with in this book but whose significance for the nationalisation process of Europe should at least be mentioned.

[16] HJ Berman, *Law and Revolution. The Formation of the Western Legal Tradition* (Cambridge, Harvard University Press, 1983) 113, for example considers the Catholic Church as the first modern Western state.

[17] J-H Halpérin, *Entre nationalisme juridique* (n 3), 13.

[18] P Grossi, *L'Europa del diritto* (Roma, Laterza, 2007) 95–6, refers in particular to François Hotman.

[19] CA Cannata, *Lineamenti di storia della giurisprudenza europea. II. Dal medioevo all'epoca contemporanea* (Torino, Giappichelli, 1976) 89. First plans of codification in the Netherlands did not even aim at repealing existing customary law; for a history of codification in that country, *see* JHA Lokin and WJ Zwalve, *Hoofdstukken uit de Europese codificatiegeschiedenis* (Den Haag, Boom, 2006) 271 ff.

[20] PAJ van den Berg, *The Politics of European Codification. A History of the Unification of Law in France, Prussia, the Austrian Monarchy and the Netherlands* (Groningen, Europa Law Publishing, 2007) 25.

remained relatively indifferent to private law for quite a long time.[21] Such a relative indifference also contributed to the autonomous emergence of that set of transnational rules commonly termed *lex mercatoria*. It took nationalism to lead to a complete nationalisation of private law.

At the same time, the personality of law principle that so strongly characterised the medieval era was challenged in the eighteenth century, when the idea that the foreigners dwelling on the soil of a given country had to adapt and be subject to the law and authority of that country became predominant.[22] It was another sign of the coupling of private law and the nation-state as a community of individuals indissolubly linked to a given territory. National thought led to epochal political and social changes in continental Europe, starting in France, but did not lead to the same spectacular outcomes in England, a country that was already unified and in which absolutism *à la française* did not exist anymore. Under these circumstances, the concepts of state and nations are—just like in pre-revolutionary France—less distinct than in the languages of countries that experienced nationalist revolutions. Private law there continued to be administered by the Court system, but its contents remained mainly customary. The civil codification, the favourite instrument of civic nationalism contemplated first in England and accomplished later in France, did not manage to cross the English Channel.

The meaning of this historical transformation can be understood from different angles and our appraisal of the role of nationalism in the development of European private law can vary accordingly. If one likes to underline the substantial unity and cosmopolitan character of the *ius commune* as a common system of law understood by everyone with a knowledge of the Latin language in Europe, nationalism appears as the blamable phenomenon that destroyed that unity. On the other hand, if one considers that besides its frequent depiction as a kind of legal golden age, *ius commune* was characterised by heterogeneity in all parts of Europe, nationalism should be considered more favourably as the element that destroyed legal pluralism within given territories, though recreating it at a higher level. This is, after all, one of the key features of nationalism which is reflected in the legal systems—a particular dynamic of inclusion/exclusion which implies the standardisation and creation of unity on the inside but at the same time a differentiation from everything which exists outside the national borders.

In continental Europe, it was therefore the emergence of the national idea that led to a shift from a statist to a national conception of private law. The phenomenon appeared most notably in France and Germany, where it initially took two different forms before spreading throughout Europe. Now, our attention should be drawn to the events that took place on the continent. In Chapter 1 it has been noted that nationalism studies have drawn a strong distinction between two nationalist forms, often described in geographical terms: western—most notably

[21] P Grossi, *Mitologie giuridiche della modernità* (Milano, Giuffrè, 2007) 27.
[22] J-H Halpérin, *Entre nationalisme juridique* (n 3), 14.

French—and eastern—most typically German—manifestations. According to this dichotomy, nationalism has developed in the western part of Europe as a civic phenomenon, while in eastern countries it assumed an ethno-cultural connotation that soon paved the way for the infamous xenophobic and racist movements of the twentieth century. This distinction should however not be exaggerated and certainly not considered as an alternative between positive and negative nationalist expressions.[23] It is nonetheless useful as an instrument to conceptualise events that took place in different countries. That difference is indeed detectable, at least at an early stage, in the processes of nationalisation of the private law of France and Germany as well. It was in this period and in these contexts that some of the most basic legal concepts of modern jurisprudence evolved, most notably the idea of codification, that still carry the signs of the cultural context that gave rise to it. The French *Code civil*, the first codification in the modern understanding of the word, is clearly a product—though an indirect one—of the revolution and civic nationalism.

The task of nationalism in France was more restricted than in other countries. While in other experiences nationalism had to perform the function of creating a unitary state—previously instilling a national consciousness in the people dwelling in those territories according to modernist theories or just awakening it according to primordialist theories—nationalism had a less ambitious programme in France. A sole state had already been established, so that the function of nationalism mainly consisted in the overturning of the governing class through the substitution of a new historical subject: the nation. The historical importance of this operation explains why such a change had to be realised by means of a revolution. The pre-existence of a politically unified state also explains why French nationalism took a civic form: there was no need to rely on ethnic elements to define the category of the French, while it was necessary to lay down the principles on which the new society had to be organised. A civil codification had the function of organising society in a new way and served as the manifesto of the new bourgeois classes. Though the French codification is not the perfect translation of the ideals of the revolution in legal terms, as it was drafted and eventually enacted under the determinant influence of Napoleon, it still shows the signs of the tension between rising legal nationalism and enlightened cosmopolitanism that characterised the era, in which the tensions between France and the other European states also increased.[24]

The events that took place in Germany were even more multi-faceted and civic understanding of the nation was opposed to ethno-cultural pulsations that soon got the upper hand in a context of strong political hostility to France. It is thus useful to look at the legal and historical events that happened in Germany,

[23] *See* Chapter I, 1.2.6: 'Is There a Good and a Bad Nationalism?'.

[24] J-H Halpérin, *Entre nationalisme juridique* (n 3), 14.

occasionally referring to experiences in other countries, the development of which have been strongly influenced by the cultural and political events in Germany.

2.1.2 Between Civic, Cultural and Ethnic Nationalism: Germany

In Germany, where a united nation-state existed only in the minds of a few liberal patriots but not in reality, a form of ethno-cultural nationalism was developed, thanks to the extremely popular work of Johann Gottfried Herder, and developed against the intellectual background of German Romanticism. *Ethnos* and culture were thought to be the only common roots upon which a national consciousness could have been built and finally used to give rise to a national state. Furthermore, they could have easily been employed to form a national identity based on an opposition between the German and the French, as German nationalism arose in the first place as a reaction against 'cultural humiliation' by the French[25] and, of course, as a political defence from their perilous neighbour country.

Civic nationalism was furthermore associated with the ideals of French rationalism. As such, it could not hope to be successful in Germany in a period during which, after the pre-Romantic movement of *Sturm und Drang* prepared an intellectual reaction against Enlightenment classicism,[26] Enlightenment came also to be associated politically with revolution. Those events marked a strong break in the nationalistic developments of the two countries; while in the first phase the French Revolution was judged positively in Germany even by several Romantic thinkers, that was not the case after 1792–93.[27] The violent shift in the course of the revolution ended up discrediting even the theoretical works of the Enlightenment thinkers, most of whom had passed away by that time and could not offer intellectual guidance any more.[28] In the cultural arena, the political principles of the revolution were famously criticised and rejected notably by the conservative Edmund Burke, while in France, François-René de Chateaubriand attacked even the theoretical foundations of Rationalism and the Enlightenment. Politically, the Congress of Vienna of 1814 and 1815 took over the task of erasing the Napoleonic era by bringing history back to before the French Revolution.[29] At the same time, however, the Congress of Vienna precluded the possibility of a united German nation-state, creating a weak German confederation (*Deutscher*

[25] RN Stromberg, *European Intellectual History since 1789* (Englewood Cliffs, Prentice Hall, 1981) 26.

[26] Ibid, 13 and 41.

[27] D Grimm, *Deutsche Verfassungsgeschichte, 1776-1866: Vom Beginn des modernen Verfassungsstaats bis zur Auflösung des Deutschen Bundes* (Frankfurt am Main, Suhrkamp, 1988) 52 ff.

[28] RN Stromberg, *European Intellectual History* (n 25), 18 and 13.

[29] In the field of private law, however, the Bourbon Restoration failed in its attempt. The impact of the French codification had been so considerable that numerous states chose to enact a codification of their own, usually based on (when not merely translated from) the Napoleonic code itself; with particular regard to the Italian pre-Unitarian states, *see* CA Cannata, *Lineamenti di storia della giurisprudenza europea* (n 19), 139 ff.

Bund) instead, a multi-coloured jumble of inhomogeneous states often in contrast to one another. In this context, German ambitions to form a sole nation-state had to choose between Rationalism—viewed as typically French and thus the expression of a state extremely dangerous to German interests—and political Romanticism—developed in particular in Germany (though imported from England and France) and easily employable to foster the awakening of a national consciousness. It is understandable that, especially under the political climate of the Bourbon Restoration, liberal patriots inspired by the Enlightenment became a minority and Romantic nationalists gained the upper hand. Despite the schematic simplification that opposes western and eastern models of nationalism, enlightened patriots thus also existed in the German context, but their voice was soon overwhelmed by Romantic ideas and ethno-cultural nationalism.

Needless to say, these ideas had a strong impact on the understanding of the law. While in newly parliamentarianly organised countries the elected bodies and the legislation that they passed were seen as the expression of national unity, consuetudinary law was viewed as the expression of the spirit of the people in those nations that had not managed to organise themselves in the form of a state yet, like Germany[30] (while the Italian case seems more complex, as will be shown later).[31] In Germany, the opposition between civic and ethno-cultural understandings of the nation is already perceivable in the probably best-known legal quarrel ever, a discussion which, under the veil of the technicality of private law theory, was animated by high political fervour and had extremely important practical implications for German and European history: the *Kodifikationsstreit* between Anton Friedrich Justus Thibaut and Friedrich Carl von Savigny. Far from being a pure academic debate concerning two technical models of law, the discussion has to be collocated in its exact historical and political context, a context that should always be considered when the arguments of these authors are employed or referred to, even at the present time. While that dispute can be read as a clash between a patriotic-nationalist and a conservative pan-European idea, it seems possible to read it in its entirety as the clash of two intellectual positions both indebted to nationalist suggestions in different forms. Engaging in that latter reading appears necessary for our purposes because, even if we were to concede that Savignian ideas were expression of a purely European spirit and therefore incompatible with the suggestions of a world order organised on the basis of the principle of nationality, the apparent paradox of why a concept inescapably indebted to Savigny soon became the pivotal element of nationalist rhetoric remains to be explained. Savigny's theories in particular have often been discussed and even employed to support different claims advanced by modern authors, often beyond the original intentions of that scholar. It is certainly not the aim of this chapter to profess new views unduly based and legitimised on the reference to older theories, but

[30] AM Hespanha, *Introduzione alla storia del diritto europeo* (Bologna, il Mulino, 2003) 203–4.
[31] *See* this chapter, II.1.4.4: 'Diffusion of the *Volksgeist* Theory'.

rather to highlight the cultural and intellectual background in which those ideas developed, with a particular reference to the influence of nationalism.

German territories had experience of the concept of a civil code, the most widely exported legal product of the Napoleonic era and indirectly of the French Revolution and Enlightenment. The circulation of the ideas stemming from the Enlightenment in Germany had been easy: cultural and political elites in the German territories were particularly interested in the French civilisation. It was the period in which French was spoken and written by all educated people in those territories, while German was unwisely reviled as the idiom for 'soldiers and horses'.[32] The works of the French thinkers were thus known and appreciated among these elites and this is how the early ideas of first Rationalism and then Romanticism managed to circulate in the German territories. However, such a fascination for French ideas was doomed to an early death.

The case of Prussian codification, although well known, is still telling in this sense. Enlightenment had been quite successful also among the highly educated sovereigns of Prussia, who undertook an ambitious design of legal codification. This effort eventually led to the creation of the Allgemeines Landrecht für die Preußischen Staaten (ALR) of 1794, whose political success was nonetheless relative. On the one hand, the enlightened ideas that pervaded the codification soon lost their charm after the shift to terror during the revolution in the years when the ALR was still being drafted and finally promulgated. In this sense, its ideological premises were at odds with the new course of Prussian politics, as those ideas that initially seemed so attractive to the Prussian elites had now become extremely dangerous to them, putting their very existence at risk. On the other hand, the ALR did not even gain the complete favour of the German liberal patriots,[33] so that in the end it did not manage to become a model for German legal unity. It was already too old when it was born.

Technically different and politically more successful than the ALR was the French code, which also circulated in several German regions. Unlike Prussia or Austria, where several attempts had been made to come up with a code that was in the end perceived as the culmination of a long trend towards the separation from the *ius commune*,[34] the revolution determined a break with the past in France, creating a more ambitious code that did not aim at a mere integration of medieval common law as the ALR did; it was rather a ' powerful unifying wave which wrecked ancient particularisms'.[35] Following Napoleon's territorial conquests, the *Code civil* circulated in the Rheinish territories. In this region, that code had been highly appreciated and the local populations intended to maintain it even after

[32] According to the impression that Voltaire got travelling in the German territories; P von Polenz, *Geschichte der deutschen Sprache* (Berlin, Walter de Gruyter, 2009) 102.

[33] F Wieacker, *Industriegesellschaft und Privatrechtsordnung* (Frankfurt am Main, Athenäum-Fischer-Taschenbuch-Verlag, 1974) 82.

[34] J-H Halpérin, *Entre nationalisme juridique* (n 3), 10.

[35] Ibid, 10.

Napoleon's fall, principally due to the economic advisability of keeping the same legislation as France and the Low Countries,[36] as well as because it was considered more advanced and liberal than the Prussian code. In this sense, the *Code civil* paradoxically became the guarantee of the political independence of the local institutions in those territories.[37]

Thus, the Germans had already become acquainted with and appreciated the clarity of the *Code civil*, as evidenced by the case of the duchies who deliberately adopted the code. Liberal patriots considered it as a symbol of progress. The ideal of the liberal codification soon gained support more than the *Code civil* itself in the academic sphere. Indeed, while in our day, French codification is commonly regarded as an outstanding code by German scholars,[38] it was still too close to a dangerous foreign power to be simply proposed as the codification of the German territories at that time. Most German patriots pleaded instead for a codification on the model of the French but authentically German. If it is true that the homogenisation required by nationalism necessarily requires the exclusion of some subjects and dangerously benefits from an externalisation of the evil, many German patriots had found their useful nemesis in the French. The German *Vaterland* is there, '*wo jeder Franzmann heißet Feind, wo jeder Deutscher heißet Freund, das soll es sein!*' ('where every Frenchman is called enemy, where every German is called friend, that shall it be'), in the words of the patriotic poet Ernst Moritz Arndt. As soon as German nationalism took a clearly anti-French connotation, it became clear that the *Code Napoléon* would not have a place in the German nation. On 18 October 1817, a group of patriots from several German cities—mostly students and professors—gathered in Eisenach to celebrate the 300th anniversary of the Lutheran Reformation and burned 28 books of non-nationalist and reactionary authors, including the *Code civil*. In the academic debate, among the advocates of a codification for German law (not limited to private law issues) an authoritative voice was that of Thibaut, renowned professor at the freshly re-founded University of Heidelberg. In 1814—the same year as the Congress of Vienna—he published his famed pamphlet *Über die Nothwendigkeit eines allgemeinen bürgerlichen Rechts für Deutschland*.

2.1.3 Civic

Several scholars believed that the legislator has the power to create private law rules and that these can be employed as an instrument to shape society. Thibaut's position stands out inasmuch as it assumes that legislation can also be used as a

[36] W Schubert, 'Das französische Recht in Deutschland zu Beginn der Restaurationszeit (1814–1820)' (1977) 94 *Zeitschrift der Savigny-Stiftung für Rechtsgeschichte. Germanistische Abteilung* 129–84, 146.

[37] U Eisenhardt, *Deutsche Rechtsgeschichte* (Munich, Beck, 2008) 302 ff.

[38] F Wieacker, *A History of Private Law in Europe: With Particular Reference to Germany* (Oxford, Clarendon Press, 1995) 273.

means of achieving political unity in the German territories. In modern terms, we could say an instrument of nation building. This view was an expression of a progressive movement linked to the ideas of the French revolution,[39] therefore a civic nationalist manifestation. To achieve the aim of a legal and political unity, the codification Thibaut pleaded for had to be general (*allgemein*): it should encompass the whole of law—similarly to the ALR—and be the same for all the territories, performing the role of an authentic liberal constitution for Germany. The codification would therefore represent the ideal occasion to carry out a throrough liberal reform of civil, criminal and procedural law[40] for the entire nation. In this sense, Thibaut's view evidences national concerns that make his conception diverge from those of other jurists, exemplified by Nikolaus Thaddäus von Gönner, who accepted the idea of private law codification exclusively within the borders of the existing German states, rejecting the liberal principles which inflamed Thibaut.

According to the Heidelberg professor, there were two fundamentally intertwined reasons for such a necessity, one political and the other technical. On the one hand, legal unification would be a first step towards political integration and thus a triumph over particularism and fragmentation of the German nation in a myriad of small political units. Even if political unity would not come, the Code would still contribute to nation building:

> Schon die bloße Einheit wäre unschätzbar. Wenn auch eine politische Trennung Statt finden muß und soll, so sind doch die Deutschen hoch dabey interessirt, daß ein brüderlicher gleicher Sinn sie ewig verbinde, und daß nie wieder eine fremde Macht den einen Theil Deutschlands gegen den andern missbrauche. Gleiche Gesetze erzeugen aber gleiche Sitten und Gewohnheiten, und diese Gleichheit hat immer zauberischen Einfluß auf Völkerliebe und Völkertreue gehabt.[41]

The classic economic argument in favour of unification appears in Thibaut's argument: transactions across borders become impossible or extremely costly if economic actors have to deal with several obscure different legal systems.[42]

[39] CA Cannata, *Lineamenti di storia della giurisprudenza europea* (n 19), 167.

[40] AJF Thibaut, *Über die Nothwendigkeit eines allgemeinen bürgerlichen Rechts für Deutschland* (Heidelberg, Mohr & Zimmer, 1814) 12.

[41] 'Mere unity is invaluable. Even if a political separation must take place, Germans are most interested that a fraternal spirit will connect them forever, and that never again shall a foreign power set one part of Germany against another. But the same laws produce the same customs and habits, and this equality has always had a magical influence on people's love and loyalty', AFJ Thibaut, *Über die Nothwendigkeit* (n 40), 32.

[42] 'Außerdem macht der bürgerliche Verkehr jene Einheit fast zu einer schreyenden Nothwendigkeit. Unsre Deutschen Länder können allein durch einen lebhaften, inneren, wechselseitigen Verkehr ihren Wohlstand erhalten, und von dem schneidenden Volksegoismus, den der Französische Code ausspricht, darf bey uns durchaus nichts gehört werden. Ist also keine Gleichheit des Rechts, so entsteht das fürchterliche Unwesen der Collision der Gesetze, wobey denn noch wieder der leidige Umstand eintritt, daß es, nach Hert, wenigstens hundert und drey und dreyßig Streitfragen über jene Collision gibt, die armen Unterthanen also bey ihrem Verkehr in solche ewige Stockungen gerathen, und in ein solches Labyrinth von Unsicherheit und Schwanken verstrickt werden, daß ihr ärgster Feind sie nicht übler berathen könnte. Die Einheit des Rechts würde dagegen den Weg des Bürgers von dem einen

The preservation of a non-unified legal system only lends advantage to shrewd lawyers, to the detriment of the citizens—a point that had been already used by Jeremy Bentham to advocate the idea of a codification of law.[43] This argument had been successful just a few years earlier in France and was doomed to become a *leitmotif* more than a century later in Europe.

On the other hand, only a civil code could ensure a systematic private law where every question can be answered in a single and unequivocal way. Even German academia would benefit from the codification of law, which would substitute the countless series of confused laws and definitions that law students had to learn by heart at that time.[44] Thibaut's liberal nationalist attitude also merges with technical considerations of the qualities a good legal system should exhibit clearly emerging from his appraisal of the laws in force in Germany. These no longer respond to the needs of the nation; instead, the only viable solution appears to be the elaboration of a German private law code, '*ein einfaches National-Gesetzbuch, mit Deutscher Kraft im Deutschen Geist gearbeitet*', ('a simple national code, elaborated with German strength in a German spirit')[45] since such German spirit was reflected neither in Canon nor in Roman law. Now, it was time for the legislator to take charge to give systematic expression to it. Roman law in particular was considered inappropriate because it was elaborated by different and decadent civilisations according to their own requirements:

> Die letzte und hauptsächlichste Rechtsquelle bleibt daher für uns das Römische Gesetzbuch, also das Werk einer uns sehr ungleichen fremden Nation aus der Periode des tiefsten Verfalls derselben, die Spuren dieses Verfalls auf jeder Seite an sich tragend![46]

Justinian's work was thus mainly accused of being the codification of the latest Roman law, that of an already decadent civilisation, distant from the splendour of classic Rome. Using the terminology adopted by Thibaut, the object of criticism is the Roman *code* rather than Roman *law*. In this sense the author shows another link to the cultural context in which he developed his ideas: the Enlightenment's rejection of the past indeed did not extend itself beyond the Middle Ages. Roman and Greek civilisations continued to be used as civic models and idealised, as it strikingly emerges looking also at the neo-classic pictorial art of the age of the revolution. But Thibaut's argument is even more radical: regardless of the Roman legal geniality which had been so much appreciated by Leibnitz, between the

Lande in das andre eben und sicherer machen, und schlechte Anwälde würden nicht mehr Gelegenheit finden, bey dem Verkauf ihrer Rechtsgeheimnisse die armen Ausländer schändlich auszusaugen und zu misshandeln', AFJ Thibaut, *Über die Nothwendigkeit* (n 40), 32–4.

43 HLA Hart, 'Bentham and the Demystification of the Law' (1973) 36 *The Modern Law Review* 2–17.

44 Ibid, 27.

45 Ibid, 25–6.

46 Ibid, 15: 'Therefore, the last and principal source of law remains for us the Roman code, ie, the work of a very dissimilar foreign nation, from the period of its deepest decline, which shows the traces of this decline on each of its pages!'

minds of Roman and modern German jurists there seems to be an almost insurmountable cognitive wall. Roman law remains the product of a civilisation that is considered to be very different from the German—it is a *foreign* law. As a result, even the celebrated Corpus Juris remains '*zu dunkel, zu flüchtig gearbeitet und der wahre Schlüssel dazu wird uns ewig fehlen*' ('too obscure, too elusive, and the true key to it will be missed forever').[47] A similar criticism was also directed against classic Germanic law,[48] so that in the end, issuing a brand-new codification—following the examples of the Prussian ALR, the Austrian ABGB and above all, the French *Code civil*—appeared to be the best solution.

It was inevitable that this pamphlet, which so firmly attacked both Roman and Germanic law, would cause the strong reaction of the jurists who would have given rise to the Historical School of Law, focusing exactly on Roman and Germanic law. A *Schandschrift*[49] somehow *ungelehrt und unwissenschaftlich*, was Friedrich Carl von Savigny's severe judgment on Thibaut's book.

2.1.4 Cultural

The publication of Thibaut's work in 1814 on the necessity of a German private law codification gave Savigny the occasion to bring out a polemic pamphlet in that same year, the famed *Vom Beruf unsrer Zeit für Gesetzgebung und Rechtswissenschaft*. In this pamphlet Savigny brought the normative anti-Thibaut argument to the fore, which was that there was no necessity to adopt a common codification. He based his argument on the descriptive theory, inspired by Herder and based on Hegel, of law as a product of the nation's spirit, the *Volksgeist*—to employ a term that soon became popular in German cultural circles and was adopted only later by Savigny. While the civic nationalism of Thibaut brought him to advocate a code that would have nationalised law in Germany similar to what had happened in France, Savigny defended the status quo, in this sense appearing as an opponent of nationalisation processes and possibly a champion of legal Europeanism. In order to defend his position, nonetheless, Savigny employed arguments often borrowed by cultural nationalists, elaborating a theoretical framework that was rooted in the intellectual period of his time. It is therefore necessary to devote our attention to this concept, which cannot be so easily detached from the sparkling cultural environment of those years, to which nationalism is inextricably related.

The opinions of the two famous German scholars strongly diverge on many aspects: Thibaut argued that the laws existing in Germany were not appropriate to

[47] Ibid, 15 ff.

[48] Ibid, 13.

[49] Letter to Achim von Arnim, 20.9.1814 in A Stoll, *Friedrich Karl von Savigny: Ein Bild seines Lebens mit einer Sammlung seiner Briefe. Bd 2: Professorenjahre in Berlin 1810–1842* (Köln, Heymann, 1929) 117.

the needs of the population and that only the legislator could enact a rational and systematic code. He believed in the force of Reason and enlightened governments and that it was time for the German nation to enact a liberal constitution. This optimistic view could never have been shared by Savigny, pessimist by nature also because of his particularly unhappy lot: while Thibaut could describe his childhood as one of the happiest periods of his entire life, Savigny was orphaned early and while the former—jurist and musician—could organise magnificent choirs at his home in Heidelberg, the latter had difficulty in maintaining any sort of durable friendships.[50] Unlike Thibaut, Savigny had no trust in enlightened sovereigns and maintained that the idea of a liberal code which breaks with the past is purely illusory: law is not the individual's act of free will but rather the actual product of a long historical process. The present itself is nothing more than the '*Fortsetzung und Entwicklung aller vergangenen Zeiten*' ('continuation and evolution of all past times').[51] In this sense, Germans did not have to pursue the path distinguished by Thibaut to have '*ein eigenes, nationales Recht*'.[52] Germans therefore had to pursue the way of their ancestors instead of ceding to the revolutionary temptation to deliberately create new rules. After all—as a legal historian put it—the nation is an entity in which the dead command the living.[53] The methodological consequence of this interpretation of the past was that modern law also had to be studied historically, a methodology that Savigny himself applied particularly in his works on Roman law from the Middle Ages and in the present. The programmatic manifesto of the German Historical School of Law was set and the nationalist element was coessential to it.[54]

Savigny's view on law is therefore inherently conservative: legal and social change cannot be produced by the will of a few people in a brief period of time but only through a slow evolution. The political consequence is that there were no historical justifications for revolution but only for reforms.[55] His understanding of law perfectly matches his political conservatism, his distrust of Enlightenment and abhorrence for revolution, a feeling which was particularly widespread in Germany after the turning-point represented by the Reign of Terror. In this respect, regardless of its alleged technical qualities (that Savigny could not really appreciate), the codification had to be refused chiefly as an instrument of domination used by Napoleon to fetter nations.[56] In Savigny's rejection of liberal ideals

[50] H Hattenhauer, *Thibaut und Savigny: Ihre programmatischen Schriften* (Munich, Vahlen, 1973) 10 ff.

[51] FC von Savigny, 'Über den Zweck dieser Zeitschrift' (1815) 1 *Zeitschrift für geschichtliche Rechtswissenschaft* 1–17, 3.

[52] FC von Savigny, *Vom Beruf unsrer Zeit für Gesetzgebung und Rechtswissenschaft* (Heidelberg, Mohr und Zimmer, 1814) 133.

[53] AM Hespanha, *Introduzione alla storia del diritto europeo* (n 30), 213.

[54] CA Cannata, *Lineamenti di storia della giurisprudenza europea* (n 19), 157.

[55] E Wolf, *Grosse Rechtsdenker der deutschen Geistesgeschichte* (Tübingen, Mohr, 1963) 480.

[56] FC von Savigny, *Vom Beruf unsrer Zeit für Gesetzgebung und Rechtswissenschaft* (n 52), 57–8: 'Ihm [Napoleon] diente der Code als ein Band mehr, die Völker zu umschlingen, und darum wäre es für uns verderblich und abscheulich gewesen, selbst wenn er allen innern Werth gehabt hätte, der ihm fehlt'.

lies another point of contrast, not only with Thibaut but with several Germanists of the Historical School of Law, notably the illustrious Jacob Grimm. The rejection of the code is therefore not just a simple defence of a pan-European legalism, as in particular, modern scholars who want to highlight predominantly the European character of Savigny like to stress, but more significantly a rejection of a French instrument and thus a way to highlight a differentiation between Germany and France. But those two elements—continuity with the European tradition and differentiation from France—are not in opposition but rather, as will be further discussed in subsequent chapters, complementary in the cultural nationalist thought of that time: not even the intellectuals who fostered the idea of nation, exemplified by Rousseau, denied the existence of deeper cultural similarities between the different European nations and even some common principles governing their institutions, sometimes even more clearly than Savigny, but storiography has nonetheless associated their name with the rising national idea.

2.1.4.1 Intellectual Background

Savigny's arguments echo Hegel's philosophy on several points.[57] Although Hegel at first showed at least some sympathy for the social claims of the Jacobins, the idealist philosopher soon became highly critical of the idea that belonging to a nation could be a matter of choice and to Rousseau's social contract theory, based on a very different understanding of 'common will', as well as on a confusion between state and civil society.[58] The theoretical foundations of civic nationalism were therefore refuted. Hegel did not see law as the imposition of a particular political power; according to him, this is rather the product of the natural evolution of a given community, otherwise state and *Volksgeist* would disunite, with the result that imposed law would encounter resistance from the *Volk*. Hegel would not elaborate on this conception until the point of becoming a theorist of nationalism[59]—at least not one who demanded the ethnic homogeneity of nations—but still articulated arguments that could be easily employed by more explicit nationalists, less interested in philosophy and more concerned with politics.

[57] While an indirect influence of *The Phenomenology of Spirit* (published in 1807) cannot be excluded and rather seems plausible, it is still unclear to what extent the thought of Hegel directly influenced Savigny, *see* C Mährlein, *Volksgeist und Recht. Hegels Philosophie der Einheit und ihre Bedeutung in der Rechtswissenschaft* (Würzburg, Königshausen und Neumann, 2000) 126–27. Moreover, a limited intellectual dialogue among the authors occurred, as references in Hegel's *Philosophy of Right* of 1820 show. In the end, the ideas of Hegel and Savigny show on several aspects interesting points of contact, so that it seems justified to make limited references to the thought of the idealist philosopher in the following pages.

[58] On some similarities and differences between the theories of Rousseau and Hegel, *see* M Pawlik, 'Hegels Kritik an der politischen Philosophie Jean-Jacques Rousseaus' (1999) 38 *Der Staat* 21–40.

[59] The interpretations as to the relation between Hegel and nationalism are many and divergent, wavering between those who deny that the national question played any role within Hegel's system and others affirming the opposite; on this point *see* A von Bogdandy, 'Hegel und der Nationalstaat' (1991) 30 *Der Staat* 513–35, 514–15.

Savigny's view was more radical: he negated the possibility of altering private law on the part of the state, rejecting therefore the idea of a code of law. In this respect, there is a great divergence between Savigny's and Hegel's views, since Hegel praised the idea of a codification.[60] Compared to Hegel, Savigny was more exposed to the influence of Romanticism, and in this respect, the divergence from Hegel—who moreover looked with great interest at 'enlightened' Prussia[61] where law had already been codified in 1794—can be explained. Although he himself was too realistic to be a Romantic,[62] Savigny found the cultural ground on which his assumptions could be based in German Romanticism. At least the 'second phase' of Romanticism (1805–30s), a phase more nationalistically focused on the folkish Germanic roots, supposedly played a significant role in the development of Savigny's thought, as the collaboration with the brothers Grimm attests. The author somehow imported the views of Romantic poets and philosophers into the legal discipline, with whom he also came in personal contact, in particular after his marriage to the sister of the poet Clemens Brentano.

While followers of the Enlightenment rejected the past and most particularly the Middle Ages—ideologically looked upon as an obscure era of ignorance—Romantics valued it. By the same token, Savigny thought that a separation between past and present is purely deceptive. According to this view, the historical method allows to go to the roots of a legal system and '*jeden gegebenen Stoff bis zu seiner Wurzel zu verfolgen, und so sein organisches Prinzip zu entdecken, wodurch sich von selbst das, was noch Leben hat, von demjenigen absondern muß, was schon abgestorben ist, und nur noch der Geschichte angehört*'.[63] In this way, the dimension of time becomes relative; there are no breaks in the validity of law and historical sources on which the jurist focuses. These sources can be used to answer today's questions of law while Savigny seems to be able to discuss all kinds of legal issues with ancient scholars as if they were sitting on the other side of his desk.[64] This position could give even formal legitimacy to Roman law in the new state, as the authority of Justinian work had been purely de facto: as a matter of fact, since it

[60] GWF Hegel, *Elements of the Philosophy of Right* [1820] English translation, edited by A Wood and HB Nisbet (Cambridge, Cambridge University Press, 1991) 241; *see* RP Horstmann, 'Hegels Theorie der bürgerlichen Gesellschaft,' in L Siep (ed), *GWF Hegel. Grundlinien der Philosophie des Rechts* (Berlin, Akademie Verlag, 2005) 208.

[61] On the reasons for Hegel's interest in the Prussian state, *see* F Beiser, *Hegel* (New York, Routledge, 2005) 222–23; A von Bogdandy, 'Hegel und der Nationalstaat' (n 59), 528–29.

[62] The non-Romantic character of Savigny is highlighted by P aker, *Europa und das römische Recht* (München, Biederstein Verlag, 1947), 260.

[63] FC von Savigny, *Vom Beruf unsrer Zeit für Gesetzgebung und Rechtswissenschaft* (n 52), 117–18: to trace every established system to its root, and thus discover an organic principle, whereby that which still has life, may be separated from that which is lifeless and only belongs to history', from the translation by A Hayward, FC von Savigny, *Of the Vocation of Our Age for Legislation and Jurisprudence* (London, 1831) 137.

[64] On the dimension of time in the thought of Savigny *see* M Bretone, *Diritto e tempo nella tradizione europea* (Bari, Laterza, 2004) 70 ff.

was issued, the Corpus Juris had never had any formal legal authority.[65] Of course, the question as to the validity of Roman law would have sounded like a heresy at the time of the glossators,[66] but it now became a rational problem that cropped up in the era of the modern state. What is more, it was allegedly the circle of the Romantic poets that transmitted the idea of the *Volksgeist* to Savigny,[67] initially based on the Hegelian concept of *objektiver Geist*. Savigny used, though not explicitly, the concept to affirm that also law, just like language and art, expresses a collective spirit shared by the whole nation.

Law became rooted in the German nation as a result of the *Volksgeist* theory; the idea that legal rules can respond to a universal rationality and be valid in all contexts is rejected. While theorists of natural law claimed that the legislator has to issue laws that could be valid for all times and peoples,[68] Savigny discards any form of universalism. Savigny's refusal of rationalism makes his 'rough' understanding of the *Volksgeist* more coherent than that of Hegel, whose relation to historicism remained ambivalent, held back by the challenging aim to uphold the authority of reason.[69]

Cultural nationalism could not accept the idea of a law that is non-historical and universal, undifferentiated and exportable without consideration of the specific characteristics of a nation,[70] so that if there is no universal reason supporting the law, then law can only be particular to every single community. This affects both private and public law. To speak of an ideal form for the state is nonsensical, since there is not a universal form that can be ideal worldwide without taking into consideration the community that establishes it. Under the rising German nationalism as expressed in the thought of Herder, such a community could only be a national one. It is in this period that 'culture' becomes 'unquestioningly, national culture, held to be different *a priori* from other cultures and singled out by the nation's underlying characteristic individuality'.[71] In this respect, it is rather Herder the intellectual who more strongly influenced Savigny.[72]

[65] R van Caenegem, *European Law in the Past and the Future. Unity and Diversity over Two Millennia* (Cambridge, Cambridge University Press, 2002) 17.

[66] N Jansen, 'Das gelehrte Recht und der Staat', in R Zimmermann (ed), *Globalisierung und Entstaatlichung des Rechts. Teilband II. Nichtstaatliches Privatrecht: Geltung und Genese* (Tübingen, Mohr Siebeck, 2008) 173–74.

[67] H Hattenhauer, *Thibaut und Savigny* (n 50), 27.

[68] An overview of these positions in J Schröder, 'Zur Vorgeschichte der Volksgeistlehre. Gesetzgebungs- und Rechtsquellentheorie im 17. und 18. Jahrhundert' (1992) 109 *Zeitschrift der Savigny-Stiftung für Rechtsgeschichte. Germanistische Abteilung* 1–47, 20 ff.

[69] F Beiser, *Hegel* (n 61), 263.

[70] AM Hespanha, *Introduzione alla storia del diritto europeo* (n 30), 212.

[71] J Leerssen, 'Imagology: History and Method', in M Beller and J Leerssen (ed), *Imagology. The Cultural Construction and Literary Representation of National Characters. A Critical Survey* (Amsterdam, Rodopi, 2007) 19.

[72] E Wolf, *Grosse Rechtsdenker der deutschen Geistesgeschichte* (n 55), 475, where a sentence from a letter that Savigny wrote in 1807 is also cited: 'Ich habe in der letzten Zeit viel in Herders Schriften gelesen und mich sehr daran erfreut'.

2.1.4.2 *The* Volksgeist *Theory*

The idea that legislators cannot regulate private law was, of course, not new in the European context, and even less an invention of Savigny; the view was already implied by those adhering to Natural law following a tradition that went back to the Ciceronian principle *neque opinione sed natura constitutum esse ius.*[73] But, Natural law itself was rejected by the Historical School of Law. In the attempt to overcome the dualism between a practical and a purely speculative jurisprudence, Gustav Hugo had already rejected the idea that law could be reduced to statutory form[74] and instead underlined the context-dependence of legal rules,[75] expressing his views in the same years in which, some miles to the west, the Bastille was collapsing. According to the same line of reasoning, Savigny—who had indeed been strongly influenced by Hugo himself[76]—concluded some years later, when the revolution was already brought to an end by Napoleon and after the Congress of Vienna strove to move history back in time, that it is impossible for the law to be modified by the mere discretion (*Willkühr*) of some legislator;[77] law—just like language—is something that spontaneously arises from the spirit of the people. How then could the will of a single person alter what centuries of tradition have created? In this respect the new German Historical School distanced itself from both the Law of Reason and legal positivism.

In reality, not even Portalis, the architect of the French code, implied that the codification would have made it possible to elaborate new laws *ex nihilo* only justified by the arbitrary decisions of the political power. In particular, when it came to more sensitive issues like family law, the legislator '*doit consulter les mœurs, le caractère, la situation politique et religieuse de la nation qu'il représente*' ('should consult the customs, the character, the political and religious situation of the nation that he represents').[78] However, after such a 'consultation', the legislator would still have the power to intervene in private law creating rules. On the contrary, Savigny conceived the role of the legislator as a non-creative one, although still not completely superfluous. According to this view, the function of the legislator is limited to the reorganisation and systematisation of an already existing consuetudinary law: what Germany needed was not codifications emulating the French model but rather mere compilations of German law. The exhortation of Herder seems to have been taken: 'If you must imitate, please imitate the people

[73] Cicero, *De Legibus* [52 BCE] Liber I, 28.

[74] F Wieacker, *A History of Private Law in Europe* (n 38), 302.

[75] In his *Lehrbuch eines civilistischen Cursus* of 1799, Hugo gives a famous example to explain his point, explaining that polygamy can be legally justified among those populations where women's 'beauty and fertility' does not last long. Quoted also by J Schröder, 'Zur Vorgeschichte der Volksgeistlehre' (n 68), 31.

[76] JEG de Montmorency, 'Savigny', in J MacDonell and E Manson (eds), *Great Jurists of the World* (London, John Murray, 1913) 563.

[77] FC von Savigny, *Vom Beruf unsrer Zeit für Gesetzgebung und Rechtswissenschaft* (n 52), 11.

[78] J-É-M Portalis, *Discours préliminaire du premier projet de code civil. Motifs et discours prononcés lors de la publication du code civil* (Bordeaux, Éditions Confluences, 2004) 37.

of your own country and do not make yourself ridiculous or contemptible by imitating foreign nationalities'.[79]

Given the complexity of the legal system, this work would have necessarily required the contribution made by the legal scholars. However, at that particular point, German legal scholars were not yet 'ready' to help the legislator issuing good statutes and this is the basic reason why, in Savigny's view, codification or even compilation plans had to be abandoned. Codification could take place one bright day in the distant future, but until then, legal scholars would have the task of interpreting the *Volksgeist* and making the legal system work properly and evolve. The real oracles of the *Volksgeist*, the only ones legitimated to interpret it and speak in its name, are thus the educated lawyers; the origin of law is popular, but law in itself is a professorial and elitist issue. Insofar as it maintains that political power is not legitimated to alter private law, Savigny's view does not significantly differ from the view that spread in the years previous to the creation of the first modern states. Until this point, Savigny merely defends a very ancient view of law as something intangible by the will of people, rejecting the developments under French Enlightenment just like Hugo did. Indeed, although it is commonly accepted that the Historical School of Law introduced the idea of *Volksgeist* in the legal discourse, it is possible to identify analogous theories much earlier; in particular, the idea that 'unwritten laws' are better than 'written laws' and that political organisations should be made according to the characteristics of particular populations is older.[80] Initially, the only relevant difference would seem to be that while the Historical School spoke of *Volksgeist*, previous thinkers preferred to employ Latin words like '*indoles*' or '*ingenium populi*'. The expression '*ingenium populi*' in particular became common in the seventeenth century,[81] not by coincidence, in the period that will lead to the formation of the modern states, while during the medieval era analogous considerations were infrequent. Furthermore, particular characteristics were more usually assigned to wide groups of people: northern Europeans, southern Europeans, Asians etc—'populations' rather than 'nations'. Consider for instance, Aristotle, who already spoke of 'the character of the citizens', distinguishing Northern and Asian populations from the Hellenic race. According to the philosopher, the characteristics of each of these groups had political repercussions, so that for example only the Hellenic race had the characteristics (high spirit and intelligence) that made it possible for them to develop their particular institutions. Interestingly, nonetheless, Aristotle recognised that

[79] JG Herder, *Fragmente über die neuere deutsche Literatur*, quote translated by RR Ergang, *Herder and the Foundations of German Nationalism* (New York, Columbia University Press, 1931) 154–55.

[80] J Schröder, 'Zur Vorgeschichte der Volksgeistlehre' (n 68), 1–47.

[81] Ibid, 7. 9: 'Festzuhalten ist, daß sich bereits im frühen 17. Jahrhundert auch in Deutschland eine Art "Volksgeistlehre" ausbreitet und daß diese Lehre zwar einerseits eine durch Bodins Klimatheorie ausgelöste Modeerscheinung ist, andererseits aber auch ihre Wurzeln in der zeitgenössischen Gesetzgebungstheorie hat, die möglichst an die natürlichen Gegebenheiten anzuknüpfen empfiehlt. Zu den—sie offenbar begünstigenden—Randbedingungen gehört eine allgemeine Skepsis gegenüber jeder Art von Gesetzgebung.'

people's characteristics diverged even among Hellenic tribes themselves.[82] The novely of the *Volksgeistdenken*, which furthermore underwent a radicalisation in the first years of the nineteenth century contextually with the beginning of the era of Restoration,[83] lies in its intertwining with the concept of nation.

The difference between Savigny and older legal theories could not be grasped—and Savigny would be reductively viewed as a mere legal reactionary—without references to the nationalist theory. As modernist studies on nationalism in particular have pointed out,[84] it is questionable whether people in the Middle Ages thought of themselves as parts of an organic living community coinciding with the modern concept of nation. As already said, private law was at that time far from being national, and its source was of course not the power of the state. The sources of such intangible legal rules were looked for in several elements such as God, Nature or even the will of people, but not in the nation, which is a comparatively modern construct. This new element appeared in the legal debate only after the creation of modern states contextually with the diffusion of nationalism: at the beginning of the nineteenth century the concept of *Nationalgeist* made its appearance in law.[85] The national idea first appeared in the work of Montesquieu, then spread in the German context through thinkers like Moser[86] and only later became the fulcrum of the theory of law of Savigny. The Savignian *Volksgeist* furthermore appears to be even more radical than its direct precursor (also in this aspect, a contrast between 'Romantic' cultural and 'Enlightened' civic nationalism could be perceived), since neither Montesquieu's '*esprit de la nation*' implied the futility of a positive legislation and was rather even determinable by legislation[87] (though the basic principle remains that it is the law that should follow the characteristics of the people and not the other way round, or the risk of despotism would arise), an idea shared also by Rousseau.[88] In Savigny's view, on the contrary, if it is not the *Willkühr* (discretion) that makes law, it is the '*gesammte Vergangenheit der Nation*' ('entire past of the nation').[89] Law is now seen as expression of a *national* character formed through the centuries, according to a view that

[82] Aristotle, *Politics* [350 BCE] English translation by B Jowett (Mineola, NY, Dover, 2000) 270–71.

[83] T Würtenberg, *Zeitgeist und Recht* (Tübingen, Mohr, 1987) 55.

[84] The remark of EJ Hobsbawm on our cognitive limits remains valid: 'what Herder thought about the Volk cannot be used as evidence for the thoughts of the Westphalian peasantry', *Nations and Nationalism since 1780. Programme, Myth, Reality* (Cambridge, Cambridge University Press, 2012) 48.

[85] In particular by Franz von Zeiller, cited in J Schröder, 'Zur Vorgeschichte der Volksgeistlehre' (n 68), 19.

[86] Who wrote in 1766 'Von dem deutschen Nationalgeist'.

[87] 'Plusieurs choses gouvernent les hommes, le climat, la religion, les lois, les maximes du gouvernement, les exemples des choses passées, les mœurs, les manières ; d'où il se forme un esprit général qui en résulte. A mesure que dans chaque nation une de ces causes agit avec plus de force, les autres lui cèdent d'autant', C-L de Montesquieu, *De l'esprit des loix*, vol 2 [1748] (London, 1777) 189.

[88] 'Il est certain que les peuples sont, à la longue, ce que le gouvernement les fait être', J-J Rousseau, 'Discours sur l'économie politique' [1755] in *Œuvres de JJ Rousseau. Ouvrages de politique. Partie I* (Lyon, 1796), 284.

[89] FC von Savigny, 'Über den Zweck dieser Zeitschrift' (n 51), 6.

was inspired by Herder and, to a lesser extent, Schelling.[90] 'Savigny follows Herder: Herder praising the creativity of the folk; Savigny seeking to protect the product of the folk, its common and customary law [...] Codification, a Benthamite rage, was an instance of the lack of veneration for the past that seemed to Romanticists to mark all their opponents'.[91]

Savigny's understanding of the catchy word *Volksgeist* is thus a personal one resulting from the eccentric combination of Hegel's idealism and Herder's nationalism. The term *Volksgeist* alone could therefore be misleading: for instance, the will of the *Volk* could also be expressed as an act of parliamentary will, as also Hegel thought. However, under Herder's influence,[92] Savigny developed an organicist conception of the *Volk* and claimed that people are a cultural and traditional subject, so that if the parliament moves away from those traditions, its acts would not represent the 'will' of the nation any more. In this point Savigny's thought departs from that of Hegel, who now seems even closer to Thibaut's considerations on Roman law. While Hegel's conception of law—fundamentally not dissimilar from Montesquieu's—exalted the link between society and legal rules acknowledging the role of positive law, the nationalist *Volksgeistdenken* goes further and deduces the impossibility of legal codification, only admitting compilations of rules under particularly limitative conditions. *Volksgeist* represents now law's origin and source of legitimacy: law is not deliberately created by the reason of man but originates instead from the spirit of a *Volk*.[93]

Nonetheless, when referring to peoples who exist—like the Germans—instead of historical communities—like the Romans—this line of reasoning can lead to reactionary results. What if the majority of the people democratically express a 'will' which moves away from tradition? The only way to solve this contradiction is to assume that the only real 'oracle' of the *Volksgeist* is not the *Volk* but rather the cultural elite of lawyers, or even more drastically, refuse democracy.

2.1.4.3 Volksgeist *and Language*

The cultural nature of this nationalist form emerges also from the continuous references to language. Employing arguments already used by Hugo, Savigny compares law and language,[94] This is not a mere stylistic or rhetoricical analogy; the argument rather collocates itself in a precise theoretical context, inasmuch as

[90] F Wieacker, *A History of Private Law in Europe* (n 38), 284 ff.

[91] JB Halsted, *Romanticism* (New York, Harper & Row, 1969) 28.

[92] A direct influence of Herder on Savigny has been acknowledged among others by P Koschaker, *Europa und das römische Recht* (n 62), 196; E-W Böckenförde, 'Die Historische Rechtsschule und das Problem der Geschichtlichkeit des Rechts', in E-M Böckenförde, *Recht, Staat, Freiheit* (Frankfurt am Main, Suhrkamp, 1991), 18 ff, F Wieacker, *A History of Private Law in Europe* (n 38), 284 ff.

[93] C Mährlein, *Volksgeist und Recht* (n 57), 19.

[94] FC von Savigny, *Vom Beruf unsrer Zeit für Gesetzgebung und Rechtswissenschaft* (n 52), 19.

it follows Fichte's linguistic philosophy as well as Herder's ideas on language[95] and that language is necessarily tied to the characteristics of the people it is spoken by.

> By whom and for whom was the French language constructed? By Frenchmen, and for Frenchmen. It expresses ideas and relations which are peculiar to their world, and to the course of their life; it expresses them in the manner which their local circumstances, the fleeting moment and the mood of their soul at that moment indicate. Outside of this area the words are only half understood or not at all; they are ill applied or, where the subjects are wanting, altogether inapplicable and thus uselessly learned.[96]

These considerations with reference to language are employed in the legal debate as well. Through Savigny the nationalist 'primordialist' image often used by Fichte and Herder—the nation as an organic (though exclusively cultural) creature with some characteristics of its own, life and eventually death—penetrates into the German jurisprudence:

> Aber dieser organische Zusammenhang des Rechts mit dem Wesen und Character des Volkes bewährt sich auch im Fortgang der Zeiten, und auch hierin ist es der Sprache zu vergleichen. So wie für diese, giebt es auch für das Recht keinen Augenblick eines absoluten Stillstandes, es ist derselben Bewegung und Entwicklung unterworfen, wie jede andere Richtung des Volkes, und auch diese Entwicklung steht unter demselben Gesetz innerer Nothwendigkeit, wie jene früheste Erscheinung. Das Recht wächst also mit dem Volke fort, bildet sich aus mit diesem, und stirbt endlich ab, so wie das Volk seine Eigenthümlichkeit verliert.[97]

With this understanding of law as the product of history and tradition, Savigny added to the Romantic *Weltanschauung* and stimulated the interest of other German patriots like the famed linguist and philologist Jacob Grimm, a student and friend of Savigny (at least until Grimm became one of the *Göttinger Sieben*),[98] who later praised Savigny's work (the legal scholar had sent a copy of his famous manuscript to the brothers Grimm in order to get feedback), further developing the theory:

> Das Recht ist wie die Sprache und Sitte *volksmäßig*, dem Ursprung und der organisch lebendigen Fortbewegung nach. Es kann nicht als getrennt von jenen gedacht werden,

[95] For the difference between a Hegelian and a Herderian conception of language, *see* A von Bogdandy, 'Hegel und der Nationalstaat' (n 59), 526.

[96] Quote and translation from RR Ergang, *Herder and the Foundations of German Nationalism* (n 80), 163.

[97] FC von Savigny, *Vom Beruf unsrer Zeit für Gesetzgebung und Rechtwissenschaft* (n 52), 11: 'But this organic connection of law with the being and character of the people, is also manifested in the progress of the times; and here, again, it may be compared with language. For law, as for language, there is no moment of absolute cessation; it is subject to the same movement and development as every other popular tendency; and this very development remains under the same law of inward necessity, as in its earliest stages. Law grows with the growth, and strengthens with the strength of the people, and finally dies away as the nation loses its nationality', translation by A Hayward (n 63) 27.

[98] The Göttinger Seven were a group of German professors of the University of Göttingen who had been fired after protesting against the king of Hannover, Ernest Augustus. The king had abrogated the liberal Constitution of 1833 that had been drafted among others by Friedrich Christoph Dahlmann, one of the Göttinger Seven and future drafter of the Constitution of the German Empire of 1849.

> sondern diese alle durchdringen einander innigst vermöge einer Kraft, die über dem Menschen liegt. So unsinnig es wäre, eine Sprache oder Poesie *erfinden* zu wollen, ebensowenig kann der Mensch mit seiner einseitigen Vernunft ein Recht finden, das sich ausbreite frisch und mild, wie das im Boden gewachsene.[99]

The influence of Jacob Grimm on Savigny—of the brilliant pupil on the (just six years older) master—seems more than plausible. Wilhelm Grimm also expressed his particular interest for the theory on the popular origin of law, manifesting the intention to apply the same hypothesis to other fields of investigation, in particular literature and philology.[100] This contributed to the development of the modern *Germanistik*, the systematic study of the German language, literature and culture in historical perspective.

2.1.4.4 Diffusion of the Volksgeist *Theory*

Right after its publication, Savigny's pamphlet provoked a debate in Germany in which numerous criticisms were raised.[101] The *Volksgeist* theory managed to prevent codification in Germany only for almost a century: ultimately, at the beginning of the twentieth century, the German civil code came into force. Politically, Savigny's success seems therefore relative. Regardless of the academic fortune of his theories and the vivacious debate they started, it can be seriously questioned whether the theory of the *Volksgeist* has left a considerable mark on German private law by shaping its contents in a distinctive way. We could even wonder whether—from this point of view—the importance of this idea is not overestimated.[102]

Notwithstanding, Savigny's influence has been—and still is—fundamental to the German and the European legal culture in another sense. His greatest success is the preservation of law within a cultural dimension, safeguarded by the elite of

[99] J Grimm, 29 October 1814, in I Schnack and W Schoof, *Briefe der Brüder Grimm an Savigny aus dem Savignyschen Nachlaß* (Berlin, Erich Schmidt, 1953) 172: 'Law, like language and customs, is *popular* in its origin and in its organic development. It cannot be imagined separately from those as they all permeate one another by virtue of a force superior to man. To want to *invent* a language or poetry would be as foolish as men wanting to conceive with their incomplete reason a law which may spread freshly and mildly, as the one grown in soil'.

[100] 'Ich kann sagen, dass es unsere Absicht ist, den Ursprung der Poesie auf solche Weise darzustellen, als ein nicht von dem vollen Leben überhaupt getrenntes Gemeingut des Volks, dessen Anfang irdische Augen nicht sehen können und welcher darum, wie bei allem Lebendigen, geheimnisreich ist', W Grimm, 12 December 1814, in I Schnack and W Schoof, *Briefe der Brüder Grimm an Savigny* (n 100), 183.

[101] F Wieacker, *Industriegesellschaft und Privatrechtsordnung* (n 33), 87.

[102] H Coing, 'Savignys rechtspolitische und methodische Anschauungen in ihrer Bedeutung für die gegenwärtige deutsche Rechtswissenschaft', in H Coing, *Gesammelte Aufsätze zu Rechtsgeschichte, Rechtsphilosophie und Zivilrecht*, vol 1 (Frankfurt am Main, Vittorio Klostermann, 1982) 181. Moreover, the Volksgeistlehre has also been considered not fundamental in the whole system of Savigny and not the most important reason for his rejection of the idea of codification, *see* P Caroni, 'Savigny und die Kodifikation. Versuch einer Neudeutung des "Berufes"' (1969) 86 *Zeitschrift der Savigny-Stiftung für Rechtsgeschichte. Germanistische Abteilung*, 97–176, and of the same author, 'La cifra codificatoria nell'opera di Savigny' 81–5.

the legal writers and protected from the mere will of the legislator, in a period in which legal positivism threatened to reduce the whole of law to the form of a statute. In the era of German nationalism, this was only possible by also making law part of that *Volksgeist* that inflamed German patriots who demanded the unity of the nation: putting emphasis on the national character of law, its roots in popular traditions and customs, its link to the natural evolution of language and history.[103] From this moment the cultural idea also conquers the law.

The doctrine of *Volksgeist*, as well as the methodology employed by the Historical School of Law, enjoyed almost immediate success abroad. This was partially due to Savigny's fame: he attracted a great number of young students from different parts of Europe willing to follow his lectures in Berlin.[104] More importantly, however, the doctrine was expedient in various countries, as it could perform several political functions: legal scholars were now reinstated as central figures within the legal system, a role that the boldness of the legislator had attempted to obliviate. The *Volksgeistdenken* could be used with the aim not only of opposing the codification but even legitimising legal systems in a traditional way. So while nationalism was at least initially just one of the factors that influenced the development of the *Volksgeist* idea, the theory proved to serve nationalist purposes in an exceptional way and a large part of its success lies in this. We can rapidly follow the journey of the *Volksgeist* in the discourses of legal scholars in a number of countries, on the old and the new continents, noteworthy experiences that exemplify the fortune of the concept, before we focus on the development of the concept in its German homeland again until the events linked to National Socialism.

2.1.4.5 ... In Europe

It has already been observed that the idea that law chiefly emerges as custom rather than legislation spread particularly in those nations that could not organise themselves in the form of a nation-state. This should be a fortiori the case for those communities provided with a strong cultural and linguistic identity that claimed their nature of nation against a centralist state, as in the case of Catalonia. It is therefore not surprising to discover that Savigny's theories were favourably accepted in that part of Europe.

The *Volksgeistdenken* rapidly permeated the work of several Catalan scholars—in particular Manuel Durán y Bas—who got to know Savigny's thought mainly through French translations.[105] Following Savigny, these scholars affirmed

[103] E Wolf, *Grosse Rechtsdenker der deutschen Geistesgeschichte* (n 55), 532.

[104] Nonetheless it would be reductive to claim that legal scholars in other countries just repeated Savigny's ideas and that the only renowned legal school in Europe at that period was the one established in Berlin; *see* P Caroni, 'La cifra codificatoria nell'opera di Savigny' (1980) 9 *Quaderni fiorentini per la storia del pensiero giuridico moderno* 69–111, 92–5.

[105] M Figueras Pàmies, *La Escuela Jurídica catalana frente a la Codificación española. Durán y Bas: su pensamiento jurídico-filosófico* (Barcelona, Bosch, 1987) 115.

that law is something that develops naturally from the people and is linked to particular contexts and historical periods (thus complying with *Volksgeist* and *Zeitgeist*). In conclusion, the law can only be a national one,[106] which implied the need to maintain a separate law for Catalonia. The reason for such diffusion is indeed political, since the thesis of the German Historical School could be easily employed by Catalan scholars to defend their own autonomy and legal system against the plans of legal unification based on the laws in force in the region of Castile.[107] In this sense, the political concerns of Catalan lawyers did not differ from those of Savigny.[108] The main problem with codification seemed to be that '[g]iven the lack of Catalan political power, it was thought that legislation on Catalan civil law should not be left in the hands of non-Catalans'.[109] Durán y Bas, who later became Minister of Justice in 1899, could obtain that the Spanish Civil Code of 1889 left traditional Catalan law 'provisionally' untouched. Still in the twentieth century, Catalonia managed to maintain its autonomy from Spanish law and gradually embarked upon autonomous projects of compilation and codification, always in light of the idea that

> Civil law represented, together with the language, one of the most important cultural products of the Catalan people, one of the principal exponents of their identity as a people, and therefore one of the essential reference points in identifying Catalonia as a product of a specific historical process.[110]

The Savignian theories represented an outstanding instrument of legitimation for those communities that had fought to gain independence from larger empires and affirm themselves as nation-states. This was in particular the case with Hungary, which restored its old traditional laws in 1861, riding the wave of the 'spring of nations' of 1848.[111] Hungarian legal scholarship soon absorbed the methodology of the Historical School and the *Volksgeistdenken*, so that expressions like 'law of nation' and 'national character' became common for almost a

[106] Ibid, 171–82, where in particular the thought of Durán y Bas is analysed.

[107] 'Nineteenth-century opposition to the codification process had its roots in the ideology of the historical school of law and its rejection of codification. This influence is clear in the setting up in Barcelona of a "Spanish Committee" linked to the Savigny Foundation of Berlin, under the honorary presidency of Pere Nolasc Vives I Cebrià, although Duran y Bas was effectively its leader', F Badosa Coll, '"... Quae ad ius Cathalanicum pertinent": The Civil Law of Catalonia, ius commune and the Legal Tradition', in HL MacQueen, A Vaquer and S Espiau Espiau (eds), *Regional Private Laws and Codification in Europe* (Cambridge, Cambridge University Press, 2003) 159.

[108] M Figueras Pàmies, *La Escuela Jurídica catalana frente a la Codificación española*, p 114: 'Las circumstancias concretas de Cataluña se parecían, cada vez máz, a las de Alemania, en 1841, cuando la codificación hacía peligrar las instituciones civiles alemanas. Es por ello que los juristas catalanes se acogieron a la escuela histórica para la defensa de su derecho civil.'

[109] F Badosa Coll, '"...Quae ad ius Cathalanicum pertinent"' (n 109), 160.

[110] This quote from the Commission for the review of the Compilation in the early 1980s can be found in N De Gispert I Català, 'The Codification of Catalan Civil Law', in HL MacQueen, A Vaquer and S Espiau Espiau (eds), *Regional Private Laws and Codification in Europe* (Cambridge, Cambridge University Press, 2003) 164.

[111] *See* I Zajtay, *Introduction à l'étude du droit hongrois. La formation historique du droit civil* (Paris, Libraire du Recueil Sirey, 1953) 155 ff.

century, contributing—together with more dramatic historical events—to delay the codification of civil law by several years.[112] Curiously enough, German legal theories spread so decisively in the Hungarian context that a first draft of civil codification in 1900—just like the more successful commercial code of 1875—met with strong criticisms for being too 'German',[113] a style contested in particular by practitioners, who longed for less abstract rules.[114]

Italy is the country in which the political situation was most easily comparable to the German. Given this similarity, one would expect an almost exact replication of Savignian arguments in the peninsula, but surprisingly enough, the *Volksgeistdenken* did not spread to Italy immediately.[115] Not even those scholars who knew and appreciated Savigny's work and adhered to a nationalist understanding of the relation between nation and law, like the famed private international lawyer and politician Pasquale Stanislao Mancini, embraced the anti-codification argument. On the contrary, those authors claimed that a code would be the perfect instrument for the nation to create a law of its own.[116] They thus advocated a national idea of law to be realised by means of codification. This was a vision much closer to—though not necessarily derived from—Thibaut's view and Hegel's thought. This is quite surprising: if we consider that Italy, even more than Germany, was fragmented by a myriad of different states while cultural and poltical elites were operating to instil national consciousness and achieve political unity, one would expect a legal evolution comparable to the German one.

The difference can, however, be easily explained: it has already been said that even in Germany at the beginning of the nineteenth century there were strands of civic nationalism, but the cultural nationalism that is more easily detectable in Savignian theories gained the upper hand mainly because of the general hostility towards France and its enlightened ideas. The political situation in Italy was quite different. Savigny's pamphlet was circulated among Italian legal scholars very late, when a translation was published in 1857, more than 40 years after its publication in Germany.[117] In those years, Italy was about to achieve political unity, under the rule of a French-speaking monarchy clearly inspired by the French ideals. A civil codification was therefore considered to be an excellent instrument for gaining legal unity, while only conservatives critical of the Enlightenment could have found Savigny's ideas appealing. By then, most Italian pre-Unitarian states already had their laws codified, as an effect of the penetration of the *Code civil* both

[112] K Gönczi, 'Die deutsch–ungarischen Rechtsverbindungen von der Frühen Neuzeit bis in die Gegenwart: Wissenstransfer, Kodifikationen und liaisonmen' (2000) 46 *Osteuropa-Recht* 215–29, 223–24.

[113] A Harmathy, 'A Survey of the History of Civil and Commercial Law', in A Harmathy (ed), *Introduction to Hungarian Law* (The Hague, Kluwer, 1998) 13–14.

[114] I Zajtay, *Introduction à l'étude du droit hongrois* (n 113), 172.

[115] On this point, *see* C Ghisalberti, *La codificazione del diritto in Italia. 1865–1942* (Roma, Laterza, 1985) 5 ff.

[116] Ibid, 7, with further references.

[117] Ibid, 7.

ratione imperii and *imperio rationis* in the peninsula. Plainly, Savignian arguments against codification may have sounded very naïve and exaggerated to the ears of lawyers who were well acquainted with codifications,[118] although private law unification, associated with a reform of property in various areas, soon determined evident social and economic dramatic changes.

Nonetheless, while the *Volksgeist* could not offer any appealing argument to object to the codification of law, it still represented a solid theoretical justification for affirming the need of a nationalisation of law, so that the idea that private law and *Volk* are intrinsically connected became a 'definitive acquisition of contemporary culture'[119] in a few years. This understanding is already evident in Mancini's thought. This author adhered to what we would today call a classical primordialist understanding of the nation—typical of that historical period[120]—according to which the nation is something really existing based on objective criteria like '*la Regione, la Razza, la Lingua, le Costumanze, la Storia, le Leggi, le Religioni*' ('the territory, the race, the language, the customs, the history, the laws, the religions'),[121] and with features of its own that necessarily reflect on the contents of the law. As a scholar of international law, Mancini was also concerned with the issue of transnational unification of law. His nationalist understanding of law, however, prevented him from advocating international unification. The imposition of a sole legal regime had been feasible in the Italian nation, but would be impossible within a broader geographical context; substantive laws necessarily differ among nations, and the idea of a universal legal system seemed neither feasible nor desirable. According to Mancini, consequently, not international unification but rather only private international law—though a particularly liberal one—could make up for the necessary fragmentation of the global legal order,[122] in which any nation had the obligation—deriving from an overarching universal human law—to respect the other legal orders.[123]

2.1.4.6. … In the USA

While our primary focus is Europe, a brief divagation overseas could be beneficial and instructive. The impact of the *Volksgeist* doctrine was not limited to Europe. Curiously, while we could gain the impression that Savigny's *Volksgeist* did not manage to prevent codification in the long run at home and did not even convince

[118] Ibid, 9: 'In questo clima di rinnovato fervore per la codificazione, le rievocazioni spesso retoriche del non più vigente diritto comune fatte da qualche giurista sorpassato o da qualche romantico nostalgico di un antico primato della cultura giuridica italiana erano destinate ad apparire come prive di senso per l'assoluta mancanza di concretezza'.

[119] B Leoni, *Il problema della scienza giuridica* (Torino, Giappichelli, 1940) 16.

[120] J-H Halpérin, *Entre nationalisme juridique* (n 3), 69.

[121] PS Mancini, *Diritto internazionale. Prelezioni con un saggio sul Machiavelli* (Napoli, Marghieri, 1873) 27.

[122] E Jayme, *Pasquale Stanislao Mancini. Internationales Privatrecht zwischen Risorgimento und praktischer Jurisprudenz* (Ebelsbach, Verlag Rolf Gremer, 1980) 41.

[123] J-L Halpérin, *Entre nationalisme juridique* (n 3), 71.

the neighbouring Italians as to the undesirability of codification, it accomplished its plan much further away, in the United States of America. In the second half of the nineteenth century, indeed, the *Kodifikationsstreit* reappeared in the state of New York, where professor David Dudley Field, moved by concerns analogous to those of Thibaut—though without the intention of unifying private law in the whole federation—embarked upon the project of drafting a code. A Code of Civil Procedure had previously been drafted by Field and already enjoyed a discrete success in the Western states, where the bar was 'young and open-minded',[124] while Eastern states chose autonomous reforms of procedural law. However, that code of procedure—per se the 'greate[st] affront to the common-law tradition can be imagined'[125]—was 'only one part of a larger, bolder plan to codify the whole common law'.[126] Such an ambitious plan could not avoid provoking a strong resistance. In the re-enactment of the German *Kodifikationsstreit*, the role of Savigny was seemingly played by Professor James Coolidge Carter who, representing the Association of the Bar of the City of New York, fiercely opposed the civil codification proposed by Field, giving rise to a debate which resulted in the victory of Carter's view.[127]

It is ascertained that Savigny's theories played an important role in Carter's argumentation, and the latter clearly resembles the former. Carter, too, thought that legal rules originated in popular standards of justice[128] which vary in different states and nations,[129] while codes are the expression of 'the arbitrary power of the sovereign', which is furthermore typical of despotic systems.[130] To be sure, the very idea of a code which professes to know beforehand how future and unknown cases have to be solved is arrogant, which is the 'habit common to all pretenders in every science to fail to observe the necessary limitations of the human faculties; they assert an ability to know the unknowable, and to do the impossible'.[131] There are of course some differences between the positions of the American and the German scholar and—as often happens—the view of the follower is more radical than that of the forerunner. One of these differences is however crucial and needs to be addressed specifically.

[124] LM Friedman, *A History of American Law* (New York, Simon & Schuster, 1973) 394.

[125] Ibid, 391.

[126] Ibid, 403.

[127] M Reimann, 'The Historical School against Codification: Savigny, Carter, and the Defeat of the New York Civil Code' (1989) 37 *The American Journal of Comparative Law* 95–119.

[128] JC Carter, *The Proposed Codification of Our Common Law* (New York, *Evening Post* Job Printing Office, 1884) 5: 'Whoever glances over the varying systems of law exhibited by civilized States, will perceive that in some, as in England and with us, the great body of the rules which determine the rights of men in respect to their persons and property, have never been directly enacted in statutory form. They have their origin in the popular standard, or ideal, of justice, as applied to human action, and the usages and practices sanctioned by it'.

[129] Ibid, 91.

[130] Ibid, 6.

[131] Ibid, 33.

While in Germany a civil code would have had a unifying function, in the American context the codification could have been a threat to legal unity: each state could have enacted its own civil code, harming a national legal unity that would have been better served by a common law. Even the attractive possibility of unifying the laws of all English-speaking states would have been compromised by codification.

> That a private law transaction between men in New Jersey and Ohio should be governed by a different law from that which would rule the same transaction in New York, must be a great evil. [...] What more desirable condition, what more impressive spectacle can there be, than that of fifty States of a great continent, and Empires beyond the seas, all appealing to the same law, and aiming to drown all dissent in one concurring voice? And what more mischievous condition than that all these States and nations should have Codes, each differing from every other, without any conceivable agency for bringing them into unison; but gravitating, by a law of their being, into infinite diversity?[132]

This argumentation is definitely closer to Thibaut's legal sensibility than to Savigny's. As already touched upon, Field had no intention of unifying the laws of the whole federation while Carter was concerned with the issue of legal unity. Subsequently, importing Savigny's theories to the different context of the United States of America lends inconsistency to Carter's argument: if it is true that law originates in popular standards which differ in different nations, how could so many different states appeal to the same law and what would be wrong with several codes representing each nation's standard of justice? Indeed, Carter had to claim that while standards of justice can differ, 'right, reason and justice are, however, everywhere the same';[133] even more, a 'native sense of justice' exists 'in the breasts of all men'.[134] Keeping in mind these fundamental diversities, the 'roles' of these scholars in the American *Kodifikationsstreit* should be inverted, and the Field–Thibaut and Carter–Savigny analogy reconsidered.

It is impossible to tell whether the state of New York would now have its law codified without the influence of Savigny; however the significance of the *Volksgeist* theory cannot be underestimated, as it is shown by the positive reactions to Carter's argumentation. Already with regard to the previous Procedural Field Code, many a legal scholar considered the imposition of a single code on different states impracticable, taking the different social and business conditions between states into consideration.[135] As Lawrence Friedman pointed out, 'lawyers could attack code pleading more easily when it was possible to identify it with an alien,

[132] Ibid, 91–2.
[133] Ibid, 91.
[134] Ibid, 91.
[135] LM Friedman, *A History of American Law*, 395, referring in particular to HH Ingersoll, 'Some Anomalies of Practice' (1892) 1 *The Yale Law Journal* 89–94.

and in this case, a hated culture'.[136] Carter as well seems to have exploited such feelings. This argument seems biased by nationalism,[137] in particular,

> Carter succeeded in presenting Field's attempt as a drastic and dramatic legal measure, as if enacting a civil code would sweep the common law away wholesale, and replace it with a foreign legal system. Carter succeeded in presenting himself as a defender of the American legal heritage, while portraying Field as a presumptuous lawyer who threatened to abolish one of the most remarkable accomplishments of American culture. Even though it is clear that Field did not attempt to do this.[138]

Indeed, Field's idea of codification was different from the European idea Carter (and even legal historians) ascribed to the former.[139] While it is well known that legal academia in the US greatly profited from the migration of several German lawyers in the twentieth century, the immediate reception of a German theory at such a stage of the American legal history surprises. There are several reasons why the *Volksgeist* theory, though distorted, so rapidly spread in that very dissimilar context. It is not revealing to note that the *Volksgeist* theory fitted better in a common law system such as the American system than a civil law system exemplified by the German: at that time both systems were not codified and based on a 'common law' (the American common law and the German *gemeines Recht* based on the *Rezeption* of Roman law). Rather, the conservative philosophy underlying Savigny's position met the favour of the American middle class: Savigny's distrust of the democratic legislative matched with the American distrust of state authority; the control of the legislator over private law was furthermore seen as a sort of economic dirigisme opposed to American laissez-faire ideology, occurring at the time when state interventions in private law notably increased.[140]

2.1.5 From Cultural to Ethnic

The form of nationalism to which Savigny's thought shows links was exclusively cultural. Even Hegel—who believed in the 'natural' character of nations and considered a degree of homogeneity within them as necessary—proposed cultural criteria of identification rather than purely ethnic criteria.[141] In the same way, Savigny was certainly not a theorist of the race as it also emerges from other parts

[136] Ibid, 396.

[137] A Masferrer, 'Defense of the Common Law against Postbellum American Codification: Reasonable and Fallacious Argumentation' (2008–10) 50 *The American Journal of Legal History* 355–431, 420.

[138] Ibid, 420.

[139] Ibid, 423 ff.

[140] M Reimann, 'The Historical School against Codification' (n 129), 107 ff.

[141] A von Bogdandy, 'Hegel und der Nationalstaat' (n 59), 517: 'Der Nation als durch ethnische und andere natürliche Umstände bestimmte Gruppe kann in Hegels Geistphilosophie, die gerade der Prozeß des Abarbeitens der natürlichen Umstände ist, keine große Bedeutung zukommen'.

of his rich work.[142] On the (quite uncertain and indeterminate) ground of culture, it could have been possible to build unexpected relations; the philosopher Hegel could write that '*bei den Griechen fühlen wir uns sogleich heimatlich, denn wir sind auf dem Boden des Geistes*' ('among the Greeks we feel ourselves immediately at home, for we are in the region of Spirit'),[143] while the legal scholar Savigny employed the identical reference to the *Geist* to establish a relation between the Romans and German law.

Without a cultural rather than an ethnic understanding of the nation, Savigny's conception of Roman law as the new historical law of the German spirit could not be fully understood and became self-contradictory,[144] incapable of explaining how the law of the Romans, deliberately received just a few centuries earlier, could have become the 'traditional' law of a Germanic nation. The refusal to accept ethnic interpretations of the nation, and thus the characterisation of the *Volksgeist*, in exclusively cultural terms appears to be a consequence of the political ideology of Savigny. Even if it is true that the various 'national consciousnesses' in Europe arose mainly through the juxtaposition of certain territorial groups, prior to its ethnic and violent shift, nationalism did not yet advocate the superiority of a given nation and was mainly aimed at building nation-states that aggregated people rather than divided them. In this sense, nationalism could be a universal ideal with the aim that all nations would give rise to independent states. This made it possible for several nationalists—the most famous, albeit particularly unfortunate case, is represented by the poet and Romantic hero George Gordon Byron—to take up arms for the independence of other nations. Such a (in reality quite troublesome) appeasement of nationalism and internationalism can be detected in the legal thought of Savigny, whose system of private international law, which seemed to do without that concept of nationality which was, on the contrary, prominent in Mancini's thought,[145] was particularly open—similar in this to that of Mancini—to the application of foreign rules.[146] This was evidently based on the conviction that, despite their differences, all European nations were part of the same legal and moral tradition.

This approach however could not last long, given the difficulty of keeping aggressive and non-aggressive forms of nationalism separated. While German nationalism initially remained of a cultural and linguistic nature it already turned to ethnic elements and to the rhetoric of the ancestral Arian origin in the 1830s.[147]

[142] J-L Halpérin, *Entre nationalisme juridique* (n 3), 58.

[143] GWF Hegel, *Vorlesungen über die Philosophie der Geschichte. Werke in zwanzig Bänden.* Vol 12 [1837] (Frankfurt am Main, Suhrkamp, 1970) 275.

[144] F Wieacker, *A History of Private Law in Europe* (n 38), 305–6 and 312.

[145] H Muir Watt, 'Private International Law Beyond the Schism' (2011) 2 *Transnational Legal Theory* 347–427.

[146] J-L Halpérin, *Entre nationalisme juridique* (n 3), 48 ff.

[147] T Benes, 'From Indo-Germans to Aryans. Philology and the Racialization of Salvationist National Rhetoric, 1806–30', in S Eigen and M Larrimore (eds), *The German Invention of Race* (Albany, NY, State University of New York Press, 2006) 168 and 176.

In jurisprudence, the argument of Savigny with regard to Roman law very soon provoked reactions, already criticised by Rudolf von Jhering, who highlighted the inherent contradiction of that argument.[148] Indeed, even if one adheres to a cultural conception of the nation, it is a fact that Roman law was deliberately adopted in Germany in the sixteenth century for an 'arbitrary' political decision. A fracture thus occurred between Savigny and the Germanist wing of the Historical School, more interested in discovering the authentic Germanic roots in ancient law and which affirmed eventually that the reception of Roman law had been a real national disaster for Germany, a decision to be regretted by any patriot.[149] The contrast later took on a more political form.

In line with the involution of the German political context, the concept of *Volksgeist* started undergoing a process of redefinition that emphasised racist instead of purely cultural elements. This aspect is already perceivable in the thought of Savigny's 'successor' Georg Friedrich Puchta,[150] who thought of the *Volk* in ethnic rather than cultural terms,[151] though admitting that immigrants could be nationalised over time,[152] adhering to primordialist nationalist views pursuant to which a nation could only have a natural instead of an artificial basis.[153] We are on the eve of the degeneration of nationalism, the moment after which an absolutely negative assessment was linked to that principle, which still shapes our way of looking at it and reading the historical and intellectual events involving nationalism before that transformation.

2.1.6 Racist

Point 19 of the NSDAP programme stating that '*das der materialistischen Weltordnung dienende römische Recht*' ('the Roman Law serving a materialistic world order') had to be replaced by '*ein deutsches Gemeinrecht*' ('a German common law') almost represents a gloomy logical consequence of the shift from a

[148] R von Jhering, *Geist des römischen Rechts auf den verschiedenen Stufen seiner Entwicklung* [1852] (Leipzig, Breitkopf & Härtel, 1907) 3 ff. 'Denn was hat das römische Recht mir der "gesammten Vergangenheit der modernen Nationen, innersten Wesen und ihrer Geschichte" zu thun?' 4; 'Möge sie auch noch so viel äußere Gründe und Ursachen namhaft machen, die uns jene Thatsache pragmatisch erklären sollen; so lange sie den Gedanken der Nationalität des Rechts als ausschließlich berechtigten und maßgebenden aufstellt, bleibt der Widerspruch, in dem ihre Lehre sich zur Reception des römischen Rechts befindet, ewig ein ungelöster—durch das Thor der Nationalität kommt das römische Recht nie in unsere Wissenschaft hinein' 5.

[149] This was in particular the idea of Georg Beseler. Nonetheless, Beseler appreciated that the Reception of Roman Law managed to establish a common law for the entire nation, while its criticism was mainly inspired by the political concern of a democratic nature that the abandoning of traditional German law aggravated the split between the law of the jurists and the law of the people. *See* F Wieacker, *Industriegesellschaft und Privatrechtsordnung* (n 33), 88–9.

[150] *See* C Mährlein, *Volksgeist und Recht* (n 57), 130 ff.

[151] GF Puchta, *Cursus der Institutionen* [1841] (Leipzig, Breitkopf und Härtel, 1875) 17.

[152] Ibid, 17.

[153] GF Puchta, *Das Gewohnheitsrecht*, vol 1 (Erlangen, Palm, 1828) 134.

cultural to an explicitly racist criterion of nationality. The programme of the NSDAP was in this respect of a purely negative nature. It did not propose anything for the future besides the abandoning of the already existing and only showed a strong nationalist attitude,[154] rejecting the legacy of Roman law. In the German racial nation there was no room whatsoever for the law of a Mediterranean civilisation and now that the nation was defined in racist terms, Savigny's focus on the culture could no longer represent an argument strong enough to 'save' Roman law. Questionable reinterpretations of history were the only way in which legal scholars could have saved Roman law. In this attempt, one could have argued that the first Romans were all in all a Nordic civilisation,[155] as someone[156] in fact did. But these arguments only represented the exacerbation of an existing trend in the comparative studies of the second half of the nineteenth century. Strongly conditioned by an ethnic national conception and making use of the categories of comparative linguistics, scholars traced the ethnic roots of the modern Germans back to the ancestral Indo-European populations (in the German language known as *indogermanisch*, without anyway any racist connotation), a group from which both Germanic and Roman populations originated, so that even Roman law could be looked upon as not entirely alien.[157]

To 'save the reputation of Roman law', it could also have been argued that the Latin system presented all the qualities ascribed to Germanic law, but this intermediate position was overwhelmed by those who sustained the superiority of traditional German law.[158] While it praised figures like Eike von Repgow, the father of the *Sachsenspiegel*,[159] Nazi propaganda already condemned Roman law, inevitably considered as a foreign system.[160] As a more serious and realistic strategy, one could emphasise the fact that the influence of Roman law on German legal doctrine had been merely methodological but did not touch its deeper Germanic

154 C Mährlein, *Volksgeist und Recht* (n 57), 174–75.

155 The idea of the Romans as a Nordic civilisation is even more absurd if one only considers that—leaving aside the debated question as to what the influence of other ancient legal systems has been on Roman law—most of the celebrated Roman lawyers were ethnically of African or Middle-Eastern descent, *see* PG Monateri, 'Black Gaius. A Quest for the Multicultural Origins of the "Western Legal Tradition"' (2000) 51 *Hastings Law Journal* 479–564, 501.

156 H Frank, 'Die Zeit des Rechts' (1936) *Deutsches Recht* 1 ff, 2, quoted in A Somma, 'Da Roma a Washington', in PG Monateri, T Giaro and A Somma, *Le radici comuni del diritto europeo. Un cambiamento di prospettiva* (Roma, Carocci, 2005) 202. On the controversial figure of Hans Frank, *see* RC van Caenegem, *European Law in the Past and the Future* (n 65), 112–20.

157 PG Monateri, 'Black Gaius' (n 157), 490–96.

158 RC van Caenegem, *European Law in the Past and the Future* (n 65), 110–11.

159 K-P Schroeder, *Vom Sachenspiegel zum Grundgesetz. Eine deutsche Rechtsgeschichte in Lebensbildern* (München, Beck, 2001) 18.

160 P Koschaker, *Europa und das römische Recht* (n 62), 311 ff.

spirit,[161] as Roman law has just contributed to the '*Verwissenschaftlichung*'[162] of German law. This point had never been raised during the age of the *Rezeption*: at that time, critics could have had good reasons to sustain that the law of a foreign civilisation should not be imported to the very different German context, but as a matter of fact this argument was never used.[163] It was only nationalism—already Thibaut accused Roman law of being alien, as seen above—and, in particular, ethnic nationalism, that could introduce the element of the nation in the legal discourse that brought the foreign nature of the Roman system to the fore. Such an alien nature was of course far less perceptible to those living in the Middle Ages, in a period in which nations had not yet been fully 'awakened', and which became increasingly more evident only later, when the efforts to establish fully independent nation-states were augmented; Roman law already started being criticised as extraneous to the needs of that country in sixteenth century France.[164]

Of course, these problems could easily be avoided in the Italian context under Fascism. Given the prevailing racist understanding of the nation under Fascism, Roman law could be rhetorically exalted as a perfect legal system, typically Italian. According to this view, Roman law had been later plundered and improperly changed by different ethnic groups that, with their alterations, contributed to the distortion of that originally perfect legal system. The pure law of the Romans—a true *Roman* rather than *Latin* law[165]—could hence be used to give traditional legitimacy to the present state of the legal order and the new Italian civil codification, occasionally underlining also the contribution of the Catholic doctrine for

[161] *See* M Stolleis, '"Fortschritte" der Rechtsgeschichte in der Zeit des Nationalsozialismus', in M Stolleis and D Simon (eds), *Rechtsgeschichte im Nationalsozialismus* (Tübingen, Mohr, 1989) 193; T Giaro, 'Diritto romano attuale. Mappe mentali e strumenti concettuali', in PG Monateri, T Giaro and A Somma, *Le radici comuni del diritto europeo* (n 158), 94.

[162] In Wieacker's original words, 'Wir verstehen daher die "Rezeption" besser unter dem Bilde nicht der Aufnahme eines stofflichen Fremdkörper, sondern eines Entwicklungsprozesses: nämlich als eine Verwissenschaftlichung des deutschen Rechtswesens', F Wieacker, *Privatrechtsgeschichte der Neuzeit unter besonderer Berücksichtigung der deutschen Entwicklung* (Göttingen, Vandenhoek & Ruprecht, 1952) 66. Also C Schmitt, *Die Lage der europäischen Rechtswissenschaft* (Tübingen, Internationaler Universitäts-Verlag, 1950) 10 warns that, 'Die europäische Bedeutung der Wiedergeburt des römischen Rechts im Mittelalter und der Einfluß der Wissenschaft vom römischen Recht in den verschiedenen Ländern und Epochen sind in keiner Weise identisch mit der Frage des "positiven Geltens" von Sätzen und Begriffen, die man im Corpus Juris Justiniani gefunden hatte'.

[163] P Koschaker, *Europa und das römische Recht* (n 62), 147 ss; F Wieacker, *A History of Private Law in Europe* (n 38), 93, highlights that the view that a foreign set of rules had been adopted 'was fostered by the romantic, nationalistic view of German legal history, which led people to suppose that in adopting "Roman" law the Germans had taken over something foreign and given up something of their own'. CA Cannata, *Lineamenti di storia della giurisprudenza europea* (n 19), 78–9: 'La recezione del diritto romano non fu sentita in Germania come adozione di un diritto straniero; un giudizio di questo genere è stato enunciato assai spesso, e divenne una proposizione programmatica del Nazionalsocialismo, ma esso è recente, ideologicamente viziato, e storicamente falso; la recezione ebbe bensì i suoi avversari, ma l'argomento tratto dalla natura "straniera" del diritto romano non fu mai usato'.

[164] P Grossi, *L'Europa del diritto* (n 18), 95–6.

[165] D Grandi, *Tradizione e Rivoluzione nei Codici Mussoliniani* (Roma, Tipografia delle Mantellate, 1940) 10.

contingent reasons of political opportunism.[166] Looking at two different 'nations' as sources of legitimacy, both the Italian and the German fascist experiences shared the same racist approach on which a disastrous cooperation could be based.[167]

However, while it was relatively easy for Italians to claim a continuity with the Roman experience, this was more complicated for the Germans, whose traditions in the study of Germanic law was much less consolidated. Instead of the repudiated Roman law, Nazi scholars now employed Germanic law—putting emphasis in particular on the duties of the individual toward the community[168]—to provide the new regime with a legal–theoretical underpinning. Nevertheless, the legal philosophy of the Third Reich remained basically unclear and undeveloped. The task of providing National Socialism with a proper legal theory that could finally contribute to 'give the German people a German law'[169] was later undertaken by a group of legal scholars known as the School of Kiel. Among them, two of the future leading figures in German jurisprudence, the aforementioned Franz Wieacker and the very young Karl Larenz—at that time more interested in questions of general jurisprudence than private law. Some of Larenz's writing from that period[170] leave no doubt that the school was trying to harmonise the German legal system with the principles of National Socialism.

The aim of the regime was to awaken and exalt the German nation, and to this end Germany needed an autochthonous jurisprudence—freed from the harmful contaminations of foreign ideologies—in which the *Volk* had to play a central role.[171] The cornerstone of the new national socialist society had been identified through the refusal of individualism and the promotion of an ethnic understanding of the nation. The fact that one had to be a Christian was already an old and implicitly anti-Semitic claim of German nationalists,[172] but now this principle assumed a clearer racist connotation. Point 4 of the NSDAP programme[173] was repeated in the proposed reformulation of section 1 of the civil code, the new section of which had hence to read: '*Rechtsgenosse ist nur, wer Volksgenosse ist;*

[166] *See*, with several references, A Somma, 'Da Roma a Washington' (n 158), 204 ff.

[167] D Grandi, 'Diritto romano-fascista e germanico-nazista di fronte alla rivoluzione del secolo XX', in *Monitore dei tribunali*, 1941, 3 ff, quoted in A Somma, 'Da Roma a Washington' (n 158), 209: 'Voi, camerati nazional-socialisti intesi a realizzare la più pura tradizione del germanismo e della razza tedesca e noi fascisti strenui propugnatori del Diritto romano che è il diritto della nostra razza italiana, siamo strettamente legati dalla chiara unità del nostro avvenire'.

[168] Ibid, 280.

[169] C von Schwerin, *Grundzüge der deutschen Rechtsgeschichte* (Munich, Duncker & Humblot, 1934) VIII.

[170] The three important writings of Larenz from the National Socialist period are *Deutsche Rechtserneuerung und Rechtsphilosophie* from 1934, *Volksgeist und Recht and Rechtsperson und subjektives Recht* from 1935.

[171] HH Jakobs (1993) 'Karl Larenz und der Nationalsozialismus' 17 *Juristen Zeitung* 805–15, 809.

[172] J Katz, *From Prejudice to Destruction: Anti-Semitism, 1700–1933* (Cambridge MA, Harvard University Press, 1980) 77.

[173] Staatsbürger kann nur sein, wer Volksgenosse ist. Volksgenosse kann nur sein, wer deutschen Blutes ist, ohne Rücksichtnahme auf Konfession. Kein Jude kann daher Volksgenosse sein.

Volksgenosse ist, wer deutschen Blutes ist' ('only a member of the *Volk* can be a legal subject; only one who is of German blood can be a member of the *Volk*').[174] The category of the subjective right was rejected and the predominance of the general over the individual interest ('*Gemeinnutz vor Eigennutz*', point 24 of the NSDAP programme) was affirmed instead.

In other words, the aforementioned shift from the liberal patriotism of the Mazzinian phase to the nationalism of 1880–1914,[175] also reached its peak in legal theory. The contrast to Savigny's legal theory is indeed clear, as this was more indebted to Kantian individualism[176] as well as a cultural understanding of the nation. This circumstance also made it difficult to employ Savignyian categories for the ends of the regime. Such was in particular the case of the concept of *Volksgeist*, a Hegelian idea Larenz had to adulterate in order to bridge Hegelianism and Nazi ideology,[177] moreover adding a new racial component to the concept of spirit. Particularly hard was the conciliation of *Volksgeistdenken* and *Führerprinzip*, an operation that earned Larenz criticism and even suspicion from the Nazis, resulting in a growing tension and open protests against the legal scholar.[178] The problem was that if all law organically stems from the people, then the role of the *Führer*—just as Savigny had argued with regard to the democratic legislator—becomes unclear and fades away. Indeed, Larenz uses words that do sound very familiar to affirm that the legislator '*ist gehalten, seine Entscheidung im Einklang mit den Sitten und dem sittlichen und rechtlichen Gemeinbewußtsein der Nation zu treffen*' ('is required to take his decisions in harmony with the customs and the moral and legal collective conscience of the nation').[179]

That conclusion is nonetheless irreconcilable with the *Führerprinzip*, according to which the word of the leader matters, above law and the interpretation given by lawyers and judges. The contradiction can only be resolved by resorting to the almost metaphysical argument that *Führer* and *Volk* coincide:

> Er gehorcht nicht einer an ihn gerichteten Norm, sondern dem Lebensgesetz der Gemeinschaft, das in ihm Fleisch und Blut gewonnen hat. Sein Wille ist mit der Gemeinschaft eins, weil in ihm der Privatmann völlig ausgelöscht ist, und er nichts anderes als das Gemeininteresse will. Ihm ist alle Verantwortung anvertraut, denn für ihn und durch ihn ist die Gemeinschaft die lebendigste Wirklichkeit.[180]

[174] K Larenz, 'Rechtsperson und subjektives Recht', in G Dahm, ER Huber and K Larenz, *Grundfragen der neuen Rechtswissenschaft* (Berlin, Junker und Dünnhaupt, 1935) 241.

[175] EJ Hobsbawm, *Nations and Nationalism since 1780* (n 85), 102.

[176] F Wieacker, *A History of Private Law in Europe* (n 38), 282.

[177] C Mährlein, *Volksgeist und Recht* (n 57), 210.

[178] HH Jakobs, 'Karl Larenz und der Nationalsozialismus', 807.

[179] K Larenz, *Deutsche Rechtserneuerung und Rechtsphilosophie* (Tübingen, Mohr, 1934) 33.

[180] Ibid, 44, 'He does not obey the norm but the living law of the community, which in him became flesh and blood. His will is one with the community, because the private citizen is completely erased in him, and he does not want anything more than the common good. He has complete responsibility, for through him and for him the community becomes the most vivid reality'.

As a result, people, nation and 'king' are once again indistinguishable from each other, just like during the period in history when civic nationalism rose up against the king's totalitarian conviction that '*l'État c'est moi*'. The only difference is that this time the nation coincided with a much more despicable 'king' than the monarch dethroned by nationalism in France.

The classical tension between legislator (be it a parliament or a dictator) and lawyers, ingrained in any modern legal system, reappeared; however this happened in a particularly acute way in the German context, where the lawyer's position had traditionally played a central role in the legal system, due to the extreme nature of the new political development. Strikingly, both cultural and ethnic nationalism continuously represented the *Volk* as the source of legitimacy of power, but never as power holder itself: provided that it is the 'spirit' of the people that gave legitimacy to political power, the interpretation and determination of what this spirit demands remained up to others to decide: the elite of the lawyers, as in Savigny, or the *Führer*, as under Nazism. This highlights the anti-democratic nature of these particular forms of nationalism. In this respect too, the lesson of French civic nationalism is rejected: the people are not holders of the power and the *Volk* is used as a mere justification. Only post-war constitutions—notably the German *Grundgesetz*—would overturn this development, clearly stating that all powers stem from and belong to the people.

On a closer look, thus, the concept of *Volksgeist* was not the best instrument employable to give legitimacy to the National Socialist idea (and this is not the first example of the difficult reconcilability between a 'purely' nationalist idea and fascist ideologies, as touched upon in the first chapter). However, this did not prevent the racist propaganda of the regime misusing the concept of *Volk*. Just like Nazi propaganda insisted on Germanic symbols, the pivotal element in the new understanding of law became the *Volk*, obsessively recurring in the words of Nazi scholars, while the *Volksgeist* theory had already successfully spread among the scholars who manifested at least some sympathy for the developing national socialist ideology.[181] In the end, the importance of that term was sacred even in the choice of name for the civil code the regime was planning to put into force: the *Volksgesetzbuch*. The BGB was indeed considered too liberal and 'foreign', as it was based primarily on Roman law. It was thus part of that '*der materialistischen Weltordnung dienende*' ('serving the materialistic world order') law which had to be replaced by a Germanic legislation. The project of *Volksgesetzbuch*, however, had no particular luck, since the first draft was published already too late, in 1942.[182] This, furthermore, only encompassed basic general rules, with the first book dedicated to the law of the persons, whereas the definitive code had to be

[181] *See* H Fehr, *Schweizerischer und deutscher Volksgeist in der Rechtsentwicklung* (Frauenfeld, Von Huber, 1926). On Hans Fehr, *see* RC van Caenegem, *European Law in the Past and the Future* (n 65), 104–105.

[182] J Hedemann, H Lehmann and W Siebert, *Volksgesetzbuch: Grundregeln und Buch I: Entwurf und Erläuterungen* (München, Beck, 1942).

composed of eight books. In the project, the Nazi ideals already expressed in the NSDAP programme convert to a series of rules characterised by more propagandistic and rhetorical than truly normative content. The principles focus obsessively on the primacy of the general over the personal interest,[183] the idea that individual behaviors should serve the community[184] and furthermore try to promote solidarity[185] and even honour[186] exclusively among the German *Volksgenossen*. Regardless of the fact that those legislative projects have been abandoned, however, that historical and legal experience has left a number of traces even in today legal orders.[187]

2.1.7 Back to Culture

As already shown, the contrast between *Volksgeistdenken* and *Führerprinzip* could only be solved through baroque interpretations that ultimately consecrate the priority of the latter over the former. This solution could not be maintained any more in a world that experienced the cruel meaning of the *Führerprinzip*. The relation between natural, cultural and positive law urgently needed to be redefined. Already during the late ruinous years of the Nazi experience, Carl Schmitt—who had initially endorsed the *Führerprinzip*—travelled around Europe now advocating in a series of conferences the primary role of legal science as source of law above the legislator.[188] A pure and simple return to Savigny was impossible,[189] but the old opponent of German codification—whose thought had been overshadowed in the years of the triumph of legal positivism—could now again have something important to say for Europe as a whole, for '[*d*]*ie europäische Rechtswissenschaft braucht nicht mit den Mythen vom Gesetz und Gesetzgeber eines gemeinsamen Todes zu sterben*' ('European jurisprudence need not die a common death with the myths of the law and of the legislator').[190]

However, the legal doctrine which is most indicative of this new course in changed post-war Europe is the famous 'Radbruch formula': when positive laws conflict in an intolerable measure with justice, then laws lose their validity so that

183 '1. Oberstes Gesetz ist das Wohl des deutschen Volkes'.

184 '11. Volksgenossen können sich zur Förderung gemeinsamer Ziele zusammenschließen, die dem völkischen Kultur-, Arbeits- und Wirtschaftsleben dienen'.

185 '15. Kein Volksgenosse darf einen Vertrag zur Ausbeutung eines anderen Volksgenossen ausnützen'. Intuitively, the contract whereby a foreigner gets exploited would have been perfectly valid.

186 '13. Wer eine Verpflichtung übernommen hat, muß seine Ehre darin sehen, sie auch in schwieriger Lage zu erfüllen; die Vertragstreue ist die Grundlage des Rechtsverkehrs'.

187 C Joerges and N Singh (eds), *Darker Legacies of Law in Europe. The Shadow of National Socialism and Fascism over Europe and its Legal Traditions* (Oxford, Hart Publishing, 2003).

188 C Schmitt, *Die Lage der europäischen Rechtswissenschaft*. *See* also M Barberis, *Europa del diritto* (Bologna, il Mulino, 2008) 25–31.

189 Ibid, 25.

190 Ibid, 32. Translation by GL Ulmen (1990) 23 *Telos. A Quarterly Journal of Critical Thought* 35 et seq., 70.

'people owe them no obedience, and jurists, too, must find the courage to deny them legal character'.[191] This was elaborated in 1945 by the legal philosopher Gustav Radbruch, a former legal positivist who radically broke with positivism and drew closer to natural law as a reaction to Nazism.[192] That idea soon spread into the consciousness of the jurists who witnessed analogous political events.[193] The formula thus marks the overcoming of a strong legal positivism which would have required judges and citizens to obey the formal validity of Nazi laws[194] and the return to the ancient idea that the legislator—might he be a democratic parliament or a dictator—simply does not have the power to change law as he prefers according to his personal discretion, producing thereby statutes which are *willkürlich* (as in the German original).[195] The Savignyian idea of cultural *Volksgeist* as a limitation to the power of the legislator seems to reappear and the identification of law and will of the legislator is rejected, since Radbruch also claims that '*das Recht ist eine Kulturerscheinung*' ('law is a cultural phenomenon'),[196] while the ultimate end of law is justice, the conception of which may vary among eras and nations, mainly seen as cultural subjects who possess collective consciousness.[197] The nation becomes once again cultural and the racist elements that appeared in the German legal discourse shortly after Savigny and came to their heyday under Nazism have been removed.

However, Radbruch only touches upon the issue of the cultural origin of law and does not deepen his appraisal of the relation between nation and culture; culture seems to remain non-historical in a neo-Kantian fashion.[198] Indeed, in

[191] G Radbruch, 'Five Minutes of Legal Philosophy (1945)' (2006) English translation 26 *Oxford Journal of Legal Studies* 13–15, 14.

[192] '"An order is an order", the soldier is told. "A law is a law", says the jurist. The soldier, however, is required neither by duty nor by law to obey an order whose object he knows to be a felony or a misdemeanor, while the jurist—since the last of the natural lawyers died out a hundred years ago—recognizes no such exceptions to the validity of a law or to the requirement of obedience by those subject to it. A law is valid because it is a law, and it is a law if, in the general run of cases, it has the power to prevail. This view of a law and of its validity (we call it the positivistic theory) has rendered jurists and the people alike defenseless against arbitrary, cruel, or criminal laws, however extreme they might be. In the end, the positivistic theory equates law with power; there is law only where there is power.' G Radbruch, 'Five Minutes of Legal Philosophy' (n 193), 13.

[193] For Italy, *see* D Barbero, 'Negazione della legge ingiusta come valore giuridico e resistenza' (1949) *Iustitia* 25 ff.

[194] It can be discussed whether legal positivism can legitimise even Nazi laws or whether, on the contrary, the Nazi state represented the denial of legal positivism. Indeed, according to this legal philosophy, there is a strong distinction between law and morals, while on the contrary Nazism abolished that difference: as Hitler himself made clear already in 1933 speaking at the Juristentag of Leipzig, 'der totale Staat wird keinen Unterschied dulden zwischen Recht und Moral', in a context in which legalistic guarantees disappeared and the Nazi principle was established that 'Recht ist, was dem Volke nützt', in M Domarus, *Hitler. Reden und Proklamationen 1932–1945*, vol 1 (Wiesbaden, Löwit, 1973) 305.

[195] G Radbruch, 'Fünf Minuten Rechtsphilosophie', in G Radbruch, *Rechtsphilosophie* (Stuttgart, Koehler,1973) 327.

[196] Ibid, 164.

[197] Ibid, 150.

[198] P Cliteur, *Natuurrecht, cultuurrecht, conservatisme. Grondslag van de democratische rechtsstaat* (Leeuwarden, Universitaire Pers Fryslân, 2005) 394.

twentieth-century democratic Germany, an easy return to Savigny's view was not thinkable: a unitary state had now been built, and this was not merely a night watchman but rather regulated society with a number of interventions which made nineteenth-century codifications appear old-fashioned and the idea of a purely inactive legislator completely untenable. The proper functioning of this state presupposes citizens' democratic participation and a certain degree of legal formalism represents a guarantee against arbitrary excesses of the political power.

More generally, the end of the Second World War marks a moment of crisis for nationalist theory, now associated with chauvinism and seemingly fated to be overcome by a new humanitarian internationalism that drew its inspiration from the Enlightenment. In order to single out what the limitations to the power of the legislators are, Radbruch therefore resorts to the open catalogue of rights offered by natural law and the law of reason, only indicatively listed in the declarations of rights of enlightened inspiration.[199]

2.1.8 The Impact on Today's Legal Systems

While the model of the *trias politica* is accepted in all countries belonging to the so-called Western legal tradition, a superficial comparative analysis reveals the extent to which some differences exist with regard to the relation between the diverse state powers and legal sources even within the group of civil law systems. These differences can also be explained on the basis of a long historical development, as the effect of the events we have considered thus far.

The civic conception of the nation that originated in France basically limited itself to transferring the same type of political power from the head of the sovereign to the hands of the citizens, so that law now represented the will of the nation instead of the mere will of the sovereign. In particular, the instrument through which the will manifested itself is the formal statute, though now issued through democratic procedures unrolled in a parliament. Thereby, the centrality of the democratic statute—authoritative but not authoritarian anymore—becomes a feature of the new legal system as derived from the revolution, which necessarily required a moment of rupture with the past. Expressing the will of the nation, the statute tends to be 'sacred'—similar to the word of a sovereign drawing his power from a divine investiture. This is a consequence that does not lead to surprise in a nationalistic system, given that nationalism has gained the function of 'civic religion' in the society.[200] Having executed the king, nationalism becomes a religion that celebrates the Nation as God, whose word is revealed through the statute. There are no priests in this religion: the nation is both God and the elected people,

[199] G Radbruch, 'Five Minutes of Legal Philosophy' (n 193), 14–15.

[200] BC Shafer, *Faces of Nationalism. New Realities and Old Myths* (New York, Harcourt Brace Jovanovich, 1972) 257.

thus no mediums are required. In this context, any 'oracles of the law', to use John Dawson's expression,[201] would only risk misunderstanding and falsifying the will embodied in the statute. Their function is thus better limited; the judge becomes the mere mouth of the law, while the legal scholar simply explains what the statute says, primarily for educative reasons and in order to inform new judges.

One of the most characteristic features of the French civic national legal system has remained quite evident and concerns the delicate relationship between legislative and judiciary power. Since the nation was embodied with absolutist powers—not different from those in the hands of the king before his beheading—which were expressed in a 'sacred' statute, it was impossible to allow other bodies to alter or otherwise limit the statute. A system of control on the constitutionality of statutes analogous to those developing in Austria or even in the United States—where too, the principle of judicial review introduced by the Supreme Court in 1803 in the famous case *Marbury v Madison* initially met strong criticisms from important founding fathers—was not easily conceivable. The French system rather maintained the less incisive control exercised by the *Conseil d'Etat*, an ancient institution that has in the first place advisory and administrative functions and is not totally independent from the other powers. Only in 1958 did the new French Constitution introduce the *Conseil constitutionnel*, an institution analogous to the constitutional courts of Germany and Italy but less intrusive in parliament's sovereignty, due to its particular control of constitutionality on statutes which have not entered into force yet—more precisely: after the act has been issued by the parliament but before it is promulgated by the president of the republic. What is even more telling, only a limited number of political powers could refer to the *Conseil constitutionnel*: the president of the republic, the prime minister, the presidents of the national assembly and the senate and a group of at least 60 deputies or 60 senators; noticeably not the judiciary power or the citizens directly. Only more recently, a reform of 2008 entered into force in 2010[202] has introduced fundamental changes to this system, establishing that the *Cour de Cassation* and the *Conseil d'Etat* can refer to the constitutional council even after a parliamentary act has been promulgated.

These developments have reduced the differences between the French and the German legal systems, as this latter has had a quite different evolution. As already shown, Savigny defended the very much older view that law is not a product of will; what in France was called general will, was considered by Savigny in Germany—the peak of a long series of authors with similar views on the relation between law and statute—as mere '*Willkür*'. The role of the legislative is played down and the legislator can only draw from the existing body of private law. This conception brings the German experience closer to the English: 'strangely enough, Savigny's arguments fit the common law tradition better than his own, civilian,

[201] JP Dawson, *Oracles of the Law* (Westport, Greenwood Press, 1978).
[202] Loi constitutionnelle 23 July 2008.

culture'.[203] Of course, when one of the legal sources is weak, the other competing sources will almost automatically become stronger.[204] The only 'oracle of the law' in this context is the jurist, in particular the legal scholar who has now the task of building the 'system'. The judge, on the contrary, is required to comply with the authority of academic writings for the sake of legal certainty.[205] In this respect, the German experience strongly differs from common law systems, where the terms of the relation between judge and academic lawyer are completely overturned and even the expression 'legal doctrine'—intended as referring to the whole of the opinions of the jurists—seems odd.[206] Although it is true that judges continue to gain importance and authority even among non-lawyers, this is also due to their strongly theoretical and conceptual academic education, which makes a 'learned jurist' out of almost every practising lawyer.[207] This aspect is also manifest if one looks at the 'judges' who form the German Federal Constitutional Court, generally leading academics. This court represents indeed another important feature distinguishing the German from the French model that can be explained historically. The history of German constitutionalism is much more ancient. Even in a context characterised by the absence of a constitutional charter, some constitutional functions were already recognised by the *Reichskammergericht*, the institutional role of which made up for the lack of a centralised German state.

2.2 PRIVATE LAW AS A NATION-BUILDING TOOL

Nationalism as an ideology does not seem to have the normative power to shape the contents of private law in a distinctive way, with the telling exception of rules mostly related to the treatment of non-nationals.[208] It is impossible to single out a number of rules which typify a 'nationalist private law' in the abstract that we could find in the law concretely enacted in particular countries under nationalist influences. This nonetheless does not imply in any way that private law as such is irrelevant in a nationalist perspective. The evidence that we have drawn from history rather shows a strong correlation between nationalism and the nationalisation of private law. Even from a more analytical perspective, it is clear that private law is connected to the concept of nation. A primordialist perspective—as exemplified in the organicist theories inspired by Herder—would insist on the derivation of private law from the (spirit of) the nation, arguing that law—just

[203] M Reimann, 'The Historical School against Codification' (n 129), 108.

[204] On these dynamics, *see* RC van Caenegem, *Judges, Legislators & Professors. Chapters in European Legal History* (New York, Cambridge University Press, 1987) and with particular reference to legal scholarship in Germany, S Vogenauer, 'An Empire of Light? Learning and Lawmaking in the History of German Law' 64 *Cambridge Law Journal* 481–500.

[205] S Vogenauer, 'An Empire of Light?' (n 206), 498.

[206] Ibid, 627–63, 631.

[207] Ibid, 654.

[208] *See* this chapter: 2.2.2 'Homogenisation by Exclusion'.

like language and traditions—is a characteristic feature of the national organism. A modernist perspective would highlight how rhetorical this construction is and would rather invert the terms of the debate: it is not the law that stems from the nation but the other way round. Law contributes to the creation of the nation as a means of social change. The key concept to understanding the relation between nationalism and law is no longer organicism but rather instrumentalism.

It was the French Revolution that introduced the idea that private law could be used not only as an instrument to regulate social and economic relations among citizens but also more generally as a tool to govern society as a whole. The civil codification issued under Napoleon brought about a new political project, enabling a new economic and social bourgeois order in which all individuals were considered to be equals and joined in the new egalitarian category of 'citizen', which replaced previous feudal class-based distinctions. The code, which standardised the legal treatment applicable to all citizens, was in this sense the most powerful legal instrument of that civic nationalism that had just transferred the political power from the king to the nation. In Germany, a civil codification would have had a slightly different function. Since a centralised state did not exist, the code would have created at least a common sense of belonging to a German nation among all German citizens and facilitated the edification of a new German nation-state, as in the hope of Thibaut.

The civil codification, beyond its importance as a legal instrument, played a role that is commonly described in nationalism studies as 'nation-building'. While in a classic primordialist perspective the already existing nation strives for unity and eventually produces an act which announces the 'awakening' of the nation, in a modernist perspective the civil code can be used to create a new consciousness among people as to their condition as nationals. From a modernist perspective, it could be said that the unification of private law represents a nation-building technique comparable to the standardisation of culture by means of language and literature,[209] the 'invention of tradition'[210] and forms of 'banal nationalism'.[211] The question is now how private law can serve as a nation-building technique; in other words, how can it promote homogeneity within the nation, in line with the tendency inaugurated by newly formed nation-states that utilise law as a tool to achieve social objectives?[212] This requires a sociological approach to law: while classical legal philosophers have seen communities as the creators of law, legal sociologists have shown that, among all the functions it has as an instrument of social change, law can also be employed as a tool to create those communities,[213]

[209] B Anderson, *Imagined Communities: Reflection on the Origin and Spread of Nationalism* [1983] (London, Verso, 2006) 46.

[210] EJ Hobsbawm, 'Introduction: Inventing Traditions', in EJ Hobsbawm and T Ranger (eds), *The Invention of Tradition* (Cambridge, Cambridge University Press, 1983).

[211] M Billig, *Banal Nationalism* (London, Sage, 1995).

[212] BZ Tamanaha, 'Understanding Legal Pluralism: Past to Present, Local to Global' (2008) 30 *Sydney Law Review* 375–411, 381.

[213] R Cotterrell, *Law's Community* (Oxford, Clarendon Press, 1995).

although it is certainly wise not to overestimate the actual role of law in those social dynamics.

2.2.1 Homogenisation by Inclusion

We have already noted that in order to build national communities, nationalism acts on two different sides: on the external side it creates differentiation; on the internal side it creates homogenisation. In this sense, law has to show two characteristics: it must be different from that of other nations, and it should create a homogeneous community within the nation. The sentiment of belonging to a national community can thus be fostered—or, according to modernists, even created—through the politics of integration through law.

In the view of Gellner,[214] nationalism was a phenomenon that fostered the transition from a static agrarian to a dynamic industrial society, a shift which is coherent with the tendency to move 'from status to contract' already identified in legal history. In this sense, the creation of a common set of legal rules mainly incorporated in a civil codification had the function to permit a higher mobility of the workers required by the new model of division of work and create more opportunities to contract across borders. It is well known that in particular the French civil and commercial codifications represented the economic charter of the new bourgeois society that arose from the industrial revolution. In a common legal framework it is indeed easier for merchants to enter economic transactions, for they will be able to rely on uniform legal rules. This would also serve the interest of the nation, since the economic relationships between communities would have increased the wealth of nations.

In another sense, it is sometimes alleged that an economic community will necessarily bring about a political community, since the economic transactions among different peoples will increase the possibility of knowing each other's culture, develop a common solidarity[215] and possibly even merge into a single community. This is also the sense of the above-mentioned words of Thibaut, who was concerned with the edification of a common German consciousness that foreshadowed political unity. However, this view is typical of the liberal nationalism of the nineteenth century, which still considered nationality a category of inclusion rather than exclusion and could not even suspect the turn that nationalism was about to experience within a few years. Nowadays, such an optimistic view is more often objected to, while some highlight that a common economic space does not automatically lead to a common cultural and political space, and

[214] *See* Chapter 1: 1.1.4.2 'Reasons for Nation-building'.

[215] A Sen, *Identity and Violence. The Illusion of Destiny* (New York, Norton, 2006) 147, referring to D Hume, *An Enquiry Concerning the Principles of Morals* [1751] (La Salle, Open Court, 1966) 25.

even less to a sense of identity.[216] Moreover and paradoxically, the contact with different cultures may more easily increase differences,[217] giving people awareness of their cultural specificities and occasionally feeding nationalist sentiments.[218] At the foundations of this pessimistic reflection already lies the perception that nationality has become a matter of *cultural* belonging, very different from the *civic* conception of nationality envisaged by the French revolutionaries and Thibaut.

Regardless of the sociological consequences produced by the interplay of different populations put into contact with one another by facilitated market relations, it is historically ascertained that unification of law, in particular by means of civil codifications, has also had a strong symbolic reason, as one of the '*sommi fattori dell unità*' ('supreme factors of unity'),[219] as the fascist rhetoric declared. Modern legal historians can state that, though 'an exclusive codification does not necessarily bring about legal unity',[220] nonetheless 'the fact that in the course of the nineteenth century European states were able to become nations was at least partly due to the introduction of uniform codifications';[221] in other words, the sociological importance of civil codification—as just one instance of legal national homogenisation—is that it has been 'a means for the state to assert its domination by shaping and controlling the law'.[222] This already emerges from several European continental experiences—in Germany, where the new civil code could give an answer to the demands summarised in the slogan '*ein Volk, ein Reich, ein Recht*', and in France where the *Code civil* was considered by Napoleon as his most important and lasting work, the symbolic authority of which remains even today and strongly conditions the way in which lawyers perceive French law in relation to non-national normative orders.[223] Generally, unification of law and civil codifications have been employed as a means to affirm the character of a state which has been recently created or rebuilt and its authority over the population

[216] A-M Thiesse, *La création des identités nationales: Europe XVIIIe-XXe siècle* (Paris, Éditions du Seuil, 1999) 16.

[217] From an economic perspective it has also been pointed out that the process of economic integration in Europe, instead of leading to a convergence of values, may lead to the opposite result 'as a result of increased specialization' of the countries; L Bovenberg, 'Unity Produces Diversity: The Economics of Europe's Social Capital', in W Arts, J Hagenaars and J Halman (eds), *The Cultural Diversity of European Unity. Findings, Explanations and Reflections from the European Values Study* (Leiden, Brill, 2003) 414–15.

[218] W Connor, 'Nation-building or Nation-destroying?' (1972) 24 *World Politics* 319–55, 329.

[219] G Vacca (1866) *Relazione ministeriale al Re sul codice civile del Regno d'Italia* (Torino, Stamperia Reale) XIII.

[220] PAJ van den Berg, *The Politics of European Codification*, 6.

[221] Ibid, 25.

[222] C Varga, *Codification as a Socio-Historical Phenomenon* (Budapest, Akadémiai Kiadó, 1991) 334.

[223] R Michaels, 'Code vs Code. Nationalist and Internationalist Images of the Code Civil in the French Resistance to a European Codification' (2012) 8 *European Review of Contract Law* 277–95; R Sefton-Green, 'French and English Crypto-nationalism and European Private Law. An Exercise in Sentiment and Reason' (2012) 8 *European Review of Contract Law* 260–76.

living on its soil, as an instrument of 'internal colonisation'.[224] This is evident in the aforementioned cases, as well as in many other nations: in Italy, where fascism undertook an ambitious programme of reform of all codifications; in socialist Germany, where the DDR decided to deviate from the excessively bourgeois BGB by issuing a new *Zivilgesetzbuch* and, more recently, also in the Central and Eastern European countries, where new civil codifications and new constitutions characterised the birth of new democratic post-communist states which had the goal of a rapid adhesion to the European Union. This was the case of states exemplified by Romania, where the new era was opened by the execution of the old despot—almost a gruesome constant in history—or Estonia, where the new private law codifications were also 'based on the experience of developed democracies which would also allow for close international cooperation'.[225] The situation of the Catalan nation/nationality in Spain has already been touched upon; here it is significant to note than even recently, a former Catalan Minister of Justice explicitly advocated law's nation-building function, stating that '[a]t the beginning of the twenty-first century, I am convinced that the Catalan codification movement must represent an effort to attain normality and to affirm ourselves as a nation'.[226]

2.2.2 Homogenisation by Exclusion

In the case of homogenisation by legal *exclusion*, legal rules will tend to give outsiders less favourable treatment than insiders, as insiders are those who have the characteristic feature which is assumed to be the main criterion of nationality (for example, those who speak the French language or profess the Christian religion) and outsiders are those who do not.

In order to operate policies of homogenisation based on exclusion it is first necessary to make a distinction. It is necessary thus to distinguish insiders and outsiders, in order for the legal rule to prescribe a different treatment. While the civic nationalism of the first phase was chiefly an integrative movement—which aimed in the first place at the integration of several feudal classes into the general category of the citizen—violent nationalism of the second phase became mainly exclusive. Given a racist interpretation of the nation, for example, someone of Jewish origin would not be allowed to marry an 'Arian' person, as took place in Nazi Germany and fascist Italy: the Italian code of 1942, indeed delegated 'special

[224] P Cappellini, 'Il codice eterno. La forma-codice e i suoi destinatari. Morfologie e metamorfosi di un paradigma della modernità', in P Cappellini and B Sordi (eds), *Codici. Una riflessione di fine millennio* (Milano, Giuffrè, 2002) 19.

[225] P Varul, 'The Creation of New Estonian Private Law' (2008) 1 *European Review of Private Law* 95–109, 99.

[226] N De Gispert I Català, 'The Codification of Catalan Civil Law' (n 110), 169.

legislation'—the infamous race laws of 1938[227]—to list the circumstances of race and nationality that could constitute impediments to the marriage. Still within the Italian legal experience, the contrast becomes striking if we consider the change since the civil code of 1865 that already read that '*lo straniero è ammesso a godere dei diritti civili attribuiti ai cittadini*' ('foreigners are granted the same civil rights as citizens').[228]

Rules on citizenship usually translate nationalist criteria of nationhood into legal language. Here, it could be referred to the (in reality not so linear) opposition between *ius sanguinis* and *ius soli*. However, in modern private international law inspired by trans-nationalism more than nationalism, both criteria usually coexist, though in variable measures, in the legislation of the same country.[229] As a general tendency, what is more, it is possible to notice how modern politics in naturalisation law links citizenship with the concept of culture,[230] as a clear symptom of the inclination to overcome the use of ethnic and civic criteria of nationhood in favour of the category of culture.

Rules distinguishing people on the basis of their nationality are indeed not frequent in modern private law systems,[231] since private law rules tend to be general and abstract. This kind of rules, nonetheless, are usually more articulated and involve different levels of 'abstraction': the legal subject is normally split up in a long series of categories such as 'landlord', 'tenant', 'seller', 'buyer', or, more recently

[227] A brief historical account of the legal treatment of religious minorities (in particular the Jews) in Italy written before the race laws of 1938 were issued is offered by M Roberti, *Svolgimento storico del diritto privato in Italia*, vol 1 (Padova, Antonio Milani, 1935) 184–202.

[228] In this regard, also the Austrian Code of 1811 should be mentioned. J-L Halpérin, *Entre nationalisme juridique* (n 3), 26 explains that, 'le Code autrichien de 1811 pose, d'abord, le principe de l'égale admission des étrangers et des nationaux aux droits civils, ainsi que de leur égale soumission aux obligations imposées par l'Etat. La condition de réciprocité est, certes, essentielle, mais elle n'intervient que pour trancher les cas douteux devant les tribunaux: l'étranger doit alors prouver que son Etat traite également les sujets autrichiens. Tout ce qui touche la capacité personnelle des étrangers doit être jugé selon les lois de leur domicile, ou à défaut de leur naissance'. Moreover, also in the Kingdom of the Netherlands a statute of 1838 acknowledged foreigners' civil rights without any condition of reciprocity, J-L Halpérin, *Entre nationalisme juridique* (n 3), 30.

[229] Such an approximation takes place since '[w]hile traditional ius sanguinis countries (Belgium, Germany, Greece) have introduced or extended ius soli provisions for second- and third-generation immigrants, classic ius soli countries (UK, Ireland) have limited these provisions'; besides this, however, the concrete regulations of citizenship in Europe are so different that it is still difficult to speak of a 'unspecified process of convergence', MP Vink and G-R de Groot, 'Birthright Citizenship. Trends and Regulations in Europe' (2010) *EUDO Citizenship Observatory* 1–36, 4 and 33.

[230] *See* L Orgad, '"Cultural Defense" of Nations: Cultural Citizenship in France, Germany and the Netherlands' (2009) 15 *European Law Journal*, 719–37. For a fierce criticism of these practices, considered ineffective mechanisms of perpetuation of prejudices and of questionable utility within the context of the European Union, *see* D Kochenov, 'Mevrouw De Jong Gaat Eten: EU Citizenship and the Culture of Prejudice' (2011) *EUI Robert Schuman Centre for Advanced Studies Working Paper No 2011/06* 1–21.

[231] In this sense, referring to contract law, G Mäsh, 'Le droit communautaire des contrats et son influence sur le droit national des Etats membres', in G Mäsh, D Mazeaud and R Schulze (eds), *Nouveaux défis du droit des contrats en France et en Europe* (Munich, Sellier, 2009) 18. The question whether private law rules make distinctions between nationals and non-nationals has become of practical relevance since the EC treaty prohibits this sort of discrimination in the EU.

'consumer' (or even 'vulnerable consumer'). It could then also be technically conceivable to have a further specification with regard to the nationality of the subject. But although a legal rule which distinguishes on the basis of nationality is imaginable, there are not many examples in private law systems; the 'exclusion' of non-nationals is carried out upstream at the constitutional level. The constitutions of several new Member States provided an example, inasmuch as they prohibited the sale of land to foreigners.[232]

2.2.2.1 Constitutional Aspects

It is significant to note that whereas a rule in which discrimination operates on the grounds of ethnicity would be considered unconstitutional nowadays in Europe, the same is not self-evident with regard to discrimination on the basis of nationality: even post-Second World War constitutions often consider nationality differently. Whereas an ethnicity-grounded discrimination denies a subject rights he or she is legally entitled to enjoy, nationality or, more correctly, citizenship, is the prerequisite for acknowledging those rights and duties (whose violation can represent a discrimination). International law, within certain limits, does not interfere with national discretion in this respect. The political question nonetheless remains: on the basis of what criteria are some rights acknowledged to some persons and denied to others? The question is still debated: what rights should be acknowledged to every human being? Already between the two World Wars, it could be noticed that '*die Menschheit ist auch heute weit davon entfernt, friedlich und reinlich zu trennen, welche Rechte und Befugnisse dem Inländer als Bürger des Staates vorbehalten und welche allen Mitmenschen eröffnet sein sollen*',[233] as an inheritance from the period in which the word foreigner basically meant 'enemy'.[234]

While a differentiated legal treatment between citizens and foreigners can be politically and legally justified on pragmatic economical grounds, when we turn to social rights, the rights which involve expenses for the state and can therefore not always be provided to everyone but often only to (some) co-nationals,[235]

[232] A Albi, *EU Enlargement and the Constitutions of Central and Eastern Europe* (Cambridge, Cambridge University Press, 2005) 64, 73, 110.

[233] H Sperl, *Nationalismus, Internationalismus und Rechtsordnung* (Wien, Hölder, 1924) 5: 'even today mankind is far from differentiating peacefully and clearly which rights and prerogatives are reserved to the native as a citizen of the state and which ones should be granted to all fellow humans'.

[234] Ibid, 5.

[235] So for example, Article 20.3 of the Dutch Basic Law. The differentiation in the treatment between nationals and foreigners remains, however, a particularly intricate legal issue, so in EU law, it can be questioned whether directive 2004/38/CE—in the part in which it allows Member States to refute social benefits to non-citizens looking for a job—is really compatible with Articles 12 and 39 of the Treaty, *see* L Raimondi, 'Cittadini dell'Unione europea in cerca di lavoro e principio di non discriminazione: osservazioni in margine alla sentenza Vatsouras' (2010) 2 *Il Diritto dell'Unione Europea* 443–62.

it is more striking that discrimination can arise with regard to liberal 'negative' rights that are traditionally looked upon as 'non-expensive', inasmuch they do not require a positive action from the state.[236] Older and even more recent constitutions tend to distinguish fundamental rights of every human being and fundamental rights of the citizens; so for example, whereas 'everyone has the right to life and to the inviolability of his person' (Art 2.2. GG) and 'all persons are equal before the law' (Art 3.1. GG), only 'All Germans have the right to assemble peacefully and unarmed without prior notification or permission' (Art 8.1. GG) and, once again, only 'all Germans have the right to form associations and societies' (Art 9.1. GG). This kind of differentiated legal treatment is laid down, of course, not only in the German constitution, which is cited here just as an example, but also in the basic laws of just about all European states.[237] Indeed, the presence of *corps intermédiaires*—representing a possible competitor for the monopoly of violence and undermining nations' assumed homogeneity—on the soil of the state have always represented a worry for nationalists,[238] and even modern democratic societies have not completely overcome this worry, so that in their constitutions they reproduce the provisions already laid down in much older basic laws. So, for example, the aforementioned articles of the German *Grundgesetz* directly derive from the liberal '*Grundrechte des Deutschen Volkes*' elaborated in the *Paulskirche* in Frankfurt am Main shortly after the revolutions of the 'Spring of Nations' in 1848 and fully in the spirit of German patriotism.[239] However, as was already discussed in Chapter 1, nationalism in Europe witnessed 'over the course of the nineteenth

[236] In reality, from this viewpoint, the distinction between liberal and social rights is not completely justified, since also liberal rights of freedom require in modern democracies expensive actions by the state; *see* S Holmes and CR Sunstein, *The Cost of Rights. Why Liberty Depends on Taxes* (New York, Norton, 1999).

[237] National constitutions are normally even more restrictive (although their provisions have to be combined with international rules). So for example, from a brief overview of national constitutions in Europe we find provisions like 'Belgians are equal before the law' (Art 10.2 Belgian Constitution), 'All Greeks are equal before the law' (Art 5, Greek Constitution), 'Spaniards are equal before the law' (Art 14, Spanish Constitution), 'Luxembourgers are equal before the law' (Art 11, Chapter II: 'Luxembourgers and their rights', Luxembourger Constitution), or 'All citizens have equal social status and are equal before the law' (Art 3, Italian Constitution), 'All citizens shall be equal before the law' (Art 6.2, Bulgarian Constitution), 'All citizens enjoy the rights and are subject to the duties laid down in the Constitution' (Art 12 of the Portuguese Constitution. In Art 13, several grounds of discrimination are prohibited, but no reference to nationality is made), 'All federal nationals are equal before the law' (Art 7.1, Austrian Constitution).

More 'universalist' are the constitutions of Finland (Art 6), Estonia (Art 12), Latvia (Art 91), Malta (Art 32: 'Every person in Malta is entitled to the fundamental rights and freedoms of the individual'), the Netherlands (Art 1: 'all persons in the Netherlands shall be treated equally in equal circumstances'), Poland (Arts 30, 31 and 32), Slovenia (Art 14).

As to the right of association, only 'universalist' constitutions do not subordinate these rights to nationality requisites; *see* the basic laws of Finland (Art 13), Estonia (Art 48; nonetheless only Estonians may be members of political parties), Latvia (Arts 102 and 103), Malta (Art 42), the Netherlands (Arts 8 and 9), Poland (Arts 57 and 58), and Slovenia (Art 42).

[238] A Vincent, 'Liberal Nationalism: An Irresponsible Compound?' (1997) 45 *Political Studies* 275–95, 287.

[239] O Kimminich, *Deutsche Verfassungsgeschichte* (Baden-Baden, Nomos, 1987) 342 ff.

century, a slow, inexorable shift from the left of the political spectrum towards the right',[240] so that categories like '*citoyen*' and '*Deutsch*', born as means of inclusion and extension of rights, soon evolved into categories of exclusion.

Considering the German legal experience, a constitutional right is thus acknowledged to those who belong to the nation but denied to outsiders. This concern politically justifies the category of rights acknowledged exclusively to nationals—as they are called, *Deutschenrechte*—within that of fundamental rights and consequently those constitutional provisions which guarantee the legitimacy of a hypothetical secondary rule which denies (or acknowledges under stricter conditions) foreigners a right which is constitutionally guaranteed to insiders (in so far as they do not find protection under different and more general constitutional provisions). Indeed, whereas ordinary legislation grants foreigners the freedom of association,[241] the formation of *Ausländervereine* is still subjected to a differentiated legal treatment[242] justified by reasons of protection of the internal and external security.[243] Furthermore, although some legal authors[244] have pleaded for an extension of the constitutional provisions limited to German citizens also by means of an extensive interpretation of the Basic Law, the German Constitutional Court has rejected this solution thus far.[245]

2.2.2.2 A Brief Digression: Non-discrimination in Europe

Already in the past, anti-discrimination legislation has been adopted as an instrument 'to promote peaceful revolution in social relations',[246] and thus as a tool of integration 'by inclusion'. In the light of the process of constitutionalisation of private law, prohibitions of discrimination have started slowly moving from the area of public to the field of private law. The drafts for a European codification are quite indicative of this tendency. Representing a real though very controversial innovation compared to traditional private law codifications and even a progress from the point of view of social justice,[247] in the DCFR (Art II.-2:101)

[240] J Leerssen, *National Thought in Europe: A Cultural History* (Amsterdam, Amsterdam University Press, 2006) 215.

[241] § 1 I Versammlungsgesetz.

[242] § 14 Vereinsgesetz.

[243] B-O Bryde in I von Munch and P Kunig, *Grundgesetz-Kommentar. Vol. 1. Präambel bis Art. 19* (München, Beck, 2000) 613.

[244] A Bleckmann, *Allgemeine Grundrechtslehren* (Köln, Heymann, 1979) 110 ff.

[245] With regard to the Deutschenrecht laid down in article 12 of the Basic Law, the Constitutional Court (BVerfGE 78, 179) affirmed: 'Jedoch kann auch die Selbstverständlichkeit, daß Ausländer Träger von Menschenrechten sind, nicht zu einer—wenn auch eingeschränkten—Anwendung des Art 12 Abs. 1 GG auf diesen Personenkreis führen, soll die ausdrückliche Entscheidung des Grundgesetzes, die Berufsfreiheit nur deutschen Staatsbürgern zu gewähren, nicht unterlaufen werden'.

[246] R Cotterrell, *The Sociology of Law. An Introduction* (London, Butterworths, 1992) 44 and 53 ff.

[247] MW Hesselink, *CFR & Social Justice* (Munich, Sellier, 2008) 41; C Mak, 'The Constitutional Momentum of European Contract Law. On the Interpretation of the DCFR in Light of Fundamental Rights' (2009) 17 *European Review of Private Law* 513–30. For the same reason, the acknowledgment of this right in private law is criticised by those who adhere to the view that private law should

non-discrimination has become an authentic right, namely the 'right not to be discriminated against'.

Nevertheless, echoing the wording of articles 10 and 19 of the Treaty on the Functioning of the European Union, this provision also limits itself to prohibiting discriminations on the grounds of sex, racial or ethnic origin. Once again, the element of nationality or citizenship, unlike the elements that can be used to found the political concept of nationality like ethnicity, is not explicitly taken into account. Even non-discrimination can thus reveal itself as an instrument of integration 'by legal exclusion', when considered from the perspective of those belonging to the non-protected categories. An express prohibition of discriminations based on nationality is contained in article 18 of the Treaty, which nonetheless limits the principle 'within the scope of application' of the Treaty itself; that means that 'nationality', as clarified by the Court of Justice,[248] only refers to the 'European nationality', so that discriminations against third-country nationals are not covered—although a broader interpretation of the article would still be possible and, in the opinion of some, desirable.[249] Article 18 limits itself to broadening the notion of nationality: functionally considering the European Union a sort of federation, its principle of non-discrimination is comparable to internal constitutional provisions proclaiming equality before the law of all 'citizens'. In a 'Euronationalist' perspective the nation-building strength of this principle is clear:

> No other aspect of Community law touches the individual more directly or does more to foster that sense of common identity and shared destiny without which the 'ever closer union of the peoples of Europe', proclaimed by the preamble of the Treaty, would be an empty slogan.[250]

It is against this legal framework that directives against discrimination have been issued. Hence, at first sight, the choice of the DCFR does not surprise, even less if we consider that both Directive 2000/43 on 'equal treatment between persons irrespective of racial or ethnic origin' and Directive 2000/78 on 'equal treatment in employment and occupation', while prohibiting discrimination on grounds of

disregards issues of distributive justice and limit itself to corrective justice, also in order not to harm the principle of legal certainty: H Eidenmüller, F Faust, HC Grigoleit, N Jansen, G Wagner and R Zimmermann, 'Der Gemeinsame Referenzrahmen für das Europäische Privatrecht. Wertungsfragen und Kodifikationsprobleme' (2008) 11 *Juristen Zeitung* 529–84, 535.

[248] Court of Justice, Criminal Proceedings against Ibiyinka Awoyemi, C-230/97, para 29: 'A national of a non-member country […] may not effectively rely on the rules governing the free movement of persons which, in accordance with settled case-law, apply only to a national of a Member State of the Community […]'.

[249] *See* B De Witte, 'The Past and Future of the European Court of Justice in the Protection of Human Rights', in P Alston, *The EU and Human Rights* (Oxford, Oxford University Press, 1999) 859–85; C Hublet, 'The Scope of Article 12 of the Treaty of the European Communities vis-à-vis Third-Country Nationals: Evolution at Last?' (2009) 15 *European Law Journal* 757–74.

[250] Opinion of Advocate General Jacobs, 20 October 1993, ECJ joined cases C-92/92 and C-326-92.

race or ethnic origins and (in the case of Directive 2000/78) also religion, belief, disability, age, or sexual orientation, allow it on grounds of nationality.[251]

Nevertheless, while this solution can be understandable at the constitutional/international level, where citizenship has the function of defining which subject has rights, whose violation can give rise to discrimination, the non-inclusion in rules meant to govern private relations is normatively more controversial since there is apparently no reason to tolerate a nationality-grounded discrimination in the sphere of private autonomy. Of course, the exclusion can be technically justified since Art 19 of the Treaty would have not conferred a sufficient legal basis to also include (third-country) nationality-based discriminations, given the narrow interpretation of Art 18. However, it is questionable if, after the Treaty of Lisbon, there is still no sufficient legal basis for a prohibition of nationality-grounded discrimination, as the EU Charter of Fundamental Rights expressly mentions 'membership of a national minority' as a prohibited ground of discrimination (Art 21). What is more, numerous Member States have included 'nationality' (although the question sometimes remains open as to whether this only refers to national origin or also citizenship) in the list of prohibited grounds of discrimination[252] when implementing EU legislation. What is more, the DCFR does not even completely draw from the consolidated EC Treaty, 'forgetting' to mention further 'classical'[253] grounds of discrimination cited in the Treaty such as religion or belief, disability, age and sexual orientation, also mentioned by the Directive 2000/78 on 'equal treatment in employment and occupation'. This restrictive choice of the DCFR can hardly be justified, for 'one should not discriminate between different grounds of discrimination'.[254] Even more, if one considers that the inclusion of the EU Charter of Fundamental Rights in the Lisbon Treaty has 'enlarged' the legal basis for anti-discrimination policies, providing a merely exemplificative non-exhaustive list of prohibited grounds of discrimination, a policy choice which is coherent with the innovation entailed in Art 20, which reads—differently from most national constitutions—that '[e]veryone is equal before the law'.

The impression thus is that the DCFR—in order not to restrict excessively the principle of contractual freedom[255] and not to take a position in highly

[251] 2000/43/EC Art 3(2); 2000/78/EC Art 3(2).

[252] D Schiek, L Waddington and M Bell, *Cases, Materials and Text on National, Supranational and International Non-Discrimination Law* (Oxford, Hart Publishing, 2007) 63 ff.

[253] *See* N Bamforth, M Malik and C O'Cinneide, *Discrimination Law: Theory and Context* (London, Sweet & Maxwell, 2008) 565 ff.

[254] MW Hesselink, *CFR & Social Justice* 41. Also the participants in the Working Group on 'Non-Discrimination' within the Acquis Group share the view that 'it is impossible to distinguish between the different forms of discrimination when [formulating] a general principle', though finding the solution in 'adopting a relative instead of an absolute prohibition of discrimination', S Leible, 'Non-Discrimination' (2006) 6 *ERA-Forum Special Issue on European Contract Law—Developing the Principles for a 'Common Frame of Reference' for European Contract Law* 76–89, 82.

[255] Inasmuch as non-discrimination interferes with the decision not to conclude a contract, it is a "new level" of limitation to freedom of contract, H Rösler, 'Schutz des Schwächeren im Europäischen Vertragsrecht. Typisierte und individuelle Unterlegenheit im Mehrebenenprivatrecht' (2009) 73 *Rabels Zeitschrift für ausländisches und internationales Privatrecht* 889–911, 906. However, the limitation is

political disputes[256]—only aims at prohibiting more evident sexual and racial discriminations, and therefore, with regard to nationality issues, is still compatible with liberal forms of (European) nationalism.

2.3 THE DENATIONALISATION OF PRIVATE LAW

It is now clear that the idea that all law derives from the nation is a comparatively recent by-product of nationalism. Legal positivism determined the overlap of state and law while nationalism determined the overlap of nation and state. The combination of these views has brought about a political era in which almost all legal concepts are marked by the nation-state. Nonetheless, it was already believed decades ago that such an era of *Staatlichkeit* had come to an end.[257] If one considers the implication for law it appears clear that, on the one hand, the nation-state does not seem to be the only creator of private law any more; on the other hand, the homogeneous application of law within the nation can be jeopardised by a decrease in homogeneity within the nation-state itself. While the traditional view conceives the state as the fundamental source of law, in recent years this view has been challenged by the phenomenon of legal pluralism in its many forms.[258] The model of the sovereign homogeneous nation-state which is organised according to its own national law started already showing flaws after the world wars, and is now aggravated by the astonishing development of communication technologies.[259]

Subsequently, and in line with the trends of the so-called economic globalisation, private law has witnessed a gradual process of internationalisation, a process did not progress regularly but that has slowed down occasionally, subsequently accelerated and altered in its forms due to the historical events that took place during the twentieth century. In particular, the establishment of the European communities first and the European Union later has led and is still leading to sensible modifications also in national private law systems, which have occasionally given rise to episodes of resistance and even 'renationalisation' of European law. Against this framework, the question as to whether this new context should require

relative, since in the view of the Working Group on 'Non-Discrimination' within the Acquis Group 'a right to enter into a contract should not be part of the remedies; because such a right would be in strong contrast to the principle of freedom of contract', S Leible, 'Non-Discrimination' (n 256), 85.

[256] Ibid, 81: 'There is no need to incorporate a further-reaching prohibition of discrimination into the Common Frame of Reference. Every prohibition on discrimination based on other grounds than gender, race or ethnic origin would be purely political'.

[257] C Schmitt, Foreword (1963) to *Der Begriff des Politischen* [1932] (Berlin, Duncker & Humboldt, 2009) 10.

[258] *See* HP Glenn, 'The Nationalist Heritage', in P Legrand and R Munday (eds) *Comparative Legal Studies: Traditions and Transitions* (Cambridge, Cambridge University Press, 2003) 97 ff.

[259] M Stolleis 'Vormodernes und postmodernes Recht' (2008) 37 *Quaderni fiorentini per la storia del pensiero giuridico moderno* 543–51, 548.

lawyers to change their 'conception of law, very much based on the nation-state experience, so as to meet the different conditions of global governance'[260] arises.

2.3.1 Before and after the Wars: Faith and Distrust

The phenomenon of legal globalisation is not new. Its significance for national private law already became evident at the end of the nineteenth century: as the economy became more global, law had to respond to the needs of the contracting parties in different countries. It was in this period, already characterised by technological and scientific development, that international trade increased and the phenomenon of 'globalisation' in its modern forms emerged. A definitive shift from a rural economy to an economy based on mass production and distribution took place:[261] capitalism was now mature enough to move from a local to a global dimension. According to the Marxist perspective, imperialism would have been the highest stage of capitalism, as in the famous words of Lenin.[262]

But legal globalisation has assumed very diverse faces. Firstly, during the heyday of colonialism, it coincided with legal colonialism: national law was simply imposed on other countries. This happened explicitly by means of transplants of domestic legal concepts or even through private international law provisions which favored the application of domestic law abroad, while the local laws and customs of the colonised countries—frequently despised by the colonising forces—could only find a limited application in local disputes provided they were not repugnant to the principles of the Europeans.[263] However, in the relations between economically advanced countries, legal globalisation took on a different aspect. These nation-states freely established uniform rules dealing with legal issues which were particularly significant for trade, so that a considerable number of international conventions on issues relevant for private law appeared. The legal instrument adopted for this particular kind of 'internationalisation of decisions' was the international convention, that is, a form of 'negotiated agreement'[264] which allowed states to elaborate common solutions to common problems while respecting the independence and autonomy of the states involved. Particularly important conventions of uniform law were created and enacted before the outbreak of the Second World War with the explicit intent of overcoming the

[260] JM Smits, 'Democracy and (European) Private Law: A Functional Approach', in MG Faure and A van der Welt (eds), *Globalization and Private Law. The Way Forward* (Cheltenham, Edward Elgar, 2010) 19.

[261] MJ Bonell, 'Comparazione giuridica e unificazione del diritto', in G Alpa, MJ Bonell, D Corapi, L Moccia, V Zeno-Zencovich and A Zoppini, *Diritto privato comparato. Istituti e problemi* (Roma, Laterza, 2004) 4.

[262] VI Lenin, *Imperialism, the Highest Stage of Capitalism: A Popular Outline* [1917] English translation (London, Lawrence & Wishart, 1948).

[263] AO Ilumoka, 'Legal Imperialism and Chauvinism: Lessons from Africa', in *Impérialisme et chauvinisme juridiques/Imperialism and Chauvinism in the Law* (Geneve, Schulthesse, 2004) 39 ff.

[264] K Goldmann, *Transforming the European Nation-State: Dynamics of Internationalization* (London, Sage, 2001) 15 ff.

difficulties linked to the diversity of legislations. Tellingly, these international instruments mainly dealt with the law of transport and the law of payments.[265]

Legal globalisation was the result of collaboration rather than imposition; the key word to describe denationalisation of law in this period is internationalism. In that moment, nationalism had already conferred on the state the exclusive monopoly on law production and the idea of a world order based on independent nation-states gained momentum; prior to the First World War nationalism had still been a liberal phenomenon. This may contribute to explaining the seeming paradox[266] that so many uniform law conventions were signed exactly in the years in which the idea of national law became dominant and several states adopted a civil codification. It was above all the needs of the economy that forced law to a non-national dimension. In a way, national codifications arrived a bit too late: nationalism created the nation-state when this was necessary for the new economic order; however, when civil codifications finally accomplished their end, economic actors were already looking beyond their national boundaries. In this context, the idea of legal unification was perceived as achievable: from different sides it was openly spoken of as a worldwide private law[267] in terms that were in no way utopian, as even the contributions from the first congress of the comparative law association in Paris in 1900 testify.

The attention paid to the interests of business, which coincide with the interest of the state economic system, even forced expanding fascist regimes to find a compromise between legal nationalism and international cooperation.[268] In a spirit of friendly relations between nations, French and Italian jurists worked together in order to come up with a sole codification for the contract law of both countries. But the project, published in 1927, was doomed to failure for easily understandable reasons. At the dawn of the new world conflict, comparative law became the preferred instrument to promote the knowledge of domestic law in other countries, favoring the relations between those—like Germany and Italy—that were ideologically akin.[269]

In the years before the rise of the Nazi power, the German Professor Ernst Rabel drafted an accurate comparative study on the law of sale in which the hypothesis of a global unification of laws was also addressed. His 1929 study incited the freshly established International Institute for the Unification of Private Law (Unidroit) to engage in the unification of this area of law. However, after the not particularly successful experience of the 1964 Hague Sales Conventions, the United Nations

[265] The most important that deserve to be mentioned are the International Convention for the Unification of Certain Rules of Law relating to Bills of Lading signed in Brussels in 1924, the Warsaw Convention for the Unification of Certain Rules Relating to International Carriage by Air of 1929, and the Convention portant loi uniforme sur les lettres de change et billets à ordre of 1930.

[266] MJ Bonell, 'Comparazione giuridica e unificazione del diritto' (n 263), 4.

[267] *See* VE Zitelmann, *Die Möglichkeit eines Weltrechts* (München-Leipzig, Duncker & Humblot, 1916). *See* also WLPA Molengraaff, 'De dageraad van het wereldrecht' (1899) 63 *De Gids* 89–113.

[268] A Somma, *I giuristi e l'Asse culturale Roma–Berlino*, 313 ff.

[269] Ibid, 323 ff.

Convention on Contracts for the International Sale of Goods was finally signed in Vienna only in 1980, at the end of a long and complex elaboration.[270] Such a hiatus between the first draft and the final version can be explained by the outbreak of the world wars. Those conflicts have not only materially delayed the works of the commissions, but rather and more importantly, have led to dramatic changes in the previous world order and the rise of new political contrasts (North vs South, West vs East) which have left their mark on the process of private law unification.[271]

The events linked to the Second World War stopped the processes of legal internationalisation for a comparatively short period of time. At the end of the 1960s, the distinguished comparative lawyer David noted that 'this nationalization of the law is distressing from the intellectual point of view, and even from the practical point of view it is contrary to all common-sense in the world of today',[272] but timid allusions to the desirability of a private law for all of Europe not limited to the nation-states are even older and were quite widespread in those years.[273] Although nationalisation of private law took place just a few decades earlier—an extremely short period of time, measured by the yardstick of history—it was already maintained that private law nationalisation was unsuitable for the needs of 'the world of today'. In what way was 'the world of today' so different from the world of Portalis, Thibaut and Savigny, as well as that of jurists from dictatorships, who revived the national roots of the legal systems of their countries?

The events linked to the wars led to a shrinkage of the weight of national sovereignty.[274] Following the conflict, more voices in Europe pleaded for a limitation of the power of the nation-states, in the belief that by doing so the risk that these states would reiterate the same mistakes would be reduced. After 1945, the number of international organisations grew exponentially to more than 300.[275] International treaties increasingly established ad hoc institutions with the aim of guarding the specific performance of the obligations arising from the treaties. The change, however, was not only quantitative but also qualitative. The model of internationalisation by means of negotiated agreement was overcome in some

[270] B van Zelst, *The Politics of European Sales Law. A Legal-Political Inquiry into the Drafting of the Uniform Commercial Code, the Vienna Sales Convention, the Dutch Civil Code and the European Consumer Sales Directive in the Context of the Europeanisation of Contract Law* (Alphen aan den Rijn, Kluwer Law International, 2008) 87 ff.

[271] MJ Bonell, 'Comparazione giuridica e unificazione del diritto' (n 263), 4–10; B van Zelst, *The Politics of European Sales Law* (n 272), 87 ff.

[272] R David, 'The International Unification of Private Law', *International Encyclopedia of Law*, vol II ch 5 (Tübingen, Mohr, 1969) 180.

[273] For references, *see* EA Kramer, *Europäische Privatrechtsvereinheitlichung. Institutionen, Methoden, Perspektiven* (Saarbrücken, Europa-Institut der Universität des Saarlandes, 1988) 3 ff.

[274] 'Der Nationalstaat war ein "echtes Idol" und die Souveränität war seine Krone. Die Erfahrungen des Ersten Weltkrieges hatten ihn nicht erschüttert und die Diktaturen von rechts und von links haben dieses Ideal zwischen den beiden Kriegen nur noch allmächtiger werden lassen. Während des Zweiten Weltkrieges jedoch war dieses Ideal überall in Europa zusammengebrochen', LJ Constantinesco, *Das Recht der Europäischen Gemeinschaften I. Das institutionelle Recht* (Baden-Baden, Nomos, 1977) 83.

[275] K Goldmann, *Transforming the European Nation-State* (n 266), 15.

parts of the world by a new 'supranational decision-making' mechanism,[276] which in some contexts was also interested in a process of democratisation. The key word to describe denationalisation of law in this period is supranationalism. The clearest example of these tendencies is European legal integration.

2.3.2 Denationalisation and Renationalisation

It has been said that the question as to the legal nature of the European communities is as old as the European communities themselves.[277] The reason why thus far this question has only obtained the answer 'neither confederation nor federation', at first sight quite unsatisfactory, is that the European project still carries traces of the historical period in which it developed. As a reaction to the nationalist excesses of the Second World War, the European communities express a new type of institutional (but not necessarily political) nationalism still based on the persistent will of all Member States but also on an innovative capacity to bind those states and occasionally their citizens, which has developed and increased over time. The tension with the nationalist principle is clear inasmuch as the voting mechanisms of the EU would allow a decision to be taken without the consent of the representatives of the nation that will be affected by that decision (dissociation of political and national unit). In order to avoid that this mechanism would allow the newly established institution to take the upper hand, national courts elaborated a series of well-known limitations. It must be thus remembered that according to the German Constitutional Court, the source of legitimacy of the European Union is twofold and cannot be solved through sole initial consent to the treaty (*Legitimation*), but must persist and be expressed in the possibility to participate democratically in the decision-making process exercising an influence (*Einflußnahme*).[278] The tension between European and domestic law is particularly clear with regard to constitutional law issues and has already determined a delicate contrast between the Court of Justice of the European Union and several European constitutional courts, a contrast which could also easily re-emerge in unpredictable ways. However, tensions have not characterised only constitutional issues, a considerable degree of 'resistance' to Europeanisation has also affected private law, consisting both in an opposition to the development of competences in private law to the European level and in the implementation and interpretation of European law through national categories, something which can lead to 're-nationalisation'.

[276] Ibid, 15 ff.

[277] C Busse, *Die völkerrechtliche Einordnung der Europäischen Union* (Köln, Heymann, 1999) 33.

[278] In the Maastricht decision the Court stated that 'Das Demokratieprinzip hindert mithin die Bundesrepublik nicht an einer Mitgliedschaft im einer—supranational organisierten—zwischenstaatlichen Gemeinschaft. Voraussetzung der Mitgliedschaft ist aber, daß eine vom Volk ausgehende Legitimation und Einflußnahme auch innerhalb eines Staatenverbundes gesichert ist'.

The term 'resistance' has been used by numerous authors[279] with slightly different meanings to describe heterogeneous phenomena that nonetheless share a lack of readiness of Member States to open up their domestic system to rules and principles elaborated at a non-national level. In this sense, speaking of resistance can be very misleading, since it seems to allude to a clear and unitary strategy of antagonism between a domestic and a European system in a world scenario possibly characterised by competition between legal orders. Quite on the contrary, resistance involves different actors and strategies that could also be moved by very different concerns. As a scholar attentive to the dynamics of European law puts it, 'resistance to private-law harmonization does not mobilise *en bloc* all components of each legal system (courts, legislators and legal scholars). Rather, it takes unpredictable, uneven forms and is, therefore, much harder to detect'.[280] Resistance is rather 'some national discomfort with any European attack on the "internal coherence" of the civil-code structure (or of its equivalents in non-codified systems)'.[281] The definition can only be vague and generic, inclusive of several different tendencies. Ten years later, another scholar spoke of resistance in a more narrow sense with regard to the minimalistic approach chosen by certain Member States with regard to the implementation of directives in national codes, as opposed to different strategies termed 'surrender' and 'segregation'.[282]

In particular, legislative and judicial forms of resistance can be distinguished. The first type is the 'discomfort' suffered by national legislators, who tend to deviate from European prescriptions in order to reduce their effect on the domestic systems. Judicial resistance, on the contrary, is the 'discomfort' felt by national judges in the application of European rules. In particular the strategies that have been adopted by national legislators to implement European directives in the field of private law can often be seen as efforts to renationalise Community law. The choices of the legislators seem indeed due to policy considerations[283] and conceive the desire to maintain the decisions taken at the national level, even when these evidently conflict with those taken at the European level. Even when implementation strategies[284] do not imply formal infringements of EU law, they seem

[279] *See* for instance D Caruso, 'The Missing View of the Cathedral: The Private Law Paradigm of European Legal Integration' (1997) 3 *European Law Journal* 3–32; O Lando, 'The Principles of European Contract Law and the Lex Mercatoria', in J Basedow (ed), *Private Law in the International Arena/Privatrecht in der internationalen Arena. Liber Amicorum Kurt Siehr* (The Hague, TMC Asser Press, 2000) 395; MW Hesselink, 'The Ideal of Codification and the Dynamics of Europeanisation: The Dutch Experience' (2006) 12 *European Law Journal* 279–305; R Sefton-Green, 'DCFR, the Avant-projet Catala and French Legal Scholars: A Story of Cat and Mouse?' (2008) 12 *Edinburgh Law Review* 351–73; M Heidemann, 'International Commercial Harmonisation and National Resistance. The Development and Reform of Transnational Commercial Law and its Application within National Legal Culture' (2010) 21 *European Business Law Review* 227–44.

[280] D Caruso, 'The Missing View of the Cathedral' (n 281), 14.

[281] Ibid, 14.

[282] MW Hesselink, 'The Ideal of Codification' (n 281), 295 ff.

[283] D Caruso, 'The Missing View of the Cathedral' (n 281), 17.

[284] For an overview on the procedures adopted in different Member States for transposing EU directives, *see* B Steunenberg and WJM Voermans, *The Transposition of EC Directives: A Comparative Study*

to aim at making the latter more consistent with domestic law, preserving the internal coherence of the national system,[285] especially with the aim of safeguarding the ideal of codification,[286] but also more substantively particular economic interests.[287] The defence of the internal coherence of private law is a concern in particular for legal scholars who, in several countries, have been critical about plans for the Europeanisation of private law, in particular when these interfere with the tradition and the structure of national codes.[288]

Several explanations may be found to explain why legal orders tend to maintain their systems and leave specific codifications as unaltered as possible: economic reasons (it could also be argued that legal practitioners may oppose ambitious projects of Europeanisation because they would be forced to become familiar with a totally new instrument,[289] furthermore reducing a legal diversity from which they could economically benefit by selling their technical knowledge of foreign law[290]), inertia bias, social acceptance of older norms[291] and even the idea that what has been reached through long and strenuous effort is particularly valuable in itself and should therefore be maintained. With their usual succinct

of Instruments, Techniques and Processes in Six EU Member States (Leiden University, Leiden/Research and Documentation Centre of the Ministry of Justice Paper, 2006); H Schulte-Nölke, C Twigg-Flesner and M Ebbers, *EC Consumer Law Compendium. The Consumer Acquis and its Transposition in the Member States* (Munich, Sellier, 2008).

[285] *See* for instance, C Amato, 'Case Note. Article 1469-sexies of the Italian Civil Code: A Tale of National Resistance' (2005) 1 *European Review of Contract Law* 240–45, 241.

[286] MW Hesselink, 'The Ideal of Codification' (n 281), 279–305.

[287] This is particularly evident in the case of the implementation of the Directive on Takeover Bids, which was adopted in 2004 under the EU Financial Services Action Plan after a long and complicated elaboration. Due to the impossibility of reaching a consensus as to its most controversial and divisive aspect—the neutrality rule—the directive granted leeway for the Member States to adopt or reject that rule. According to the report of the Commission—18 Member States opted for the neutrality rule, but for only one of them (Malta) this represented an innovation. In conclusion, the Report on the implementation of the Directive on Takeover Bids, SEC (2007) 268, 10 noticed that '[a] large number of Member States have shown strong reluctance to lift takeover barriers. The new board neutrality regime may even result in the emergence of new obstacles on the market of corporate control. The number of Member States implementing the Directive in a seemingly protectionist way is unexpectedly large'.

[288] *See* Y Lequette, 'Le Code européen est de retour' (2011) 3 *Revue des contrats* 1028–44.

[289] W Snijders, 'Building a European Contract Law: Five Fallacies and Two Castles in Spain' (2003) 7(4) *Electronic Journal of Comparative Law*; O Lando, 'The Principles of European Contract Law and the Lex Mercatoria' (n 281), 395.

[290] Discussing a scenario in which competition between legal orders makes it possible for private parties to choose the applicable law, A Ogus, 'The Contribution of Economic Analysis of Law to Legal Transplants', in JM Smits (ed), *The Contribution of Mixed Legal Systems to European Private Law* (Antwerp, Intersentia, 2001) 28. *See* also U Mattei, 'The Professional Project. Scholars', in U Mattei, *The European Codification Process. Cut and Paste* (The Hague, Kluwer Law International, 2003) 75.

[291] The idea that an older law is per se better than a recent one due to the fact that the code of behavior made obligatory by the law gets accepted by people over time goes back to Aristotle: 'For the habit of lightly changing the laws is an evil, and, when the advantage is small, some errors both of lawgivers and rulers had better be left; the citizen will not gain so much by making the change as he will lose by the habit of disobedience. The analogy of the arts is false; a change in a law is a very different thing from a change in an art. For the law has no power to command obedience except that of habit, which can only be given by time, so that a readiness to change from old to new laws enfeebles the power of the law', *Politics*, 81.

and incisive jargon, behavioural economists and law and economics scholars call this latter aspect the *endowment effect*, which, combined with *path dependence*, determines a favour for the status quo, a conservatism from which it is very difficult and costly to escape. Without resorting to abstruse mathematical formulae, a classical legal scholar already expressed the sense of the concept with regard to the idea of codification in a much more vibrant way many decades ago, long before the creation of the European communities:

> Un Code, une fois promulgué, acquiert un prestige tel qu'il voile, pur un temps, aux yeux des jurisconsultes, le jeu de l'évolution du Droit. Ce prestige tient à deux causes : à la grandeur de l'effort nécessaire pour mener à bien l'œuvre de codification, et a l'avantage que présente pour le commerce juridique la condensation des lois en articles brefs et précis. De là naît la tendance à considérer l'œuvre nouvelle comme un monument définitif, indestructible, dont il faut respecter l'ordonnance, auquel on ne doit toucher qu'avec circonspection, et lorsqu'une modification en a été reconnue absolument indispensable. Aussi les projets de réforme sont-ils pendant de longues années vus avec défaveur et combattus par ceux mêmes qui ont pour mission d'interpréter la loi.[292]

More explicitly, other commentators have complained about the risk of dislocating the political unit from the national to the supranational level: because of an extensive Europeanisation of national law and the generalisation of European consumer law solutions to the status of general law, the interpretation of key areas of the national legal system will be delegated to the Court of Justice of the European Union, so that, in the future the rules of the BGB—in the case of Germany—will be developed not by the praxis of the German courts but by the European judges.[293] This outcome is considered undesirable and a consequence of a legal science that, inspired by an excessive legal positivism,[294] has cut off the links with the *ius commune*, natural and Roman law that lie at the basis of all other legal systems of Europe, forgetting the legacy of Savigny.[295] Similar concerns were already famously expressed in England by Lord Denning, who denounced that '[o]ur sovereignty has been taken away by the European Court of Justice. It has made many decisions impinging on our statute law and says that we are to obey its

[292] H Capitant, *Introduction à l'étude du droit civil* (Paris, A Pedone Editeur, 1929) 87–8: 'Once enacted, a code gains such prestige that it obscures for some time the dynamics of legal evolution in the eyes of lawyers. Such prestige is due to two elements: the major effort required to achieve a codification and the practical advantage of condensing the law into short and clear articles. Hence the tendency to consider the new creation as a definitive, indestructible monument, whose coherence has to be safeguarded and which should be altered circumspectly only when a modification becomes absolutely indispensable. During many years, therefore, projects of reform are seen unfavourably and are opposed by those whose mission is to interpret the law'.

[293] MJ Schermaier, 'Una superficiale e arbitraria modifica del BGB? Perché la riforma dello Schuldrecht si è rivelata un insuccesso' (2005) 9 *Contratto e impresa/Europa* 898–919, at 906.

[294] Ibid, 900.

[295] Ibid, 918. This severe judgement is referred to the German reform of the Schuldrecht not only for having improperly generalised European consumer law, making it the basis of the new German general contract law, but also for having taken Europeanisation as an excuse to make more general negative changes in the BGB, that could only found a justification in 'legal politics propaganda' (917, with reference to the Münchner Kommentar zum BGB, Vor § 275 par. 25).

decisions instead of our own statute law… Our courts must no longer enforce our national laws. They must enforce Community law… No longer is European law an incoming tide flowing up the estuaries of England. It is now like a tidal wave bringing down our sea walls and flowing inland over our fields and houses—to the dismay of all'.[296]

It has been pointed out that the resistance offered by legislators and governments is nonetheless stronger than the resistance offered by judges, who on the contrary:

> Have often used the leverage of EC law to denounce or even make up for the shortcomings of their own national systems. By complying with Brussels rule even beyond the mandates of their own States' legislators, courts have experienced a veritable institutional empowerment.[297]

This is comprehensible, since while legislators' resistance affects the formation of law before this comes into force, judges can only react afterwards, so that their ability to 'resist' is more limited. This is not to say that resistance cannot be given by the judiciary, even if this is less easily detectable. Occasionally, also the judiciary has expressed the concern that European law—including the case-law of the European Court—may have a disruptive effect on the internal consistency of national law, especially when it comes to politically sensitive issues.[298] In some jurisdictions, therefore, the highest courts have often resorted to a strict formalism in order to limit the influence of European law on the domestic provisions. In this sense, the alleged neutrality of formalism has become a suitable means of resistance.[299] National judges may indeed quite easily use 'renationalising' interpretations of European law, intentional or merely consequences of a physiological homeward bias. Resistance at this level can take different but more subtle forms—often not easily detectable—such as rejection and avoidance,[300] and often judges can be led to an interpretation of community law in light of their particular national system.

The particular reluctance to refer to the Court of Justice of the European Union of certain constitutional and highest national courts is quite striking, even if it is impossible to conclude that this aversion is necessarily an expression of hostility against European law.[301] This path has been followed in particular by the German

[296] Court of Appeal, Bulmer vs Bollinger [1974] Lord Denning.

[297] D Caruso, 'The Missing View of the Cathedral' (n 281), 25.

[298] J Kokott, 'Report on Germany', in A-M Slaughter, AS Stone Sweet and JHH Weiler (eds) *The European Courts and National Courts—Doctrine and Jurisprudence. Legal Change in its Social Context* (Oxford, Hart Publishing, 1998) 124; KJ Alter, *The European Court's Political Power. Selected Essays* (Oxford, Oxford University Press, 2010) 201.

[299] D Caruso, 'The Missing View of the Cathedral' (n 281), 29.

[300] L Niglia, 'The Non-Europeanisation of Private Law' (2001) 4 *European Review of Private Law* 575–99, 580 ff. According to this author, the reluctance of national courts is such that the Europeanisation of private law appears as a normative discourse of legal scholarship rather than reality, 598–99.

[301] MP Broberg and N. Fenger, *Preliminary References to the European Court of Justice* (Oxford, Oxford University Press, 2010) 57; C Kilpatrick, 'Community or Community of Courts in European

Bundesverfassungsgericht and by the Italian *Corte Costituzionale* for a long time. The latter is an institution whose approach to European law seems to have been characterised by 'a sort of procedural mutual exclusion between EC law and domestic constitutional law',[302] a 'rebelliousness'[303] formally justified on the basis of the argument that the Constitutional Court is not a 'court' or a 'tribunal' in the sense in which Article 267 TFEU speaks of and is therefore not legitimated to refer to the European Court.[304] In this case too, thus, a 'strict formalism' has been the way chosen to maintain the separation of European and domestic law. However, following the example given by the Belgian and more recently the Austrian Constitutional Courts, the Italian *Corte Costituzionale* changed its approach and referred for the first time to the Court of Justice in 2008,[305] with a decision which has been considered as the beginning of a new dialogue between the Italian and the European Court.[306] It is generally acknowledged that in some countries even high courts are unwilling to refer to the European Court for primary ruling—a striking tendency which, far from being just the consequence of a mere judicial unawareness of European law,[307] can also be explained by political and economic reasons which can become manifest in contract law issues too[308] as even a 'cultural stickiness' that hampers adaptation when important changes take place.[309]

At this point, one could wonder how many of these strands of resistance exemplify widespread tendencies in all national societies. Are the opinions of Lord Denning representative of a national cultural trait?[310] The intricate relation between legal cultures and the more general national culture will deserve further analysis and can be effectively investigated only in the scholarly debate on European private law.

Integration? Sex Equality Dialogues between UK Courts and the ECJ' (1998) 4 *European Law Journal* 121–47.

[302] F Fontanelli and G Martinico, 'Between Procedural Impermeability and Constitutional Openness: The Italian Constitutional Court and Preliminary References to the European Court of Justice' (2010) 16 *European Law Journal* 345–64, 357.

[303] M Panebianco, 'La recente giurisprudenza comunitaria della Corte costituzionale', in *Studi in Onore di Modestino Acone*, vol I (Napoli, Jovene, 2010) 153.

[304] Italian Corte Costituzionale, Ordinanza 536/1995.

[305] F Fontanelli and G Martinico, 'Between Procedural Impermeability and Constitutional Openness' 345–64; E Happacher, 'Der italienische Verfassungsgerichtshof und das Vorabentscheidungsverfahren gemäß Art 234 EGV: neue Entwicklungen' (2009) 22 *Jahrbuch für Italienisches Recht* 149–62.

[306] F Teresi, 'Finalmente inizia il dialogo tra la Corte costituzionale e la Corte europea [Nota a C. Cost. 15 aprile 2008, n. 102; ord. C. Cost. 15 aprile 2008, n. 103]' (2008) 17 *Nuove Autonomie* 129–33.

[307] KJ Alter, *The European Court's Political Power* (n 300), 201.

[308] G Comparato, 'Behind Judicial Resistance to European Private Law', in H-W Micklitz and Y Svetiev (ed) *A Self-Sufficient European Private Law—A Viable Concept?, EUI Working Paper 2012/31* 97–113.

[309] Eg. the Italian judge F Bile, 'La Corte di cassazione di fronte al diritto comunitario', in N Lipari (ed), *Diritto privato europeo e categorie civilistiche* (Napoli, Edizioni Scientifiche Italiane, 1998) 208.

[310] The idea that the Court of Justice is some kind of foreign institution adjudicating on issues of national competence is indeed quite widespread among English Eurosceptics, *see* for example C Booker and R North, *The Castle of Lies. Why Britain Must Get Out of Europe*, (London, Duckworth, 1996) 195.

Chapter 3

Why Private Law Should be National

THE PROCESS OF Europeanisation of private law has often run into resistance on the part of the Member States. Such resistance, as it has been said in the Chapter 2, is based on the concern of not compromising the national interest and the systematic coherence of the national legal system, and primarily offered by means of a 'renationalisation', consisting in the reshaping of European rules in a way that fits the economic or symbolic needs of the nation-state and maintains the decisional power at the national level. The concern that it is the European legislator or judge who decides upon potentially significant matters of domestic law has been repeatedly expressed with suspicion, but the 'political' reasons behind this behaviour remain mostly unexplained. While the reasons that lie behind the resistance of legislators and judges are often hidden and can be examined only with uncertainty, legal scholars have started an extensive debate on the feasibility and desirability of a highly harmonised European private law, in which the political and economic implications of such options are discussed and where objections to denationalisation are explicitly formulated. This chapter therefore is focussed on that debate to analyse some recurring arguments of resistance to the Europeanisation of private law, with the intent to identify and expose the links between those arguments and the nationalist political principle and therefore the impact of this latter on the development of European private law.

Several authors have manifested concerns about the possibility that a common European law will substitute the variety and richness of local laws, employing economic, political and cultural arguments to support their views. This makes the debate a highly multi-disciplinary one, in which the variety of approaches allows consideration of the phenomenon of denationalisation of private law from several perspectives. In this discussion, several positions can be identified, which in their complexity cannot be simplistically reduced to a catchy linear opposition between those who are 'in favour' and those who are 'against' Europeanisation. On the contrary, there are a wide range of standpoints, from a strong opposition *tout court* to any attribution of competences in the field of private law to the European level (even based on the idea that any form of imitation or legal transplants is simply impossible)[1] to—at the other extreme—the claim of the necessity of a mandatory

[1] P Legrand, 'The Impossibility of Legal Transplants' (1997) 4 *Maastricht Journal of European and Comparative* Law 111–24.

European civil codification.[2] Intermediate views underline the risks that a unified or highly harmonised private law would imply; at the same time they do not object to but rather endorse a Europeanisation of legal science, intended as a condition for the establishment of a new generation of truly European lawyers.[3] Quite on the contrary, in the views of other authors, it is exactly the plurality of legal orders that would allow for those learning and borrowing processes that would promote Europeanisation in this sense.[4] Many an author also seems to appreciate the idea of optional instruments,[5] which are, as in the already mentioned Common European Sales Law, a set of substantive rules that parties could be free to adopt as the system governing their transborder transactions.

Not dissimilar from the well-known quarrel between Savigny and Thibaut as to the desirability and feasibility of a nationalisation of German private law, all these positions as to the desirability and feasibility of a Europeanisation of national laws[6] are based upon certain assumptions as to the role of private law in contemporary societies and could be inspired by several economic and political ideologies. The idea of an optional instrument, for instance, could be linked to the belief that contract law should chiefly serve as a tool to facilitate economic transactions, and in this sense it seems rational to offer contracting parties the last word as to the utility of that instrument. The idea of a *hard* pan-European civil code, on the other hand, could be inspired by a statist vision that aims to create a kind of new super multinational state out of the European Union, or rather, a reaction to trends favouring neoliberal forms of competition between legal orders. Focusing on political ideologies, what is the role of the nationalist ideology in this discourse? Various arguments employed in the debate seem to share traits with the assumptions of given political theories, including liberal nationalism. Such influence could be easily explained since, as we have seen in the Chapter 2,

[2] U Mattei, 'Hard Minimal Code Now: A Critique of "Softness" and a Plea for Responsibility in the European Debate over Codification', in S Grundmann and J Stuyck (eds) *An Academic Green Paper on European Contract Law* (The Hague, Kluwer Law International, 2002).

[3] MG Faure, JM Smits and H Schneider (eds), *Towards a European ius commune in Legal Education and Research: Proceedings of the Conference Held at the Occasion of the 20th Anniversary of the Maastricht Faculty of Law* (Antwerp, Intersentia, 2002); A Flessner, 'Rechtsvereinheitlichung durch Rechtswissenschaft und Juristenausbildung' (1992) 56 *Rabels Zeitschrift für ausländisches und internationales Privatrecht* 243–60.

[4] *See* R van den Bergh, 'Private Law in a Globalizing World: Economic Criteria for Choosing the Optimal Regulatory Level in a Multi-Level Government System', in MG Faure and A van der Welt (eds), *Globalization and Private Law. The Way Forward* (Cheltenham, Edward Elgar Publishing, 2010).

[5] Among others, *see* JM Smits, 'Towards a Multi-Layered Contract Law for Europe', in S Grundmann and J Stuyk (eds) *An Academic Green Paper on European Contract Law* (The Hague, Kluwer Law International, 2002) 397 ff; G Wagner, 'The Economics of Harmonization: The Case of Contract Law' (2002) 39 *Common Market Law Review* 995–1023, 1018; V Reding, 'Warum Europa ein optionales europäisches Vertragsrecht benötigt' (2011) 19 *Zeitschrift für Europäisches Privatrecht* 1–6.

[6] The literature as to the Europeanisation of private law is already boundless; however, the basic viewpoints in this debate can be found in particular in the collective works of A Hartkamp, MW Hesselink, EW Hondius, C Mak and E du Perron (eds), *Towards a European Civil Code. Fourth and Expanded Edition* (The Hague, Kluwer Law International, 2011), and S Grundmann and J Stuyck (eds), *An Academic Green Paper on European Contract Law* (The Hague, Kluwer Law International, 2002).

nationalism has been one of the ideological forces that have contributed to the shaping of the modern understanding of law and its relation to the state.

In this chapter, some of the arguments used in the debate on Europeanisation to resist in particular unification or *forced* harmonisation of private law will be analysed in order to verify whether nationalist ideology also plays a role therein.[7] The concept of forced harmonisation is taken to mean the approximation of private law systems by means of mandatory or optional legal instruments and not also forms of spontaneous 'bottom-up' convergence. Keeping in mind that resistance to forced harmonisation does not necessarily entail a rejection of—and can even be functional to—the Europeanisation of law in a broader perspective, it is evident that we can only refer to 'nationalist arguments' rather than 'nationalist scholars'. Some authors have explicitly advocated a non-nationalist position; this however does not necessarily exclude that some of their arguments may echo in their structure at least liberal nationalist positions, widespread in legal studies for the reasons that have been seen and will be further investigated. This situation is again in large part due to the uncertain understanding of 'nationalism', which still today many a scholar would equate with a necessarily negative attitude, from which it is necessary to be distanced, rather than more neutrally with a legitimate political principle. At the same time, it is evident that, in analysing a law which has been nationalised as a by-product of nationalism, scholars inevitably end up as hostages of a methodological nationalism which has to be recognised, and this holds true even in the transnational debate on European private law, on which the chapter is mostly focused. For these reasons, the chapter will focus on sophisticated arguments that should be associated only with nationalism upon a closer examination of their structure and function.

It should also be repeated that given the positive nature of this book, the aim of the chapter is not to challenge the validity of the arguments presented, suggesting that these are *wrong* for whatever reason, but rather to show their political and ideological associations. It does not claim that the arguments of resistance rest on false assumptions, but rather on specific political assumptions, the validity and reasonableness of which can be further debated in light of political theory, as the chapter also tries to do, addressing political theories other than nationalism too. Consequently, the approach adopted here is mainly analytical, and the reader should be cautioned that the analysis will at certain points appear to take unexpected paths in the deepening—some may even like to say: deconstruction—of the considered arguments. It is hoped that at the end of that progression, the various pieces will fall into place and the general picture become clear.

Although various arguments have been put forward, in this chapter only three of them will be considered: the economic, the social, and the cultural arguments.

[7] It is opportune to clarify that, since the goal of this chapter is to discuss European private law rather than European private lawyers, some references will also be made to non-European literature whose impact on the development of European private law is nonetheless self-evident, despite the limitation of this book to discussing nationalism and private law in Europe.

It will also be suggested that the first two arguments tend to flow into the third one. The reason for such limitation is twofold: on the one hand, those are the most recurring arguments, not only in the legal debate but also, as the reader will easily recognise, in more general political discussions. Therefore, although the contributions of individual authors in particular are discussed, the choice for those contributions is not anecdotal, as they are highly representative of general arguments which are widely employed in legal and political debates and therefore highly influential. On the other hand, it is exactly in those arguments that the link to the liberal nationalist principle as analysed in the previous chapters most clearly emerged. Throughout this chapter, therefore, it will be shown how they relate to one another and what the 'political philosophy' of these positions is, by means of a comparison with the theory of nationalism as opposed to the theories of communitarianism and cosmopolitanism for the methodological reasons that have been explained earlier.

The argumentative structure of the next sections is as follows: each argument employed in legal studies to object to the further attribution of private law competences to a supranational level is presented, subsequently these arguments are more critically examined in the light of insights originating from the political theories of communitarianism and the cosmopolitan idea of 'multiple identities'; through this juxtaposition, it will emerge what the assumptions are on which both the considered legal arguments and the (liberal) nationalist political principle—as it has been examined in the Chapter 1—are based.

3.1 THE ECONOMIC ARGUMENT

Combining insights from law and economics, several commentators have pointed out what the limits of denationalisation should be and what are the reasons to halt, or even invert,[8] the process of Europeanisation. A particular role is played by the economic argument of decentralisation, according to which decentralised legislation presents a series of advantages on centralised forms of governance. On the basis of this argument, drawing specifically on the work of highly influential economists exemplified by Tiebout and Hayek, several legal scholars have affirmed that the harmonisation or even unification of private law systems in Europe represents a hazard, while the same argument is often employed in political discussions as well. However, other commentators have already expressed the suspicion that behind many of those economic arguments 'there is a fear of colonization, loss of hegemonic status, or cultural decline'.[9]

[8] R van den Bergh, 'Forced Harmonisation of Contract Law in Europe: Not to be Continued', in S Grundmann and J Stuyk (eds), *An Academic Green Paper on European Contract Law* (The Hague, Kluwer Law International, 2002) 268.

[9] U Mattei, 'The Comparative Law and Economics Approach to the European Civil Code. An Introduction', in U Mattei, *The European Codification Process. Cut and Paste* (The Hague, Kluwer Law

Is it then possible that ideological concerns inspire economic arguments? Economic models indeed can give the impression of being technically neutral and therefore, somehow 'true'. At any rate, it is clear nowadays that also 'technical' economic arguments may conceal concerns of a political nature, and a comparison with political arguments in order to identify what their reciprocal influences are is therefore justified.

3.1.1 The Ideal Locus of Private Law in the European Context

In the debate on the Europeanisation of private law, the point has been made that the European bodies should not expand their competences into the field of private law, since that would imply moving away from the preferences and needs of the citizens. This would probably aggravate the democratic deficit within the European Union and, what is more, would lead to inefficient regulation. In fact, what guarantees that 'the more remote European legislator is in a better position to assess what consumers in a particular Member State really want'?[10] In establishing what governance level is more appropriate to regulate the interests of private citizens, it should be taken in consideration what the capacity of each level is to interpret those interests. In Gellnerian terms, at what level of governance should the political unit be located?

Since it is reasonably more difficult to guess the preferences of a large number of people than those of a more limited group, some authors have manifested doubts as to the idea of devolving the competence to regulate private relationships to a supranational level, assuming that the European legislator will be less informed about the needs and preferences of citizens than the national lawmaker; the former is further away from the citizens, whereas the latter has a more direct contact with them and can understand what they really want and what is better for them. The main issue therefore seems to be the knowledge of the needs and preferences of citizens or at least the availability of such information.

3.1.1.1 Normative Implications of the Argument

Imaging a hierarchical two-layer system, it is suggested that the 'more remote' level has an inferior knowledge of the interests of the citizens, while 'the local level has the best information on local problems and on the preferences of citizens'.[11] According to this line of reasoning, two alternative normative consequences follow.

International, 2003); U Mattei, 'Why the Wind Changed. Intellectual Leadership in Western Law' (1995) 42 *American Journal of Comparative Law* 195–218.

[10] R van den Bergh, 'Forced Harmonisation of Contract Law in Europe' (n 8), 252.

[11] MG Faure, 'How Law and Economics May Contribute to the Harmonisation of Tort Law in Europe', in R Zimmermann (ed), *Grundstrukturen des europäischen Deliktsrechts* (Baden-Baden, Nomos, 2003) 38.

In the first place, attribution of competences in the field of private law on the supranational level should be avoided *tout court* or subjected to a particularly strong burden of proof: private law legislation should be enacted at the regulatory level that is the nearest to the citizens, while an attribution of this competence to a higher level should be excluded or admitted only as the *extrema ratio*, possibly when empirical data show that the benefits of centralisation would outweigh its disadvantages. In plain words, the competence for private law should be 'moved to a higher level only when there is a good reason'.[12] The idea, of course, sounds familiar to European lawyers: that is the sense of the principle of subsidiarity that requires the centralised bodies to intervene—provided that a legal basis exists—when decentralised bodies cannot achieve the objective.[13] Or such is, at least, one of the interpretations that can be given of that principle. In contrast to what the European institutions claim, several authors involved in the debate on harmonisation sustain that the real need for moving private and, more specifically, contract law, to a higher level lacks empirical evidence, so that, in conclusion, that 'good reason' seems not to exist or at least not to be sufficiently weighty to win the burden of proof in favour of decentralisation. It is true that the centralist idea behind the projects of private law harmonisation, ie that diversity of laws represents an obstacle to the creation of a well-functioning common market, lacks of univocal evidence. Researches have recently highlighted why, for very different reasons including psychological motives, the reasoning of the European institutions should be rejected,[14] but even this counter-argument that diversity of laws does *not* hinder the market sometimes often seems to lack empirical evidence.[15]

At any rate, in the view of opponents of Europeanisation, even if empirical data were to confirm—or theoretical arguments were to convince—that good reasons for centralisation actually exist, a mandatory supranational harmonisation should still be considered the last resort: a classical international negotiation between states may produce more efficient results, since the idea that private parties should be better left free to negotiate their own interests would be applicable also in this case, in which the role of private actors would be played by states.[16] This idea is familiar in politics, as it reflects the 'first guiding principle' uttered by

[12] MG Faure, 'Economic Analysis of Tort Law and the European Civil Code', in A Hartkamp, MW Hesselink, EW Hondius, C Mak and E du Perron (eds), *Towards a European Civil Code. Fourth and Expanded Edition* (The Hague, Kluwer Law International, 2011) 985; MG Faure, 'How Law and Economics May Contribute' (n 11), 38. This position was supported also by the UK government in its response to the first communication by the Commission.

[13] Art 5 TEU.

[14] *See* the contributions in JM Smits (ed), *The Need for a European Contract Law. Empirical and Legal Perspectives* (Groningen, Europa Law Publishing, 2005); G Low, 'The (Ir)Relevance of Harmonization and Legal Diversity to European Contract Law: A Perspective from Psychology' (2010) 18 *European Review of Private Law* 285–307.

[15] MW Hesselink, 'An Optional Instrument on EU Contract Law: Can it Increase Legal Certainty and Foster Cross-border Trade?', in MW Hesselink, A van Hoek M Loos and A Salomons (eds) *Groenboek Europees contractenrecht: naar een optioneel instrument?* (Den Haag, Boom, 2011) 12.

[16] R van den Bergh, 'Forced Harmonisation of Contract Law in Europe' (n 8), 258.

Margaret Thatcher, according to which, 'willing and active cooperation between independent sovereign states is the best way to build a successful European Community', while 'to try to suppress nationhood and concentrate power at the centre of a European conglomerate would be highly damaging and would jeopardise the objectives we seek to achieve'.[17] In this sense, an interstate negotiation eventually resulting in an international treaty that responds to the exigencies of both contracting states would be preferable to a supranational system that could occasionally bind even unwilling Member States. This reasoning can also justify the increasing use within the European Union of new 'non-authoritative' modes of governance, such as the so-called Open Method of Coordination. From this point of view, however, one may even think that the entire European community should be better disestablished and the state of private law should better return to the stage prior to supranationalism, in the era characterised—as seen before—by the 'trust in nations'.

As a less radical solution, if a given area of law—let us say consumer law, which is the object of much of European private law regulation—which aims to be effective and efficient were to be enacted at a non-national level, that could only be a 'non-interventionist' law. Given the impossibility for the more remote legislator to know the preferences of the citizens, it should be concluded that the legislator should not be too interventionist. In the multi-level system of European private law, fields like consumer law—intended as an 'interventionist law'[18]—should consequently be competence of the local level—ie the national—for in order to protect the interests of consumers, the legislator has first to know what those needs and interests are. In this view, legal rules can be distinguished between facilitative and interventionist, with the category of interventionist law generally overlapping with what legal scholars have traditionally known as mandatory law. The core of the distinction is clearly explained by Grundmann and Kerber:

> *Facilitative law* encompasses two different groups of functions, which both help to save transaction costs: (1) One group encompasses the functions of the legal order that help the parties to *enforce contracts* ('pacta sunt servanda'; including the services of the court system). (2) The second group consists of supplying *legal standard solutions* ('default rules') for typical transaction or cooperation problems. If the legal order is capable of offering good legal standard solutions for many different typical problems, the parties can save bargaining (and therefore transaction) costs by using those standard solutions instead of writing thick contracts.[19]

The harmonisation of such facilitative rules should not present particular difficulties, since inasmuch as they just facilitate commerce, they are normally viewed

[17] M Thatcher, 'The European Family of Nations' [1988] in M Holmes (ed), *The Eurosceptical Reader* (New York, Saint Martin's Press, 1996) 91.

[18] R van den Bergh, 'Forced Harmonisation of Contract Law in Europe' (n 8), 252.

[19] S Grundmann and W Kerber, 'European System of Contract Laws—A Map for Combining the Advantages of Centralised and Decentralised Rule-making', in S Grundmann and J Stuyck (eds), *An Academic Green Paper on European Contract Law* (The Hague, Kluwer Law International, 2002) 297.

favourably by every market actor and do not lead to serious contrasting interests. For instance, both parties to a contract will agree (at least when they initially sign a contract) that what they have negotiated and put down in their agreement will have to be performed. These are, according to the terminology employed by Ogus, 'homogeneous products', 'as to which there is unlikely to be a significant variation in preference as between market actors in different jurisdictions'.[20] On the contrary, interventionist rules imply policy choices that are likely to differ and are therefore not suitable for harmonisation.

This conclusion from a law and economics perspective is quite striking for legal scholars, as they would more likely sustain that it is exactly the differences in mandatory rules that represent an impediment in the international commercial relationships, while facilitative rules (notably including default rules) do not imply this problem; thus, even if the market requires the abolition of the mandatory character of several private law rules, the remaining mandatory rules should be better harmonised as far as possible.[21] What is more, even facilitative laws are less 'neutral' than they are occasionally presented by some law and economic scholars, so that also the drafting of mere default rules can be a sensitive matter of preferences. In this sense, Grundmann and Kerber indeed consider the argument of heterogeneous preferences to hold true for both mandatory and facilitative law, or to be even more important in the case of the latter.[22] Especially those who adhere to a free-market economy ideology and affirm that it is competition that should 'influence the behaviour of those demanding, and those supplying, law reform'[23] will more likely downplay the need for harmonisation of interventionist law foremost. This indeed entails mainly mandatory rules that limit private autonomy, so that 'interventionist' rules eventually tend to alter the natural dynamics of the economic forces and do not fit into a classical Smithian model. Indeed, if 'there is no doubt from an economic point of view that markets need an institutional framework in the form of mandatory rules in order to ensure the efficient working of the markets', it is also true that 'there is much discussion to what extent mandatory rules are necessary and helpful for solving problems of market failure or for attaining additional aims (beyond economic efficiency)'.[24]

But what does all this mean for the development of a harmonised system of contract law in Europe? This rather abstract point has particularly important consequences and can be explained by way of a concrete example: a chief feature

[20] A Ogus, 'Competition between National Legal Systems: A Contribution of Economic Analysis of Comparative Law' (1999) 48 *International and Comparative Law Quarterly* 405–18, 410.

[21] This concept is expressed in particular by E McKendrick, *The Creation of a European Law of Contracts. The Role of Standard Form Contracts and Principles of Interpretation* (Deventer, Kluwer, 2004) 47.

[22] S Grundmann and W Kerber, 'European System of Contract Laws—A Map for Combining the Advantages of Centralised and Decentralised Rule-making' (n 19), 300–1.

[23] A Ogus, 'The Contribution of Economic Analysis of Law to Legal Transplants', in JM Smits (ed), *The Contribution of Mixed Legal Systems to European Private Law* (Antwerp, Intersentia, 2001) 27.

[24] S Grundmann and W Kerber, 'European System of Contract Laws' (n 19), 297.

of the European system of consumer law is represented by the right of withdrawal which is acknowledged to consumers under certain circumstances. Although it is manifest that this right is beneficial to single consumers making up for their allegedly weaker position in front of the business, economic analysis confirms the intuitive impression that in a way such legal remedy is detrimental to the general category of consumers. The right of withdrawal implies costs for the businesses that will later be borne by the consumers themselves, in the form of higher prices for the goods and services they purchase.[25] Some consumers could thus actually prefer to give up their right of withdrawal—in particular when they can reasonably foresee that they will not need to make use of it—and instead pay less and, maybe, consequently buy more. This is, however, impossible under European consumer law, since the right of withdrawal is a mandatory rule that cannot be contractually given up. Would consumers generally prefer to be entitled to withdraw from their contracts, paying a little more for this right or rather give up this opportunity and spend less money? And would businesses prefer to maintain a mandatory right of withdrawal or 'liberalise' it and offer more competitive prices for their services? It is necessary to know the answer to these questions as to personal preferences before the policy choice whether the right of withdrawal should be mandatory can be made.

As it is argued that this choice cannot be efficiently or democratically made by the 'higher' legislator in a way that satisfies everyone's interests—given that 'national preferences regarding the level of protection are likely to differ'[26]—it follows that the supranational legal intervention should rather be minimalistic, possibly enacting the institutional framework which is necessary to promote competition between national systems, since '[g]enerally, more legislators are better than one'[27] as long as there are no information deficiencies and people are allowed to choose from a wide range of applicable legal regimes,[28] as the well-known Tiebout model[29] actually requires. In the opposite case, that 'interventionist' legal regime will probably be ineffective and inefficient, and 'any uniform regulation has to be an unsatisfactory average solution'.[30] Nonetheless, the deeper justification of the basic assumption behind these considerations—that the national legislator is in a better position to interpret the interests of the citizens—remains obscure. What does it mean that a 'distant' legislator knows less about those preferences? And what are the risks of a supranational legislation? The reasons why the 'more remote' legislator is considered less able to enact private law legislation than the national legislator still need to be investigated, and several hypotheses can be formulated.

[25] R van den Bergh, 'Forced Harmonisation of Contract Law in Europe' (n 8), 252.

[26] A Ogus, 'Competition between National Legal Systems' (n 20), 418.

[27] R van den Bergh, 'Forced Harmonisation of Contract Law in Europe' (n 8), 256.

[28] R van den Bergh, 'Private Law in a Globalizing World (n 4), 60.

[29] C Tiebout, 'A Pure Theory of Local Expenditures' (1956) 64 *Journal of Political Economy* 416–24.

[30] S Grundmann and W Kerber, 'European System of Contract Laws' (n 19), 301.

3.1.1.2 The Challenging Nature of Distance Relationships

It is a particular concern that the attribution of some competences to a 'higher' regulatory level will produce results that do not take into account the interests of those who are at the 'lower' level; as Faure puts it in his discussion of the regulatory level for environmental law (a field that was traditionally considered particularly in need of centralisation), 'the further away from the citizens concerned the decision making takes place, the greater the risk is that a countervailing power, taking into account the interests of the citizens, may be lacking'.[31] Distance, in this view, leads to serious problems of legitimacy, accountability and transparency.[32] The point is expressed in particularly clear terms in a series of critical articles in which the author deals with the idea of tort law harmonisation. In these writings,[33] the aims of the advocates of centralisation are condemned as being inherently paternalistic and, in a way, also dangerously imperialistic: when advocates of harmonisation argue that a given legal solution is preferable over the one adopted in a given legal system, they are *de facto* substituting their personal policy evaluation for the one that was democratically formed and expressed by the inhabitants of that country.[34] The point is also made by Ogus: 'If the argument is for harmonization at a higher level of protection than that provided in some jurisdictions, why should the preferences of their citizens for lower standards at a lower cost be overreached?'.[35] In plain terms, it could also be true that certain national legal system do not protect consumers in an efficient way, but who are foreign observers to judge and say that such a system should be changed, when people actually chose it? National legislators and judges—as contestable as their concrete activity can be—are better informed about the preferences of their own co-nationals; surely better than some obscure bureaucrat in Brussels. Steering clear of easy rhetoric on people's preferences, Ogus admits that national rules could also not reflect the real inclinations of citizens, but still, if already the national legislator failed in understanding them, no doubt that a foreigner will be even less able.[36]

Given these different orders of difficulty, one can posit that decentralisation should at least be the starting point (coherently with what the principle of subsidiarity requires), while centralisation should bear the burden of proof. Thus, the subsidiarity principle should be taken 'seriously'.[37]

[31] MG Faure, 'Globalization and Multi-level Governance of Environmental Harm', in MG Faure and A van der Walt, *Globalization and Private Law*, 407.

[32] Ibid, 407.

[33] MG Faure, 'Economic Analysis of Tort Law and the European Civil Code' (n 12), 977 ff; MG Faure, 'Towards a Harmonized Tort Law in Europe? An Economic Perspective' (2001) 8 *Maastricht Journal of European and Comparative Law*, 339–50; MG Faure and T Hartlief, 'Naar een harmonisatie van aansprakelijkheidsrecht in Europa? Een kritisch rechtseconomisch perspectief' (2003) *Nederlands Juristenblad* 170–177.

[34] MG Faure, 'Economic Analysis of Tort Law and the European Civil Code' (n 12), 985.

[35] A Ogus, 'Competition between National Legal Systems' (n 20), 417.

[36] A Ogus, 'Competition between National Legal Systems' (n 20), 418.

[37] MG Faure, 'Economic Analysis of Tort Law and the European Civil Code' (n 12), 985.

> [E]ven if one were to agree with these critics of the preference argument that national legislators and judges are not capable of producing legislation which really reflects the preference of the citizens, there is still no reason to assume that the European legislator would do better in that respect. Why should we assume that European bureaucrats in Brussels would be more able to find out what the preferences are of the Portuguese than Portuguese legislators and judges could? Here one can notice that the supporters of harmonisation are in fact of the opinion that they would know better than national legislators or judges what is good for the European citizens.[38]

The argument in favour of harmonisation is therefore paternalistic and dangerous, while the starting point should remain that national legislators are in a better position to make regulations that reflect the preferences of their own citizens.[39] The argumentative strength of these considerations is definitely greater when they refer to the Europeanisation of tort law, a field in which the 'good reasons' to confer the competence to a higher regulatory level seem to be less evident than in contract law, despite the fact that European institutions also started to indicate tort law as a possible area of harmonisation by means of an optional instrument.[40] The normative consequence is again that the European legislator should abandon the design of harmonising European legal systems when there are differences in the legal systems that can be explained by different preferences.

Nevertheless, it is suggested that it would be possible to unify rules that, also by means of a comparative functionalist analysis, would appear to be an expression of similar policy considerations on what is preferable.[41] In this sense, the normative consequence is quite limitative: only harmonise what is already converging. The reason for this possibility, again, is that where a convergence can be detected, one has to assume that people in those countries share the same preferences, so that there would not be any 'imposition' by third foreign subjects but rather a mere technical simplification. In the opposite case, of course, the motto should sound like: 'where preferences differ: don't touch!'[42]

[38] Ibid, 985. In the Dutch version, published with T Hartlief, the argument sounds: 'Zelfs wanneer men met die critici zou aannemen dat nationale wetgevers (en rechters) niet in staat zijn om op voldoende wijze wetgeving (en rechtspraak) te produceren die daadwerkelijk correspondeert met de preferenties van de eigen burgers, dan is er nog steeds geen enkele reden om er van uit te gaan dat de Europese bureaucraten in Brussel beter in staat zijn te achterhalen wat de preferenties zijn van—in dit geval—de Portugezen. Liefhebbers van harmonisatie weten eigenlijk beter dan de nationale wetgevers of rechters wat goed is voor de burgers.' (MG Faure and T Hartlief (2003), 'Naar een harmonisatie van aansprakelijkheidsrecht in Europa?' (n 33), 172.). Note that in this version, it is spoken of 'citizens' in general and not 'European citizens'. This slight difference incidentally lets a question arise: if it is comprehensible that the Portuguese legislator is more apt to know the preferences of the Portuguese citizens, why should he also know better the preferences of the 'European' citizens? If a 'European' citizen exists, shouldn't a European legislator exist too on the basis of the same argument?

[39] Ibid, 172.

[40] *See* European Commission's Green Paper on policy options for progress towards a European Contract Law for Consumers and Businesses, COM(2010) 348, final, 4.3.4.

[41] MG Faure and T Hartlief (2003), 'Naar een harmonisatie van aansprakelijkheidsrecht in Europa?' (n 33), 175.

[42] MG Faure, 'Economic Analysis of Tort Law and the European Civil Code' (n 12), 992.

3.1.1.3 Democracy Issues

Legislators might easily be incompetent corrupt politicians completely uninterested in and unaware of the real needs of citizens, while an hypothetical technical commission formed by distinguished international experts may have a perfect knowledge of the issues at stake, but still this circumstance would not imply that the legislator should be relieved of their functions and duties and abdicate in favour of some scientific committee, stakeholders associations or study group on a European civil code. As long as we are dealing with democratic systems—the only imaginable option within the European Union constitutional framework—the legislator remains the only subject democratically legitimated to take any decision on those issues. In contemporary legal orders, there is indeed an intrinsic and inescapable connection between legitimacy of law and democratic processes.[43] The argument presented by Ogus and Faure among others thus reminds us of the democracy issues connected to the process of harmonisation and warns the legal scholars from more or less conscious paternalistic bents and professorial intellectual arrogance. From this perspective, the argument is convincing and in no way refutable by anyone who genuinely supports the democratic ideal; if the alternative presented is between a law which is an expression of the democratic choice of the people on the one hand, and a set of obscure legal rules drafted by some foreign bureaucrat without any legitimation whatsoever on the other hand, no doubt that the Portuguese legislator—to heed the example made by Faure—has to be preferred over the nameless bureaucrat located in Brussels: the former simply is the only policymaker who is democratically legitimated. All the more, considering that there is not even evidence that technocracies are more efficient than democracies.

In this sense, though it is partially true what critics of the democracy approach like to repeat, that is that civil codifications and other important statutes have historically been drafted by restricted circles of technicians instead of by politicians (whether democratically elected or not)—at least in most cases[44]—democracy still requires an involvement, prior or posterior, of legitimated representative bodies in the drafting of any legal rules, including those of European private law.[45] No wonder that, in this perspective, private law should remain a national competence and the arguments against Europeanisation may sound slightly

[43] *See* on this aspect J Habermas, 'Über den internen Zusammenhang von Rechtsstaat und Demokratie', in UK Preuss (ed), *Zum Begriff der Verfassung, die Ordnung des Politischen* (Frankfurt am Main, Fischer, 1994) 83.

[44] The French *Code civil* can be considered a partial exception, as it is well known that Napoleon personally participated and in several parts (particularly in family law) strongly influenced the work of the technical commission; in more recent years, the Dutch parliament has also been actively involved in the drafting of the new civil code of the Netherlands.

[45] *See* B van Zelst, *The Politics of European Sales Law. A Legal–Political Inquiry into the Drafting of the Uniform Commercial Code, the Vienna Sales Convention, the Dutch Civil Code and the European Consumer Sales Directive in the Context of the Europeanisation of Contract Law* (Alphen aan den Rijn, Kluwer Law International, 2008) 244–45.

nationalistic. It has already been observed that nationalism may also represent an instrument of democratisation, inasmuch as it gives an answer to the complicated and essential question as to what is the *demos*; indeed, the nation. A defence of the nation can more deeply mean a defence of democracy. The political unit with regard to private law, thus, coincides with the national unit.

If one rejects nationalism in any way, and thus also its controversial but undeniable democratic function, the view that only local legislators are legitimated to draft private law rules becomes disputable. Criticising the 'democracy thesis' of those who plead for a democratic process in the drafting of private law rules, Smits for instance affirms that 'in an increasingly globalizing and interconnected world, there is no necessary relationship between the nation-state and the legitimacy of law',[46] with the consequence that democratic legitimacy 'does not have to come about through territorial entities such as national parliaments. There are other methods of legitimating law',[47] such as, for instance, competition between legal orders. If a given legal regime meets the favour of citizens involved in commercial transactions and is thus chosen as applicable law, the role of parliamentary bodies that are representative of the citizens seems superfluous. This would have as a consequence that 'the mere fact that a democratic process took place is then not enough to conclude that a rule is sufficiently legitimate'.[48] This could be one of those cases in which instead of regulating the market, law is legitimated by the market itself.

As an attempt to rethink law in post-nationalist categories, this provocative view is surely stimulating and coherent; however, it remains highly contestable. Even if contract law mainly contains rules that may be derogated from, any contract law system also imposes mandatory provisions—and this is particularly the case in European consumer law, as the previous example on the right of withdrawal has pointed out. Can the determination of such rules be left to the competitive mechanism—that is the free choice of contracting parties? The idea that private subjects can contractually create a new legal order that imposes mandatory rules and negative consequences on third subjects without these parties being involved is simply non-democratic and rather distressing—though de facto not absurd. For these reasons, it seems that such rules cannot be left to freedom of choice or jurisdictional competition; in other words, the market. The lack of state involvement in legitimating these rules stands in the way of the elevation of any project of private law rule to the status of applicable law, a fortiori if merely optional,[49] while

[46] JM Smits, 'Democracy and (European) Private Law: A Functional Approach', in MG Faure and A van der Welt, *Globalization and Private Law*, 24.

[47] Ibid, 27.

[48] Ibid, 22.

[49] R Goode, 'The Harmonization of Dispositive Contract and Commercial Law—Should the European Community Be Involved?', in EM Kieninger (ed), *Denationalisierung des Privatrechts? Symposium anlässlich des 70. Geburtstages von Karl Kreuzer* (Tübingen, Mohr Siebeck, 2005) 27–28 and 23.

different legitimacy mechanisms do not seem so far to offer sufficient guarantee of a democratic control over the law-making process.

In this sense, even the idea of a European codification or an optional instrument can help bring the production of legal rules—that are today often elaborated by the 'business community'—back to a democratic dimension,[50] while the suggestion that such a business community can basically legitimise itself makes the very usefulness of a codification doubtful. The idea of a post-national private law that needs no classic democratic legitimacy is on a closer look inherently libertarian, since such a legal system would have to renounce mandatory rules, whereby the lack of such rules is revelatory of an ideological agenda aimed at giving a marginal role to the state and, therefore, politics.[51] In this sense, for those who fear such an anti-statist agenda, the idea of a non-optional supranational instrument to be called 'code' becomes on the contrary quite appealing, provided that instead of following a market functionalist approach it entails those solidarity elements that have been seemingly developed by the national courts of Europe.[52]

Nevertheless, even repudiating the suggested idea that national parliaments are already obsolete, the unfeasibility of unification of European private law should not be looked upon as the necessary consequence of the interesting objections raised by law and economics scholars. The coincidence of nation-state and democracy is just a historical coincidence, not even perfectly brought about in the same way in the world, while in fact those categories remain conceptually distinct and democratic procedures do not necessarily have to take place at the national level.[53] Within a democratic federal or confederal multi-layer system in which every regulatory level is provided with democratic legitimacy, the question as to the optimal level of legislation cannot be easily solved resorting to the democracy thesis.

It has been noted earlier, that if the alternative is between a democratically elected local legislator and some kind of a-national undefined bureaucrat, there is not much room for discussion and there would not be anything else to do other than to acknowledge that in this particular historical moment, democracy is better served by nationalism than by Europeanisation. But what if the alternative is between a democratically elected legislator and another lawmaker provided with democratic legitimacy too? This is basically the situation we face today in the European multi-level governance system. For sure, the question as to the democratic legitimacy of the European Union is an old and highly controversial issue, which has recently again become a hotly debated topic and whose examination goes far beyond the scope of this book, as it would need a specific account as to

[50] S Rodotà, 'Il codice civile e il processo costituente europeo' (2005) 23 *Rivista critica del diritto privato* 21–33, 28.

[51] *See* M Barcellona, 'Per un codice civile europeo', in M Meli and MR Maugeri (eds), *L'armonizzazione del diritto privato europeo. Il piano d'azione 2003* (Milano, Giuffrè, 2004) 187.

[52] A Somma, *Diritto comunitario vs diritto comune europeo* (Torino, Giappichelli, 2003) 15.

[53] *See* J Habermas, *Zur Verfassung Europas. Ein Essay* (Berlin, Suhrkamp, 2011) 49–55.

its implications for private law. It is common knowledge that the powers of the European Parliament, the only body provided with direct democratic legitimacy, are limited if compared to those of other institutions. On the other hand, the European Parliament has shown itself to be capable of exercising a considerable pressure and control over the functioning of the other institutions, showing powers that are unknown even to various national parliaments.[54] Leaving aside the question as to the improvement of democratic legitimacy within the European system, however, the democratic legitimacy of European rules could not be questioned for our purposes, also taking into account the numerous judgments of several European constitutional and supreme courts that already confirmed the compatibility of EU law with the democratic principles under certain conditions. There are many more than a single model of democracy, and one may still have very good and numerous reasons to deem the national legislator as 'more democratic' than the European one, but then it would become arbitrary to consider the democracy argument decisive to oppose the Europeanisation of certain private law rules (such as the 'interventionist' ones) and not of other (such as the 'facilitative' ones), when both are created through the same procedures.

In conclusion, if both the Portuguese legislator and the European 'bureaucrat' are democratically legitimated, the answer to the question as to who knows the preferences of citizens better is less self-evident and should be answered by referring to arguments other than democratic legitimacy.

3.1.1.4 Heterogeneity of Preferences

The reason to oppose attribution of competences to a higher regulatory level cannot be exclusively an issue of democratic legitimacy. The main problem with centralisation appears to be that the decisions taken at the centre would disregard the preferences of people on the periphery, that are more likely to be reflected by the legal rules elaborated at a decentralised level, regardless of the democratic legitimacy of this latter. If a uniform legal regime were to be applied in several different contexts and reflect the interests of many different groups, there is the concrete risk that only one group—undoubtedly the more powerful or overrepresented one—will be able to instill its values and interests in the legal rules, while the other groups will have to accept a decision they could not contribute to make. This quite concrete concern already gives rise to episodes of legislative resistance both at the European and the national level; the interest of a state are not necessarily the interest of another Member State and, limiting ourselves to private law, some legal concepts that are particularly appreciated in given contexts—think of good faith—might not meet the favour of other nations.

At the level of scholarly discourse this concern is explicitly addressed and discussed in detail. What critics of harmonisation fear is that a unified legal

[54] R Bin and P Caretti, *Profili costituzionali dell'Unione Europea* (Bologna, il Mulino, 2009) 94.

system will reflect the preference of only one specific people at the expense of the interests of all other peoples, so that harmonisation ends up determining the imposition of the preferences of someone on someone else.[55] If this is true, legal diversity appears as a preferable solution, since 'diverging rules may satisfy a greater number of preferences'.[56] So for example, bearing in mind the example made with regard to the preference as to the options pay-more-and-withdraw and pay-less-and-do-not-withdraw, 'citizens in different jurisdictions may have different preferences regarding the level of protection to be imposed and the price to be paid for it'.[57] On the basis of these considerations while developing the new field of comparative law and economics, Ogus has intended to challenge the 'orthodox' view that convergence of national laws is always desirable and should be obtained even by means of mandatory international instruments.[58]

Another author, Helmut Wagner, has stated that 'variety of regulations or laws reflects variety of preferences',[59] but the reasons why a citizen, say a consumer, may prefer a given solution and another consumer in another country a different one are not a matter of mere personal preferences: rather it is in the first place the 'economic structures' that are not identical in different countries. Consequently, each country needs a special legal system of its own that fits its specific needs. The normative conclusion this time is even more drastic for substantive private law than the one considered before. While Faure advised to harmonise only those aspects which are already converging in order to respect the policy choices behind those rules, in Wagner's view harmonisation should only focus on procedural law,[60] since, as no one would object, differences in procedural systems may indeed represent a considerable obstacle in the establishment of a well-functioning common market much more than differences in substantive laws. But given these premises, the conclusion appears to be even too moderate: do procedural rules not reflect the preferences of the citizens as well? If so, those rules should not be harmonised either, or national preferences as to the procedural system would otherwise be disrespected. Moreover, it could be incidentally noted that already in the past, differences in preferences and social conditions have been considered an obstacle to the unification of procedural rules, as was the case in the United States when the possibility of enacting a common code of civil procedure was discussed.[61] In other words, there seems not to be any conceptual reason why procedural rules should be more suitable for harmonisation than substantive rules. If the argument

[55] MG Faure and T Hartlief, 'Naar een harmonisatie van aansprakelijkheidsrecht in Europa?' (n 33), 176.

[56] R van den Bergh, 'Private Law in a Globalizing World' (n 4), 92.

[57] A Ogus, 'Competition between National Legal Systems' (n 20), 416.

[58] Ibid, 406.

[59] H Wagner, 'Economic Analysis of Cross-Border Legal Uncertainty. The Example of the European Union', in JM Smits (ed), *The Need for a European Contract Law. Empirical and Legal Perspectives* (Groningen, Europa Law Publishing, 2005) 39.

[60] Ibid', 42.

[61] *See* Chapter 2: 2.1.4.6 '...In the USA'.

of heterogeneous preferences is correct, then it should be valid always, and not be conveniently employed only to advance or oppose a given economic agenda.

Those who plead for a 'market of legal rules' within the European Union would necessarily reject the hypothesis of unification, since this would frustrate the most basic conditions of Tiebout's model. From this perspective, cultural pluralism is also a value to be safeguarded rather than an obstacle to the efficiency of the market, as this would 'encourage each region to increasingly specialize in its comparative advantages, which are in part shaped by its specific social capital'.[62] In this sense, as Goode put it addressing the European institutions, varieties of contract laws in Europe should be considered an asset, inasmuch as it allows contracting parties to 'have a wide range of choice and select their own law or that of another legal system with which they feel comfortable'.[63] Heterogeneity of preferences—rather than democratic legitimacy—seems to be thus the fundamental rationale for decentralisation. However, once it has been clarified that heterogeneous regulations should correspond to heterogeneous preferences, it still remains to be seen why exactly decentralised legislators are in a better position to understand what those preferences are.

These argumentations constitute the application of theories that had previously been elaborated in economics and occasionally already inspired some policy choices. It is therefore necessary to delve into that disciplinary field to further explore the assumptions and implications of the argument, before we can come back to the legal field.

3.1.1.5 The Decentralisation Theorem in Economics and Politics

The factors that could justify centralisation or decentralisation have been extensively described in the economic literature. In particular, centralisation seems to be a preferable option in the presence of strong inter-state externalities, 'if there is a risk of "race to the bottom" or if significant scale economies and/or transaction cost savings can be achieved by increased legal uniformity'.[64] However, the advantages of a 'forced' or 'negotiated' harmonisation (as the one that would be achieved by means of international agreements rather than by supranational instruments) are overshadowed by the benefits of decentralisation. According to this view, decentralisation—intended as devolution of power and responsibility over policies from the national to the local level[65]—is the guarantee that the necessities of all individuals will be properly dealt with. Local agents will be better informed about the needs of citizens and will therefore be more able to take good

[62] L Bovenberg, 'Unity Produces Diversity: The Economics of Europe's Social Capital', in W Arts, J Hagenaars and J Halman (eds), *The Cultural Diversity of European Unity. Findings, Explanations and Reflections from the European Values Study* (Leiden, Brill, 2003) 412.

[63] R Goode, response to COM(2001) 398, at para 11.

[64] R van den Bergh, 'Private Law in a Globalizing World' (n 4), 80.

[65] MS De Vries, 'The Rise and Fall of Decentralization: A Comparative Analysis of Arguments and Practices in European Countries' (2000) 38 *European Journal of Political Research* 193–224, 196.

decisions; moreover, they will have stronger incentives to take people's interests into account,[66] so that an 'agency problem' is less likely to occur than in a centralised system.[67] The reason seems to be that if the geographical distance between lawmakers and citizens is reduced, it will be easier for the citizens to track the activities of their representatives and keep them in mind the next time they are called to the polls. This holds true also from the point of view of the enforcement of legal rules, whereby decentralisation seems to be preferable as it reduces the distance between those who are subjected to the law and those who should apply it. On the contrary, in a centralised system such distance would hinder a proper application of legal rules and very likely lead to inefficiencies.

Oates has made a strong case for decentralisation in the economic literature.[68] Discussing the subject of fiscal federalism, this author suggested that regional governments are more apt to adopt regulations that reflect the preferences of regional citizens, while a central government could only give a uniform regulation that would disrespect regional interests. Thus, without spillovers, a decentralised system has to be preferred. This is commonly known as Oates' decentralisation theorem. In 2003, two other scholars, Besley and Coate,[69] built upon that argument and brought it to more radical conclusions: if Oates' formulation left 'unclear why a government charged with providing public goods in a centralised system cannot differentiate the levels according to the heterogeneous tastes in each district',[70] these authors suggested that even if this was the case—ie if the central government were to adopt differentiated regulations—these would anyway be inefficient as the centralised and differentiated rules elaborated by representatives of local regions at the centralised level could only take into account the interests and preferences of the citizens of one specific district: 'The fact that costs are shared in a centralized system, creates a conflict of interest between citizens in different jurisdictions'.[71] From the argument, a pessimistic idea follows which is however not limited to a centralised model but rather to the entire democratic process, as it is assumed that regulatory bodies—as they should express the interests of several different subjects within the centralised system—will be characterised by a conflict of interest that will give rise to unsatisfactory or inefficient regulations. In simpler terms, in a centralised—but actually in any democratic—system, some

[66] WE Oates, 'An Essay on Fiscal Federalism' (1999) 37 *The Journal of Economic Literature*, 1120–49.

[67] R van den Bergh, 'Private Law in a Globalizing World' (n 4), 62, states that 'decentralization may thus be advocated because it reduces the agency problem', specifying in a footnote that 'there are, naturally, intermediate solutions between full decentralization and full centralization. Decentralized information gathering can help to remove much of the information asymmetry faced by central regulatory agencies. An obvious alternative to the choice between centralization and decentralization is the co-existence of national and supranational procedures'.

[68] WE Oates, *Fiscal Federalism* (New York, Harcourt Bruce Jovanovich, 1972).

[69] T Besley and S Coate, 'Centralized versus Decentralized Provision of Local Public Goods: A Political Economy Approach' (2003) 87 *Journal of Public Economics*, 2611–37.

[70] Ibid, 2612.

[71] Ibid, 2628.

minorities will always have to bear the costs of rules that affect everyone but are de facto decided by the majority.

Going further back in history, we see that this argument had been already formulated by the libertarian economist Friedrich August von Hayek with the aim of explaining the ideal distribution of competences within a federal state. A recipient of the Nobel prize for economics in 1974 (with Gunnar Myrdal), Friedrich Hayek has left an important mark on contemporary politics and economics and his thought still plays an important role even in the debate on the Europeanisation of private law.[72] Hayek developed the argument in 1945 in his famed article *The Use of Knowledge in Society*[73] in which, starting from the consideration that knowledge (or at least *some* knowledge) in society is generally dispersed rather than concentrated, he suggested that decentralisation is a more desirable option, as it better fits the dispersed nature of knowledge. On the contrary, centralised organs would not be efficient since they would not be able to concentrate all the knowledge they need in order to come up with good decisions. The inefficiency of a centralised system, indeed, lies in the fact that knowledge should be transferred from the periphery to the centre, where a decision should then be made, following a time-consuming and most likely wasteful process. In this perspective, decentralisation will ensure an optimal and more rapid use of knowledge:

> If we can agree that the economic problem of society is mainly one of rapid adaptation to changes in the particular circumstances of time and place, it would seem to follow that the ultimate decisions must be left to the people who are familiar with these circumstances, who know directly of the relevant changes and of the resources immediately available to meet them. We cannot expect that this problem will be solved by first communicating all this knowledge to a central board which, after integrating *all* knowledge, issues its orders. We must solve it by some form of decentralization because only thus can we ensure that the knowledge of the particular circumstances of time and place will be promptly used.[74]

From this moment on, the decentralisation theorem enjoyed considerable fortune also in politics, inspiring the activity of many an influential leader and indirectly already playing a role within the process of Europeanisation. Inspired by these considerations and mixing them with concerns of protection of national decision-making power from foreign dominance, Margaret Thatcher expressed her doubts as to a centralised and invasive model of European Communities somehow comparable to socialist regimes:

> But working together does *not* require power to be centralised in Brussels or decisions to be taken by an appointed bureaucracy. Indeed, it is ironic that just when those countries such as the Soviet Union, which have tried to run everything from the centre, are

[72] MW Hesselink, 'A Spontaneous Order for Europe? Why Hayek's Libertarianism is not the Right Way Forward for European Private Law', in H-W Micklitz and F Cafaggi (eds), *European Private Law after the Common Frame of Reference* (Cheltenham, Edward Elgar Publishing, 2010) 123–46.

[73] FA von Hayek, 'The Use of Knowledge in Society' (1945) 35 *American Economic Review* 519–30.

[74] Ibid, 524.

> learning that success depends on dispersing power and decisions *away* from the centre, some in the Community seem to want to move in the opposite direction. We have not successfully rolled back the frontiers of the state in Britain, only to see them re-imposed at a European level, with a European super-state exercising a new dominance from Brussels.[75]

In light of these considerations, it seems that decentralisation should be preferred inasmuch as it confers the decisional power to those subjects who are more informed about the issue they have to decide on. In other words, availability of information is greater at a higher degree of physical proximity to the object to be understood.

3.1.1.6 Problematic Aspects for European Private Law

Considering the particular historical moment in which Hayek wrote his article on the use of knowledge in society as well as the political views of the author, it is easy to see that the theory also aimed at creating a limit against centralist tendencies of the government that in Hayek's view would have eventually led to a socialist despotic state. While the knowledge thesis has been sometimes used uncritically to object to any form of economic and political centralisation, oddly enough, the argument of knowledge could be used both to promote and oppose processes of decentralisation, that furthermore more usually depend on political and historical contingencies than on economic calculations:[76] in practice, centralisation or decentralisation are usually not chosen because of their economic efficiency but rather for political reasons.

If the main issue is the availability and efficient use of knowledge, the argument of knowledge does not necessarily lead to the conclusion that decentralisation should be preferred and could also represent a solid justification for the attribution of some competences to a federal, supranational or, theoretically, even a foreign authority when it is more likely that such authority will be more informed than the local institutions and can therefore take more efficient decisions. In this light, the argument does not self-evidently coincide with a democratic argument. This conclusion, of course, is not satisfactory if we adhere to the view of Besley and Coate, since even if the central or foreign governance level had more information, its regulations would be irremediably marked by conflicts of interest and thus inefficient. But, as already touched upon, this is an intrinsic characteristic of any pluralistic system.

Furthermore, the premise of Hayek's 1945 paper—as well as most of his work—is that knowledge in society is dispersed, but it can also be thought that certain kinds of knowledge are not dispersed in a geographical sense that justifies decentralisation. In other words, Hayek's idea cannot be generalised to the point

[75] M Thatcher, 'The European Family of Nations' (n 17), 91–2.
[76] MS De Vries, 'The Rise and Fall of Decentralization' (n 65), 202 ff.

of comprehending *any* form of knowledge and *any* economic or political activity. Keeping this in mind, the extension of this economic argument in the discussion on the feasibility of a harmonised system of European private law gives rise to some questions.

3.1.1.7 Geographical Proximity

The argument we have taken into account seems to be fully employable only as far as geographically localised problems are concerned. Only in this case, a strong link between availability of information and physical proximity can be built. Pollution is a clear example, as the knowledge of relevant factors (atmospheric conditions and so on) is more likely to be decentralised.[77] This circumstance could justify a decentralised enforcement of legal rules in the first place, which is requested by reasons of efficiency, but even democracy concerns could require decentralisation with regard to the elaboration of substantive legal rules. In this case it is fully democratic that the inhabitants of the region where a political decision will produce its effects should have the right to contribute to the making of that decision, and contest that decision if it negatively affects only that community.

However, as the importance of the geographical element decreases, the need for decentralisation seems less compelling. Already the reason why 'it is more difficult for firms to hide or misrepresent information to decentralized agencies than to a more remote agency'[78] does not seem self-evident—as if it were possible to understand the balance sheet of a corporation just by passing by in front of the corporation building. The opposite may be true: in a centralised and restricted context, it is easier for those who are controlled and those who should control to build interpersonal relations that could occasionally lead to regulatory capture, dishonest agreements and eventually seriously prejudice law enforcement. There is already some evidence that this factor can frustrate the correct enforcement of substantive private law.[79] An analogous problem of regulatory capture may arise since 'national authorities may be inclined to favour national interests', which is indeed looked upon as one of the arguments that could speak in favour of

[77] R van den Bergh, 'Private Law in a Globalizing World' (n 4), 62.

[78] Ibid, 62.

[79] CJ Milhaupt, 'Beyond Legal Origin: Rethinking Law's Relationship to the Economy: Implications for Policy' (2009) 57 *American Journal of Comparative Law* 831–45, 843–44: 'In 2005, the South Korean legislature enacted a provision permitting class action lawsuits for securities fraud claims. Debate over the provision was dominated by the fear of meritless "strike" suits. As a result, measures were taken to circumscribe the procedure and reduce its potential for abuse. Yet since enactment of the provision, only one class action lawsuit has been filed—in 2009—against a small company. Why? Probably because the South Korean legal profession is still so small and tight-knit, and links between the major law firms and major corporate clients are so strong, that it is not economically prudent from a long-term perspective to represent plaintiffs in this type of litigation, however strong the particular claim. In other words, South Korea lacks the entrepreneurial lawyers and attorney fee mechanisms that make class action litigation viable—and subject to abuse—in the United States'.

centralisation even by law and economics scholars that more explicitly advocate decentralisation.[80]

Furthermore, geographical proximity could justify the decentralisation of the enforcement of legal rules, but the drafting of substantive law implies even more complicated problems: if decentralisation allows law to cope better with the needs of the local communities, what about needs which are not common to a particular local community but rather to a social group, for example consumers? Where are the consumers on the map? Not being a geographical community, it could be argued that decentralisation makes little sense in this case. Moreover, in the presence of externalities or other reasons that could justify centralisation, it would be sensible to opt for the centralisation solution, so that competence could be assumed by the highest hierarchical authority. Is this conclusion in favor of centralisation in contradiction with the Hayekian model? State's activities are very diverse in their nature and could require different levels of decentralisation. This aspect is also looked upon as a flaw of a general comprehensive economic model by Besley and Coate themselves:

> One weakness of the analysis is that we have assumed that the only function of decentralized and centralized governments was providing the public goods in question. In reality, both levels of government determine numerous issues and hence the political consequences of transferring responsibility for one area of spending are likely to be much more subtle than our analysis suggests.[81]

The reasons that support decentralisation in a given state's areas of activity cannot be generalised to the point of comprehending *any* imaginable activity. There exist differences between issues of trade, environmental protection, monetary policies, financial regulation and so on, and each of those fields can have a different optimal regulatory level. In this line of reasoning, we could wonder whether contract law falls under the decentralisation theorem: looking at the real world of practice, after all even decentralised systems like Germany or Switzerland are strongly centralised with regard to private law.

If we consider this aspect, a new criticism of the decentralisation argument in the debate on Europeanisation of private law could come from a Hayekian perspective, strangely enough. Speaking of a federal nation-state, Hayek indeed distinguished for instance legislation from government, claiming that 'it is not really necessary always to have both legislative assemblies and governmental assemblies on the same level of the hierarchy'.[82] Here, Hayek was not concerned exclusively with economic policies: the focus is broader and Hayek aimed at describing *the political order of a free people.* It is thus spoken of a multi-level government system in which the degree of centralisation can vary according to the activity to be

[80] R van den Bergh, 'Private Law in a Globalizing World' (n 4), 62.

[81] T Besley and S Coate, 'Centralized versus Decentralized Provision of Local Public Goods' (n 69), 2628.

[82] FA von Hayek, *Law, Legislation and Liberty. Vol 3. The Political Order of a Free People* (London, Routledge & Kegan Paul, 1979) 132–33.

performed by the state (legislation, enforcement, etc). Needless to say, Hayek is considering a federal state, but this line of reasoning could be valid also in the context of the European multi-level system,[83] which is of course no federal state in legal terms but something at least comparable to that in politological terms.[84] Discussing the possible impact of Hayek's theories for the development of a harmonised private law system in Europe, it has already been suggested that even the most centralist idea of a European civil code could fit in the Hayekian system.[85]

Here it could be useful to make a distinction between legislation and enforcement of legal rules. It is conceivable that one of these activities can be assigned to a particular subject, the one which is more competent or informed, whereas the other one can be located at a different governmental level (leaving aside the question as to the public or private nature of the law enforcement). Basically, as the enforcement of law is a more concrete activity which can materially take place in a specific space and time, it is more suitable to be assigned to a more localised unit, whereas legislation, its task being the elaboration of 'general and abstract rules', could be less dependent on concrete circumstances which are related to a specific territory. While it seems to move towards centralisation with regard to the drafting of substantive private law rules, the EU system adopts decentralisation with regard to the enforcement of those harmonised provisions, completely matching the Hayekian model.

Nevertheless, the reasons that support decentralisation in the case of substantive rules also hold true with reference to the enforcement of law—in particular the benefit represented by the learning processes allowed by legal diversity—so that some law and economics scholars claim that both activities—legislation and enforcement—should be better located at the decentralised level.[86] Then why what is possible within a federal state—as conceived by Hayek—is not within a supranational institution—like the European Union?

3.1.1.8 A Slippery Slope to Balkanisation

Taking on the normative advice formulated by several law and economics authors, one could think that the efficiency of enforcement and legislation increases with increasing decentralisation. If this is true, where should we set the limit? While in the specific context of European law the decentralisation theorem implies the maintenance of the status quo or even a return to a fully national law, the argument could be pulled further to the point of legitimating a further decentralisation, which would have as a result the creation of regional systems of private law.

[83] MW Hesselink, 'A Spontaneous Order for Europe?' (n 72), 140.

[84] *See* Introduction: I.3.2 'European Union as a Multinational and Multi-level System'.

[85] MW Hesselink, 'A Spontaneous Order for Europe?' (n 72), 140.

[86] R van den Bergh, 'Forced Harmonisation of Contract Law in Europe' (n 8), 255; R van den Bergh, 'Private Law in a Globalizing World' (n 4), 62.

There are indeed good reasons to think that even within several countries, both preferences and economic structures diverge to a point that national law would be inefficient and non-democratic, as it disregards regional preferences. It is clear that within several European states, local identities are sometimes so marked[87] that local preferences should be considered not only to object to the attribution of national competences to a supranational level, but even of local competences to a national level of governance. The same holds true if one relates preferences to objective economic structures (so, for example, if one maintains that certain consumers prefer lower levels of protection not because this is what they actually wish but rather because they cannot afford the economic consequences of a mandatory right of withdrawal) that strongly vary within most European nations. In other words, the decentralisation theorem transplanted within the legal debate could be used to affirm that even national codifications are inefficient, and would build a convincing argument for decodification or even secession.

The point is not exclusively theoretical; indeed, already in the past national law has been criticised for very similar reasons. A historical example can help to highlight the point. In France, one of the arguments used to affirm the need to maintain the prerogatives of the provincial parliaments was that monarchy would have become despotic if the *corps intermédiaires* were deprived of their rights; these groups 'considered themselves representatives of the nation' and claimed that it was rather necessary to restore the 'corporate freedom' of local institutions; whereby freedom basically meant political competence.[88] This idea was advanced by Montesquieu in particular and, ironically enough, was advocated initially even by Portalis, when he was still a member of local parliaments as opposed to his eventual rise to the position of 'architect' of French codification.[89] It was indeed the period in which even Portalis, in quite conservative terms long before Savigny, could argue that 'the dangerous ambition to make a new civil code' had to be given up, and it was rather necessary to go back to Roman law, the law of all nations.[90] The argument of 'corporate freedom'—that 'provided a political-theoretical argument against centralisation of the authority to make laws and against the introduction of legal unity'[91]—did not achieve the aims of avoiding a codification of French law, but in the course of the eighteenth century became quite popular, evolving in the theory of federalism.[92] If that argument had been successful in those years, one can presume that no codification of French law would have taken place and the history

[87] MW Hesselink, 'The Politics of a European Civil Code' (2004) 10 *European Law Journal* 675–97, 678 ff.

[88] PAJ van den Berg, *The Politics of European Codification. A History of the Unification of Law in France, Prussia, the Austrian Monarchy and the Netherlands* (Groningen, Europa Law Publishing, 2007) 2930 and 267–68.

[89] Ibid, 30.

[90] RC van Caenegem, *European Law in the Past and the Future. Unity and Diversity over Two Millennia* (Cambridge, Cambridge University Press, 2002) 66; J-L Halpérin, *L'impossible Code civil* (Paris, PUF, 1992) 252–53.

[91] PAJ van den Berg, *The Politics of European Codification* (n 88), 30.

[92] Ibid, 30.

of European law would have been very different. It is, to say the least, ironic that the *Code civil* passed from being viewed as an instrument that disrespected local peculiarities and preferences to the manifestation of those preferences, as it is nowadays intended in the modern discourse on European private law. This consideration opens up an intricate problem: does national law express the preferences and interests of the citizens or does it also deceive local interests? More fundamentally, are preferences homogeneous within the nation or can they vary within it?

3.1.2 The Argument in Light of Different Political Theories

The transposition in the legal discourse of the decentralisation theorem elaborated in the economic literature leads to affirming that, since preferences vary among countries, it is convenient not to unify or further harmonise private law or at least some aspects of it, such as mandatory rules. Approximation of laws would overlook national preferences impeding a beneficial competition between legal orders as well as valuable inter-state learning processes. At the same time, as it has been shown, the application of that argument in the context of European private law gives rise to a few questions.

Summing up some of the controversial aspects of the arguments employed, it is on the one hand claimed that preferences vary among countries and therefore a centralised system would disregard these element resulting in inefficient legislation. However, the cultural variety within Europe and even the Member States may lead us to think that preferences may vary not only among but also within nations. To claim, on the contrary, that conflicts of interest will arise only in the case of centralised legislation at the European level but not also within a national pluralistic system seems to imply that the interests within that system are basically homogeneous. History shows that this line of reasoning was used even to object to national codification; thus how can the same argument now support the idea of a national legislation? On the other hand, it is said that decentralisation should be preferred because local institutions are 'closer' to citizens and have therefore a better knowledge of their needs and preferences, so being able to come up with better decisions. However, only in some cases does geographical vicinity seem to be synonymous with availability of knowledge. What about communities that are not geographically based? Here, there could be strong reasons to support centralisation, as the rationale for decentralisation fades out. Why should private law legislation be national (ie decentralised) also in these cases? All these open questions can be answered only by adopting a broader perspective and inquiring into political theories.

3.1.2.1 Communitarian and Cosmopolitan Perspectives

It should be noticed that the objections that have been raised so far against the economic argument are not extemporaneous but rather rest upon certain views which have already been extensively discussed by political scientists. In particular, these objections are based on the positions advocated by the philosophies of communitarianism and cosmopolitanism. The objection based on the idea that preferences can vary also *within* nations is a classic communitarian argument, while arguing that preferences can vary also *beyond* and *across* nations is a point connected to a particular kind of cosmopolitanism. Both philosophies can be opposed to nationalist assumptions.

Most definitely, nationalism and communitarianism share various features, in particular they both sustain that the decisional power (the political unit, in Gellnerian terms) should be acknowledged to a specific homogeneous group. The radical distinction however concerns the qualification of this group, which is invariably the nation for nationalism while for communitarians it can be represented by different geographic or social groups. In this sense communitarianism and nationalism can clash, since according to the communitarian thought, even within the nation there are groups that are entitled to some kind of recognition. Transposed in the legal discourse, this argument implies that private law has not necessarily to be enacted at the level of the nation-state but could also be created by particular groups within the nation. Nationalism, on the other hand, takes into consideration only a particular group, indeed, the nation; in this sense the political claims of all other groups even within the nation are downplayed, denied or even, as the many notorious historical experiences reveal, repressed. In this perspective, acknowledging only one particular social unit has the practical merit of setting a limit to dangers of Balkanisation.

This point has already been made in the debate on Europeanisation, to object to the rationale of the decentralisation thesis: if we were to agree that the closer the legislator the better, then we would start a whirl of decentralisation that would most likely lead to perpetual secessions. Even if the idea of enacting local private laws can sound provocative, the argument underlying such a proposal is not and does not count as a paradox without links to the real world. Several groups that advance independence—or at least autonomy—claims against established states actually ask for a separate legislation that would better fit their needs, as already happened, for example, in the Spanish region of Catalonia. Certain legal scholars have moreover explicitly advocated a communitarian politics of recognition even in private law systems characterised by an increasing multiculturalism,[93] and in this sense, different from the typical law of homogeneous nation-states. Why then should private law operate exclusively at the national level instead of a sub-national one?

Cosmopolitans, at the other end, tend to see homogeneity beyond local and national communities. In this view, the idea that preferences differ in different

[93] JM Smits, 'Multiculturalisme en Europees privaatrecht: een pleidooi' (2000) 17 *Nederlands Tijdscrhift voor Burgerlijk Recht* 289–92; JM Smits, 'Legal Culture as Mental Software, or: How to Overcome National Legal Culture?', in T Wilhelmsson, E Paunio and A Pohjolainen (eds), *Private Law and the Many Cultures of Europe* (Alphen aan den Rijn, Kluwer Law International, 2007) 141–51.

countries does not automatically lead to the necessity of fragmentation of the world order in a myriad of differentiated political units. We could trace back the thought of Amartya Sen to the philosophy of cosmopolitanism; his idea of multiple identities[94] in particular represents a strong argument for assuming that even if some preferences may be different in different countries, there are still indefinite numbers of other ways in which preferences may differ. Given the fact that personal identity is not determined exclusively by national belonging but rather a multitude of different group allegiances, it could be concluded that—following these identities—also people's preferences are not determined (only) by their nationality but also—and sometimes even more evidently—by their other identities of different natures: local, social, political, sexual and so on.

Transposing this line of reasoning to legal studies, the conclusion can be drawn that it makes little sense to claim that private law should be national because this reflects the preferences of the people, since there is no reason to consider those preferences depending exclusively on national identity. So, following the recurring example of a consumer, there are good reasons to believe that, independent of their nationality, most consumers share some basic preferences rooted in their identity as consumers, in certain cases overarching their identities as Portuguese, German, English and so on. Quite on the contrary, nationalist ideology tends to deny or at least underestimate such a plurality of identities, arguing that the national identity is the one that most notably shapes human identity.[95] Why then should private law operate exclusively at the national level?

3.1.2.2 Nationalist Perspective

Only liberal nationalists seem to be able to delineate a coherent theoretical justification in opposition to the points raised from a communitarian and a cosmopolitan perspective. As already mentioned in the first chapter, the liberal nationalist philosopher Miller claims that thinking that assigning responsibility for the rights and welfare of the 'Swedes to other Swedes' is convenient because of reasons of administrative ease and physical proximity would be a mistake.[96] The reason why they are 'better informed' than outsiders is rather that there is a *cultural similarity* between co-nationals.[97]

> Why does it make sense to assign responsibility for the rights and welfare of Swedes to other Swedes? […] Two bad answers to this question are physical proximity and administrative ease. Neither of these has any intrinsic connection with nationality. Physical proximity suggests taking responsibility for those in your locality regardless of their nationality. Administrative ease brings us back once again to states, as the institutions that are currently most effective in protecting rights and delivering welfare; but it

94 A Sen, *Identity and Violence. The Illusion of Destiny* (New York, Norton, 2006).

95 *See* Chapter 2, 1.3.2. 'Nation and Culture Coincide': 'Nationalism'.

96 D Miller, *On Nationality* (Oxford, Clarendon Press, 1995) 63.

97 Ibid, 63.

> provides no answer to such questions as, 'Why should the boundaries of the states be located here rather than there?' 'Why not have sub-national or supra-national units performing these tasks?' A better answer is that cultural similarities mean that co-nationals are better informed about one another than they are about outsiders, and therefore better placed to say, for example, when their fellows are in need, or are deprived of their rights.

Once this point, which is 'the strongest argument that can be given, from a universalistic point of view, for acknowledging special obligations to compatriots',[98] has been made, it makes no sense to ask whether it is fair that the state only takes care of its citizens' needs; if it did otherwise, its legislation would be on the one hand detrimental to its own citizens and, on the other hand, inefficient for outsiders—whose inscrutable real needs would not be understood by another nation-state. Knowledge is divorced from geographic proximity and comes to coincide with culture.

Such emphasis on the cultural element is easily explicable, since having abandoned criteria like *ethnos*, religion, and language, nationalists assumed a subjective/objective cultural criterion in order to determine who belongs to the nation. People sharing a culture also share a nationality.[99] The argument thus becomes to some extent circular: co-nationals know better each other's needs because they share the same culture, ie because they are co-nationals. This is a circularity which is determined by an alleged overlap between personal and collective identity: the nationalist theory of identity is built upon the assumption that each nation has a unique character, from which national characteristics stem and are shared by every citizen.[100] Given their theories on identity and culture which ignore the relevance of sub-national and supranational divisions and identities, liberal nationalists can simply pay no attention to questions like who is 'closer' to a non-geographical community or whether it is not more efficient to enact regional private laws to mirror better the interests of more restricted infra-national communities—those communities, in a liberal nationalist perspective, are simply irrelevant, as the political unit can only coincide with the national one. In this sense, the nationalist argument, mainly based on the assumption of the cultural similarity between citizens, may justify why even private law should be maintained national, avoiding furthermore the risk of a legal Balkanisation.

3.1.2.3 Cultural Similarity and the Economic Argument

The time has come to draw the threads of our discourse together. Provided that the philosophies of nationalism, cosmopolitanism and communitarianism would offer different answers to the question as to whether private law should be better

[98] Ibid, 63.

[99] D Miller, *Citizenship and National Identity* (Cambridge, Polity Press, 2000) 127.

[100] BC Shafer, *Faces of Nationalism. New Realities and Old Myths* (New York, Harcourt Brace Jovanovich, 1972) 249.

placed at the national or the European level, the question now arises whether the economic argument employed in the debate on Europeanisation can be linked to (liberal) nationalism—that is, if it presents the features of the nationalist argument. The reason why liberal nationalists deem the national level as the best governance level is not that there is some kind of geographical proximity—as the Hayekian model seems on the contrary to assume—but rather a cultural similarity within the nation. Since liberal nationalism bases its conclusions on an alleged cultural similarity of co-nationals, it should be verified whether also the economic argument as it has been used in the debate on Europeanisation assigns *cultural similarity* the pivotal role.

Probably with the intent of making up for one of the alleged weak points of economics—that is, to create abstract models that forget the particular specificities of certain contexts—law and economics authors who used the decentralisation theorem to object to Europeanisation indeed seem to put particular emphasis on the element of culture. While liberal nationalists speak of a kind of general culture that binds all nationals, legal scholars speak of a particular 'legal culture', which seems to be highly dependent on the nation. For instance, legal culture is present in the views of Gerhard Wagner, who acknowledges that legal diversity reflects different preferences that are expressions of cultural diversity[101] and therefore pleads for a European system characterised by more competition between legal orders instead of unification of contract law.[102] A similar point is made by Rachlinski, who adheres to the idea that different legal rules 'might be' the expression of different cultural norms. However, he adds an interesting perspective to the debate: different laws can be the product, more than different legal cultures, of different 'cognitive errors', but also these cognitive errors are mostly dependent on the national context and the particular national history: 'mistakes in judgment about risk, in particular, are so sensitive to context that minor variations in a nation's history or lawmaking process creates differential sensitivity to cognitive errors'.[103] Helmut Wagner emphasises the fact that preferences are not only a matter of personal predilections but also have a more objective dimension: variety of regulations or laws reflects variety of preferences, which in turn depends on different economic structures. The normative conclusion of this author is that harmonisation is not only undesirable, but rather radically impossible. He expresses in behavioral terms an argument which now sounds familiar to our ears:

> Harmonization of behavioral structures, and therefore of the forms of realization of formal law, cannot be ordered from above simply through a formal decree. In other words, uniformity of law cannot be created by just imposing rules through public policy.

[101] G Wagner, 'The Virtues of Diversity in European Private Law', in JM Smits (ed), *The Need for a European Contract Law. Empirical and Legal Perspectives* (Groningen, Europa Law Publishing, 2005) 1–24.

[102] Ibid', 15–16.

[103] JJ Rachlinski, 'The Psychology of Conflict of Laws', in JM Smits (ed), *The Need for a European Contract Law* (n 101), 111.

> Compliance with the law requires more than just rules. It must match the legal culture of a country.[104]

The point clearly echoes Savigny's criticism that the 'arbitrariness' of the legislator cannot affect the law, which is rather an expression of the 'spirit of the nation'—the *Volksgeist*, evidently defined in cultural terms and whose conceptual and historical links to German cultural nationalism have already been extensively discussed. Starting from the consideration that preferences are heterogeneous because they reflect diversity of economic structure, Wagner ends up alleging that rules are something more: the expression of a particular culture insensitive to the change imposed by political power. More exactly, such culture is the legal culture of a country so that culture—in its 'legal' version—and nationality come to coincide. But such harmony of nationality and culture is exactly the point on which liberal nationalist assumptions depend. Preferences are the expression of different 'cultures and lifestyles', while culture is assumed to be national. Consequently preferences are thought to be so strictly linked to the nation that 'the arguments in favour of decentralization become the more powerful the larger is the number of nations involved'.[105] There is no room for sub-national or non-national preferences.

The importance of the consequences that stem from the argument of legal culture are pivotal, since it is argued that the congruence of culture and nation makes it impossible for the legislator to modify rules that are rooted in the 'culture of the country'. The concept of legal culture would therefore deserve a specific account, which is furthermore highly needed if one considers the indeterminateness of the idea. This would of course go far beyond the aims of law and economic scholars, who therefore just tend to accept the interpretation that has been given by other scholars. Van den Bergh, for instance, refers[106] to the ideas made famous by the comparative lawyer Pierre Legrand, whose conclusion consists in the 'impossibility of legal transplants' because of the cultural roots of private law rules. Legal culture therefore hinders plans for legal harmonisation in several ways and the economic costs to supersede this obstacle would outweigh the benefits of harmonisation, which is for sure a strong counter-argument, even if economic data were to confirm the need of harmonisation which is propagandised in particular by the European Commission. In conclusion:

> The transaction cost savings stressed by the Commission may be outweighed by the costs of formulating uniform principles, reaching agreement on common principles, formulating new rules in accordance with these principles and subsequently adapting national legal systems. The latter costs should not be underestimated, since private law is deeply entrenched in national legal culture: the legal language, the conceptual structure and procedures may vary significantly across jurisdictions.[107]

[104] H Wagner, 'Economic Analysis of Cross-Border Legal Uncertainty' (n 59), 42.
[105] R van den Bergh, 'Private Law in a Globalizing World' (n 4), 92.
[106] R van den Bergh, 'Forced Harmonisation of Contract Law in Europe' (n 8), 254.
[107] Ibid, 254.

At last, thus, the economic argument flows into a 'cultural argument' that intends culture mainly in national terms and according to which cultural diversity among nations determine different preferences and impedes the application of laws which are expressions of different cultural traditions. Even the more explicitly economic dimension of contract law is 'conditioned by and embedded in cultural understandings and identity',[108] so that it becomes clear that the whole process of Europeanisation will have to deal with the diversity in legal cultures of the Member States. The degree to which such 'cultural argument' can in turn be related to nationalism must be further investigated.

3.2 THE SOCIAL ARGUMENT

Those who employ the economic argument to oppose Europeanisation assume that divergences in preferences in different nations would require different private laws instead of a unified or highly harmonised supranational system. A similar point, anyway, could also be made to affirm that a highly harmonised legal system would produce results that are not only inefficient from an economic perspective, but even undesirable from a viewpoint mainly concerned with different values, like first and foremost social justice. This is a concern in particular for those who advocate that private law should contribute to the establishment of a society that pursues not only economic welfare but also ideals of justice and that it is now time for the European institutions to move on from the classic market-functionalist approach.[109]

Among scholars interested in the subject of European private law, the social argument has hardly ever been employed to object to the European harmonisation project *tout court*; nonetheless, those who are particularly concerned with the dimension of social justice have often proved to perceive plans of forced harmonisation as a possible danger to the social character of private law of Europe. This position is actually even more widespread outside the scholarly legal debate, where a form of left-wing Euroscepticism has developed, based on the concern that the European Union is the Trojan horse for neoliberal politics detrimental to social justice. What is then the relevance of the social dimension for European private law? Keeping the example which has been made previously, the choice for a given level of consumer protection, that underlines several rules of consumer law such as the ones that make the right of withdrawal non-disposable, attains for sure at economic evaluations—as law and economic scholars have already pointed out—but even more importantly also at basic considerations of justice. Several

[108] R Sefton-Green, 'Social Justice and European Identity in European Contract Law' (2006) 2 *European Review of Contract Law* 275–86, 277.

[109] Study Group on Social Justice in European Private Law, 'Social Justice in European Contract Law: A Manifesto' (2004) 10 *European Law Journal*, 653–74; H Collins, 'La giustizia contrattuale in Europa', in A Somma (ed), *Giustizia sociale e mercato nel diritto europeo dei contratti* (Torino, Giappichelli, 2007) 105.

mandatory contract law rules are indeed aimed at restraining private autonomy in order to ensure the protection of those subjects that under certain circumstances are presumed to be 'weaker' than other contracting parties. In this sense, rules that aim to make up for such an imbalance and re-establish a contracting equilibrium can be considered social contract law.[110]

However, people could have different preferences; some might think that the consumers' inexperience and informative deficit makes it 'fair' to derogate from the principle that agreements must be kept, while others might dispute this view, calling upon the authority of ancient legal principles. The unfair terms directive offers an even clearer example: while the text provides a list of terms that can be considered unfair, it is first necessary to understand what is concretely meant by the concept of 'unfairness' referred to by the directive. From this point of view, the specification that a term is unfair when it determines in a specific case a significant imbalance in the parties' rights is not completely satisfactory, as we still need a preliminary conception of fairness in order to consider an imbalance significant for the purposes of the directive. As a result, what is considered an unfair term somewhere could be acceptable somewhere else, leading to problems for legal uniformity in Europe. In other words, the 'idea of just' is not univocal but rather can change in different opinions and contexts. A unified legal regime—say, a European norm deeming the invalidity of a particular contract term or establishing a non-disposable right of withdrawal for weak contracting parties—could only entail *one* of these different ideas of what is just, so that the imposition of that rule on people who do not share the same value would end up producing *unjust* results.

This can have important practical consequences in the dynamics of the harmonisation process; if their aim is to establish a uniform system, European institutions will have to opt for one specific idea of justice through a political decision. It is exactly this aspect that leads to concerns among those interested in justice; it has been pointed out that given the market-functionalist approach of the Commission,[111] it is likely that European rules could be less protective than national ones, resulting in a de-socialisation of private law. For instance, Nordic systems seem to be more protective of the weaker party than other European legal orders and if European rules were to mirror the values—therefore the idea of justice and consequently the level of consumer protection[112]—of Central, Southern

[110] T Wilhelmsson, *Social Contract Law and European Integration* (Aldershot, Dartmouth, 1995).

[111] B Lurger, 'The Common Frame of Reference/Optional Code and the Various Understandings of Social Justice in Europe', in T Wilhelmsson, E Paunio and A Pohjolainen (eds) *Private Law and the Many Cultures of Europe* (Alphen aan den Rijn, Kluwer Law International) 197.

[112] For sure, justice, solidarity and consumer protection cannot be seen as synonyms, in particular '[c]onsumer protection is not a measure of social policy in the traditional sense. It does not only concentrate on the protection of the really poor and needy', B Lurger, 'The "Social" Side of Contract Law and the New Principle of Regard and Fairness', in A Hartkamp, MW Hesselink, EW Hondius, C Mak and E du Perron (eds), *Towards a European Civil Code. Fourth and Expanded Edition* (The Hague, Kluwer Law International, 2011) 369.

or Eastern Europeans countries, the impact of European law on Nordic laws would be detrimental to consumers. Such European rules would be perceived as unjust in those countries, almost certainly leading to resistance. This risk is actually concrete: even if the academic project of the CFR acknowledges justice the status of fundamental principle, there are still completely different understandings of the meaning of the concept of justice,[113] while the DCFR seems to opt for the traditional notion of corrective justice, in so doing showing quite a conservative approach.[114] This would furthermore create a dangerous path, as in the scenario of the competition between legal orders a process of imitation could arise, possibly fostered by the creation of a new optional legal regime. In this sense, even empirical data seem to confirm that forms of 'social dumping' could crop up.[115] More in general, European directives seem to delineate a concept of justice that is functional to the access of the market, and can therefore be termed access justice, in possible and easy contrast with national understandings.[116]

However, results perceived as being unjust would be produced even in the opposite case—in other words, if particularly elevated standards of justice were imposed on people whose conception of those values is different. This would be the case if European rules were to introduce solidarity elements in a context that favours a more individualistic approach, as it seems to be the case with the English common law or more recently with the new Member States. This seems to point to the conclusion that attenuation of legal diversity in matters of social justice will produce per se unjust results.

3.2.1 Social Justice in the European Context

It is necessary to address briefly the question of social justice in private law, in order to understand what the practical relevance of the theoretical discussion is. At first sight, the problem could seem exclusively theoretical, as 'justice' is one of those redundant words that abound in the speeches of philosophers and politicians, but that would be out of place in the reasoning of a private lawyer. The question of social justice is nonetheless only one of the aspects of the question as to the political nature of private law, while discussions as to the social character of private law in Europe are particularly deep-rooted and of substantial practical

[113] H Eidenmüller, F Faust, HC Grigoleit, N Jansen, G Wagner and R Zimmermann (2008) 'Der Gemeinsame Referenzrahmen für das Europäische Privatrecht. Wertungsfragen und Kodifikationsprobleme' 11 *JuristenZeitung* 529–84, 671.

[114] MW Hesselink (2008) *CFR & Social Justice* (Munich, Sellier) 62.

[115] J Rutgers, 'Het (a)sociale gezicht van Europa: kanttekeningen bij het optioneel instrument' in MW Hesselink, A van Hoek, M Loos and A Salomons (eds), *Het Groenboek Europees contractenrecht: naar een optioneel instrument?* (The Hague, Boom, 2011) 125–32.

[116] H-W Micklitz, 'Introduction. Social Justice and Access Justice in Private Law', in H-W Micklitz (ed), *The Many Concepts of Social Justice in European Private Law* (Northampton MA, Edward Elgar Publishing, 2011) 3–57.

relevance. It would here suffice to mention the well-known and fierce criticism of Otto von Gierke to the first draft of the BGB, blamed for being too individualistic and insensitive to the social question, which led to the introduction of the two famous 'drops of socialist oil' in the definitive version of that code. Though it is indeed only after the development of a mature form of capitalism and the consequent rise of socialism that the 'social question' started affecting more and more private law,[117] it cannot be denied that the pursuit of some idea of justice has always represented one of the objectives also of any private law system. This for sure still leaves open the question as to what model of justice has to underlie private law—the traditional view being that this should only be some kind of commutative justice in an Aristotelian sense.

While this is not the place to tackle the intricate issues of social justice in private law, it can be noticed here that within the European context the topic has become particularly topical, at least after the publication in 2004 of a Manifesto for Social Justice in European Contract Law,[118] elaborated and undersigned by numerous European comparative and private law scholars. The Manifesto in particular denounces the technocratic approach adopted by the European bodies with the aim of hiding from the citizens the real political issues[119] and blames the institutions for chiefly pursuing an economic agenda that disregards social issues;[120] in this sense, European rules are mainly thought to foster trans-border commerce, leaving aside aspects of social justice.[121] The European Union admittedly appears as 'unbalanced in that the economics enjoys primacy over social concerns'.[122] But while it is understandable that the European communities—born as an international organisation with limited competences in the field of the economy—at least initially issued rules aimed at achieving economic objectives, in the actual scenario which is characterised by an enlargement of competences and the swift towards a quasi-federal structure, there is a concrete risk that the Europeanisation of more and more aspects of private law will lead to a system exclusively inspired by the idea of efficiency rather than justice—which has always been ingrained in private law. As the Manifesto states,

> The Commission, quite properly, addresses issues within the framework of its own competence and the powers of the European Community. It is extremely doubtful that the European Treaty confers powers on European institutions to enact a European law of

[117] *See* G Solari, *Socialismo e diritto privato. Influenza delle odierne dottrine socialiste sul diritto privato* [1906] (Milano, Giuffrè, 1980).

[118] Study Group on Social Justice in European Private Law, 'Social Justice in European Contract Law: A Manifesto', 653–74.

[119] Ibid, 655–56.

[120] The criticism that 'a discussion on the political, economic and social implications of contract law was almost completely avoided' had already been made by B Lurger, 'The "Social" Side of Contract Law and the New Principle of Regard and Fairness', 380.

[121] Study Group on Social Justice in European Private Law, 'Social Justice in European Contract Law: A Manifesto' (n 118), 660–62.

[122] H-W Micklitz, 'Failure or Ideological Preconceptions—Thoughts on Two Grand Projects: The European Constitution and the European Civil Code' (2010) *EUI Working Paper 2010/4* 1–25, 3.

> contract, once this project is understood as setting an agenda that necessarily goes beyond measures of integration of the single market. Thus, to progress any further with any rapidity, the agenda has had to be confined to an examination of technical problems, and more fundamental political questions have had to be suppressed. But there is a real danger that, by ignoring these political issues, we will end up with a lop-sided European contract law: one that furthers market integration, but is inadequate to secure social justice.[123]

But given the problems represented by the difficult compatibility of justice and harmonisation, how would it be possible to promote justice through European private law? In the words of the Manifesto, the creation of a harmonised system of law that takes into account questions of social justice is not only possible but even desirable. Interestingly enough, the Manifesto considers that 'a shared vision of social justice in the market order would provide the basis for greater approximation of national laws'[124] still respecting the cultural diversity of the states. This is indeed remarkable, as the basic objection to harmonisation from the social perspective would seem to be that if a 'shared vision of social justice' lacks and rather there are several visions linked to the cultural specificities of the different Member States, it becomes impossible to achieve harmonisation and to respect social justice at the same time.

Unfortunately, the concrete way in which such a reconciliation of shared values and respect for diversity—if it exists—should be brought about is not explicitly addressed by the Manifesto, so that opinions as to this pivotal aspect diverge even among the members of the Social Justice Group itself. The generic words adopted by the Manifesto indeed allowed different and opposite views to coexist within the group itself, where at least two main different currents of opinion were represented: those considering that respect for differences and the preservation of diversity of culture is per se an aspect of justice, and those sustaining that cultural diversity and social justice are rather separated issues.[125] The idea that preservation of cultural diversity is in itself a matter of justice is sustained in particular by Sefton-Green[126] while it is denied by Collins, who rather argues that '[w]e do not need to conserve the differences between national private law systems for the sake of social justice'. However, while the question whether diversity is part of justice is debated, the idea that where conceptions of justice are different harmonisation should not intervene is more widespread.[127]

[123] Study Group on Social Justice in European Private Law, 'Social Justice in European Contract Law: A Manifesto', 664.

[124] Ibid, 673.

[125] On this fracture within the Study Group, *see* H Collins, 'Does Social Justice Require the Preservation of Diversity in the Private Laws of Member States of Europe?', in T Wilhelmsson, E Paunio and A Pohjolainen (eds), *Private Law and the Many Cultures of Europe* (Alphen aan den Rijn, Kluwer Law International, 2007) 155 ff.

[126] R Sefton-Green, 'Social Justice and European Identity in European Contract Law' (n 108), 275–86.

[127] H Collins, 'Does Social Justice Require the Preservation of Diversity?' (n 125), 175.

3.2.1.1 Normative Implications of the Argument

Analogously to what we have seen with regard to the economic argument, two normative consequences can be derived in order not to produce unjust results by means of Europeanisation. In the first place, the process of 'forced' legal harmonisation—by means of mandatory interventions of the European institutions—should be stopped, in order to avoid the imposition on people of legal rules that they would perceive as being unjust. As national systems show divergences in underlying values, in particular the idea of a uniform code is not particularly appealing.[128] As an alternative, Europeanisation could continue only at the cost of overlooking questions of social justice or dealing with those questions only at a particularly abstract level. Rather than a suggestion, this second scenario is depicted as a risk for the movement towards higher harmonisation and even a particularly concrete one, if one only considers the specific dynamics of Europeanisation, which tend to generalise (and at the same time instrumentalise) minimum liberal principles included in the 'bourgeoisie' codifications of the Member States. In this sense, a return to liberalism would be the 'price to be paid' for a 'harmonized Europeanisation' which at this point sounds less appealing than a more social-justice-friendly fragmented one.[129]

In both cases, the social argument does not exclude the possibility of a future agreement between the Member States—similar to the idea advanced in law and economics to favour international rather than supranational instruments—that permits to elaborate a common scheme of social justice, which would also be an important step on the way toward the construction of a European identity.[130] However, as long as 'the differences between national legal systems reveal divergent views about desired patterns of social welfare', the promotion of social justice can only 'encourag[e] further dialogue' instead of requiring imperative political interventions.[131] Harmonisation in this area should not be abandoned, but rather postponed. Practically, this would amount to an exclusion of social contract law from the European level and its allocation at the national one, where it has traditionally resided. The historical trend—evident to political scientists—of consigning social solidarity to the nation-state is therefore confirmed also in the debate on social justice in private law.[132]

[128] R Sefton-Green, 'Cultural Diversity and the Idea of a European Civil Code', in MW Hesselink (ed), *The Politics of a European Civil Code* (The Hague, Kluwer Law International, 2006) 71–88, 79.

[129] T Wilhelmsson, 'Private Law in the EU: Harmonized or Fragmented Europeanisation?' (2002) 10 *European Review of Private Law* 77–94, 84 ff.

[130] R Sefton-Green, 'Social Justice and European Identity in European Contract Law' (n 108), 286.

[131] H Collins, 'Does Social Justice Require the Preservation of Diversity?' (n 125), 175. In the same sense JM Smits, *The Good Samaritan in European Private Law: On the Perils of Principles without a Programme and a Programme for the Future* (Deventer, Kluwer, 2000) 45, declares to 'believe in as much uniformity as is possible without sacrificing national moralities in Europe'.

[132] J Habermas, 'The European Nation-State and the Pressure of Globalization' (1999) 235 *New Left Review* 46–59, 57.

3.2.1.2 Absence of a European Model of Justice

Allegedly, harmonisation of social contract law could be satisfactorily realised only if there were a consensus in Europe as to fundamental values such as the protection of weaker parties. It is therefore suggested that until Member States reach a sufficient agreement as to certain values—not all of them easily sharable by all states—mandatory intervention is not a desirable option.[133] In other words, a highly harmonised system of law requires the existence of a common social and cultural background[134] without which uniform rules would necessarily disrespect this particular relativistic dimension of justice.

Nowadays, if uniform rules were to be established, we would have to admit that there exists something as a common European idea of justice or a whole of sufficiently shared values exist: this is something that some authors both in sociology and legal studies tend to deny, affirming that not even in Europe is the 'European social model' universal,[135] or more radically, that there are some insuperable differences as to those values.[136] Critics claim that the proposed idea of a Europeanisation of tort law rests upon the idea that different national ideas of justice—one French, one German, one Dutch and so on—should be replaced by a sole European justice,[137] which nonetheless does not seem to exist at the present day. Not even in contract law can one find a uniformity of views as to the idea of social justice that should inspire rules. While European Union law seems to be developing a new concept of justice which is different from the traditional 'social' understanding of the nation-state and rather qualifies as 'access'

[133] R Sefton-Green, 'Cultural Diversity and the Idea of a European Civil Code' (n 128), 87–88.

[134] R Goode, 'Contract and Commercial Law: The Logic and Limits of Harmonisation' (2003) 7(4) *Electronic Journal of Comparative Law*.

[135] R Dahrendorf, *Why Europe? On the Purposes of the EU after Enlargement* (Maastricht, Universiteit Maastricht, 2004) 17: 'It is of course not the model of the United Kingdom. Nor is it the model of most of the new members of the European Union, because they are far too poor to introduce the kind of welfare state that is characteristic of older members of the European Union. So one can have doubts about the importance of the European social model. Still, it is a subject that concerns Europeans—and if one reads carefully, a subject that appears in the treaty'.

[136] R Sefton-Green, 'Cultural Diversity and the Idea of a European Civil Code' (n 128), 78–79.

[137] MG Faure and T Hartlief 'Naar een harmonisatie van aansprakelijkheidsrecht in Europa? Een kritisch rechtseconomisch perspectief', (n 33), 176: 'Waarom zou een Duits slachtoffer van een ongeval in Spanje minder vergaand moeten worden beschermd in het Spaanse aansprakelijkheidsrecht dan "thuis"? In het verlengde van het voorgaande ligt een argument dat voor voorstanders wellicht belangrijker is dan zij in eerste instantie willen toegeven: verschillen behoren als zodanig te worden vermeden, juist omdat wij inmiddels in een Europees verband samenleven waarin geen ruimte meer zou bestaan voor een Franse, Duitse of Nederlandse rechtvaardigheid. Wij hebben zojuist als typisch voorbeeld van een dergelijke benadering Magnus en Fedtke opgevoerd. Waar men dan kennelijk vanuit gaat is dat er zoiets bestaat als een "Europese" rechtvaardigheid die aanspraak op algemene gelding kan maken'. Also MW Hesselink, *CFR & Social Justice. A short study for the European Parliament on the Values underlying the draft Common Frame of Reference for European Private Law: What Roles for Fairness and Social Justice?* (Munich, Sellier, 2008) 27, points out that a lower degree of Europeanisation is the price to be paid for higher (local) foreseeability.

justice,[138] conceptions of social justice at the national level continue to diverge.[139] Wilhelmsson, for instance, distinguished different 'varieties of welfarism'[140] that reflect on contract law systems too. These varieties are characterised by different policy choices made in striking a balance between the opposite values of contractual freedom and fairness. According to this view, it seems that at the present day 'no agreement exists among Member States on where to draw the line between the two principles of contractual freedom and regard and fairness: the strong liberal traditions of some Member States are confronted with traditions of strong social protection of others'.[141]

3.2.1.3 Fundamental Rights, Justice and Harmonisation

In order to verify whether a convergence exists at the operational level of the legal rule, it is of primary importance to look at the activities of the courts rather than just at the black letter rule, and this holds true also for those who intend to verify whether shared conceptions of justice exist in the European systems. Certainly, in civil law jurisdictions judges' hands are relatively tied, since their main task is the application of statutes they do not create. However, even adhering to a strictly positivist vision of the legal system, the judiciary can still play a fundamental role in instilling social values in private law in the rooms of autonomy courts still have in those systems. General clauses are a typical example of such room for autonomy, as they still need to be filled with contents that are not laid down in statutes. An instrument which is increasingly employed by judges in order to fill those rooms of autonomy and achieve just outcomes consists in making reference to overarching and super-primary principles of the legal orders and for this purpose, a particular importance has been assumed in recent years by the category of fundamental human rights that are normally laid down in national constitutions and international conventions.[142]

While it is in general evident that a process of 'constitutionalisation of private law' is underway in Europe,[143] it is still discussed whether the *Drittwirkung* of

[138] H-W Micklitz, 'Introduction. Social Justice and Access Justice in Private Law' (n 116); KP Purnhagen, 'The Architecture of Post-National European Contract Law from a Phenomenological Perspective—A Question of Institutions' (2011) *CSECL Working Paper* 25 1–19.

[139] *See* H-W Micklitz (ed), *The Many Concepts of Social Justice in European Private Law* (Northampton MA, Edward Elgar Publishing, 2011).

[140] T Whilhelmsson, 'Varieties of Welfarism in European Contract Law' (2004) 10 *European Law Journal* 712–33.

[141] B Lurger, 'The Common Frame of Reference/Optional Code and the Various Understandings of Social Justice in Europe' (n 111), 192.

[142] *See* C Mak, *Fundamental Rights in European Contract Law. A Comparison of the Impact of Fundamental Rights on Contractual Relationships in Germany, the Netherlands, Italy and England* (Alphen aan den Rijn, Kluwer Law International, 2008).

[143] Ibid, on the development of the theories of direct and indirect effect in particular 46 ff. On the constitutionalisation of contract law, A Colombi Ciacchi, 'The Constitutionalization of European Contract Law: Judicial Convergence and Social Justice' (2006) 2 *European Review of Contract Law* 167–80.

constitutional provisions should be direct or rather indirect. In the former case, these norms will directly address private citizens so that the distinction between public and private is overcome; in the latter case, on the contrary, constitutional provisions will address citizens only through private law rules that will have to be interpreted in light of those overarching principles. In this latter strategy general clauses play a particular role. Tort law also clearly benefits from a dialogue with constitutional principles, as has happened notably in Italy, so that for example the list of constitutionally protected interests of several charters of rights can help the judge and the interpreter understand which damages can be recovered.[144]

Thus, while the legislator instills social justice mainly by means of mandatory rules, judges instill social justice by mainly interpreting open clauses in light of constitutional provisions and fundamental rights. Making use of this technique, judges have contributed to nuancing the traditionally conservative character of private law systems and introducing elements of solidarity.[145] Such use of fundamental rights in case-law represents an interesting development from a historical perspective. While early socialists criticised the concept of human rights—in particular those laid down in the revolutionary *Déclaration des droits de l'Homme et du Citoyen*—as an essentially bourgeois concept elaborated to hallow individualistic principles to the detriment of the working classes,[146] in contemporary legal systems fundamental rights have evolved into a more social 'second generation' and have been mainly employed by judges (also constitutional judges) to restrict individualistic principles in order to ensure solidarity and protect the weaker subjects. If this is true, then a form of harmonisation of social contract law could spontaneously take place or at least be more easily achieved by means of supranational instruments. Indeed, not only comparative private lawyers have made efforts to identify a 'common core' of the European systems: public lawyers also discuss the existence of a European 'constitutional heritage',[147] which is an expression frequently employed by the Court of Justice of the European Union to underline how the European institutions respect fundamental rights that Member States already recognise.

That convergence can be achieved by means of the activity of national courts is, however, not self-evident, and two criticisms can actually emerge. In the first place, it remains to be seen whether such a constitutional heritage in Europe actually exists or is rather a rhetorical formula used to advance the process of construction of a European identity. If it is true that most European constitutions take their roots in the same historical period or exhibit ideological links, some aspects may still diverge in particular when it comes to the most controversial social rights and the definition of the role of the welfare state. The enlargement

[144] C Mak, *Fundamental Rights in European Contract Law* (n 142), 38 ff.

[145] G Alpa, *L'arte di giudicare* (Roma, Laterza, 1996) 3 ff.

[146] *See* K Marx, 'Zur Judenfrage', in K Marx and F Engels, *Werke. Band 1* (Berlin, Karl Dietz Verlag, 1988) 364–67.

[147] A Pizzorusso, *Il patrimonio costituzionale europeo* (Bologna, il Mulino, 2002).

of the Union to include Central and Eastern countries—for whom constitutions mostly symbolise the transition from a different political context from the one experienced in Western countries—can only increase this complexity.[148] In the second place and more importantly, even if constitutions show similar wordings, the concrete interpretation of those provisions may take diverging paths in different jurisdictions. Needless to say that such risk is not theoretical at all, considering that constitutional provisions are by their very nature broad and principles need to be balanced with each other. The basic question is, therefore, whether the fundamental rights and values that are laid down in international conventions and national constitutions can 'represent a "common core" of European principles and values that could further the harmonization of the contract laws of EU Member States'.[149] In this respect, while some scholars think that a certain degree of convergence can already be detected in the judgments of different courts in Europe,[150] other commentators warn that constitutional values are not reliable instruments for achieving unity, as they are such general concepts that their understanding essentially differ in different Member States.[151]

The problem could seem to be exclusively technical: given that a uniform interpretation is not provided by any court, national interpretations have no guidance and therefore diverge. In this case, a central court with the aim of providing a uniform interpretation could at least reduce the problem, but at the present day a similar institution does not exist and it is very unlikely that it will be created in the near future, as it would first have to obtain the legal competence to interpret national constitutional provisions, which does not seem constitutionally and politically viable. But more importantly, these divergences do not appear to be merely accidental; they are rather expressions of diverging policy considerations; indeed '[o]ur constitutions are said to encapsulate fundamental values of the polity and this, in turn, is said to be a reflection of our collective identity as a people, as a nation, as a state, as a Community, as a Union'.[152] If this is indeed true, it would not suffice to confer the authority of interpreting these provisions to a supranational court (which is, as already said, a politically titanic undertaking), as this would amount to an imposition of certain values on people who do not share

[148] 'The enlargement decision has been the single most important constitutional decision taken in the last decade and arguably longer. For good or for bad, the change in the number of Member States, in Europe's population size, in its geography and topography and its cultural and political mix are all on a scale of magnitude which will make the new Europe a very, very different polity independently of any constitutional structure adopted', according to JHH Weiler, 'A Constitution for Europe? Some Hard Choices' (2004) 40 *Journal of Common Market Studies* 563–80, 564.

[149] C Mak, 'Harmonising Effects of Fundamental Rights in European Contract Law' (2006) 1 *Erasmus Law Review* 59–79, 61.

[150] A Colombi Ciacchi, 'The Constitutionalization of European Contract Law' 177–78, concludes that 'national courts all across Europe tend to refer to Constitutions and human rights to promote social and distributive justice, equality, democracy and laicism in contract law. This is true both for the horizontal application of social rights and traditional fundamental rights and liberties.'

[151] JM Smits, 'Human Dignity and Uniform Law: An Unhappy Relationship' (2008) *TICOM Working Paper 2008/2* 2–10, 10.

[152] JHH Weiler, 'A Constitution for Europe?' (n 148), 569.

them. In this sense, the fact that interpretations diverge in Europe would be not only due to the technical circumstance that a central authority in charge of giving a uniform version is lacking.

The differences in fundamental values then reflect on private law when judges employ constitutional concepts to give substance to open rules like good faith, good morals and so on. If it is true that 'the norm that contracts against public policy should have no effect may be universal, [...] it should be filled with *national* [*sic*] conceptions of what these fundamental principles mean'.[153] Critics then argue that even if the category of fundamental rights can be employed to 'warn' the interpreter in exceptional situations in which the outcome of legal rules is too severe or unjust, as a matter of facts these concepts remain 'inherently vague',[154] maybe too much to fit into the systematic coherence of a private law system. The new list of fundamental rights of the Charter of Nice is not much help in this sense.[155] As there is no universal conception as of yet, 'we should stop claiming that the use of fundamental rights in private law offers any real guidance in the harmonization process';[156] by the same token, concepts like human dignity or public policy are 'essentially local and we should not try to harmonize them on basis of common principles or rules'.[157]

3.2.1.4 The Stance of European Law

The idea that differences in the interpretation of constitutional concepts are a manifestation of different fundamental values in societies seems to inspire the case-law of the Court of Justice of the European Union, as the famous *Omega* case shows. Specifically, this was not exactly a private law case, but its implications for that field of law too are self-evident. On that occasion, on the basis of the public law clause of public policy (*öffentliche Ordnung*), German authorities impeded the commercialisation of a laser game for the simulation of killing of people, considered to be offensive of the 'human dignity' that is guaranteed by the German Constitution. As in the concrete case, this decision amounted to a limitation on the freedom to provide services and of movements of goods guaranteed by the European treaties, the national judge who had to adjudicate the issue referred to the Court of Justice in order to know whether it was 'compatible with the provisions on freedom to provide services and the free movement of goods contained in the Treaty establishing the European Community for a particular commercial activity—in this case the operation of a so called "laserdrome" involving simulated killing action—to be prohibited under national law because it offends the values enshrined in the constitution'. Confronted by the question, the European Court

[153] JM Smits, 'Human Dignity and Uniform Law' (n 151), 7.
[154] Ibid, 10.
[155] JHH Weiler, 'A Constitution for Europe?' (n 148), 586–77.
[156] JM Smits, 'Human Dignity and Uniform Law' (n 151), 6.
[157] Ibid, 10.

recognised the legitimacy of the prohibition of commercialisation of the game in Germany, confirming its previous case-law pursuant to which the protection of constitutional values may limit European fundamental freedoms and added that respect for human dignity is a common principle shared by all European countries. At the same time, nevertheless, the Court avoided inferring the existence of a general European understanding of human dignity, specifying that '[i]t is not indispensable in that respect for the restrictive measure issued by the authorities of a Member State to correspond to a conception shared by all Member States as regards the precise way in which the fundamental right or legitimate interest in question is to be protected'[158] and that 'the specific circumstances which may justify recourse to the concept of public policy may vary from one country to another and from one era to another'.[159]

In light of this judgment, although the protection of human dignity can be said to be part of the European constitutional heritage—as we can find this or analogous principles laid down not only in the German *Grundgesetz* but in many other charters—its concrete relevance for the interpretation of ordinary rules end up varying between different countries. In the specific case, for instance, the decision of the German authorities could be justified by the fact that Germany may be more sensitive when it comes to constitutional values and human dignity probably because of its dramatic history,[160] while other countries like the United Kingdom may be more liberal and allow the game, although protection of human dignity is obviously a value in both nations. The reference to the 'specific circumstances' that differ between 'countries' and 'eras'—which per se pretty much resembles the ideas of *Volksgeist* and *Zeitgeist*—alludes to the fact that even values which are more or less universal end up taking different shapes when applied in different contexts.

The 'localist' decision of the European court can be read in political terms too. The solution is, of course, moderate and aimed at avoiding important domino repercussions for the European system. The Court of Justice would have otherwise created a common European interpretation of human dignity valid for all countries. Furthermore, interpreting a concept which is laid down in a national constitution, it would have ended up invading an extremely sensitive area of competence of the national institutions and in particular the constitutional courts, likely giving rise to new tensions between the European judge and the national highest courts. In this sense, the judgment of the Court should not be taken as a statement as to the necessarily localist nature of general concepts like human dignity and the resulting impossibility of elaborating trans-national notions of it. The case is, rather, telling of a new tendency on the part of the Court of Justice: less exuberant than some time ago, the Court is in this particular historical

[158] Court of Justice, Omega, C-36/02, para. 37.

[159] Ibid, para. 31.

[160] S Sánchez Lorenzo, 'What Do We Mean when We Say "Folklore"? Cultural and Axiological Diversity as a Limit for a European Private Law' (2006) 2 *European Review of Private Law* 197–219, 211.

moment more interested in a constitutional dialogue with Member States rather than in imposing politically important decisions on them. In this sense, it prefers to refer to the constitutional values of the Member States rather than directly stating what those values entail.[161]

In this light, European projects of directives or other instruments that contain open norms—good faith, unconscionability, good morals, etc—would not really help the process of harmonisation. This tendency to employ open norms has been the object of several criticisms based on the habitual twofold argument that on the one hand, the vagueness of these provisions necessarily increases legal uncertainty,[162] and on the other hand, general clauses represent the delegation of the task of defining standards of justice from the legislator to non-democratically legitimated judges.[163] As a matter of fact, not even the academic projects of private law codification/compilation seem to take a clear position with regard to this aspect. It is difficult to imagine how the trend of the Court of Justice could be reconciled with the dispositions contained, for instance, in the DCFR. This instrument indeed limits itself to establishing the nullity of those contracts that infringe 'a principle recognised as fundamental in the laws of the Member States of the European Union'.[164] Not even other academic projects of European codification directly cope with this aspect. The Gandolfi Code, for example, reads that contracts should have a lawful content that is not contrary to mandatory rules laid down in the code itself, 'in Community or national laws, nor to public policy or morals',[165] while comments do not explicitly address the issue of the national or supranational nature of the concepts. The proposal for a Common European Sales Law even plainly ignores the question, not referring to public policy and good morals. The (deliberately?) vague wording of the DCFR had immediately led to doubts and questions as to the correct interpretation of the rule, in particular as to what these fundamental principles are, or, in other words, 'from where' these come: are these principles common to the Member States, so that they should be acknowledged in all countries, or can they also be national ones (similar to mandatory rules)?[166] Despite the vagueness of the wording, the commentary to the DCFR makes some points clear, to begin with specifying *what*

[161] LFM Besselink, 'National and Constitutional Identity Before and After Lisbon' (2010) 6 *Utrecht Law Review* 36–49. On the judicial dialogue between national and supranational courts, A Torres Pérez, *Conflicts of Rights in the European Union. A Theory of Supranational Adjudication* (Oxford, Oxford University Press, 2009) 112 ff.

[162] H Eidenmüller, F Faust, HC Grigoleit, N Jansen, G Wagner and R Zimmermann, 'Der Gemeinsame Referenzrahmen für das Europäische Privatrecht', 69. *See* also A Zoppini, 'La concorrenza tra gli ordinamenti giuridici', in A Zoppini (ed), *La concorrenza tra ordinamenti giuridici* (Roma, Laterza, 2004) 33–34.

[163] H Collins, 'La giustizia contrattuale in Europa' (n 109), 100–1.

[164] Article II.-7:301 DCFR.

[165] Art 30, *Avant-projet, Code europeen des contrats* (Milano, Giuffrè, 2004).

[166] On this aspect, *see* JW Rutgers, 'The Draft Common Frame of Reference, Public Policy, Mandatory Rules and the Welfare State', in A Somma (ed), *The Politics of the Draft Common Frame of Reference* (Alphen aan den Rijn, Kluwer Law International, 2009).

fundamental principles are (a concept which is, already in the introduction to the DCFR, 'susceptible to different interpretations'[167]): these are here general 'constitutional' principles like those laid down in the ECHR and the Treaty of Nice. The commentary—echoing the PECL—explains that the aim of the provision is:

> To avoid the varying national concepts of immorality, illegality at common law, public policy, *ordre public* and *bonos mores* [*sic*], by invoking a necessarily broad idea of fundamental principles found across the European Union, including EU law [...] Merely national concepts as such have no effect under the Article and may not be invoked directly, although comparative study can give further help in the identification and elucidation of principles recognized as fundamental in the laws of the Member States.[168]

While the conception of fundamental principles is therefore pan-European and does not take into account local variations, it still admits that '[t]he public policy underpinning principles recognised as fundamental may change over time, in accordance with the prevailing norms of society as they develop'.[169] Thus, a social understanding of certain values can evolve, but not vary among countries: the *Zeitgeist* remains, while the national *Volksgeist* is ignored. In this sense, the DCFR goes much beyond the Court of Justice in *Omega*.

3.2.2 The Argument in Light of Different Political Theories

The idea that a strong sense of solidarity does not exist amongst the European countries along with a shared understanding of justice and that this represents an obstacle for European economic integration has been expressed for decades in the economics and political science. It was already Hayek—an author normally opposed to nationalism—who highlighted that such flaw would result in the systematic oppression of smaller nations by larger communities, while the lurking risk remains that 'as there is less community of views, the necessity to rely on force and coercion increases':[170]

> Who imagines that there exists any common ideals of distributive justice such as will make the Norwegian fisherman consent to forgo the prospect of economic improvement in order to help his Portuguese fellow, or the Dutch worker to pay more for his bicycle

[167] Already in the outline edition C von Bar, E Clive, H Schulte-Nölke et al (eds), *Principles, Definitions and Model Rules of European Private Law. Draft Common Frame of Reference (DCFR). Outline Edition* (Munich, Sellier, 2009) 9. *See* also MW Hesselink, 'If You Don't Like our Principles We Have Others. On Core Values and Underlying Principles in European Private Law: A Critical Discussion of the New "Principles" Section in the Draft Common Frame of Reference', in R Brownsword, H-W Micklitz, L Niglia and S Weatherill (eds), *The Foundations of European Private Law* (Oxford, Hart Publishing, 2011).

[168] DCFR, vol 1, 536.

[169] DCFR, vol 1, 537.

[170] FA von Hayek, *The Road to Serfdom* (London, Routledge, 2007) 228.

> to help the Coventry mechanic, or the French peasant to pay more taxes to assist the industrialisation of Italy?[171]

The localist trend in the understanding of justice and other fundamental values that emerge in legal studies is therefore not accidental but rather coherent with general trends described in political theory and that, especially in the latest years, political practice has too often confirmed. When they affirm that Europeanisation should not extend to those areas that are sensitive to the different understandings of social justice in given societies and that cultural plurality is per se a matter of justice, legal scholars are basically repeating communitarian arguments. Opponents of harmonisation, more particularly, depart from the relativist and the tolerance thesis of communitarianism to embrace an alleged equivalence of community and nation typical of liberal nationalism.

3.2.2.1 Communitarian Perspective

The communitarian thesis as to the relativity of justice originated from a criticism of Rawls's conception of justice, blamed for being insensitive toward context specificities. In opposition to Rawls, communitarians claimed that it is impossible to elaborate a universally applicable theory of justice, for different communities will have different conceptions of what is valuable so that even their idea of justice will be dependent on their conception of the good. More specifically, the argument is twofold and based on a relativist theory sustaining that values differ from one community to another and a tolerance theory which states that those differences have to be respected and maintained; no one should interfere with the practices of other groups as this would mean acting unjustly and could lead to totalitarian degenerations.[172] As Walzer formulates this point:

> We do justice to actual men and women by respecting their particular creations. And they claim justice, and resist tyranny, by insisting on the meaning of social goods among themselves. Justice is rooted in the distinct understandings of places, honors, jobs, things of all sorts, that constitute a shared way of life. To override those understandings is (always) to act unjustly.[173]

In this sense, the idea advanced in the debate on social justice in European contract law that the respect for the differences is in itself required by the idea of justice takes its roots in the communitarian thesis. Discussing Europeanisation of private law, Collins makes exactly the same criticism of communitarian[174] to the 'original position' of Rawls, which seems the position of some 'mythical figure,

[171] Ibid, 228.

[172] Of course these two assumptions can be criticised for not being consistent with each other, as also the idea of tolerance is a relativist principle that could be shared or not by certain communities, so that the tolerance thesis asserts what the relativist thesis denies: S Caney, 'Liberalism and Communitarianism: A Misconceived Debate' (1992) 40 *Political Studies* 273–89, 288.

[173] M Walzer, *Spheres of Justice* (Oxford, Basic Books, 1983) 314.

[174] MJ Sandel, *Liberalism and the Limits of Justice* (Cambridge, Cambridge University Press, 1982).

one who cannot exist in reality, for everyone has a socially constituted identity and is born to the ties of various communities such as family and groups'.[175] However, if we were to take communitarians 'seriously' we should admit that not only a supranational but even a national system of social justice is unjust, as it overrides the understanding of justice which is spread among the different communities (not to be intended in a merely geographical sense) within the nation. In this sense, the logical consequence to be drawn would be that the national legal system cannot be monistic but should rather tolerate the coexistence of different normative orders, each of them mirroring the 'shared way of life' of a different community. This is indeed the conclusion coherently drawn by Smits, who explicitly refers to the work of Walzer, when he pleads for different legal systems within a single nation and the overcoming of the traditional national narrowness of private law.[176] The communitarian argument provides a strong theoretical point against unification of law not only at a supranational level, but at a national level too, so that it could have even represented an argument against the nationalism of the past centuries. Even if at that time the philosophical trend of communitarianism was still far from arising, the argument of the differences in the 'shared ways of life' was already used to object to codification processes. The reader will recall Carter's defense of American common law against Field's project of civil codification, based on the idea that while codifications only express the will of the legislator, common law spontaneously arises from popular ideals of justice, which are considered to be national (although it has already been pointed out that the import of this Savignian theme in the particular American context led to several inconsistencies in Carter's argumentation).

In other words, communitarian theories cannot be consistently used to defend national law, unless one intends to qualify the 'relevant unit' of community as a nation. This is what liberal nationalist theories do in particular. The price to be paid is, of course, the concealment of subnational differences, obtained through the argument of the preponderance of the cultural identity over all other possible forms of multiple allegiances.

3.2.2.2 Nationalist Perspective

While communitarians speak generally of a community as bearer of specific conceptions of justice, it is liberal nationalists who more precisely demarcate the concept of community and maintain that 'the scope of social justice should be limited by the boundaries of national political communities'.[177] Chapter 1 has highlighted how liberal nationalism derives a 'morality of partiality' (that is the political and ethic justification for a favorable treatment towards co-nationals)

[175] H Collins, 'European Private Law and the Cultural Identity of the States' (1995) 3 *European Review of Private Law* 353–65, 357.

[176] JM Smits, 'Multiculturalisme en Europees privaatrecht' (n 93), 291.

[177] D Miller, *Principles of Social Justice* (Cambridge MA, Harvard University Press, 2003) 19–20.

from the idea that justice is a national concept. In this sense, Miller argues that—given that nationality is the main source of solidarity[178]—a political order that considers social justice as a value to be pursued should necessarily be national. Unlike liberals like Hayek, who conceived of social justice as a dangerous mirage that would have opened the path to totalitarianism, liberal nationalists like Miller indeed acknowledge it has a very important role in the organisation of society. Given the idea that solidarity is only possible within a national community, this position leads to the conclusion that a state should better be national, for the sake of social justice: 'Social justice will always be easier to achieve in states with strong national identities and without internal communal divisions'.[179]

This position is justified on the basis of a twofold argument: on the one hand, nationality is the most important source of identification for people, so that a genuine sense of solidarity will naturally arise only *vis-à-vis* co-nationals and, on the other hand, different nations have different conceptions of what is just. As to the first point, Miller praises communities based on nationality, noting that:

> The community that is formed in this way becomes a natural reference group when people ask themselves whether the share of resources they are getting is fair or not. They compare themselves primarily with fellow members rather than with outsiders when thinking about whether their income is too low or whether the educational opportunities available to their children are adequate. [...] Sometimes our sense of justice may be more forcefully engaged by distribution in smaller units such as workplaces, but it is very hard to imagine this happening within units *larger* than nation-states. A Spaniard who feels that he is being underpaid may be comparing himself with other Spaniards generally, or with other workers in his factory or village, but he will not be comparing himself with Germans or Americans, say.[180]

Turning to the second aspect, Miller criticises particularly the idea of a global or trans-national justice, as it endeavors to reproduce, on a supranational level, distributive mechanisms that can only work within national communities. Once political communities are organised on a national basis, particular schemes of justice will be applicable in that context but not outside it; in this sense, adopting Rawls's starting point, it is almost as if each country had 'an original position of its own'.[181]

> [N]ational political cultures include a range of shared understanding that form an essential background to principles of social justice. As I have shown, the idea of social justice presupposes that there is agreement both about the basis on which people can make just claims to resources and about the value of the resources that are being distributed. [...] Because these shared understandings are so easily taken for granted within national communities, we may overlook the difficulty involved even in specifying what

178 D Miller, *On Nationality* (n 96), 32.

179 Ibid, 96.

180 D Miller, *Principles of Social Justice* (n 177), 18.

181 As in the critical words of A Sen, 'Justice across Borders', in P De Greiff and C Cronin (eds), *Global Justice and Transnational Politics* (Cambridge MA, MIT Press, 2002) 38.

> distributive justice would mean across such communities. Finally, for social justice to become an operative ideal that guides people's everyday behavior, those concerned must have sufficient assurance that the restraint they show in following fair principles and procedures will be matched by similar restraint on the part of others. [...] Nation-states can help to provide such an assurance.[182]

The whole theory combines communitarian relativistic and tolerance thesis with a basic assumption: 'National identities tend to create strong bonds of solidarity among those who share them, bonds that are strong enough to override individual differences of religion, ethnicity, and so forth'.[183] As already discussed, this is the core of the nationalist theory of identity—the idea, in other words, that the identity of a person is chiefly determined by his national belonging. Although people can develop different kinds of moral bonds, these prove to be of a second range when compared to bonds based on national identity. The theoretical reason behind this assumption seems to be a primordialist conception of the nation, looked upon as an extended family in which people share a common ancestry and are considered to be members of the same family. It naturally follows that among them particular kinds of moral obligations should exist, similar to those keeping families together.

3.2.2.3 Fortune of Communitarian and Nationalist Conceptions

The communitarian and nationalist suggestion that the idea of justice is determined primarily nationally is particularly widespread in the political science: it is actually amazing how the nationalist principle 'somehow creeps into apparently universalist theories by the back door'.[184] In this sense, the most remarkable example is represented by the thought of John Rawls. Even though Rawls's celebrated liberal theory of justice gives the impression of being applicable generally to all peoples and countries, this is not meant to be a universal proposition.[185] Rawls himself strikingly admits that '[t]he boundaries of these schemes are given by the notion of a self-contained national community'.[186] What is more, his conception of a national community is an astonishingly archaic one, much more primordialist than those adopted later by nationalists like Miller and Tamir themselves: the community is mainly closed and self-contained—'We enter it only by birth and exit only by death'.[187] Such a conception is more difficult to reconcile even with a theory of constitutional patriotism than Miller's theories are. Moreover, unlike liberal nationalists who have made a remarkable effort in this sense, Rawls disappointingly does not even attempt to give a theoretical justification for the national

182 D Miller, *Principles of Social Justice* (n 177), 18–19.
183 Ibid, 18.
184 M Canovan, *Nationhood and Political Theory* (Cheltenham, Edward Elgar Publishing, 1996) 32.
185 A Sen, 'Justice across Borders' (n 181), 38–39.
186 J Rawls, *Theory of Justice* (Cambridge MA, Harvard University Press, 1971) 457.
187 J Rawls, *Political Liberalism* (New York, Columbia University Press, 1993) 68.

narrowness of his theory: the fact that his theory of justice can work only within a national community is taken for granted without being questioned.[188] Outside of the nation, on the other hand, an international conception of justice will only affect nation-states but not also citizens of those political communities.

Despite such limitations, Rawls's view is generally regarded as the basis for a universal theory of justice. The reason why such feature of Rawls's system was not detected by many of the commentators involved in the discourse on justice is that, according to one view, most of them 'share the same unconsidered assumptions' of Rawls.[189] This is very likely, as in particular during the 1980s communitarian theories—of which liberal nationalism appears to be a specification—were quite successful and spread in academia and politics. Rawls himself has been influenced by thinkers such as Sandel, MacIntyre and Walzer, and elaborated his theory further in the attempt to accommodate the communitarian criticism to his ideas of 'original position' and 'veil of ignorance', accused for being unrealistic abstractions insensitive to cultural specificities.[190]

Taking the aforementioned into consideration, it is not surprising that even within the realm of legal studies, several scholars concerned with the issue of social justice have ended up embracing the idea that social justice—for several reasons—can be better achieved at a national level. Though this view is dominant nowadays and appears to be strongly rooted in the reality of European political institutions too, it remains nonetheless philosophically questionable and alternatives are easily conceivable.

3.2.2.4 *Cosmopolitan Perspective*

Although it is true that mechanisms of social justice have been historically employed in particular within nation-states, the idea that transnational forms of justice are per se impossible is controversial. In the first place, the theoretical justification of a nationalist conception does not stand the criticism of modernist theories of nationalism: if nations are considered to be cultural artefacts then the idea of the extended family appears to be pure nation-building propaganda, so

[188] This aspect of Rawls's theory is critically discussed by M Canovan, *Nationhood and Political Theory* 32 ff 33 she writes: 'Given the generality and abstraction of Rawls' approach, one might reasonably expect that political frontiers, with all their implications for differential rights and benefits, must be one of the main sources of injustice with which he is concerned. However, this expectation is disappointed. Not only does it eventually emerge that Rawls is assuming for the purposes of his theory "the notion of a self-contained national community"; more seriously, he makes no attempt to justify this concession to sheer contingency or to explain why co-nationals should have special claims upon one another whereas (for example) fellow members of a superior caste do not. [...] Evidently the existing borders of states are simply given; within the boundaries of the US, citizens are to live together on terms of fair cooperation, but no explanation is given why the moral relations between individuals inside those borders should be different from their relations with individuals who happen to be outside. This omission is all the more striking because Rawls reiterates the principle that mere good fortune is not a sufficient justification for social privilege'.

[189] M Canovan, *Nationhood and Political Theory*, 33.

[190] *See* S Mulhall and A Swift, *Liberals and Communitarians* (Malden, Blackwell Publishing, 2007).

that the whole idea that solidarity can be naturally felt only towards a co-national is undermined. In the second place, theories of justice that are not limited to nationally constituted communities have already been elaborated. These theories share a cosmopolitan perspective, inasmuch as they assume that people should be considered not as nationals—and distinguished on the basis of national, social or other collective categories—but rather as persons.[191]

Inspired by these considerations, political philosophers have challenged the nationalistic assimilation of collective and personal identity and subsequently started speaking of forms of international and global justice, whose first aim is the eradication of global poverty.[192] Regardless of its practicability, this attempt is philosophically quite interesting, for thus far transnational theories of justice did not manage to pierce the veil of the nation and only contributed to a 'moralisation' of international relationships. A non-nationalist theory of justice would possibly imagine a sort of 'international original position' to which all nations would agree and that could serve to derive a standard of fairness that could guide the relations between nations rather than citizens (international justice);[193] nevertheless, it is evident that this would only serve to give (quite minimalistic) standards of justice in public international law and not to create direct links between people across nations,[194] coherently with a statist and nationalist view of the world order.[195]

Theorists of global justice—most of whom generally describe themselves as cosmopolitans[196]—on the contrary aim at a theory that can directly reach private citizens without passing through the state.[197] In this sense, it would be possible to affirm, at least at a theoretical level and without considering the viability of such solution on pragmatic grounds, that even citizens of rich countries have

[191] C Beitz, 'Rawls's Law of Peoples' (2000) 110 *Ethics* 669–96, 677.

[192] Among others, TW Pogge, 'Priorities of Global Justice', in TW Pogge (ed), *Global Justice* (Oxford, Blackwell, 2001) 6 ff.

[193] J Rawls, *The Law of Peoples* (Cambridge MA, Harvard University Press, 1999). For some interesting critical remarks on Rawls's international original position *see* TW Pogge, '"Assisting" the Global Poor', in DK Chatterjee (ed), *The Ethics of Assistance. Morality and the Distant Needy* (Cambridge, Cambridge University Press, 2004) 260 ff.

[194] The point is clearly summarised by C Beitz, 'Rawls's Law of Peoples', 694–95, opposing Rawls's model to cosmopolitanism: 'Imagine two societies, each satisfying principles of liberal justice, in a world that complies fully with the Law of Peoples. The worst-off representative person in the first society is worse off in absolute terms than the worst-off person in the second society. According to the Law of Peoples, once we are assured that each society's institutions are just, there is nothing further to be said. According to the cosmopolitan view (or anyway a plausible interpretation of it), the residual inequality is an injustice, or at least might be so under certain conditions—for example, if it were produced by aspects of the global basic structure and if there were a feasible strategy available to improve the position of the globally worse-off person—and therefore requires remediation.'

[195] 'La differenza tra l'approccio globale e l'approccio internazionale è data dal fatto che la seconda prospettiva è ancora portatrice del retaggio statalista del diritto internazionale della pace di Westfalia, anche se il diritto internazionale attuale include come soggetti sia gli individui, sia gli stati, sia altre organizzazioni di varia natura', I Trujillo, *Giustizia globale. Le nuove frontiere dell'eguaglianza* (Bologna, Il Mulino, 2007) 126.

[196] So affirms D Miller, *National Responsibility and Global Justice* (Oxford, Oxford University Press, 2007) 23.

[197] A Sen, 'Justice across Borders' (n 181), 40–41.

solidarity obligations towards citizens of poor countries and not only—as liberal nationalists seem to imply—poor co-nationals. Such obligations can only be justified if one accepts the idea that there is a 'good' that is basic or universal enough to be valuable for every human being, for the mere fact of having the identity of human being and regardless of national or community ties.

However, such a cosmopolitan theory of justice constructed upon these premises is hardly employable to create standards of social justice applicable in a more restricted regional context—as the European continent can be—in which, in comparison to other non-European countries, differences in the welfare of people are less considerable (though occasionally disturbingly significant but also growing) and the basic needs of people are generally acknowledged and already taken care of by the nation-state. Indeed, the values that are truly universal are particularly basic: for instance, a universal standard of justice can be identified in the idea that every human being should have enough food, but it is hard to isolate a universal standard of, say, consumer protection. This marks a criticism that is not new in political philosophy, a criticism directed in particular to the universalisation of social rights. Specifically, it suffices to mention Hayek's sarcastic remark concerning the inclusion of a 'right to periodic holidays with pay' in the UN Universal Declaration of Human Rights of 1948:

> The conception of 'universal right' which assures to the peasant, to the Eskimo and presumably to the Abominable Snowman, 'periodic holidays with pay' shows the absurdity of the whole thing. Even the slightest amount of ordinary common sense ought to have told the authors of the document that what they decreed as universal rights were for the present and for any foreseeable future utterly impossible of achievement.[198]

Hayek's distrust toward any allusion to social justice leads him to employ—again—an argument which is similar to those employed by the theorists of several schools of thought: firstly Romantics, nationalists and contemporary communitarians and later, more surprisingly, postmodernists and even exponents of the critical legal studies movement.[199] However, an answer that could be given to this criticism is that even the right to paid holidays is just the particular expression, probably formulated in overly Western-centric terms, of the more universal right to rest.[200] This right would not meet with objections even if granted to the Abominable Snowman as well. In this sense, universal rights have application and forms that can vary in different contexts.

But by saying this, we end up once again depending on nations as political communities in which those general and universal ideas have to be concretised and obtain a specific meaning according to particular circumstances—similarly to what the Court of Justice of the European Union has sustained in the *Omega*

[198] FA von Hayek, *Law, Legislation and Liberty. Vol 2. The Mirage of Social Justice* (London, Routledge & Kegan Paul, 1976) 105.

[199] M Barberis, *Europa del diritto* (Bologna, il Mulino, 2008), 177.

[200] Ibid, 177.

case.[201] No wonder that such a weak understanding does not alter that much and can even be reconciled with nationalist theories, especially considering that the latter do not simplistically plead for a sort of national egoism and insensitivity to the most basic needs of non-nationals—as the principle that all human beings have equal moral dignity is widely accepted[202]—but rather affirm that, although there are also obligations towards non-nationals, these are less strong than those towards fellow nationals.[203] In Miller's view, obligations towards non-nationals are indeed quite thin and can be summarised in two principles: *protecting basic rights* and *preventing exploitation*.[204] All this reinforces nationalists' convictions that an international (similar to the model of Rawls's law of peoples) or weak *global* justice is not impossible, but that at the same time *social* justice necessarily requires a more restricted political community. On the one hand, if all of these premises are true, the use of a theory of international justice for the purposes of the harmonisation process in Europe is quite disappointing, as it does not help in elaborating standards of social justice that could be applicable in all countries and indirectly ends up confirming the strength of particularistic conceptions. On the other hand, a theory of global justice based on the idea of multiple identities can basically challenge nationalistic interpretations and lead to the conclusion that differences in the conception of justice among countries are not as important as those *across* countries.

The pessimistic conclusions on the possibility of elaborating an extensive theory of global justice can indeed be drawn only if one is willing to build a global theory of justice on the basis of the most basic identity shared by people regardless of their nationality: their human nature. Since this element is extremely minimalistic, it is no wonder that the contents of a theory of justice are minimalistic as well (and thus of limited utility for the citizens of European countries in their reciprocal relations). On the contrary, the idea of plural identities allows us to imagine a potentially unlimited number of different and sometimes even conflicting allegiances. If it is true that all people share a common identity of human beings, it is also true that many other people share identities as Englishmen, women, feminists, workers, consumers, and so on. These identities

[201] Court of Justice, Omega, C-36/02, para. 31.

[202] If this is the moral claim of a 'weak' version of cosmopolitanism that is that '[t]he various good and bad things that can happen to people should be valued in the same way no matter who those people are and where in the world they live', then 'we could safely say that we are all cosmopolitans now', D Miller, *National Responsibility and Global Justice*, 28.

[203] Ibid, 28–29: 'A world in which there is a starving peasant in Ethiopia is to that extent as bad as a world in which there is a starving peasant in Poland, all else being equal. The fate of both these people makes a claim on us. But this does not by itself settle whether, as moral agents, we have an equal responsibility to respond to both claims. The fact that both cases of starvation are equally bad does not tell me whether I have more reason or less to go to the aid of the Ethiopian than to go to the aid of the Pole. On the contrary, as an agent I may well have an obligation grounded in moral reasons to act to help one of these people before the other—to take a straightforward case. I may have entered an undertaking to support food aid to Ethiopia. This obligation cannot be defeated merely by pointing out that the condition of both people is equally a matter of moral concern.'

[204] D Miller, *Principles of Social Justice* (n 177), 19.

are not necessarily linked to specific geographic territories, 'thus collectivities of many different types may be invoked as bases of commitments and obligations that reach across national borders'.[205] If one acknowledges this aspect, the idea that justice can only exist within certain nation-states has to be reconsidered, as it would imply the limitation of the idea of justice to a particular national identity regardless of all other allegiances.

In this sense, the implications for legal studies would be that instead of looking at the divergences and convergences between conceptions of justice in the different Member States—assuming that these are homogeneous within those countries—it would be useful to compare the ideas of justice espoused by different political, social or economic actors. In this sense, it is conceivable that the same idea of justice that is normally presupposed by the legislation of a particular country will be shared—or opposed—by different subjects sharing the same non-national identity in different countries regardless of their nationality.

3.3 THE CULTURAL ARGUMENT

The usual argument employed by the European Commission to foster the process of Europeanisation is that some differences in the private law systems of the Member States represent a hindrance to the establishment of a well-functioning internal market, so that, provided that there is an appropriate legal basis for the European institutions to intervene, these should be eliminated.[206] The Court of Justice already ruled on the issue in order to better define what the legal basis is, specifying that the mere existence of a difference that can theoretically hinder the market is not in itself a sufficient reason to legitimise an action by the European institutions.[207] The position of many opponents of Europeanisation goes beyond such perspective. In their view, there are differences that—even if they could represent an obstacle to the establishment of the common market—are still valuable and should therefore be preserved. What is the factor that makes a rule resistant to Europeanisation even if it can hinder the establishment of a well-functioning market?

The concept of *culture* is of particular importance in this regard. According to the cultural argument, some of the differences that can be found in the legal systems of the Member States are not accidental but rather expressions of different national cultures and in this sense, if it is true that culture is a value deserving respect, the European institutions should not extend their harmonising actions to those culturally determined aspects. To make an absurd example, one of the reasons why consumers prefer not to make the most of the internal market and purchase goods from foreign businesses is presumably that they do not have

[205] A Sen, 'Justice across Borders' (n 181), 42.
[206] Most recently, *see* COM(2010) 348 final, 1.
[207] Court of Justice, Tobacco, C-380/03.

sufficient knowledge of foreign languages; it would therefore be economically efficient to fight linguistic diversity and promote the use of a unique language in Europe at least for economic transactions (and indeed, in the perspective of the competition between legal orders, some jurisdictions have already started providing English translations for their law and opening up to legal litigations in the English language), but—imagining for a moment that this were possible—this would be highly detrimental to that cultural richness which is seen as a source of pride for Europe. In the same way, as cultural manifestations, also legal differences, often in the guise of national codifications, should not be contrasted but rather protected.

Two intertwined views lie at the basis of the cultural argument. In the first place, cultural plurality is a value in and of itself that should be conserved, while the aims of the European institutions are a threat to such a cultural diversity. The implication is that Europeanisation becomes undesirable, for legal harmonisation would imply disrespecting local cultures. In the second place, culture 'comes before law': since law is so deeply rooted in the cultural dimension of a nation, plans for Europeanisation will necessarily mean resistance due to the difficulty of transplanting law in a completely different cultural context. The implication is that Europeanisation is more than undesirable; it is simply impossible.[208]

As the previous sections have shown, even other arguments are eventually revealed to be based on the cultural argument itself; so for example, the economic argument is founded on the assumption that preferences between countries will diverge as they are rooted in different cultures, which makes the idea of forced harmonisation—as a form of centralisation—inefficient. Even the different ideas of justice found in Europe that could hinder the process of harmonisation are aspects that contribute to the making of the culture of a given nation, since 'cultural diversity is entwined with issues of social justice';[209] for instance, '[w]hat in England is regarded as a consequence of the rule of law, of victim protection or of social justice may be regarded differently in Germany because these ideas are strongly related to different cultural values'.[210] The two assumptions upon which the cultural argument is based need to be clarified; in other words we have to

[208] 'Unfortunately, a common law requires common statutes, principles and mentalities, but also a unique culture of thought. Fortunately, efficiency is too weak a flag to break the rich European cultural diversity, expressed through different languages, thought systems, mentalities and values, which even get over a unique law', S Sánchez Lorenzo, 'What Do We Mean when We Say "Folklore"?' (n 160), 219.

[209] R Sefton-Green, 'The European Union, Law and Society: Making the Societal-Cultural Difference', in T Wilhelmsson, E Paunio and A Pohjolainen (eds), *Private Law and the Many Cultures of Europe* (Alphen aan den Rijn, Kluwer Law International, 2007) 55; H Collins, 'European Private Law' (n 176), 360.

[210] C van Dam, 'European Tort Law and the Many Cultures of Europe', in T Wilhelmsson, E Paunio and A Pohjolainen (eds), *Private Law and the Many Cultures of Europe*, 78. Analogous points are made in C van Dam, 'Who is Afraid of Diversity? Cultural Diversity, European Co-operation, and European Tort Law' (2009) 20 *King's Law Journal* 281–308.

address why cultural pluralism is valuable and what the relation between law and culture is. This might bring us again outside the purely legal field.

3.3.1 Culture as a Value

In recent decades, the argument that plurality of cultures is a value in itself became popular as an important aspect of post-modernism. At least in social sciences, post-modernism is the vague denomination that is given to a series of cultural trends that share an emphasis on the importance of plurality and cultural diversities, in opposition to the abstractness and uniformity of post-war modernism.[211] According to this line of thought (or maybe more precisely, according to this sensibility), differences are considered per se positive, as an expression of the variety and imagining capacity of humans.[212] Cultural diversity is praised in and of itself regardless of the concrete contents of a given culture. Its protection is assumed as a means for guaranteeing human 'well-being'[213] and international peace,[214] while the so-called 'cultural rights' are declared 'an integral part of human rights, which are universal, indivisible and interdependent'.[215]

Similar considerations have also entered jurisprudence, in particular thanks to the American movement critical legal studies. But the post-modernism which is conveyed by scholars inspired by the critical legal studies movement can take a very different form in Europe, where 'post-modernism might become an easy legitimization of a status quo that is more often than not chauvinistic in the defence of the tradition of the nation state, of its locally produced law and of its local bar'.[216] In Europe, therefore, post-modernism, which remains a politically ambiguous denomination,[217] contributes to the preservation of the legal status quo, in this sense displaying conservatism.[218] This constitutes an interesting ideological twist, since critical studies in America generally developed as a progressive movement. Under post-modernism, the philosophical justification

[211] On post-modernism in jurisprudence, *see* U Mattei and A Di Robilant, 'The Art and Science of Critical Scholarship. Post-modernism and International Style in the Legal Architecture of Europe' (2002) 10 *European Review of Private Law* 29–59.

[212] 'In fact, the diversity of legal traditions and the diversity of forms of life in the law they embody remain the expression of the human capacity for choice and self-creation', P Legrand, 'On the Unbearable Localness of the Law: Academic Fallacies and Unsensonable Observations' (2002) 1 *European Review of Private Law* 61–76, 67.

[213] A Łopatka, 'Cultural Diversity and Cultural Human Rights', in G Doeker-Mach and KA Ziegert (eds), *Law and Legal Culture in Comparative Perspective* (Stuttgart, Franz Steiner Verlag, 2004) 216: 'As biological diversity is a common heritage of mankind, the preservation of cultural diversity is necessary for the well-being of humanity'.

[214] *See* the UNESCO Universal Declaration on Cultural Diversity of 2001.

[215] Ibid, art 5.

[216] U Mattei and A Di Robilant, 'The Art and Science of Critical Scholarship' (n 211), 57.

[217] Ibid, 30.

[218] Ibid, 29–30 and 45.

of the cultural argument can be identified.[219] Supposedly, in the first decade of the new millennium, post-modernist thought has nonetheless entered a state of crisis due to a changed geo-political world scenario in which the aprioristic praise for diversity seems to have left space for a new desire for simplicity and certainty also in law.[220] In Europe, nevertheless, the post-modernist argument of cultural diversity continues to be widely used, probably for the reason that in the context of the European Union, this is not a mere rhetorical argument but has some legal strength too. This leads to the seemingly paradoxical conclusion that, in defending pluralism, post-modernism offers the perfect legitimation for the typical product of modernism, that is, the nation-state and its law.

It is taken for granted that the treaties bind the European institutions to respect of the cultural identity of the Member States. While the Treaty of Maastricht focused on the respect of national identities, the Treaty of Lisbon has put even more emphasis on the cultural aspect in order to reassure European sceptics. The Treaty on European Union now reads that the EU 'shall respect its rich cultural and linguistic diversity, and shall ensure that Europe's cultural heritage is safeguarded and enhanced' (Art 2). This appears as one of those clearly political provisions that were determined by new trends of Euroscepticism and neo-nationalism and represents a vague, though important, counterbalance to the acquisition of competences by the European bodies. It is downright questionable whether legal diversity can be considered to fall within the scope of the provisions on cultural identities in the sense of the treaties, if only because the treaties elsewhere[221] expressly and prominently consider the approximation of national legislations as one of their aims.

But while it is disputable whether legal differences could represent a cultural value in need of protection, the inescapable vagueness of expressions such as culture makes it possible to conceive of law itself as an aspect of culture.[222] In particular, several critics of harmonisation like to remind us that 'law is essentially a cultural product',[223] so that Europeanisation in certain areas of law would not only be politically undesirable but even legally impossible, given the provisions of the treaties. These provisions are indeed explicitly referred to by several

[219] The link between post-modernism and the cultural argument is affirmed also by M Antokolskaia, 'The Harmonisation of Family Law: Old and New Dilemmas' (2003) 1 *European Review of Private Law* 28–49, 38.

[220] MW Hesselink, 'The New European Legal Culture—Ten Years On' (2011) *Centre for the Study of European* Contract Law Working Paper, 1–2.

[221] Title VII Chapter 3, TEU.

[222] The UNESCO Universal Declaration on Cultural Diversity of 2001 gives a quite broad definition: culture is 'regarded as the set of distinctive spiritual, material, intellectual and emotional features of society or a social group, and that it encompasses, in addition to art and literature, lifestyles, ways of living together, value systems, traditions and beliefs'. The lack of any reference to 'law' in this list is evident.

[223] S Sánchez Lorenzo, 'What Do We Mean when We Say "Folklore"?' (n 160), 200.

authors as challenging the existence of an appropriate legal basis for the European institutions to unify private laws.[224]

Nevertheless, while no-one could seriously question that jurisprudence represents one of the most important manifestations of human culture, it remains actually harder to consider legal rules themselves as pieces of culture in need of protection: legal rules perform specific socio-economic functions and cannot be considered as something different, as pieces of 'art' without altering their original function. If this is true, the idea that plurality is per se something positive cannot be applied to legal rules. This would be a merely esthetic vision of law, that has to be rejected in light of the consideration, expressed by other scholars, that the result is all that matters: a rule should not be 'beautiful', but only 'useful'.[225] But still, since culture cannot be understood as synonymous with 'art', law cannot so easily be disconnected from culture.

3.3.2 Interactions of Law and Culture

Less lyrically but probably more seriously, the relation between law and culture can be seen as a derivative one: law derives from the culture of a given society and in this sense, it is linked only to that society. Although it can be artificial to consider legal rules as pieces of culture themselves, rules have been generated within the specific cultural context in which they found their reason for existence. So for example, Roman law would not have elaborated something like the *actio de feris*, which dealt with damages caused by wild animals, if at a certain moment in history an increasing number of exotic creatures had not been imported from distant territories for the amusement of the rich Romans.[226] Only a cultural–historical analysis reveals the deep *raison d'être* of that rule, which would otherwise remain difficult to understand. Outside those cultural contexts, there is furthermore the risk that legal rules will lose their original meaning and effect, so for instance, the idea that it would be sufficient to transpose the institutions of highly advanced

[224] C van Dam, 'European Tort Law' (n 210), 78; S Sánchez Lorenzo, 'What Do We Mean when We Say "Folklore"?' (n 160), 198.

[225] G Alpa, 'La competizione tra ordinamenti: un approccio realistico', in A Zoppini (ed), *La concorrenza tra ordinamenti giuridici* (Roma, Laterza, 2004) 48: 'quasi che la pluralità di regole fosse di per sé un bene, un vantaggio, esprimesse un valore positivo, ed invece l'uniformità fosse di per sé un male, uno svantaggio, esprimesse un disvalore. Insomma, una concezione "estetica" degli ordinamenti che allieta lo sguardo del giurista come la pittura, la flora, la fauna, con i loro molteplici colori, allietano lo sguardo di chiunque, in un mondo che sarebbe molto più noioso se quella dimensione fosse dissolta dalla uniformità. Nella realtà delle cose, la diversità o l'omologazione sono apprezzabili per i contenuti che esse recano, piuttosto che non per le differenze o le convergenze che esse esprimono. In altri termini la norma non è bella in sé, ma è utile per la funzione che assolve. Può esser bella la forma letteraria con cui è redatta, può affascinare il suo ritmo, come Stendhal era affascinato dallo stile del Code Napoléon, ma non per il solo fatto di essere diversa da un'altra. Siamo in un'altra dimensione, che qui non rileva. Mentre ciò che rileva è il risultato'.

[226] *See* R Zimmermann, *The Law of Obligations. Roman Foundations of the Civilian Tradition* (Oxford, Clarendon, 1996) 1104.

capitalist systems to Third World countries in order to trigger the same kind of economic growth certainly appears as a superficial standpoint. In this sense, there are rules, and differences between rules that are 'culturally conditioned'.[227]

The link between law and society was emphasised in particular under the influence of Romanticism and represented a fundamental theoretical element of the Historical School of Law. Hugo's example of the link between regulation of monogamy and fertility of women could be recalled here. Generally speaking, the idea that there is a link between law and culture is neither new nor controversial in the history of thought. More recently, even comparative lawyers have emphasised the necessity of acknowledging the cultural context in which legal rules operate and 'immerge' in such a new dimension before any comparative research is undertaken. However, this dependence of law on society has hardly been considered a threat per se to possibilities of legal transplants or even unification, and there does not seem to be a necessary contradiction between those. As even the classic textbooks of the discipline report, the necessity of considering the cultural background of legal rules is part of the methodology of comparative law, while legal unification is one of its possible functions. So for example, the leading German comparative lawyer of his time, Ernst Rabel, was aware of the fact that foreign law could be understood only taking its socio-economic background in consideration,[228] but this did not prevent him from laying the foundations of a sales law regulation that could bind very different states.

A certain degree of tension nonetheless exists. As projects of unification and supranational harmonisation have more recently become more audacious, the unquestionable link between law and culture has been considered to be so close-knit that it impedes rules to travel outside the culture that generated them. As they are culturally constrained, legal rules cannot allegedly be transferred from one context to a different one without undergoing processes of alteration, giving rise to something that, in the European context, has been termed legal irritants.[229] These problems are not new and a vivacious academic debate has started as to the possibility of successful legal transplants. In the American context this debate focused on the general theory of comparative law, where in particular the ideas of Watson and Friedman were discussed.[230] The same terms of this dispute cropped up later in the European context, as the activity of the European institutions confronted legal scholars with a myriad of legal transplants every year. These transplants are even more problematic, as they can be compared to 'artificial

[227] *See* S Leible, 'Marktintegration und Privatrechtsvereinheitlichung. Notwendigkeit und Grenzen', in A Furrer (ed), *Europäisches Privatrecht im wissenschaftlichen Diskurs* (Bern, Stämpfli, 2006) 40.

[228] Ibid, 39.

[229] G Teubner, 'Legal Irritants: Good Faith in British Law or How Unifying Law Ends up in New Divergences' (1998) 61 *The Modern Law Review* 11–32.

[230] *See* LM Friedman, *The Legal System. A Social Science Perspective* (New York, Russell Sage Foundation, 1975); A Watson, 'Legal Transplants and Law Reform' (1976) 92 *Law Quarterly Review* 79–84; D Nelken, 'Towards a Sociology of Legal Adaption', in D Nelken and J Feest, *Adapting Legal Cultures* (Oxford, Hart Publishing, 2001).

transplant organs' rather than 'human'.[231] In this context, the argument based on legal culture has assumed a new and peculiar connotation.

3.3.2.1 Transferability Thesis

The idea that legal rules can be borrowed, transplanted, copied, supranationally imposed and so on—in less metaphorical terms, transferred—from one country to another has been sustained by several scholars, while historians can straightforwardly find confirmations for this thesis. As generally understood, Watson sustained that legal rules can be transplanted, noticing that even transplanted rules do not show particular differences from one country to another due to diverging cultural conditions. According to this viewpoint, in the end it can be seriously questioned whether, as 'historically conditioned their origins might be', legal rules have some 'inherent close relationship with a particular people, time or place'.[232] The link between law and people or time (*Volksgeist* and *Zeitgeist*) would appear as a mere Romantic hypothesis with no anchorage in reality. Moreover, while cultural factors may serve to explain why a given foreign rule is borrowed in some country, Sacco points out that all nations have occasionally preferred non-historical models to solutions hallowed by national culture and tradition.[233] Not even cultural differences in the mentality of those who work with legal rules seem to represent a serious obstacle for mutual comprehension, unlike diversities in rules of practical relevance: 'Commercial lawyers and businessmen in Scotland and England do not in general perceive differences in habits of thought, but only—and often with irritation—differences in rules'.[234] By the same token, one can wonder whether in the world of the large international law firms a distinction such as the one between a classically Roman concept like *causa* and the common law consideration really matters.[235] On the basis of this disillusioned view on the relation between law and culture, Lando suggested the possibility that legal unification may be achieved in the European context even through imperative instruments, including a supranational civil code. According to this understanding the cultural argument does not stand on the way towards harmonisation, for the mere reason that '[c]ontract law and commercial law are not folklore'.[236]

It appears that the existence of a link between law and culture is not radically denied by the advocates of codifications but it is not seen as an unbridgeable obstacle in processes of reduction of the legal diversity: even Thibaut was well

[231] C van Dam, 'European Tort Law' (n 210), 76.

[232] A Watson, 'Legal Transplants and Law Reform' (n 230), 81.

[233] R Sacco, *Sistemi giuridici comparati* (Torino, Giappichelli, 2002) 46.

[234] A Watson, *Legal Transplants. An Approach to Comparative Law* (Edinburgh, Scottish Academic Press, 1974) 96–97.

[235] U Mattei and A Di Robilant, 'The Art and Science of Critical Scholarship' (n 211), 47.

[236] O Lando, 'The Principles of European Contract Law and the Lex Mercatoria', in J Basedow (ed), *Private Law in the International Arena/Privatrecht in der internationalen Arena. Liber Amicorum Kurt Siehr* (The Hague, TMC Asser Press, 2000) 396.

aware of the argument founded on the '*Geist des Volkes*'—based on the thesis of Montesquieu and subsequently made famous by Savigny. Nonetheless these arguments were considered insufficient and too vague to seriously object to a precise political proposal as a civil codification for Germany.[237] In the same way, the *Volksgeist* theory did not manage to convince those lawyers who were used to working with statutes adopted from the model of foreign legislation—first and foremost the French codification—who could easily appreciate how those theoretical concerns were disproportionate in relation to the reality of practice.[238]

3.3.2.2 Non-transferability Thesis

In the American context, it was in particular Friedman, the leading exponent of the Law and Sociology movement, who highlighted how law reflects the particular characteristics of society in a given period and consequently evolves over time together with those social conditions. This idea does not imply that legal borrowing is de facto impossible, but quite on the contrary seems to suggest that imported law is normally adapted successfully.[239] In this respect, indeed, 'Friedman is as optimistic as Watson concerning the extent to which legal transfers take place successfully'.[240]

A more radical criticism has been later directed to the transferability thesis by Legrand in a series of publications in which the link between law and culture is strongly emphasised and represented as an insurmountable obstacle to legal transplants. According to this view, culture determines people's mentalities so that both the application of law and the drafting of supranational rules will always be filtered by the culturally determined mentality of the legal actors, which will also represent obstacles to their transnational circulation. Such obstacles concern in the first place the problem of legal translation and in the second place the impossibility for a concept—even if perfectly translated—to mean the exact same thing in two different contexts. Legrand resorts to the famous example made by the linguist Benjamin, according to whom the two words meaning 'bread' in German and French do not actually mean exactly the same thing in those languages, because of the very different set of ideas, images and expectations that people in different cultural contexts bind to those words.[241] If this is true in relation to

[237] This aspect is dealt with by S Leible, 'Marktintegration und Privatrechtsvereinheitlichung' (n 227), 37.

[238] *See* Chapter 2: 2.1.4.4 'Diffusion of the *Volksgeist* Theory' and 2.1.4.5 '…In Europe'.

[239] D Nelken, 'Towards a Sociology of Legal Adaption' (n 230), 13.

[240] Ibid, 13. According to R Cotterrell, 'Comparative Law and Legal Culture', in M Reimann and R Zimmermann (eds), *The Oxford Handbook of Comparative Law* (Oxford, Oxford University Press, 2006) 719, 'Watson's view of the nature and effects of legal culture is much closer to Lawrence Friedman's than to that of most contemporary cultural comparatists', while the main differences can be imputed to the fact that Friedman is mainly concerned with the 'external' legal culture of the population, while Watson with the 'internal' culture of the lawyers, which leads the latter to ignore some sociological aspects.

[241] P Legrand, 'The Impossibility of Legal Transplants' (n 1), 117.

simple concepts like 'bread', the implications for the much more complex legal system would be enormous.

In reality, the idea that black letter rules can be easily transferred while the transplant of 'law' requires a bigger effort is widespread in legal studies.[242] However, according to Legrand's view, processes of legal transplants and legal harmonisation are radically impossible, since, detached from the cultural context in which it was generated and to which it is bi-univocally tied and implanted into an alien context, law will signify something different despite the seemingly indistinguishable black letter rules. In this perspective, legal culture has become the most important and undetermined of those veiled formants defined as crypto-types.[243]

3.3.3 Law and Culture in the European Context

In comparative law, theories on the cultural origin of law warn the comparative lawyer that even when legal rules share the same wording it is necessary to look at different factors—or *formants*, in the terminology developed by Sacco[244]—to have a realistic look at the functioning of a legal system. In the light of the debate on Europeanisation, the idea casts more serious doubts on the top-down harmonisation which has been pursued so far—as this is mainly concerned with the unification of legislations, leaving the other 'formants' untouched.

The strongest use of the cultural argument to reject Europeanisation aims has been made by Legrand, whose position coherent with his premise as to the impossibility of legal transplant is amply known and does not require a new account, while it will suffice here to mention his political criticism of the state of comparative law in Europe. According to this viewpoint, since there is no specific need for suppressing differences just for the sake of universalism, the intents of the comparative lawyers aimed at discovering the existence of an ancestral common core of different legal orders are biased, since authors 'are expected to subscribe to a script of underlying unity and transcendent universalism where particularism is assumed to be secondary and fated to play but a peripheral role in the future

[242] Discussing the nature of the reception of Roman law in the German territories, already F Wieacker, *A History of Private Law in Europe: With Particular Reference to Germany* (Oxford, Clarendon, 1995) 93, explains that 'The idea of "reception" may also lead one to think, quite wrongly, that foreign law can somehow be taken over as a whole without at the same time being digested and thereby altered in the process. This fallacy results from the simplistic view that law is a kind of material substance which one can "hand on" and "pick up", whereas in fact it is a multilayered cultural interfusion of great complexity and variability, an amalgam of group processes, historical and social, intellectual and psychological'.

[243] *See* R Sacco, 'Formante', in *Digesto italiano. Discipline privatistiche. Sez. civ*, Vol VIII (Torino, UTET, 1992).

[244] Ibid, 438–42.

of human affairs'.[245] Adhering to such a 'script of transcendent universalism' is required in order to present one's credentials as a good European[246]—in other words a form of 'political correctness *à l'européenne*'.[247] Comparative lawyers in Europe, in this sense, have deliberately chosen not to see what seems manifest if one only looks at the cultural aspects of law: legal orders are not even converging.[248] In this sense, national legal cultures are jeopardised by the harmonisation process, which is not innocuously aimed at removing positivistic obstacles in the path towards the convergence of legal systems.

3.3.3.1 Normative Implications

Disregarding culture would mean disrespecting national identities. As culture is something important for the very identity of communities, 'the gains in efficiency and welfare achieved by a single market should always be balanced against the threat to meaning and identity posed by disruption of communities'.[249] Harmonisation implies a reduction of diversities and if one assumes that diversities are something valuable to a certain extent even protected by the treaties—an asset rather than a burden[250]—a considerable tension arises,[251] since as even advocates of legislative Europeanisation have to acknowledge, 'you cannot have both unity and diversity, and that also holds true of European civil law',[252] at least in theory. Sociologists too have approached the cultural dimension of the process of European integration sustaining that unification can be hampered by the existence of different and contrasting values.[253] In this sense, the normative conclusion drawn by opponents of Europeanisation who employ the cultural argument is quite radical: legal harmonisation in Europe should or even could not extend to those aspects of law that are expressions of national cultural specificities. 'If private law is a part of the culture of each Member State, this assumption—together with the proportionality principle [...]—will mean a limit for the feasibility and scope of the unification of European private law'.[254] Authors adopting a more moderate view also highlight that a possible contrast between harmonisation and

[245] P Legrand, 'The Same and the Different', in P Legrand and R Munday (eds), *Comparative Legal Studies: Traditions and Transitions* (Cambridge, Cambridge University Press, 2003) 299.

[246] P Legrand, 'On the Unbearable Localness of the Law' (n 212), 66.

[247] Ibid, 66.

[248] P Legrand, 'European Legal Systems Are Not Converging' (1996) 45 *International and Comparative Law Quarterly* 52–81.

[249] H Collins, 'European Private Law' (n 175), 358.

[250] C van Dam, 'European Tort Law' (n 210), 80.

[251] H Collins, 'European Private Law' (n 175), 353.

[252] O Lando, 'Can Europe Build Unity of Civil Law whilst Respecting Diversity?' (2006) *Europa & diritto privato* 1–18, 1.

[253] W Arts, J Hagenaars and J Halman, 'The Cultural Diversity of European Unity: An Introduction', in W Arts, J Hagenaars and J Halman (eds), *The Cultural Diversity of European Unity. Findings, Explanations and Reflections from the European Values Study* (Leiden, Brill, 2003) 4, discussing the work of the researchers that led to the European Values Study.

[254] S Sánchez Lorenzo, 'What Do We Mean when We Say "Folklore"?' (n 160), 198.

multiculturalism may reveal the flaws of Europeanisation, whose plans should be more respectful towards cultural differentiations.[255]

As long as it refers to rules that are expressions of cultural specificities, the idea that Europeanisation should not extend to culturally constrained rules surpasses the legal discourse and impacts the more general political debate on Europe. After all, the idea of a limitation of the competences of the European institutions to merely economical rather than political subjects was and still is a well-defined political idea. Coherently with this inspiration, it was originally claimed that in particular those areas of law that are more evidently political had to be excluded from harmonisation: family law and criminal law had to remain untouched by European institutions. In this regard, the concerns of the Eurosceptics and the plans of the European institutions were unlikely to collide, as the aim of the Community was initially just to establish a market, in which aspects of family and criminal law were not of primary importance. Expressions like European family law and European criminal law were discussed years later, primarily in the academic environment,[256] and only more recently aroused a concrete interest in the European institutions, turning in particular into rules concerning conflict of laws and civil procedure.[257] Thus, it comes as no surprise that the cultural argument has been expressed in particular in the discussions of family lawyers, to whom the belief as to the unbreakable link between law and culture or even religion is particularly evident, while the European institutions have generally accepted this assumption and respected the consequence thereof.[258] Against this background, the limits of private law Europeanisation should appear quite clear, with an exclusion of family law and an inclusion of contract and commercial law, which, again, are not 'folklore'.[259]

3.3.3.2 Distinguishing Cultural and Technical Aspects

The suggestion that aspects of the legal orders that are more clearly linked to national culture should not be regulated by non-national institutions echoes the economic argument that only 'facilitative' aspects of contract law should be harmonised but not also others in which important political divergences can still exist. However, in the same way as it was unclear why only certain contract law rules had to be considered as neutrally facilitative, a hypothetical distinction

[255] R Sefton-Green, 'Multiculturalism, Europhilia and Harmonization: Harmony or Disharmony?' (2010) 6 *Utrecht Law Review*, 66: 'multiculturalism does not always, nor necessarily, clash with harmonization. However, when multiculturalism does clash directly with harmonization, particularly in the case of complete harmonization, this may indicate that such harmonization is not the right model in the EU, or that we are not yet ready for it'. Insisting on harmonisation in these cases could on the contrary lead to 'legal nationalism', informally intended as a synonym of conservatism.

[256] *See* K Boele-Woelki, 'The Road Towards a European Family Law' (1997) 1 *Electronic Journal of Comparative Law*.

[257] *See* for example, Commission, Green Paper on Succession and wills, COM(2005)65.

[258] M Antokolskaia, 'The Harmonisation of Family Law' (n 219), 37.

[259] O Lando, 'The Principles of European Contract Law and the Lex Mercatoria' (n 236), 396.

between 'culturally determined' and 'neutral' legal rules—the former falling outside the competences of the European institutions and the latter being easily modifiable—proves to be tricky. Political scientists also have highlighted the idea of a distinction between economic matters—to be demanded at the European level—and cultural ones—prerogative of Member States—is imaginable in theory but still highly problematic.[260] In jurisprudence, such a clear-cut distinction has fallen apart, together with the distinction between political and technical issues of private law. If contract law rules are politically determined then cultural factors also play an important role in those, as they lie behind the political choices. The border between cultural and neutral aspects becomes even more blurred when adopting a political and ideological understanding of legal culture.[261] In the end, the 'cultural' character of a rule is not an aspect inherent in the rule itself, but is rather a value judgment linked to the political significance of that rule in a particular moment and context. Of course, an emphasis on the political nature of legal culture helps bring clarity to the otherwise extremely nebulous concept of culture; nonetheless, it shows how a mere political concern of power distribution between the different levels of a multi-layer system may lie behind a resistance to Europeanisation.

Several authors have specifically highlighted how seemingly technical aspects of legal orders are on the contrary coherent to specific cultural characteristics of particular countries. This concerns all branches of private law: labour law can easily be influenced by the pressure exercised by the crowd, but contract law rules too, such as the unilateral termination of the contract, are culturally constrained inasmuch as they are coherent with a set of values and beliefs typical of nation-states.[262] Tort law is no exception, and mechanisms such as strict liability remain controversial issues over which there is allegedly no convergence in European legal systems, as a consequence of the fact that 'in many respects national private law, for example victim protection in tort law, is such a manifestation of national culture'.[263]

In other terms, given a broad understanding of culture that also includes political factors, it becomes impossible to distinguish between political and technical, as well as culturally oriented and neutral aspects of the legal system. All rules are rooted in a certain legal tradition or have been adopted to respond to particular needs that cropped up in a society at a particular moment, so that even cultural identity 'cannot be limited conveniently to some non-economic sphere,

[260] H Mikkeli, *Europe as an Idea and an Identity* (Basingstoke, Palgrave, 1998) 225.

[261] *See* for example R Sefton-Green, 'Cultural Diversity and the Idea of a European Civil Code' (n 128), 72.

[262] R Sefton-Green, 'Cultural Diversity and the Idea of a European Civil Code' (n 128), 84. Also the Danish government, in its reponse to the first communication of the Commission, highlighted that 'closely linked with the different cultural and legal traditions of the Member States, which must be kept in mind, particularly when considering any harmonisation' (para 14).

[263] C van Dam, 'European Tort Law' (n 210), 76.

leaving Europe a free hand to implement the single market'.[264] Even more, if one only considers that economic choices also are culturally constrained, since each Member State 'has explored and constructed through its laws and social practices a different interpretation of liberalism and market economy, so that any imposed homogeneity in private law would challenge the sources of personal identity of members of that society'.[265] After all, the very idea of the *Volksgeist* explained the origin and development of the whole body of civil law and not only of family or criminal law.

Given the premise of the cultural origin of private law, the only coherent conclusion would be that the whole process of 'forced' Europeanisation should be limited or completely abandoned, and in this perspective in particular the idea of a European civil code, which is the more radical (but still the less likely) form of Europeanisation one could think of, could only be considered Machiavellian[266] or even diabolic.[267] Of all the suggested forms of approximation of laws in Europe,[268] the possibility of enacting a common civil code is indeed the option that raises the most criticisms from a 'law and culture' perspective. It is in fact alleged that such an instrument would represent an arrogant act of legal imperialism, as it would also authoritatively impose a dramatic change on the English common law system, seen as less worthy.[269] Nonetheless, even within the civil law family there is a concrete risk that the provisions of a code will reflect solutions which are typical of one specific country only. Coherently with the now widespread criticism that the German state is using a predominant influence on the European Union,[270] also the prevalence of the German component within the networks in charge of drafting and evaluating a Common Frame of Reference is well known and has already led to reactions from other countries aiming at a more important role in the Europeanisation process.[271] The problem therefore appears to be not only the enduring link between law and culture, but rather the impossibility of adopting politically shared solutions. In the impossibility of overcoming resistance based on cultural defences of the States, one strategy may be to appeal directly the citizens through the increasingly popular 'optional instruments'. For instance, an optional system of sales law, inasmuch as it does not replace national rules,

[264] H Collins, 'European Private Law' (n 175), 359.

[265] Ibid, 362.

[266] S Sánchez Lorenzo, 'What Do We Mean when We Say "Folklore"?' (n 160), 219.

[267] P Legrand, 'A Diabolical Idea', in A Hartkamp, MW Hesselink, E Hondius, C Joustra, E du Perron and M Veldman (eds), *Towards a European Civil Code. Third Fully Revised and Expanded Edition* (The Hague, Kluwer Law International, 2004) 245–72.

[268] *See* the different options in COM(2001) 398 final and COM(2010) 348 final.

[269] P Legrand, 'Against a European Civil Code' (1997) 60 *The Modern Law Review* 44–63, 56.

[270] U Beck, *Das Deutsche Europa. Neue Machtlandschaften im Zeichen der Krise* (Berlin, Suhrkamp, 2012).

[271] *See* B Fauvarque-Cosson and D Mazeaud (eds), *European Contract Law. Materials for a Common Frame of Reference: Terminology, Guiding Principles, Model Rules/Produced by Association Henri Capitant des Amis de la Culture Juridique Française and Société de Législation Comparée* (Munich, Sellier, 2008).

appears to be more respectful of cultural differences, so that even the Commission presented it as 'an innovative approach because, in line with the principle of proportionality, it preserves Member States' legal traditions and cultures whilst giving the choice to businesses to use it',[272] although this reassurance has not prevented several national parliaments from complaining about the non-compliance of the proposal with the principle of subsidiarity.[273]

3.3.3.3 Inescapability of National Categories?

The implications of the cultural constraints thesis are particularly radical and put in question the very possibility of achieving a real uniformity: the supranational rules would easily conflict with the national rules inspired by different cultural values, giving rise to resistance or even a vivid 'clash of cultures'.[274] This eventuality becomes more concrete if one agrees with Legrand that to escape one's cultural formation is radically impossible. Someone who has been formed as a German scholar, for example, will always be a German scholar even when he or she is entrusted with drafting a supranational legal instrument that he or she will probably make as abstract as possible, unconsciously repeating the features of their own national codification.[275]

Though expressed in perhaps excessively provocative terms (that easily attract fierce critics), the thesis can avail itself of a series of factual elements that seem to confirm the existence of national biases. Whether one considers it an inescapable destiny to which one is doomed by one's own culture or not, the impression that national actors try more or less consciously to steer the process of Europeanisation in a national direction is in fact strong. Even legal scholars occasionally give the impression of trying to recreate their own national categories at the supranational level, so that one could speculate that, independent of more or less political concerns, it is really 'mentalities' that are nationalistically structured. So for example, in a vivid report from a famous conference in the Hague in 1997 in which international scholars gathered to discuss the possibility of a European civil code, Mattei depicts the distinguished speakers as chauvinistic advocates of their own national codes as a model for a possible supranational codification: the Dutch presidency willing to promote its already 'cosmopolitan' code, the French already convinced of the historical superiority of the *Code civil*, the German persuaded that the general part of the BGB can still be valuable to a European Code and so on, with the exception of the English, it goes without saying, certain of the uselessness of a civil

[272] COM(2011) 636 final, 12.

[273] *See* in particular the reasoned opinions of the English House of Commons and the German Bundestag concerning a draft Regulation on a Common European Sales Law for the European Union, 2011.

[274] C van Dam, 'European Tort Law' (n 210), 80, and also H Collins, 'European Private Law' (n 175), 358.

[275] P Legrand, 'Antivonbar' (2005) 1 *Journal of Comparative Law* 13–40.

codification.[276] Each delegate expressed loyalty to the stereotype others expected them to embody. The impression that even comparative lawyers involved in the process of Europeanisation of private law are in a way biased by their national background is shared also by Markesinis, who recalls the reaction of distinguished German comparative lawyers to the proposal made at a conference in Paris to extend to Europe the French legal regime on traffic accidents,[277] a seemingly very technical topic.

All these examples of 'militant parochialism', to quote Mattei, can be optimistically considered coincidences, or the pragmatic consequence of more complex reasons than just attachment to national categories. However, from the perspective of Legrand's cultural determinism, all these behaviours find a coherent and rational explanation which goes completely beyond a simple distrust of foreign law: these behaviours are rather culturally necessary. If it is true that legal mentality conditions every activity and judgment, then German, French, and English scholars simply cannot behave differently from the way they do because such is the mentality they acquired growing up in a particular cultural context. Once you formed yourself as a jurist studying the BGB, you simply cannot avoid noticing—perhaps loathing, perhaps being fascinated by—the a-systematic character of English common law and vice versa.

3.3.3.4 Future Convergence or Eternal Divergence?

In the end, the main reason why the process of Europeanisation should be slowed down or even stopped is that cultures in Europe are still too differentiated to be authoritatively brought together in a unique legal system. As Van Dam clearly summarised, '[p]rovided that cultural values are not converging, it can be submitted that legal systems are not converging inasmuch as they are the outward manifestation of national cultures'.[278] The convergence of legal systems presupposes a convergence of national values. Such a merging of legal cultures could be obtained by means of a Europeanisation of legal education,[279] but a convergence of more general societal values seems less likely to be expected. As politics and cultures are strictly tied, the main issue is that Europe is not culturally mature enough to have its laws unified.

[276] U Mattei, 'Perché il piano d'azione privilegia i poteri forti. Critica della retorica soft', in M Meli and MR Maugeri (eds), *L'armonizzazione del diritto privato europeo. Il piano d'azione 2003* (Milano, Giuffrè, 2004) 7–8; more briefly and in less colourful terms, U Mattei, 'The Comparative Law and Econonomics Approach to the European Civil Code. An Introduction', in U Mattei, *The European Codification Process. Cut and Paste* (The Hague, Kluwer Law International, 2003) 5.

[277] BS Markesinis, 'Why a Code is Not the Best Way to Advance the Cause of European Legal Unity' (1997) 5 *European Review of Private Law* 519–24, 520–21.

[278] C van Dam, 'European Tort Law' (n 210), 76.

[279] P Müller-Graff, 'Common Private Law in the European Community', in B de Witte and C Forder (eds), *The Common Law of Europe and the Future of Legal Education* (Deventer, Kluwer, 1992) 239.

But if the creation—even by means of legislative action—of a highly harmonised system of European private law has to wait until all legal scholars (agree to the fact that they) are finally ready, it is justifiable to foresee that national codifications still have many years before them.[280] While some authors enthusiastically consider that European private lawyers are now ready to take on this demanding role, other scholars advance doubts as to such ripeness[281] as well as on the likelihood of a future convergence: allegedly there are certain cultural differences—such as the divide between civil and common law—that are simply unbridgeable.[282]

A pessimistic view on the likelihood of a future convergence is coherent with and somehow implied by the cultural argument: although culture can change slightly over time, sociologists know that the societal development is subject to path dependence, so that even if it is possible that different cultures change over time, they will do it mostly following their own paths also when under the same influences. In this sense, they cannot be expected to converge: 'Economic development tends to push societies, in a common direction, but rather than converging, they seem to move on parallel trajectories, shaped by their cultural heritage'.[283] Even the process of economic integration in Europe cannot therefore be considered sufficient to allow a common culture to blossom.

But couldn't a convergence of legal cultures in Europe be fostered by means of an authoritative legal instrument? In such a perspective, law would be intended as one of those many sociological factors that influence societies, contributing to create the values that are followed in those social organisations. Sociologists of law have already discussed this aspect and even identified a series of factors that are necessary for law to shape society. Generally speaking, if these criteria are followed, it is likely that the legal rule will steer the cultural development of society; in the opposite case, it will run against resistance. If this is true, then, cultural constraints should not be necessarily considered as a hindrance for Europeanisation, as harmonised rules could simply change culture. This view is, nonetheless, rejected by the opponents of Europeanisation who even consider the idea of using law to instil values in the population as a pure Machiavellian idea.[284] According to this understanding, law could only be harmonised at a later stage where a cultural convergence has been already achieved, but not before, in order to foster that convergence. In this sense, though authors generally recognise that culture is something that can evolve, legal culture is represented as something steady that cannot be easily changed—certainly not by law—and in this sense comes to coincide with the similar but not identical concept of 'legal tradition'.

[280] U Drobnig, 'Abschied vom BGB?' (2007) 85 *Deutsche Richterzeitung* 257–61.

[281] BS Markesinis, 'Why a Code is Not the Best Way' (n 277), 522.

[282] P Legrand, 'European Legal Systems are not Converging' (n 248), 63: 'the common law mentalité is not only different, but is actually irreducibly different, from the civil law mentalité as found in Continental Europe'.

[283] R Inglehart and WE Baker, 'Modernization, Cultural Change, and the Persistence of Traditional Values' (2000) 65 *American Sociological Revue* 19–51, 49.

[284] S Sánchez Lorenzo, 'What Do We Mean when We Say "Folklore"?' (n 160), 219.

It is not difficult to identify the historical antecedents of this argument. More exactly, this represents a new version of the *Volksgeistdenken* in the European context. In particular, the view of Legrand reveals that underlying this approach to legal culture there is 'the unspoken—yet at times almost explicit—view that law is the 'spirit of the people'.[285] In the same way, Savigny did not reject a priori the possibility of a simple compilation of German law, but rather considered that the legal scholarship was not ripe yet for such a demanding role, with the result that the project had to be postponed to an indefinite date.

3.3.4 Analysing Cultures

The debate on Europeanisation is strongly polarised when it comes to legal culture,[286] and suffers from a lack of clarity as to the very concept around which it revolves.[287] It has been repeatedly pointed out that notions like culture and legal culture are extremely vague and different interpretations can be given thereof. Anthropologists have already warned against the risk of overloading and, therefore, exhausting, the term 'culture', which is currently employed in the most different context also in quite imprecise ways.[288] A certain caution should then be used by legal scholars too, but this does not seem to be the case. It suffices here to note that the expression 'legal culture', together with its homologues in other languages, has been used in several ways in legal studies, from an almost perfect synonym of 'legal history', to an equivalent of 'legal style', an element traditionally used by comparative lawyers to distinguish between legal families. Legal sociologists have elaborated on the concept, using it in more precise ways drawing further distinctions. In particular, the notion of 'internal' legal culture conveys the more technical and confined culture of lawyers, as opposed to the 'external' legal culture which refers to the relation between law and people's habits: as in a famous definition, this latter represents 'the values and attitudes which bind the system together, and which determine the place of the legal system in the culture of the society as a whole'.[289]

[285] A Watson, 'Legal Transplants and European Private Law', in JM Smits (ed), *The Contribution of Mixed Legal Systems to European Private Law* (Antwerp, Intersentia, 2001) 15. *See* also R Cotterrell, 'Comparative Law and Legal Culture' (n 240), 722.

[286] T Wilhelmsson, 'Introduction: Harmonization and National Cultures', in T Wilhelmsson, E Paunio and A Pohjolainen (eds), *Private Law and the Many Cultures of Europe* (Alphen aan den Rijn, Kluwer Law International, 2007) 3–18.

[287] As an introduction to the different ideas on legal culture, D Nelken, 'Legal Culture', in JM Smits (ed), *Elgar Encyclopedia of Comparative Law* (Cheltenham, Edward Elgar Publishing, 2006) 372 ff.

[288] U Hannerz, *Transnational Connections. Culture, People, Places* (London, Routledge, 1996) 30 ff; for a strong critique of the concept of culture: J Abu-Lughod, 'Writing against Culture', in RG Fox (ed), *Recapturing Anthropology. Working in the Present* (Santa Fe, School of American Research Press, 1991).

[289] LM Friedman, 'Legal Culture and Social Development' (1969) 4 *Law and Society Review* 29–44, 34.

3.3.4.1 Legal Culture and Comparative Law

Unfortunately, while one can at least have some intuitive idea as to what the concept of legal culture may mean, it remains more complicated to concretely identify and distinguish cultures, 'measuring' them and making usefully employable instruments of legal analysis out of them. This engenders a considerable limit on the debate on Europeanisation, since as long as one does not have an idea as to what legal culture concretely means, there is a constant risk of using that more evocative name—which within the European context has a particular importance given the treaty provisions on the respect of cultural identities—to describe what was already known with other terms, coherently with the just mentioned and widespread tendency to abuse the term 'culture', employing it in inaccurate ways. So for example, in classifying legal culture, there seems to be a certain inclination to repeat classical categories of comparative law, distinguishing Roman–Germanic, common law, non-European and still some years ago, socialist legal cultures,[290] just like comparative lawyers have distinguished legal families on the basis of the criterion of legal style.

As it can be used to repeat the usual distinctions of comparative law, the notion of legal culture also bears the risk of being burdened by the same ideological and political biases that can affect traditional comparative research, starting from the well-known Western-centric bias and the consequent excessive attention on the common law/civil law distinction. In this sense, after a 'second generation' of comparative lawyers played down the differences between civil and common law systems in light of the functional method[291] or even historical analysis,[292] the cultural argument accentuates once again that distinction as one of the most fundamental ones; this time, nonetheless, the differentiation would not reside in the legal rules but rather in the mentality of lawyers. It is not the concrete function performed by the rules that has to be investigated to verify whether there is convergence or divergence but rather 'the nature of legal reasoning, the significance of systematisation, the character of rules, the role of facts and the meaning of rights'.[293] A slight change in the standpoint from which one observes the legal systems leads to radically different outcomes: whereas a functionalist perspective brought to light similarities, the postmodern cultural perspective highlights diversity.[294]

The notion of legal culture could therefore be employed to reaffirm at a non-positivistic level differences that already exist between positivist systems. This leads to the problem that basically any difference which can be found between two

[290] For example, HW Ehrmann, *Comparative Legal Cultures* (London, Prentice-Hall, 1976) 13.

[291] *See* K Zweigert and H Kötz, *Einführung in die Rechtsvergleichung auf dem Gebiete des Privatrechts* (Tübingen, Mohr, 1996).

[292] *See* R Zimmermann, 'Roman Law and the Harmonisation of Private Law in Europe', in A Hartkamp, MW Hesselink, EW Hondius, C Mak and E du Perron (eds), *Towards a European Civil Code. Fourth and Expanded Edition* (The Hague, Kluwer Law International, 2011) 27–53.

[293] P Legrand, 'European Legal Systems Are Not Converging' (n 248), 63.

[294] MW Hesselink, *Contractenrecht in perspectief* (The Hague, Boom Juridische uitgevers, 2004) 31.

or more legal systems may be imputed to a difference in mentalities; if culture is identified with mentality, then its analysis becomes all the more difficult and even arbitrary. There are nonetheless frameworks employable to investigate this aspect of culture that can—and indeed have been—used in legal studies.

3.3.4.2 Cultural Classifications

The vagueness of the term makes it possible to present as cultural any difference that could be more precisely explained in a political, historical or sociological way, while the knowledge we have of the different legal cultures is mostly anecdotal when not plainly based on widespread stereotypes, and tends to repeat distinctions already visible at the positivistic level. Sociologists have already tried to develop frameworks to analyse cultural diversity more precisely. One of the best employable instruments to this end is a study by the Dutch organisational sociologist Geert Hofstede, first published in 1980. Since then, the study has met with considerable fortune, used as a framework to analyse cultural diversity and, possibly, 'predict' the impact of certain behaviours in culturally different contexts.[295] The study has been regularly referred to by several scholars from different backgrounds including legal scholars, who have tried to link particular social facts such as legal rules to the general culture of the nation, coming very close to defining methodically the contents of the thus far almost mythical notion of *Volksgeist*. It therefore appears compulsory to focus here on that study in order to have a more comprehensive view on the cultural argument.

The author based his study on numerous sources but most fundamentally on an international survey conducted to investigate the business cultures of a large and transnational group of employees at a large multinational corporation. The results of the study have been published in a long series of articles and were reorganised and updated years later in a new publication.[296] The author claimed to have discovered a series of differences in the mentality not only of those who participated in the survey but, more generally speaking, among nationalities. In order to 'measure' cultures, he made use of a set of different indexes called 'dimensions of culture': power-distance, individualism vs collectivism, masculinity vs femininity, uncertainty avoidance, and long and short-term orientation.[297] In other words, the study would empirically show that different social groups

[295] 'Since the later 1980s the idea of dimensions of national cultures has become part of what Kuhn called 'normal science'. The message of the first edition of this book has been integrated into the state of the art in various disciplines dealing with culture. The four or five dimensions I introduced have become part of intercultural training programs and of textbooks and readers in cross-cultural psychology, organizational psychology and sociology, management and communications. They have also been used in a number of other areas and disciplines', as affirmed by Hofstede himself, 'Dimensions Do Not Exist: A Reply to Brendan McSweeney' (2002) 55 *Human Relations* 1355–61, 1356.

[296] G Hofstede and GJ Hofstede, *Cultures and Organizations. Software of the Mind* (New York, McGraw-Hill, 2005).

[297] These are called dimension exactly because a dimension is 'an aspect of a phenomenon that can be measured (expressed in a number)', ibid, 400.

have different values that are now identified, so that we can distinguish groups in which, for instance, hierarchical stratification is more accentuated and accepted than others, groups that are more or less individualistic, where disputes tend to be solved in a more or less friendly way, and so forth. The practical implications of those dimensions are basically unlimited, with successive generations of scholars in different fields building upon that original framework. All these features define the culture of a particular group, or, the 'software of the mind' of people.

Such software of the mind is something that people are not born with but rather grow up with, and it determines the way in which our minds work; it cannot be kept hidden and there is no easy escape from it: 'We are from the Netherlands,' say the authors of the study, 'and even when we write in English, the Dutch software of our minds will remain evident to the careful reader'.[298] Just like language, this is something which a child inevitably learns from his or her parents,[299] with the implications that 'culture reproduces itself' and cultural belonging becomes a matter of pure moulding, normally independent from personal choices. The question can crop up whether such 'mental software' can also be 'uninstalled'; leaving metaphors aside, one could ask whether new cultures can also be learnt later in life, given up or modified. Hofstede's study seems to suggest that this is theoretically possible[300] but still practically improbable. In particular, while the superficially visible aspects of culture—so-called practices—may easily vary, there is a set of more fundamental values learnt during childhood that tend to persist and replicate themselves.[301] This explains why most of the cultural features we can find in nations today were already identifiable hundreds of years ago; so for example the strong 'uncertainty avoidance' of Spain is assumed to imply a particular fear of the stranger which in turn can be considered the cause of the *Reconquista* of Spain from the Moors, a historical event that lasted centuries and was concluded only at the end of the fifteenth century.[302] In history, changes in cultures are therefore quite relative and often the results of military conquest or even consequence of pre-existing cultural values[303]—a form of path dependence—while '[r]esearch about the development of cultural values has shown repeatedly that there is little evidence of international convergence over time, except an increase of individualism for countries having become wealthier'.[304] The importance of social change is therefore downplayed.

[298] Ibid, XI.

[299] Ibid, 10.

[300] This 'open' character of the culture defined by Hofstede is emphasised in particular by JM Smits, 'Legal Culture as Mental Software' (n 93), 147–49.

[301] G Hofstede and GJ Hofstede, *Cultures and Organizations* (n 296), 11–13.

[302] Ibid, 197.

[303] Ibid, 17.

[304] Ibid, 366. This aspect also allows Hofstede to reject the criticism that the material he employed for this study was too old to properly reflect actual national cultures: G Hofstede, 'Dimensions Do Not Exist' (n 295), 1356.

3.3.4.3 Controversial Aspects of Cultural Classifications

It can be supposed that the success of the study has been also favoured by a renewed interest in the relation between diversity and globalisation in the geopolitically turbulent recent years, in which Huntington in particular advanced a theory on the clash of civilisations that met with wide success in the academic and political discourse.[305] Such fortune, anyway, should not conceal the fact that Hofstede's study has also provoked and still provokes diverse criticisms.[306]

While this is not the place to engage in a discussion as to the validity of that model or even more generally the existence and contents of national cultures or characters—those that are often striking enough to allow co-nationals to recognise each other even abroad—it is important to focus on some of those criticisms, as they highlight methodological assumptions which can be relevant in the study of nationalism. In other words, those criticisms (which are not free from criticism themselves) help us see the nationalistic relevance of cultural classifications rather than their inexactness. Therefore, the main criticisms that have been made against that framework will be presented here and subsequently applied in the context of legal studies. Considering these critical aspects, it will emerge that even if the existence of national cultures could be proven, it remains problematic to link these to specific legal developments, proving the existence of the *Volksgeist* as well as its impact on private law.

[305] *See* SP Huntington, *The Clash of Civilizations and the Remaking of World Order* (New York, Simon & Schuster, 1996). No wonder that the text on the back cover of the second edition of *Cultures and Organizations* opens with the sentence 'The world is a more dangerously divided place today than it was at the end of the Cold War'. Some years before Huntington's work was published, Hofstede insisted on the increasing importance of national identities in a world scenario characterised by escalating tensions between nations and pleaded for 'een herkenning van de actualiteit van de vraag naar nationale (juist: nationale) cultuurverschillen'. Allegedly, 'binnen een EEG die tracht zijn markten te integreren, binnen een Atlantisch bondgenootschap, Oost–West en Noord–Zuid conflicten en dialogen, spelen behalve geld en macht ook ideeën mee die aanwijsbaar van land tot land verschillen, en die we met "cultuur" kunnen aanduiden', G Hofstede, 'Commentaar naar aanleiding van J Th Leerssen "Over nationale identiteit"' (1989) 16 *Theoretische geschiedenis* 360–65, 361.

[306] Geert Hofstede himself has often replied to the criticisms directed to his work, starting vivacious discussions. Particularly animated have been the diatribes with Joep Leerssen (whose field of comparative literature has been looked down upon as a mere 'hobby', *see* G Hofstede, 'Commentaar' (n 305), 361) and Brendan McSweeney (considered a 'British accountant' with little authority to challenge a study praised by distinguished anthropologists, *see* G Hofstede, 'Dimensions Do Not Exist' (n 295), 1360 and the reply 'I am not British, nor as it happens an accountant [...] I [...] am the research director of a department of accounting, finance, and management at a leading UK research university' of McSweeney, 'The Essentials of Scholarship. A Reply to Geert Hofstede' (2002) 55 *Human Relations* 1363–72), whose works it will be here referred to. For those who observe such stimulating and energetic discussions, it can be surely an amusing relief to learn that, being Dutch, Hofstede may share a cultural trait according to which, at least, '[s]cientific opponents can be personal friends', G Hofstede and GJ Hofstede, *Cultures and Organizations* (n 296), 203.

3.3.4.4 *Culture as Nation*

Doubts have been cast already on the methodological correctness of the study,[307] but more fundamentally Hofstede's framework was heavily criticised for its primary focus on the differences between *national* cultures. This appears as intrinsically nationalistically biased, as the author admittedly devoted his studies to the 'cultural category' of the nation-state.[308] Indeed, the author identifies cultures with nations, coherently speaking of 'dimensions of national cultures' and distinguishing on the basis of these indexes national categories such as the German, the French, the Italian, the Dutch and so on.

However, it has been suggested by critics that the contrast between categories such as 'Dutch' and 'German' has an absolutising effect that diverts from subnational differences and transnational similarities.[309] This systematisation would lead to an artificial emphasis on cultural uniformity within nations that conceals the strong differentiations within those nations.[310] Certainly, nobody believes that all swans are white and expects generalisations to unfailingly describe the totality of individuals within the category, but it can be asked why those individuals get categorised and 'generalised' in a category instead of others (which could be statistically more precise) and according to which criteria. One could wonder why the differences between different regions of a country should be less significant than those between countries,[311] so that the choice for the national dimension could seem ultimately quite arbitrary, while organising the results along national lines necessarily ends up highlighting differences between nations, just like distinguishing the respondents to the questionnaires along religious or ethnic lines would have brought to light the 'cultural' diversity of those religious and ethnic groups.[312] How is this preference for the nation justifiable?

Replying to this criticism, Hofstede clarified that the reason behind such a preference for the nation is primarily methodological: no ideological reasons but simply there would be a greater availability of information regarding national cultures.[313] This, of course, opens up the question as to whether those other studies and materials employed to obtain information about nations are also biased by methodological nationalism. What is more, the methodological choice for the national unit, although imprecise, remains 'better than nothing'.[314] But these

[307] *See* B McSweeney, 'Hofstede's Model of National Cultural Differences and their Consequences: A Triumph of Faith—A Failure of Analysis' (2002) 55 *Human Relations* 89–118, 93 ff, who contests the narrow number of respondents to the questionnaires, as well as their representativeness of a general national culture rather than a specific business culture.

[308] G Hofstede and GJ Hofstede, *Cultures and Organizations* (n 296), 364. Explicitly qualifying culture as 'national' culture: G Hofstede, 'Commentaar' (n 305), 361.

[309] J Leerssen, 'Feminien en klagen, dat is twee keer hetzelfde zeggen', in *NRC Handelsblad/Opinie & Debate*, 21.11.09 9.

[310] Ibid, 9; B McSweeny, 'Hofstede's Model of National Cultural Differences' (n 307), 99.

[311] J Leerssen, 'Over nationale identiteit' (1988) 15 *Theoretische geschiedenis* 417–29, 424.

[312] *See* B McSweeney, 'Hofstede's Model of National Cultural Differences' (n 307), 102.

[313] G Hofstede, 'Commentaar' (n 305), 360.

[314] G Hofstede, 'Dimensions Do Not Exist' (n 295), 1356.

reasons alone seem rather insufficient to justify a central methodological choice with such important implications.[315] Indeed, there is something more than a mere practical reason: Hofstede also justifies his choice on the basis of the argument that people usually tend to distinguish others primarily on the basis of national identities, so that certain behaviours are labelled as 'typically American', 'typically German' and so on.[316]

In this regard, the modernist view on nationalism should be considered. The fact that people tend to see themselves as co-nationals has little to do with anthropological cultural similarity and much to do with the nation-building strategies adopted over the centuries; while it is disputable whether before nationalism people actually regarded themselves as members of the same nation, confined as they were in narrow geo-political units that did not share much with other different entities from an economic, social and occasionally even linguistic point of view. Nowadays, it is surely prudent to affirm that national identities have been created and they probably represent the primary allegiance for many people,[317] but the very idea of the existence of 'national software of the mind' handed down for centuries from generation to generation, which undergoes little or no change over centuries weakens. Timeless national cultural traits cannot exist because nations themselves are not timeless.

A national allegiance can become undeniably strong, but it is not the only conceivable allegiance as others can be imagined which, according to circumstances, can be even more relevant than national identity. Nonetheless, the relevance of these other dimensions, though recognised in theory, is deemed irrelevant in the end.[318] Of course, many distinctions and further elucidations can be made, at least in theory, but in practice concepts tend to blur and become indistinguishable. For instance, nations should be distinguished from societies (to which the concept of culture should apply in the first place),[319] '[n]evertheless, many nations do form historically developed wholes even if they consist of clearly different groups'.[320] These groups, in turn, challenge the cultural homogeneity of the nation only secondarily, and their 'national culture' in the end emerges:

> The degree of national cultural homogeneity varies from one society to another, and may be especially low for some of the newer nations [...] Even if a society contains

[315] The availability argument is considered even 'unreasonable' by J Leerssen, 'Culturele verschillen en nationale ideologieën: een naschrift' (1989) 16 *Theoretische geschiedenis* 361–65, 362.

[316] G Hofstede and GJ Hofstede, *Cultures and Organizations* (n 296), 19.

[317] In a contrast between national and supranational identities, Eurobarometer surveys show that even European citizens who have connections with more countries than the one in which they live identify themselves mainly with their nation; *see* Special Eurobarometer 346 Wave 73.3, April 2011, 87.

[318] 'The population of a nation can be differentiated on many grounds, but Hofstede claims that regardless of these divisions every national population somehow shares a unique culture', B McSweeney, 'Hofstede's Model of National Cultural Differences' (n 307), 92.

[319] G Hofstede and GJ Hofstede, *Cultures and Organizations* (n 296), 18. G Hofstede, *Culture's Consequences: Comparing Values, Behaviors, Institutions, and Organizations Across Nations* (London, Sage, 2003) 10, the author sustains that the word culture can nonetheless 'be applied to any human collectivity or category: an organization, a profession, an age group, an entire gender, or a family'.

[320] G Hofstede and GJ Hofstede, *Cultures and Organizations* (n 296), 18.

> different cultural groups (such as blacks, Hispanics, Asians and Caucasians in the United States), these usually share certain cultural traits with one another that make their members recognizable to foreigners as belonging to that society.[321]

Regardless of its validity, the representation of cultural traits as distinguished among nations is a deliberate choice based on nationalist suppositions. Interestingly, Hofstede himself recognised that an equalisation of nation and culture amounts to a largely imprecise accommodation, as admittedly nations only occasionally perfectly coincide with cultures[322] and culture is something different from *identity*.[323] For this reason and in the presence of strong subnational (mostly linguistic) differentiations, the author occasionally adopted a regional model, distinguishing for example the French-speaking from the Flemish communities within Belgium. This, however, does not always occur, not even for quite heterogeneous countries, so that a strongly statist interpretation of the nation is given.[324] On the other hand, Hofstede also speaks of cultural traits that can be found among more nations, and in this respect a particular relevance concerns the distinction in Europe between Germanic and Latin countries. However, even the focus on such a juxtaposition—which could be linked to a distinction between Latin on the one side and Germanic and Common Law legal systems on the other side—is considered by critics as a deviation. More exactly, this appears to be the legacy of ethnic stereotypical distinctions which took root in Europe ever since *L'esprit des lois* of Montesquieu, so that that opposition between *Romania* and *Germania* appears ideological rather than cultural and therefore constructed rather than objective.[325]

However, the fact that Montesquieu (and actually many others before him)[326] put emphasis on a distinction between Germanic and Latin countries proves that the distinction is quite old but definitely not that it is false. Quite on the contrary, recent political and economic developments have led that distinction to become once again a powerful (though again very ideological and inaccurate) tool to conceptualise European cultural diversity in the consciousness of people. Apart from the consideration that distinguishing cultures on the basis of nations is a highly imprecise methodological operation which shows continuity with nationalist practices, these criticisms are therefore still insufficient to reject the whole model—just like affirming that the methodology of a research is biased does not automatically imply that its outcomes are false.

321 G Hofstede, *Culture's Consequences*, 2001 (n 319), 10.

322 G Hofstede, 'Commentaar' (n 305), 360: 'ik ben me bewust van de beperkingen van het 'land' als eenheid van onderzoek'.

323 G Hofstede, *Culture's Consequences*, 2001 (n 319), 10.

324 B McSweeney, 'Hofstede's Model of National Cultural Differences' (n 307), 92.

325 J Leerssen, 'Culturele verschillen en nationale ideologieën' (n 315), 363.

326 *See* F Chabod, *Storia dell'idea d'Europa* [1961] (Roma, Laterza, 2010) 38.

3.3.4.5 Description as Explanation

The aspect that raises more doubts is rather a confusion between descriptions and explanations in dealing with cultural differentiations. The problem arises since the cultural characteristics of a given group can be described only by means of more or less precise generalisations, which lead to the extension of certain characteristics to all those who belong to the same group. In this sense, descriptive categories become somewhat 'prescriptive'.

A confusion between these descriptive and explicatory functions is deceptive, in particular considering that Hofstede's indexes are associated with a long series of very diverse cultural features: peoples with an uncertainty avoiding culture—basically all the Mediterranean and Slavic countries—for example, besides tending to escape insecurity also suffer from high stress, anxiety, worries about health and money and in general feel less happy (but, notwithstanding, they at least suffer from fewer heart attacks).[327] Following the success and on the basis of this model, diverse recent studies have attempted to show the national cultural dependence of a long series of radically different elements, mostly pertaining to marketing strategies.[328]

It is probably exaggerated to affirm that all of these characteristics derive from the 'uncertainty avoidance' level of culture, unless one considers 'uncertainty avoidance' as the generic descriptive label collectively given to a series of heterogeneous characteristics (stress, anxiety, level of precision of the laws, incidence of heart attacks and so on), rather than their cause. People in Mediterranean countries are not more anxious because of their uncertainty avoidance, but rather, since people in those countries have shown higher levels of anxiety, they can be described as uncertainty avoiding. In this light, however, the entire model disappointingly turns into a sophisticated truism: it would be in the end like affirming that being bachelor is the reason why someone is unmarried.[329] Otherwise, we would be just giving a definition of bachelor.

But even the simpler descriptive function can conceal circularity. According to a critic, even behind the apparently innocuous question 'what are the typical characteristics of the Dutch?' lurks the self-referential question—'what are the typical characteristics of the typical Dutch?'—which already presupposes a choice,[330] given that nations are so heterogeneous that it is necessary to single out the characteristics of a particular group out of all the possible identities that

[327] G Hofstede and GJ Hofstede, *Cultures and Organizations* (n 296), 194.

[328] References are made by T Wilhelmsson, 'The Average Consumer: A Legal Fiction?', in T Wilhelmsson, E Paunio and A Pohjolainen (eds), *Private Law and the Many Cultures of Europe* (Alphen aan den Rijn, Kluwer Law International, 2007) 243–68, 256.

[329] J Leerssen, 'Feminien en klagen, dat is twee keer hetzelfde zeggen' (n 309), 9.

[330] J Leerssen, 'Over nationale identiteit' (n 311), 424.

people in a country may have,[331] and elevate those as 'typical'[332] features of the national group.[333]

The two dimensions of description and explanation appear to be tightly connected. Even if Hofstede's aim is primarily to describe cultural differentiation simply reporting the findings of his study, the author abundantly gives in to the temptation of creating various examples to show how diverse individual behaviours and attitudes can be linked to those findings concerning the cultural traits of the nation. Again, even if it is not necessarily false, this operation bears the risks of oversimplification, retrospectivity and biased selection. It is in other words easier to see only those individual examples that prove the point, more or less unconsciously overlooking all those others who do not fit or even contradict the assumption made.[334] Outside of academia, nationalistically inspired populism is particularly familiar with such practices of biased selection. But this operation is even methodologically questionable, because since Hofstede affirms that cultural dimensions cannot be applied to individuals but only to populations, it is contradictory to look for validation in specific cases and deny any value to those other cases that contradict the model. In other words, while it can even be agreed that in Spain people tend to avoid uncertainty more than in other countries (just like the typical characteristic of the typical Dutch might actually be widespread in a considerable part of the Dutch population), affirming that centuries ago the Spanish expelled the Moors and the Jews *because* of their uncertainty avoidance is retrospective and conceals all the historical explanations of those events, such as the tense relations between the different confessions or pure economic and military reasons. In this sense, Hofstede has been criticised for focusing on a cultural

[331] Ibid, 423.

[332] 'In stereotyping, qualities or features that are ascribed to a given nationality are posited as typical of the nation in question, in a peculiarly double sense of the term. On the one hand, "typical" (as in "I saw a typically Spanish bullfight") means that a certain type (Spanish) is marked and characterized and that the attribute or characteristic in question (bullfight) is representative of the type at large. On the other hand, typical means that the attribute in question is salient, nontrivial, remarkable, and noteworthy and that a bullfight is something that strikes the unwary observer as something out of the ordinary', J Leerssen, 'The Rhetoric of National Character: A Programmatic Survey' (2000) 21 *Poetics Today* 267–92, 284.

[333] This leads to a mortification of plural identities: 'If somehow the average tendency of IBM employee responses is assumed to be nationally representative then, with equal plausibility—or rather equal implausibility—it must also be assumed that this would be the same as the average tendency in every other company, tennis club, knitting club, political party, massage parlour, socialist party, and fascist party within the same country. The "average [national culture] tendency" in New York City Young Marxist Club, for example, is [...] the same as in the Keep America White Cheer-Leaders Club in Smoky Hill, Kansas, USA', B McSweeney, 'Hofstede's Model of National Cultural Differences' (n 307), 101.

[334] In general, the use of the Hofstede categories implies the risk of a biased selection of the examples, *see* J Leerssen 'Feminien en klagen' (n 309); B McSweeney, 'The Essentials of Scholarship. A Reply to Geert Hofstede', 48: 'recognise everything supporting, ignore anything which contradicts'; J Leerssen, 'Culturele verschillen en nationale ideologieën: een naschrift' (n 315), 362–63, also this author notices how in *Culture's Consequences*, Hofstede adopts examples that prove its classification, minimises those who contradict it and at same point (120 of the first 1980 edition) explicitly affirms 'I have completed the picture with elements based on intuition rather than on empirical evidence' (n 319).

determinism that does not take into account the possibility of the influence of strictly non-cultural factors on society.[335]

3.3.4.6 Cultural Classifications in Historical Perspective

Are these 'risks' mere methodological mistakes due to an excessive faith in the explicatory value of a fundamentally valid model? We could certainly think so, considering in particular that generalisations inescapably require second-best accommodations and can even create inequalities, but they still remain unavoidable at least to a certain extent.[336] Nonetheless, from a broader perspective, scholars of comparative literature have pointed out that such an uncertain correlation of causes and effects is not fortuitous, but rather an authentic leitmotif in the history of the description and distinction of national groups. Hofstede's study is in this sense merely one of the most influential and best structured examples of something that has been considered a renaissance[337] of the old trend of using concepts such as culture, nation and nationality 'as explanations rather than as descriptions or explicanda', an operation which in the end gives new life to old ethnic categories.[338] At any rate, this tendency is more widespread and often based on mere intuition rather than accurate studies. For instance, the ideologist of the 'clash of civilisations' affirmed that the reason why South Korea has developed so rapidly since the 1960s while Ghana mired in the same poor economic conditions is mainly cultural, because the South Koreans are said to be hard workers while Ghanaians have other values: culture has 'to be a large part of the explanation'.[339] By the same token, the European economic crisis that started in 2008 has led to an ostensible revitalisation of the tendency to link, in a way which is as scientifically unsound as it is demagogically convenient, economic development with alleged cultural or even moral characteristics of the different nations of Europe.

Historically, such interpretations, together with the tendency to confuse description and explanation, became particularly widespread in the nineteenth century under the influence of escalating nationalist thought. This was the period in which 'the various stereotypes and assumptions concerning national peculiarities never form[ed] the topic of investigation, but always part of the interpretative tool-kit; they [were] explanations rather than explicanda',[340] used as a criterion to create a taxonomy of the different national groups similar to what naturalists

[335] B McSweeney, 'Hofstede's Model of National Cultural Differences' (n 307), 109–10.

[336] On this point, *see* in US scholarship F Schauer, *Profiles, Probabilities, and Stereotypes* (Cambridge MA, Harvard University Press, 2003).

[337] J Leerssen, 'Over nationale identiteit' (n 311), 418.

[338] J Leerssen, 'Imagology: History and Method', in M Beller and J Leerssen (eds), *Imagology. The Cultural Construction and Literary Representation of National Characters. A Critical Survey* (Amsterdam, Rodopi, 2007) 25.

[339] SP Huntington, 'Foreword. Cultures Count', in LE Harrison and SP Huntington (eds), *Culture Matters. How Values Shape Human Progress* (New York, Basic Books, 2000) XIII.

[340] J Leerssen, 'Imagology: History and Method' (n 338), 19.

did to systematise animals and plants.[341] Differences between nations had to be scientifically demonstrable, as they were thought to be rooted in nature according to the primordialist and ethno-cultural vision of nations that was endorsed explicitly during that period and often implicitly assumed nowadays. An example of this kind of biased activity concerns the nineteenth-century studies of phrenology on human skulls that would have proved scientifically the existence of differences in races, on the basis of the systematisation of the results on a supposed racial basis, a kind of 'hardware of the mind'.[342] Such a procedure was not only logically circular, but its findings were radically false, as modern researches on genetics have shown.

3.3.4.7 The Use of Cultural Classifications in Legal Studies

The use of the Hofstedian model to link differences in national cultures to specific political and legal institutions is particularly problematic. The controversial aspects that have been previously highlighted—overlap of description and explanation, circularity, concealing of subnational and transnational cultural variations, retrospectivity and so on—can materialise also in legal studies. Here the risk of confusion between descriptions and explanations is actually higher, since national legal systems already appear as different, so that there is no real need to describe a difference which is clarified after an even superficial comparative analysis. In this context, the role of the cultural dimensions would mainly be to explain those existing differences on the basis of different mentalities.

It has been underlined, for example, how the unsystematic nature of the British legal order and the absence of a written constitution in that country may be linked to the low uncertainty avoidance index scored by Britain, In other countries where, on the contrary, unforeseeable situations generate more angst, laws tend to become more and more precise in order to reduce that anxiety-provoking uncertainty, while legal reasoning becomes deductive.[343] Just like most other examples, this explanation seems at first sight convincing, as it is reasonable to assume that subjects who prefer to avoid uncertainty tend to regulate in detail several aspects of their life, also by means of laws. However, the relation does not always work bi-univocally. So for instance, if one accepts that in the case of the United Kingdom there is a relation between a low uncertainty avoidance level and the absence of a written constitution, it is then very difficult to explain on the basis of the same argument why another country that scored quite low on the same index such as the United States has elaborated the oldest written constitution in force. The cultural explanations would then need to be integrated by historical justifications. In the second place, the references to historical experiences to explain

[341] *See* J Leerssen, *National Thought in Europe. A Cultural History* (Amsterdam, Amsterdam University Press, 2006), 55–57.

[342] B McSweeney, 'Hofstede's Model of National Cultural Differences' (n 307), 112.

[343] C van Dam, 'European Tort Law' (n 210), 68, 73–74.

mental diversities often appear as not always fitting: a low uncertainty avoidance index is associated with nations that historically belonged to the former Roman Empire.[344] Again, this association raises some doubts: one could already wonder how this empire could have managed to instil in such diverse populations a feeling of 'uncertainty avoidance' without even replacing many of the local languages and traditions; but even more decisively, how is then the high level of legal diversification within countries that once belonged to that empire explainable? Here, we are in the field of pure suppositions as to the social psychology of extinct civilisations, justified with the tricky assumption that culture generally does not change over generations—an assumption which is incidentally now subjected to critical re-examination in anthropology.

In this sense, to affirm that the UK has no codification or written constitution because culturally it leans more towards 'imprecise laws' for its low 'uncertainty avoidance' appears—apart from as a partial and quite inaccurate statement which fails to consider other forms of regulation in that jurisdiction—at least retrospective, while a maybe less fascinating but more genuine diachronic cultural–historical account would bring us to allege—in something which is obvious enough to resemble a truism—that Britain gives the impression of not having as many statutes as other countries because it has neither written constitution nor codification. A purely descriptive function, on the contrary, adds nothing to what every lawyer already knows: that the UK has neither a written constitution nor codification.

It is therefore evident that the tendency to select only examples that prove the point (confirmation bias) attributed to the Hofstede model is a tempting risk for legal scholars as well, who can look into cultural systematisations to find the categories needed to justify some existing legal differences in hindsight. In this sense, basically any difference can be justified through cultural dimensions, with results that can even contradict more concrete historical explanations. This can lead to overemphasising the relevance of the *national* cultural dimensions at the expense of other cultural, as well as non-cultural, factors that could contribute to explaining legal development. For example, legal scholars can relate masculinity and strong power distance with the inclination of countries to inexactly implement European directives, and use as an example the case of the French implementation of the liability directive.[345] Such a correlation is statistically relevant, seems convincing and cannot be considered a priori wrong. However and again, this consideration alone could make the legal analyst forget other more concrete reasons behind that case of resistance, reasons that in a broad sense could be considered cultural as well.[346] What is worse, the affirmation of the cultural necessity of those behaviours could even lead authors particularly respectful of cultural

[344] Ibid, 68.

[345] Ibid, 77.

[346] *See* for instance D Caruso, 'The Missing View of the Cathedral: The Private Law Paradigm of European Legal Integration' (1997) 3 *European Law Journal* 3–32, 17.

diversification to justify the persistence of practices such as the systematic delay in the implementation of directives, something that even citizens of those countries would not be likely to deem appropriate.

In the end, culture appears to be a valuable tool to understand and analyse contemporary societies and historical events—that cannot be fully understood without looking at the cultural scenario in which they developed and continuously evolve—but it seems to lead to vague and contradictory results when, becoming a synonym of *national* mentality, it pretends to explain, let alone predict, legal developments alone.[347]

3.3.4.8 Conclusion

The controversial aspects that have been exposed could lead some critics to object even to the existence of any kind of 'national culture' or 'national characteristics'. This conclusion would go too far. Otherwise, even an obvious empirical statement such as 'Frenchmen speak French' should be considered as stereotyping, and we should close our eyes when confronted with the existence of populations in the world with extremely different traditions and customs. It is on the contrary hardly deniable that certain social or even national groups share certain traits and show a degree of homogeneity as to, for example, language, religion, eating habits, knowledge of particular facts concerning their own country etc. Only a certain level of 'cultural homogeneity' elucidates why most Germans speak German and most Spaniards speak Spanish, why most Portuguese citizens are Catholic while most Danes are not, as well as why most average Americans, confronted by the question as to who invented the telephone, would answer 'Alexander Graham Bell' while most average Italians would indicate their co-national Antonio Meucci. And, of course, the examples could include why English lawyers (and law students) primarily look into case law while French lawyers (and law students) turn to statutory law to find an answer to legal questions. These circumstances are certainly not ignored by modernist scholars of nationalism, who rather investigate the origins of these habits and cultural traits highlighting their oft-constructed nature.

However, admitting the existence of national culture is not the same as sustaining a national cultural determinism.[348] Certainly there is also a difference in explaining a cultural aspect (different perceptions as to historical events, legal method) by means of a precise documentable fact (nation-building function of public education, organisation of the law schools) and explaining precise documentable facts (legal institutions) by means of culture. Explaining culture by means of culture is even more problematic.[349] In this sense, as it cannot be said

[347] For the most recurring criticisms against the notion of legal culture, R Michaels, 'Rechtskultur', in J Basedow, K Hopt and R Zimmermann (eds), *Handwörterbuch des Europäischen Privatrechts. Band II* (Tübingen, Mohr/Siebeck, 2009) 1258.

[348] *See* B McSweeney, 'Hofstede's Model of National Cultural Differences' (n 307), 92.

[349] J Leerssen, 'Over nationale identiteit' (n 311), 419, therefore considers Hofstede's model an explanation obscurum per obscurius.

that national characters simply do not exist, even the data collected by Hofstede should not be considered *ipso facto* false and any serious attempt to shed light on this highly nebulous field must be appreciated, keeping in mind that cultural pluralism is a fact but that '[c]ulture is a construct, for which there can be no direct measure'.[350] But exactly for these reasons, a critical analysis of those data as well as a clarification as to the functions and the utility of those distinctions becomes compulsory.

In light of the criticisms that have been made, the dimensions of national culture should be considered simple accommodations that cannot pretend to explain every cultural manifestation as the 'cause' rather than the 'consequence'. In particular, there are doubts as to their predictive value[351] and even their capacity to describe flawlessly the whole society.[352] Such a predictive effect could be logically acknowledged only generalising—or more correctly, universalising—the major premise of a hypothetical syllogism until the point of creating an average uniformity within a category—the nation—at the expenses of differences among that category; this operation would save the formal validity of the syllogism, but still say nothing about its actual truth, as the major premise remains unproven and even indemonstrable.[353] But '[t]o *assume* national uniformity, as Hofstede does, is not appropriate for a study which purports to have *found* it'.[354]

To cope with such a twist, even Hofstede recognised that cultures should be considered as general tendencies in nations[355] that cannot be applied to individuals.[356] This appropriate clarification basically means that within those national cultures that are considered more or less homogeneous, people can also manifest very

[350] D Williamson, 'Forward from a Critique of Hofstede's Model of National Cultural Differences' (2002) 55 *Human Relations* 1373–95, 1380 and 1388. This author then warns that 'not to confuse Hofstede's scores with the cultural constructs for which they are only approximate measures. Hofstede's scores can only be a very rough indication of tendencies in the rich variety of cultural values', 'But to reject Hofstede's model because it does not provide a direct measure of national culture, is to reject all nomothetic research of culture', 1381 and 1388. This anyway redimensions Hofstede's claim that dimensions of culture can be measured.

[351] Hofstede is ambiguous on the possibility of 'predictions': on the one hand, it seems that this is not possible when referred to the behaviour of individuals, on the other hand, 'prediction' would be on the contrary possible in generic terms, since the cultural dimensions 'affect human thinking, feeling, and acting, as well as organizations and institutions, in predictable ways', XIX; criticised by B McSweeney, 'The Essentials of Scholarship. A Reply to Geert Hofstede' (n 306), 47.

[352] More analytically and critically on the logical steps of the Hofstedian model, *see* B McSweeney, 'Hofstede's Model of National Cultural Differences' (n 307), 99 ff. The risk that intranational differences are neglected is acknowledged even by sustainers of the Hofstedian model cricitising the critical remarks by McSweeney, *see* D Williamson, 'Foreward From a Critique of Hofstede's Model of National Culture' (n 350), 1379.

[353] As to the indemonstrable character of the cultural dimensions, the Hofstedian model escapes scientific falsifiability according to J Leerssen, 'Feminien en klagen, dat is twee keer hetzelfde zeggen' (n 309), 9. If this consideration is true, then no wonder that the 'critic of the critic' D Williamson, 'Foreward From a Critique of Hofstede's Model of National Culture', 1390 notices that McSweeney 'fails to falsify Hofstede's model' (n 350).

[354] Ibid, 100.

[355] G Hofstede, *Culture's Consequences*, 2001 (n 319), 16.

[356] D Nelken, 'Legal Culture' (n 287), 376 and 378.

different cultural values. National culture appears less and less a matter of mentality and increasingly more a matter of statistics. For these reasons, not dissimilar from prophecies—inevitably vague till the day they eventually seem to have become fulfilled—*predictions* based on national culture could be realised only in hindsight when a particular circumstance confirms the general assumptions. But while we can generally accept this limitation and still make a reasonable guess that if we meet someone from France he or she will be very likely to speak French (we nonetheless have progressively fewer chances to guess correctly in regard to more specific cultural traits), the legal researcher is confronted with further difficulties: for his or her purposes, much of the practical utility of a model based on *national* cultures has by now faded out. Legal researchers also have to take into account a further hurdle, which is that to build a direct link between general culture and legal culture is not always possible, since often legal culture appears as a bearer of values that are different from those widespread among the population in a given community, neither is it necessarily homogeneous among different branches of the legal system.[357]

On the one hand unable to exercise an unequivocal *predictive* function as to the behaviors of people or the developments of legal rules and institution and, on the other hand, imprecise in their *descriptive* function, cultural systematisations rather appear to perform a different function: a *constructivist* one. By elevating some characteristics to the range of national specificity of a given culture, they promote the definition of a cultural national model that can be opposed to others and becomes a model of identification. As far as legal studies are concerned, the pessimistic conclusion is in the end corroborated:

> The notion of the 'spirit of the people' is impossible to analyse empirically—a purely mystical idea on which nationalist or racist sentiment can easily be hung—glossing over the political struggles involved in legal development with a simple conception of unified culture as a given and as a causal factor.[358]

Such an operation of dissimulation of the 'political struggles' and the other dynamics of legal development appears clearly when one more specifically looks at the notion of 'legal culture' as it has been used in legal studies.

3.3.5 The Argument in Light of Different Political Theories

The association of legal culture with the nation and the subsequent concealment of subnational and international cultural segments, leads to represent national legal systems as culturally homogeneous, different from one another and not able

[357] T Wilhelmsson, 'Introduction: Harmonization and National Cultures', in T Wilhelmsson, E Paunio and A Pohjolainen (eds), *Private Law and the Many Cultures of Europe* (Alphen aan den Rijn, Kluwer Law International, 2007) 3–18.

[358] R Cotterrell, *The Sociology of Law. An Introduction* (London, Butterworths, 1992) 23. Critical toward the Volksgeist theory from an historical perspecitive, RC van Caenegem, *Judges, Legislators & Professors. Chapters in European Legal History* (New York, Cambridge University Press, 1987) 71–72.

to be harmonised in a supranational context. This is perfectly coherent with the nationalist strategy to create homogeneity in the internal side, differentiations from other communities, and advance political autonomy claims. In this sense, this use of the cultural argument is associable with nationalism not inasmuch as it functionally aims at impeding any transfer of competences from the national to the supranational level, but rather inasmuch as it bases its implications on an identification of culture and nation on the one hand and a representation of national culture as basically homogeneous on the other hand. It is important to notice that while culture and nations are often employed as almost synonyms, the most attentive anthropologists have already warned against that easy association, considering it an heritage of nationalism and pointing out that culture is a much more multifaceted notion.[359]

Differentiation from other nations and emphasis on internal homogeneity, which are the assumptions upon which theories on national characters presented in the previous section are based, are indeed the political assumptions of the nationalist ideology, contested by opposed ideologies.

3.3.5.1 The Nationalist Perspective

Culture is the pivotal element around which modern theories of nations revolve, lying 'at the heart of contemporary debates about identity'.[360] As already shown in Chapter 1, culture is the fundamental criterion employed in particular by liberal nationalists to construct collective identification. Such use was already observable in nineteenth century Germany, and it was more specifically the '[a]nti-Enlightenment cultural relativism, Herder-style', that 'created an ethnic taxonomy which saw 'nation' and 'culture' as the natural and fundamental, mutually interdependent units of humanity'.[361] After the disastrous experience of nationalism represented in ethnic terms, the cultural criterion met with new favour and became the key to modern liberal nationalisms. The focus on culture does not therefore appear as the feature of a former historical phase but rather a still important element for liberal nationalist theories that re-emerge at the present day.

Needless to say, no one ever claimed that people in a given nation perfectly share the same culture. This point, explicitly rejected also by Hofstede, is not even sustained by nationalists: culture is only basically homogeneous within nations, while it is undeniable that certain individuals will occasionally manifest cultural traits which are different from those of the majority of their fellow countrymen. Such homogeneity of tendency, nonetheless, is sufficient to make culture the fundamental form of identification for people. Miller is clear on this aspect:

> If we think of national culture not as implying complete uniformity but as a set of overlapping cultural characteristics—beliefs, practices, sensibilities—which different

[359] U Hannerz, *Transnational Connections* (n 288), 20.
[360] UNESCO Universal Declaration on Cultural Diversity of 2001.
[361] J Leerssen, 'Imagology: History and Method' (n 338), 18.

> members exhibit in different combinations and to different degrees, then [...] it is reasonably clear that distinct national cultures do exist.[362]

In a later work, the political theorist did not deny the existence of cultural groups internal to the nation that make the idea of a 'common nationality as implying cultural homogeneity' appear as a 'general fallacy'.[363] Indeed, the general nationalist 'assumption of an equivalence between a common culture and a shared community which jointly underpin a nation-state' has been increasingly criticised in political science[364] as excessively reductionist and for that reason not apt to represent the complexity of modern societies. Nevertheless and regardless of those criticisms, Miller continues affirming that it is the presence of such 'overlapping cultural characteristics' that makes the nation somehow homogeneous. In this view, if the state were not sufficiently homogeneous, it would become difficult to be governed and eventually regress to a totalitarian form: the existence of 'cultural homogeneity'[365] as well as 'even partially shared standards of justice'[366] are the reasons why a state works more effectively when it 'embraces just a single national community'.[367] This is basically the reason why, in the nationalist thought, national culture gives rise to political claims, legitimated also on the basis of 'empirical reasons for thinking that national cultures will be protected most effectively when nurtured by states of their own',[368] while communitarian politics of recognition, based on the argument of the existence of subnational group identities, should be in general rejected.[369]

The refusal of non-national identities is common among most nationalists; another theorist of liberal nationalism clearly closer to civic understandings of the nation, Tamir, has highlighted in this regard:

> Nationalists reject the proliferation of cultural options for two reasons. First it challenges the aspect of continuity [...], opens the way for the disintegration of national identities based on cultural similarities, and brings about a proliferation of 'private' cultures. Second, it is feared that new, modified traditions might be so thin as to lack all meaning.[370]

These concerns are rejected by this author on the basis of the assumption that 'national culture is not a prison and cultural ties are not shackles', so that even a right to 'choose' their own national group should be acknowledged to individuals.[371] This hypothetical right would have to be counter-balanced by the 'right to preserve cultural homogeneity' which has to be acknowledged to states. However,

362 D Miller, *On Nationality* (n 96), 85.
363 D Miller, *Citizenship and National Identity* (n 99), 77.
364 P Gilbert, *The Philosophy of Nationalism* (Boulder Colorado, Westview Press, 1998) 174.
365 D Miller, *On Nationality* (n 96), 90.
366 D Miller, *Citizenship and National Identity* (n 99), 78.
367 D Miller, *On Nationality* (n 96), 90.
368 Ibid, 88.
369 D Miller, *Citizenship and National Identity* (n 99), 62 ff.
370 Y Tamir, *Liberal Nationalism* (Princeton, Princeton University Press, 1993) 50.
371 Ibid, 57.

this latter right is clearly a particularly controversial one, so that in order not to legitimise chauvinistic degenerations and bring about the coveted pacification of nationalism and liberalism, the author suggests that 'it is justified for a nation to seek homogeneity by restricting immigration only if it has fulfilled its global obligation to assure equality among all nations',[372] while on the internal side, '[n] ational cultures should [...] be protected if, and only if, their members express a reflective interest in adhering to them'.[373]

Such an opening to cultural voluntarism, however, remains generally criticised by nationalists: provided that the pursuit of cultural homogeneity—the objective of what has been defined 'statist nationalism'[374]—should never degenerate into chauvinistic practices, 'the idea that I *choose* my culture is deeply problematic. I have cultural affinities with others whether I wish it or not'.[375] Miller in fact rejects the idea that belonging to a nation could be made object of subjective 'will' rather than objective 'identity'.[376] According to this line of reasoning, cultural determinism also becomes primarily national cultural determinism: national culture can explain individual choices, as the 'background' against which these can be tested and made.[377] In conclusion, only 'a national culture gives the society its distinct identity'.[378]

3.3.5.2 Legal Culture as National Legal Culture

Parallel to the nationalist approach that mainly equates cultures with national cultures, legal studies also show a strong tendency to consider legal culture in mainly national terms. This tendency has already been denounced by various scholars—Smits among others—who blamed legal sociologists like Friedman, Marryman and Clark as well as Legrand for adopting a predominantly static understanding of legal culture, pretty much resembling the *Volksgeist* idea, which conceives the existence of different 'cultural segments' within and across nations.[379]

Not even the more circumscribed debate on Europeanisation is immune from such reductionism with regard to the national dimension. So for example, limiting ourselves to the works that have already been cited, authors have analysed the tort law systems of France, Germany and England referring to the nationally organised categories of Hofstede. After having initially recognised that even within nation-states there are differences but that those differences are even larger in the context of the EU as a whole, the analysis of scholars ended up once again opposing a French idea of social justice, an English idea and so on, so that in

372 Ibid, 161.
373 Y Tamir, *Liberal Nationalism* (n 370), 37.
374 P Gilbert, *The Philosophy of Nationalism*, 31.
375 Ibid, 123.
376 D Miller, *On Nationality* (n 96), 37.
377 Ibid, 86.
378 Ibid, 95.
379 JM Smits, 'Legal Culture as Mental Software' (n 93), 142.

conclusion we do not manage to get away from the nationalist perspective even if we are conscious of its insufficiency. What is more, the image of legal cultures as something homogeneous and basically stable is increased by the fact that very little attention is given to the possibility of cultural changes, which is anyway subordinated to the idea of path dependence: even if it is possible to change cultural values, 'this requires a reinterpretation and development; the slate cannot be wiped clean'.[380] Certainly, it is clear that some particular understanding of justice or of any other value may be enshrined in the law of a particular country, but this still does not imply that those values are necessarily an expression of a general national culture.

The very idea Hofstede described of culture as a 'mental software' that has been handed down from father to son for centuries and will influence any future choice the sons make is widespread in legal studies as well; as already mentioned, Legrand has emphasised this point excluding even the possibility of a change, famously arguing that the national legal culture is a 'destiny' to which lawyers were doomed long before they set foot in a law faculty and that culture is something that has to be therefore investigated in the *longue durée*.[381]

Since the national unit is, as in Hofstede's words, methodologically 'better than nothing' for understanding cultural pluralism, the reductionist approach does not appear to be necessarily erroneous. However, admitting that nations can be culturally heterogeneous even on the inside, it is then artificial to draw a coherent conclusion against legal denationalisation based on the cultural argument: even a national legal order disrespects sub-national cultural diversity, but this—except for a few particular contexts—has not led to the conclusion that regional private laws should be enacted.

In this way, the argument of culture becomes quite conservative as it gives a cultural legitimacy to the legal status quo and paradoxically even appears as the new instrument to defend legal positivism. The distinctions between legal cultures basically follow the ones between positive legal systems (French or English legal culture) or at most legal families (civil law or common law culture),[382] hallowing them on supposedly anthropological grounds.

3.3.5.3 Cultural Homogeneity and the Legal Order

In the debate on law and culture there is a strong tendency to neglect cultural variety at a regional or subnational level. This may be due to several factors that entirely coincide with the methodological justifications given by Hofstede. In the

380 H Collins, 'European Private Law' (n 175), 358.

381 P Legrand, 'European Legal Systems Are Not Converging' (n 248), 63.

382 *See* S Weatherill, 'Why Object to the Harmonization of Private Law by the EC?' (2004) 5 *European Review of Private Law* 633–60, 650: 'I do not deny that culture is capable of embracing law and legal tradition. But I do deny that it is useful simply to take a legal system and stick the label culture on it'.

first place, especially for those who intend to make an empirical analysis on the basis of existing data, information concerning nations is more easily available than data concerning local cultures; in the second place, it is generally thought that people tend to define themselves primarily in terms of nationalities.[383] If the choice for the nation is an appealing methodological option for sociologists, it becomes almost a forced choice for legal scholars, for the reason that—ever since the nationalisation of private law as discussed in Chapter 2—legal systems have been built on a national basis, and it would be simply impossible in the present day to analyse the law without taking into account its national dimension. If you investigate a legal order, you often necessarily investigate a national one. But in a legally centralised state where the same rules are meant to be applied in the same way to the whole territory, it would be impossible to remain faithful to the *Volksgeist* idea without somehow admitting that the *Volk* of a given legal system is essentially homogeneous. Consequently, the weight of subnational cultural segments is played down and in the legal studies legal culture is constructed in national terms, only furtively admitting that not even national systems are culturally homogeneous.

Is it not too simplistic to imagine legal cultures as homogeneous within nations and not considering internal divergences and external convergences? In this regard, it is important to note that the existence of cultural differences within nation-states is not radically denied by authors who insist on the national legal culture argument. The importance of those segments rather is minimised. In particular, Legrand has addressed this issue. The author explicitly recognised that differences in legal cultures can be found even within the same jurisdiction, accepting at least in theory subnational regionalism,[384] but then again his analysis mainly opposed broader legal traditions, as a civil law culture vs a common law culture, as they are mainly expressed in the opposition between the national legal cultures of France and Britain,[385] while his focus has progressively shifted towards the national dimension over the years. The presumption seems to be that nations may be heterogeneous inasmuch as regional groups exist within them. But, what about groups that are organised on a non-geographical basis? Again, Legrand makes an interesting concession, acknowledging that 'sub-*mentalités*' or 'para-*mentalités*' can exist even within nation-states, nevertheless, also the relevance

[383] JM Smits, 'Legal Culture as Mental Software': 'Traditionally, the analysis of legal culture has been on this national level: the existence of legal cultures is usually assigned to countries or groups of countries (like the civil law and common law tradition or Nordic legal culture). Good reasons exist for this emphasis on countries. One is that it is practical: it is relatively easy to establish a person's nationality. Another is that statistics are often only available for countries and not for other segments of society. But a substantive reason also exists for this emphasis on national culture: the age-old presumption that people are indeed shaped the most by their country of origin. Although this probably was true in the past, increasing Europeanization and globalization may have made the situation different' (n 93), 144.

[384] Since 'there are clearly differences at the level of legal cultures within the same jurisdiction: Holland is not Limburg and the Trentino is not Sicily', P Legrand, 'European Legal Systems Are Not Converging' (n 248), 63.

[385] Ibid, 63.

of these minor mentalities is immediately put aside in the name of a necessarily imperfect approximation which once again coincides with the nation.[386]

In other words, the most attentive advocates of the national cultural argument are well aware of the existence of different 'cultural segments' of geographical, religious or ideological nature, as well as the idea that 'our identities are multiple',[387] but given the practical impossibility of taking all of them into account, they resort to an approximation which makes cultures appear at least mostly homogeneous within the nation. In other terms, scholars do not fully manage to escape methodological nationalism.[388]

All in all, not even nineteenth-century patriots denied the existence of subnational identities, but rather minimised their relevance, considering them to be mere expressions of 'regionalism'.[389]

3.3.5.4 Concealing Ideological Distinctions

The price to be paid for representing the legal systems in homogeneous terms is the concealment of the distinctions within those systems. Such distinctions can be understood not only as referring to the diverging cultures of particular minorities of ethnic, linguistic, religious natures and so on, in the anthropological sense that normally comes to mind when one thinks of the lack of national homogeneity. An emphasis on such contrasts between a majority and minority groups in the country would ultimately even strengthen the nationalist belief that nations are homogeneous while problems crop up only when a state is not organised on a national basis. Rather and more radically, homogeneity does not exist even within the majority, and cultural differences can in fact be linked to different social, economic or ideological categories too. Such aspects had been initially highlighted by Marxist theorists in particular, concerned with the peril that the emerging idea of national identity might have been an instrument to prevent the workers from developing a class consciousness.[390]

The way in which the emphasis on national cultures represses infra-national political dynamics is discernible even in the realm of private law. Some examples may help clarify this point. As long as one looks at legal systems from a classical positivist perspective, one is justified in affirming that national jurisdictions

[386] Ibid, 63–4.

[387] R Sefton-Green, 'Social Justice and European Identity in European Contract Law' (n 108), 282.

[388] 'Both Zimmermann and Legrand loosen ties between law and the nation state. Yet, both remain, themselves, tied to a methodological nationalism: Zimmermann in that he seeks to follow the example of the historical legal science in the codification movement; Legrand in that he deduces from the cultural features of common law and civil law their political (solipsistic) autonomy', C Joerges and C Schmid, 'Towards Proceduralization of Private Law in the European Multi-Level System', in A Hartkamp, MW Hesselink, EW Hondius, C Mak and E du Perron (eds), *Towards a European Civil Code. Fourth and Expanded Edition* (The Hague, Kluwer Law International, 2011) 277–309, 287.

[389] EJ Hobsbawm, *The Age of Capital. 1848–1875* (London, Weidenfeld and Nicolson, 1975) 86–87.

[390] *See* Chapter 1: 1.3.8 'National vs Social Identities: Notes on Socialism'.

are (more or less) homogeneous. In particular in civil law systems, codifications provide for only one answer to a question of law, while the highest court provides the correct interpretation of the rule for the whole country. From this point of view, there is little or no room for pluralism. Adopting a cultural perspective, however, such coherence of the legal order cannot be imputed to the homogeneity of the national culture anymore, although it is certainly plausible that the internal culture of lawyers shows a higher degree of homogeneity. This would fit an organicist *Volksgeist* idea, but contradicts the cultural complexity of modern societies. So, to take a clear example concerning family law, the fact that some jurisdictions have come to acknowledge same-sex marriage does not indicate that a particular idea of the marriage belongs to the culture of the nation, but rather that because of political circumstances, that particular 'liberal' cultural segment has arisen until it was eventually sanctioned in law.

Democratic procedures allow the shaping of the law according to the wish of the majority, but democratic majority is not the same as cultural homogeneity.[391] As in Smits' words,

> Even if Parliament, after long deliberation, comes up with a 'best' national solution (often in the form of a compromise), many people will still disagree with that solution. The truth is that there is no longer one ideal social arrangement; in its place, we only have competing views of what is right.[392]

Law can unquestionably be one of those social factors that influence culture—as affirmed by Rousseau and Montesquieu long ago[393]—so that it is likely that over time and under certain circumstances a particular value entailed in law will rise to the status of social cultural value, but these dynamics cannot be grasped if culture is seen as something steady. Given the impossibility of distinguishing cultural from technical aspects of law, the same holds true for contract law: the allegedly more economically liberal character of the English law of contracts seems to derive from the fact that in that procedural system almost only corporations and associations can afford the economic effort of legal procedures that reach the Supreme Court, so that the case law of that country is mainly based on business transactions.[394] This can explain distinctive 'business-friendly' features of that jurisdiction such as, notably, the refusal of a general clause of good faith, as well as the frequent choice for that legal regime in international transactions, considered

[391] Admittedly, national culture does not demand unanimity as to its contents, but statistics are at least a useful tool to get a more comprehensive view: according to a Spanish study of 2004, 26.5% of the population was against same-sex marriages, while 30% admitted they would have considered it a 'serious problem' if their sons had a homosexual relation; Centro de Investigaciones Sociológicas, Estudio n. 2568, June 2004, questions 14, 8 and 9.

[392] JM Smits, 'Beyond Euroscepticism: On the Choice of Legal Regimes as Empowerment of Citizens' (2010) 6 *Utrecht Law Review* 68–74, 72.

[393] *See* Chapter 2: 2.1.4.2 'The *Volksgeist* Theory'.

[394] H Kötz, 'The Jurisdiction of Choice: England and Wales or Germany?' (2010) 6 *European Review of Private Law* 1243–57, 1251–52.

with some reason by many English commentators as a good argument to object to Europeanisation.

Researching the historical and societal background of a legal system, a cultural analysis allows us to shed light on these and many other aspects, highlighting the cultural complexity of societies and rules behind the simplifications of positivism. Quite on the contrary, insisting on the notion of national legal culture overlooks this aspect, extending the cultural segment entailed in legal rules for the whole nation: 'national legal culture' then becomes just an easily misleading formula with the aim or result of concealing the domination of a particular cultural segment over the others, which hides and mortifies the existence of cultural pluralism—where of course, different cultural segments could also be productively analysed in terms of the Hofstedian dimensions. Furthermore, if the national legal culture argument gains normative force, the result will necessarily be the maintenance of the status quo and therefore an advantage for the cultural segment that had already established itself to the detriment of the others. This also amounts to a strategy of nation building—which is indeed an on-going process rather than the heritage of another historical period[395]—as it 'invents' a national culture drawing from a specific one, regardless of the political and economic reasons behind it. In this sense, national culture is often just the culture of those who have more power in the nation.

3.3.5.5 Non-nationalist Perspectives

The equalisation of culture and nation proposed by nationalism is rejected by several authors. Already the model elaborated by Hofstede has been criticised for the reason that it would emphasise homogeneity within the nation, downplaying important differences within it and similarities across nations. For example, it has been noticed that two small border-towns, one in Germany and the other in the Netherlands, will be much more similar to one another culturally than each would be to the capital of the country they belong to.[396]

In legal studies, Watson has made similar points in direct confrontation with the reductionism of Legrand, basically challenging the idea of a national cultural homogeneity. If the word which translates 'bread' in French means something slightly different from an analogous word in German, it must be said that even the same word in the same language can sound very different to two people within the same country.[397] By the same token, '[a] small farmer in the Belgian Ardennes will be closer in his legal conceptions to a small farmer in neighboring Germany than to a businessman from Brussels'.[398] What is implied by Watson is that there are some identities—in this case the professional identity of 'small farmer'—that

[395] J Leerssen, 'Over nationale identiteit' (n 311), 428.

[396] J Leerssen, 'Feminien en klagen, dat is twee keer hetzelfde zeggen' (n 309) at 9.

[397] A Watson, 'Legal Transplants and European Private Law' (n 285), 15–26.

[398] Ibid, 26.

can occasionally be much more important than national identities. This point introduces a new dimension into the debate: the relevance of non-geographical identities rather based on economic or sociological categories. If Legrand's thesis shares with nationalism a focus on the national dimension, Watson's position clearly transposes within legal studies the criticism of nationalism carried out by the multiple identities idea, of cosmopolitan inspiration, that has been alluded to several times in this book. It is time to address it more specifically.

This view has gained momentum in recent years, as it has been expressed notably by the Nobel prize-winner for economics, Amartya Sen, to challenge any form of reductionism of the person on the basis of which the world order is presented as an inhomogeneous jumble of ethnic, cultural and national groups possibly in conflict with one another. The strongest criticism that derives for nationalism is therefore that nation and culture do not necessarily coincide, as liberal nationalists more or less openly claim.[399] While nationalists make 'a fetish of culture',[400] cosmopolitans try to desecrate that fetish, pointing at how multi-faceted its figure is. At the basis of this argument lies the belief that '[t]he political conception of a person as a citizen of a nation—important as it is—cannot override all other conceptions and the behavioral consequences of other forms of group association'.[401]

Despite its association with the name of Sen, the idea is actually older. Another Nobel prize-winner for economics, Hayek, expressed a similar point without the uttered intention of challenging nationalist assumptions—to which he professed himself critical[402]—but rather to draw attention to the distinction between state and society:

> It is in fact very misleading to single out the inhabitants or citizens of a particular political unit as the prototype of the society. There exists, under modern conditions, no single society to which an individual normally belongs, and it is highly desirable that this should not be so. Each of us is fortunately a member of many different overlapping and interlacing societies to which he may belong more or less strongly or lastingly. Society is a network of voluntary relationships between individuals and organized groups, and strictly speaking there is hardly ever merely one society to which any person exclusively belongs. For practical purposes it may be innocuous to single out, in a particular context, some part of the complex order of often hierarchically related networks as specially relevant for the topic discussed, and to assume that it will be understood to which part of this complex the speaker or writer refers as 'the society'. But it should never be forgotten that today many persons and organizations belong to networks which extend over

[399] *See* Chapter 1: 1.3.7 'Do Nation and Culture Coincide?'

[400] B Kapferer, *Legends of People, Myths of State: Violence, Intolerance, and Political in Sri Lanka and Australia* (Washington, Smithsonian, 1998) 97.

[401] A Sen, 'Justice Across Borders' (n 181), 43.

[402] '[M]y personal position makes me unable to sympathize with any form of nationalism', Hayek wrote quite clearly in his *The Constitution of Liberty* (London and New York, Routledge, 2009) 350.

national boundaries as well as that within any nation any one may be an element in many different structures of this kind.[403]

Significantly, analogous views originally inspired the pluralist theories of the State which developed in the first half of the twentieth century, serving the more radical goal of rejecting the sovereignty of the State.[404]

The focus on the plurality of 'societies' or 'identities' permits the clarification, at least theoretically, of a controversial aspect. One could wonder whether it is really wise and convenient to blame the nationalist tendency to make cultural generalisations for presenting 'astonishingly limited and bleak understandings of the characteristics of the human beings involved'.[405] Looking for alternatives to that approach, the risk would be once again to create a new terrible cultural destiny from which it is impossible to escape: a businessperson will always be a businessperson, a farmer will always remain a farmer and so on, so that in the end we would recreate a class-based legal system which distinguishes people according to their social class, their profession or their education. Civic nationalism may be disqualified as 'reductionist', but its 'anti-hierarchical'[406] function cannot be so easily ignored: the French revolution and later the *Code civil* had at least the merit of overcoming such a class-based system. Abandoning this assumption would mean moving away from the foundations of the legal system of modern Europe and paving the way to new sweetened forms of apartheid. Is this really the direction contemporary societies are taking in the name of a deceitful anti-nationalism?

This concern might go too far. The argument of plural allegiances does not imply that non-national identities such as farmer or consumer will *always* be more important than the national identity. If it is true that our individuality is a jigsaw of multiple identities then '[n]one of them can be taken to be the person's only identity or singular membership category'.[407] As Sen alleged, these are rather multiple, occasionally conflictual and their weight changes according to the circumstances, '[f]or example, when going to a dinner, one's identity as a vegetarian may be rather more crucial than one's identity as a linguist, whereas the latter may be particularly important if one considers going to a lecture on linguistic studies'.[408] In the same line of reasoning and with regard to the relevance of these identities for law, Smits remarks that national culture may determine people's behaviour 'when they support their national football team, but does not bind them when they conclude a commercial contract'.[409]

403 FA von Hayek, *Law, Legislation and Liberty. Vol 3* (n 82), 140–41.

404 HJ Laski, *Studies in the Problem of Sovereignty* (New Haven, Yale University Press, 1917); GDH Cole, *Social Theory* (London, Methuen & Co, 1920).

405 A Sen, *Identity and Violence* (n 94), 103.

406 O Dann, 'Funktionen des Nationalismus in modernen Gesellschaften', in O Dann (ed), *Nationalismus und sozialer Wandel* (Hamburg, Hoffmann und Campe, 1978) 213.

407 A Sen, *Identity and Violence* (n 94), 5.

408 Ibid, 25.

409 JM Smits, 'Legal Culture as Mental Software' (n 93), 147.

3.3.5.6 Legal Significance of Multiple Identities

What are then the practical consequences of all these rather theoretical premises? Is it seriously conceivable to conjure the image of some kind of private intercultural law on the model of the classical private international law, which is precise enough to determine what affiliation will be more relevant for people in a particular circumstance and consequently establish which specific legal regime will be applicable? In the first place, it should be noticed that in fact this example is not completely frivolous, as modern private international law already provides for rules that perform a similar function: so for example, the provisions of the Rome I Regulation that limit the freedom of choice as to the applicable law in contracts with consumers and workers can be seen as recognition of the prevalence in certain circumstances of those identities of consumer or worker over identities based on nationality or geographical criteria—such as the place of habitual residence, that in European law already undermined the traditional criterion of nationality. Taking the aforementioned into consideration, the recognition of multiple identities does not do away with the anti-hierarchical function of nationalism determining a comeback to the 'status': differently from the identities based on status which civil codifications got rid of, the identity of a consumer is not a fixed but rather a dynamic one; for example, depending on the circumstances, everyone is also a consumer.

In the second place, there are other relevant theoretical implications. As Watson makes clear, the fact that there is no higher cultural similarity between a small farmer and a businessperson in the same country than between two farmers in different nations proves that there is no reason why private law rules should be necessarily national rather than, say, included in some common legal code (which holds particularly true if one considers that, pursuant to the regulation that has been just mentioned, parties are generally free to choose the contract law that will bind them).[410] In the context of the on-going debate on European private law, such a view lends legitimacy to the idea of an optional code that parties may be free to adopt as a legal regime additional to those of the nation-states.[411]

The same conclusion that plural identities in Europe demand more freedom of choice and optional instruments is drawn by Smits. According to this author, one should already start asking 'if the fact that people are English or live in the United Kingdom automatically implies that national English law has to apply to everything they do'.[412] In this sense, the strategy that is more attentive to the theme of the plurality of identity is *differentiation*, which allows people to opt out of their national legal system and opt for a legal regime that is more suitable to their

[410] A Watson, 'Legal Transplants and European Private Law' (n 285), 25–26.

[411] *See* MW Hesselink, 'The Case for a Common European Sales Law in an Age of Rising Nationalism' (2012) 8 *European Review of Contract Law* 342–66.

[412] JM Smits, 'Legal Culture as Mental Software' (n 93), 146.

culture,[413] something which could be moreover particularly important in an era of accentuated multiculturalism and social pluralism. The choice as to applicable legal regime, in other words, would be up to the people.[414]

While the idea of people as completely free agents who choose the legal regime that best suits their interests still provokes some doubts, to say the least—unless of course one naïvely sustains that the establishment of some kind of free-market anarchism is one of the values a legal system should strive for—the theory of multiple identities still has important implications for the debate on the Europeanisation of private law. The most important lesson to be drawn is that there is no theoretical justification to affirm that only a national system of law can reflect the culture of citizens, because such culture is in reality a set of different beliefs, notions and allegiances which are often independent of nationality and not always significant in a contract law perspective. If this is true, even subnational or supranational regulations can be suitable to mirror that culture, in particular if allegiances transcend the borders of a nation-state, then one is legitimised to speak of forms of legal unification.[415]

The supranational institutional context of the European Union already offers several examples of the ways in which different identities can reveal themselves and challenge nationalistic assumptions. As far as the institutional organisation is concerned, the European Parliament represents an attempt to supersede national distinctions and allow a political confrontation between subjects that are gathered and interact with one another on the basis of ideological rather than geographical distinctions. This does not exclude the idea that political distinctions could occasionally (actually quite often) give way to 'classical' national differentiations, which reveal themselves in cross-cutting majorities. This is normal, since identities—including the national one—gain prevalence 'according to the circumstances'. Besides, there are examples that directly concern the process of the Europeanisation of private law.

3.3.5.7 Multiple Identities and the Process of Europeanisation

In the field of contract law, some evidence of the relevance of non-national allegiances can be found, for instance, in the responses that have been given by national governments, consumer organisations, businesses and lawyers to the European Commission after the publication of the 'Communication on European Contract Law' of July 2001.[416] In the 'Communication on a More Coherent

[413] Ibid, 147.

[414] JM Smits, 'Beyond Euroscepticism' (n 392), 70 ff.

[415] Already in the 1970s Wieacker affirmed: 'Einmail ist heute der Nationalstaatsgedanke selbst geschwächt. Gewiß kann uns auch heute niemand sonst abnehmen, Recht und Freiheit im eigenen Hause zu bestellen; aber starke Interessen und Loyalitäten richten sich heute auch auf übernationale Gemeinschaften und damit auch auf eine Rechtsvereinheitlichung in größerem Maßstab', F Wieacker, *Industriegesellschaft und Privatrechtsordnung* (Frankfurt am Main, Athenäum-Fischer-Taschenbuch-Verlag, 1974) 92.

[416] COM/2001/398.

European Contract Law—An Action Plan',[417] those responses that came from various parts of Europe have been grouped together according to the social or economic function (governments, consumers, businesses, lawyers and so on)[418] of the respondents instead of their nationality. *Mutatis mutandis*, this represents the opposite choice to that made by Hofstede in his study, which on the contrary distinguished the respondents to questionnaires on the basis of their nationality. Distinguished on the basis of the function of the respondents, the reactions to the Commission even show a reasonable homogeneity within those categories. There is for instance a higher propensity for academic lawyers and legal practitioners to favour the famous proposed 'option IV'—that is, a new comprehensive European legislation—which plainly contrasts with the general disfavour of the business for that hypothesis.[419] On the contrary, it is among businesses that the idea of a minimalistic approach by the European communities seems to be favoured, while particular emphasis is put on the necessity to acknowledge freedom of contract and reduce mandatory interventions. If the results had been grouped together keeping in consideration the nationality of the respondents instead of their socio-economic function, the results obtained would have appeared to be less homogeneous. Even in that case, anyway, the results could have been different enough to allow us to speak of different average cultures in different countries, provided, of course, with the usual disclaimer as to the acceptable imprecision of the idea of cultural homogeneity.

While these circumstances do not necessarily lead to the eccentric (and in reality, likely dangerous) idea that instead of national legal regimes Europe should have 'economic' or 'sociological' codifications, they highlight the methodological reductionism that, although originating in the era of nationalism, still affects various aspects of the legal debate. The discussion on the Europeanisation of private law continues to take the nation as a starting point, implying that there is some kind of homogeneity between the members of a nation while it adopts national understanding of the concept of culture—whose functional equivalent in the legal debate became legal culture, the main argument of critics of Europeanisation. Such an approach is coherent with a nationalist *Weltanschauung*. If one assumes that a French consumer is primarily a Frenchman, and only secondly a consumer, then the preference for the national level within the European multi-level private law system is consistent with the premise. Nonetheless, if one wants to underline the identity of consumer, the conclusion would not necessarily lead in the direction of the national level and the option of a supranational regulation—may it be in the form of a contract code, a so-called optional instrument, a comprehensive directive on consumer rights, a uniform legal method and so on—would appear

[417] COM/2003/68.

[418] More precisely, respondents have been distinguished in governments (and these further distinguished in national governments), business (further distinguished in manufacturing industry, retail trade and so on), consumer organisations, legal practitioners, academic lawyers.

[419] COM/2003/68, 4.4.4, 4.4.5 and 4.4.2.

more attractive and not in contradiction with the valuable respect for cultural diversity.

3.3.6 Concluding Remarks

While in a purely Kelsenian perspective every legal rule finds its justification and reason for validity in a hierarchically superior rule—up until the *Grundnorm*—in an external perspective every rule finds a justification which resides in non-legal elements: politics, economy and, in a broader sense, culture. The analysis of legal culture is for this reason fundamental for a comparative analysis of law. In particular in the European context, fascinating attempts have been made to link legal culture with the more general societal culture, which in a way, appear as the attempt to prove scientifically the *Volksgeist*. However, the analysis of the broad concept of culture has mainly remained limited to the national dimension, coming to coincide with 'national culture', a still unclear concept distrusted by an increasing number of anthropologists and mainly employed by nationalists to found the political claim to organise states on a national basis. Such a limitation—which shows the greatest trouble in concealing cultural variety within and beyond the borders of the nation—is not necessarily false but inaccurate and almost unavoidably leads to the conclusion of the cultural undesirability or even impossibility of detaching private law from the national unit. The historical nationalisation of private law which has been addressed in Chapter 2 has led not just to the creation of distinct systems of private law in Europe, but more importantly, to the rise and establishment of methodological nationalism.

Even despite all the methodological reservations about those studies that tried to prove scientifically the existence of national characters, the importance of national identities cannot be plainly confuted, just as one cannot seriously claim that personal identity develops independently from the context in which a person lives or has lived. Quite on the contrary, everything depends on its context. It is anyway opportune that the importance of other identities is also recognized. Limiting the analysis of culture to the sole national dimension in the end appears as an arbitrary choice that can easily misrepresent reality and that cannot be seriously justified unless one accepts the unspoken nationalist assumption that the nation is our only allegiance.

Chapter 4

Euronationalism

NATIONALISM HAS THUS far been described as a multi-faceted principle that can take on different forms according to the particular context and historical moment in which it arises. More specifically, the realisation of its programmatic aim—that is, bringing the national and the political unit to overlap—can in the first place nourish progressive movements aimed at the creation of nation-states, as well as in a successive phase nourishing conservative or even reactionary movements aimed at preserving the national status quo and fostering the national interest once a nation-state has already been constructed. The indeterminacy of the concept of nation, together with the practical impossibility of ever achieving a national homogeneity, makes it easy for nationalist forms of these two types to conflict with each other, each claiming to speak in the name of a particular national group. This is particularly evident even today in the experience of certain countries in which regional groups claim a particular autonomy or even independence, so that, for instance, the dispute between Spain and Catalonia on the use of the terms 'nation' and 'nationality' to define a particular community is not only a quarrel about the most proper use of a word but reveals the presence of nationalist tensions. In this sense it becomes manifest that in the contemporary world order as organised in states, the nationalist claims of a given national unit are usually opposed to those, equal and contrary, of another unit which adopts a different understanding of nation. When dealing with nationalist manifestations it is then useful to take cognisance of the other group against which nationalist claims are directed.

As we have previously drawn an analogy between nationalist arguments and the arguments employed in legal studies that object to Europeanisation, it is opportune to verify whether such 'nationalism of resistance' is opposed to an analogous and contrary proactive nationalism based on a different understanding of the nation. In other words, the opposition occurs between a 'state nationalism' aimed at the maintenance of the political unit at the national level—within the state—and a kind of 'European nationalism' aimed at moving that political unit to a different supranational level. An influence of the nationalist ideology could be detected even behind the integration aims of the European institutions and the arguments employed by scholars who *sustain* Europeanisation. It has been suggested earlier[1] that the European Union is a new framework for nationalism to

[1] Introduction, 1.1.2: 'The Persistence of Nationalism'.

operate in a broader context rather than the superseding of nationalist schemes, so that Europeanism may easily translate into a form of nationalism in Europeanist disguise, but at the same time it can now be asked whether and to what extent the European integration process *in itself* can be considered a Euronationalist project. Such a conceptualisation should not surprise: as a legitimate political principle which can still contribute to the elaboration of political communities, the basic assumptions of nationalism can by the same token contribute to the theoretical and political elaboration of even post-national institutions.

In this chapter, therefore, some general considerations will be made with regard to the different forms and characters of Euronationalism, subsequently showing its impact on the process of the Europeanisation of private law. Quite definitely, the complex question of Europeanism cannot be disentangled *tout court* considering it an expression of a (new?) kind of pan-nationalism; on the contrary the characteristic features of the processes of Europeanisation are so peculiar that the reductionist qualification of these dynamics as nationalism necessarily appears inadequate or provocative. Bearing this in mind, anyway, some links between opposite phenomena can be shown which, looked at from this angle, may reveal some important features even with regard to the approximation of national laws.

The use of the term Euronationalism may suggest the image of a movement for the creation of a European superstate which would act as a protagonist in a future world scenario characterised by the disappearance of nations and the creation of other superstates. Sustaining the European project with the aim of establishing a superstate politically or economically opposed to other world powers would be indeed a plainly super-nationalist vision, as well as a quite ambiguous one.[2] However, coherently with the distinction between state and nation and the suggested idea that unification of law is a strategy for building the nation rather than the state, the question that has to be asked here is not whether Europeanisation projects are steps on the way to the creation of a European *state*—which would lead us to the eternal question of the federative or confederative nature of the Union—but rather, what their relevance is for the definition of a European *nation* as the basis for common political and legal institutions.

4.1 THE IDEA OF EUROPE

At first glance, the expression European nationalism refers to the complex of particular nationalist manifestations in Europe. It is therefore a collective name given to a series of different and inhomogeneous phenomena, which nonetheless share the same basic nationalist assumption. A commonality of purpose between those manifestations is made possible by the fact that, according to the liberal nationalist principle, each nation should recognise the equal right to self-determination of all other national groups, which makes nationalism a possibly universal principle

[2] R Dahrendorf, *Perché l'Europa? Riflessioni di un europeista scettico* (Roma, Laterza, 1997) 47 ff. This author rather pleads for a 'heterogeneous nation-state', 64.

with necessarily local realisation. This aspect in particular marks the difference between liberal manifestations of nationalism and the aggressive movements that gained momentum at the beginning of the twentieth century which more or less explicitly rejected that principle in the name of the overriding national interest. While in reality the indeterminacy of the notion of nation and the exclusive focus on the national interest—occasionally opposed to those of other nations—makes the pacific coexistence of different nationalist movements more complicated than nationalists like to suggest, the expression European nationalism can therefore be used to show a general unity of intentions among those groups and movements sharing the same ideology. Besides this understanding, one can also speak of Euronationalism in a very different sense, as an international movement that, given a broad interpretation of nation, aims at establishing a European state whose legitimacy is founded on a European nation. In this second sense, the political unit should come to coincide with a national one which is identified in a broader group of peoples, basically European populations, considered as a unique people. Curiously, these two conceptions are not necessarily opposed and often even complementary to each other, as they share some cultural and historical roots.

While the cultural background of modern ethno-cultural nationalism in Europe is normally identified with German Romanticism, it should also be borne in mind that the exclusive focus on one particular nation as strongly opposed to other nations in Europe was a characteristic particularly associated with the second phase of Romanticism, while its origins were actually of a more clear Europeanist inspiration, even if still opposed to the cosmopolitan idea of Europe that Enlightened intellectuals in particular sustained. One apparent example of these tendencies is Novalis's work *Die Christenheit oder Europa*, in which the cultural unity of Europe was emphasised and based on mainly religious criteria, in apparent contrast to the Voltairian secular vision of Europe.

In politics, even rising nationalism occasionally showed a clear European vocation. Firstly, the pursuit of national independence was seen as a principle valid for all European nations, so that revolutionaries of different origins could belong to the same network in order to better achieve their particularistic but common goals. As Smith puts it, 'the basic goals of nationalists everywhere were identical: they sought to unify the nation, to endow it with a distinctive individuality, and to make it free and autonomous'.[3] The political activity of Mazzini is a clear example thereof: after the disaggregation of the *Giovine Italia*, the new movement of the ideologue of the Italian Risorgimento was baptized *Giovine Europa*. The relation between Europe and the nation was nonetheless doomed to remain dramatic: as an author has highlighted:

> It is noteworthy that the two countries with the strongest traditions of Europeanism, Italy and Germany, were not unified. Both the Risorgimento and the drive for German unity exalted the idea of Europe. However, once these countries became unified, the

[3] AD Smith, 'National Identity and the Idea of European Unity' (1992) 68 *International Affairs*, 55–76, 61.

earlier enthusiasm for Europe degenerated into national chauvinism and irredentism. The universalist principles associated with Europe were overshadowed by the particularism of national cultures.[4]

Secondly, a movement for the creation of a European state—a goal for which the establishment of nation-states was considered a first necessary step—soon arose. Of course, plans for a politically united Europe, albeit and for sure hardly comparable to contemporary ones, have continued to exist at least since the fall of the Western Roman Empire,[5] though great ambiguity existed as to the determination of the borders of Europe. Limiting ourselves to more recent years, Victor Hugo, already a supporter of the independence claims of several nations in Europe, famously expressed the ideal of a United States of Europe, a new liberal and peaceful state in which European nations would have joined enthusiastically without renouncing their distinctive features.[6] In this sense, the European ideal smoothly coexisted with and completed the nationalist idea.

Between the second half of the nineteenth and the beginning of the twentieth centuries, calls for a federal state, even representing a liberal and Christian nation called 'Pan-Europa',[7] proliferated. This particular form of European nationalism remained, however, minor and politically non-influential, so that Europe remained predominately a cultural idea, evidently overwhelmed by the success of that internally oriented nationalism that soon took on a more ethnic and illiberal connotation. It was 1908 when Georges Sorel predicted that, since the idea of integrating different populations like the Europeans seemed still impracticable, in just ten years Europe would have sunk again into war.[8] He had been too optimistic: war broke out again already in 1914.

[4] G Delanty, *Inventing Europe. Idea, Identity, Reality* (Basingstoke, Macmillan, 1995) 79.

[5] H Mikkeli, *Europe as an Idea and an Identity* (Basingstoke, Palgrave Macmillan, 1998) 35.

[6] In his speech at the International Peace Congress of Paris in 21 August 1849, Hugo said: 'Un jour viendra où vous France, vous Russie, vous Italie, vous Angleterre, vous Allemagne, vous toutes, nations du continent, sans perdre vos qualités distinctes et votre glorieuse individualité, vous vous fondrez étroitement dans une unité supérieure, et vous constituerez la fraternité européenne, absolument comme la Normandie, la Bretagne, la Bourgogne, la Lorraine, l'Alsace, toutes nos provinces, se sont fondues dans la France. Un jour viendra où il n'y aura plus d'autres champs de bataille que les marchés s'ouvrant au commerce et les esprits s'ouvrant aux idées. Un jour viendra où les boulets et les bombes seront remplacés par les votes, par le suffrage universel des peuples, par le vénérable arbitrage d'un grand Sénat souverain qui sera à l'Europe ce que le parlement est à l'Angleterre, ce que la diète est à l'Allemagne, ce que l'Assemblée législative est à la France !'

On Hugo's idea of Europe, also *see* E Ousselin 'Victor Hugo's European Utopia' (2006) 34 *Nineteenth-Century French Studies* 32–43.

[7] This is the view of the movement International Paneuropean Union, the programmatic manifesto of which, *Pan-Europa* by Richard Graf Coudenhove Kalergi, was published in 1923.

[8] 'En Amérique, on a fédéré des gens tous pareils les uns aux autres, vivant dans des Etats tous pareils... La belle affaire ! Mais comment ferez-vous pour fédérer des Slaves, ou religieux ou mystiques révolutionnaires ; des Scandinaves assagis ; des Allemands ambitieux; des Anglais jaloux d'autorité; des Français avares; des Italiens souffrant d'une crise de croissance; des Balkaniques braconniers; des Hongrois guerriers? Comment calmerez-vous ce panier de crabes qui se pincent toute la sainte journée? Malheureuse Europe! Pourquoi lui chacher ce qui l'attend? Avant dix ans, elle sombrera dans la guerre et l'anarchie, comme elle a toujours fait deux ou trois fois par siècle', quoted in G Chabert,

A few decades later, in the disarray of the Second World War, Europe became even more clearly an empty word deprived of an autonomous meaning, and European unity ended up being advocated by irreconcilably different political sides. On the one hand, the pan-nationalist idea of Europe survived among nationalists in the darkest days of the continent, but it now came to coincide with a brutal Nazi empire, so that even Hitler dared speak in the name of the European culture and civilisation.[9] The idea of European unity was furthermore essential to fascist ideology,[10] and the plan of creating a federal and anti-Semitic organisation called the *European community*, integrated under the flag of the Third Reich (and from which the United Kingdom had to be excluded) was even envisaged as a concrete (albeit at that point evidently unreachable) political proposal in the manifesto of the Fascist Republican Party, as one of the last gasps of the fading Mussolinian era.[11] On the other hand, a federative supranational organisation was seen as an ideal that could transform itself as a solution to the ills Europe was experiencing in that period. In 1941 Altieri Spinelli and Ernesto Rossi wrote the famous Ventotene Manifesto by which the European Federalist Movement was founded, giving new impulse to the vision of Aristide Briand, also honorary president of the aforementioned Paneuropean movement, who had advanced the progressive idea of a *European Union* already ten years earlier. The successive creation of the European Communities first and the European Union later—the historical background of which is widely known—revitalised the aspiration, together with a European *state*, to something similar to a European *nation*, based on a series of elements shared by all European populations.

In general and even in less extreme situations than those mentioned, it is therefore manifest that the idea of a European identity has always been generic enough to be compatible with—and reproached by—both leftist and rightist political perspectives, as well as, paradoxically, an instrument for 'state-nationalist' aims. This latter point is what emerges not only after a consideration of the fascist imperialist views, but also visions expressed in a previous historical phase. The Napoleonic

L'idée européeenne. Entre guerres et culture : de la confrontation à l'union (Bruxelles, Peter Lang, 2007) 198. *See* also H Mikkeli, *Europe as an Idea and an Identity* (n 5), 89.

[9] Speech of 21 June 1941 to the German people, in F Herr, *Der Glaube des Adolf Hitler. Anatomie einer politischen Religiosität* (München, Bechtle, 1968) 379.

[10] G Delanty, *Inventing Europe* (n 4), 111.

[11] The point 8 of the Manifesto di Verona of 1944 stated: 'Fine essenziale della politica estera della Repubblica dovrà essere l'unità, l'indipendenza, l'integrità territoriale della Patria nei termini marittimi ed alpini segnati dalla natura, dal sacrificio di sangue e dalla storia […] Altro fine essenziale consisterà nel far riconoscere la necessità degli spazi vitali indispensabili ad un popolo di 45 milioni di abitanti sopra un'area insufficiente a nutrirli. Tale politica si adoprerà inoltre per la realizzazione di una comunità europea, con la federazione di tutte le Nazioni che accettino i seguenti principî fondamentali: a) eliminazione dei secolari intrighi britannici dal nostro continente; b) abolizione del sistema capitalistico interno e lotta contro le plutocrazie mondiali; c) valorizzazione, a beneficio dei popoli europei e di quelli autoctoni, delle risorse naturali dell'Africa, nel rispetto assoluto di quei popoli, in ispecie musulmani, che, come l'Egitto, sono già civilmente e nazionalmente organizzati', in R De Felice, *Autobiografia del fascismo. Antologia di testi fascisti 1919–1945* (Torino, Einaudi, 2004) 474.

idea of Europe was almost the same as his idea of a French empire,[12] while many French conveniently praised the idea of Europe exactly when European culture was most strongly inspired by the French language and civilization, with Paris that would have served as the European capital.[13] Conversely, German intellectuals often considered Europe as the quintessence of Christendom and, of course, Germanic culture.[14] Instrumental references to Europe, with the aim of fostering particular national agendas, also remain self-evident in politics. Considering the more or less explicit exploitations of the European idea, at least the merit of frankness must be given to Peter the Great, who once clearly said: 'We shall need Europe for a few decades, and then we can turn our backside to her'.[15]

In conclusion, similarly to nationalism *tout court*, Euronationalism also appears to be a concept that can take several forms in different periods and contexts, so that in this place it seems preferable to avoid trying to develop a precise and comprehensive definition of it. Rather, distinctions between Euronationalist forms could be based on the criteria already employed to define European identity—therefore distinguishing between civic, ethnic and cultural manifestations[16]—and most importantly, on the political agendas associated with that idea.

4.2 REASONS FOR EUROPE-BUILDING

Imaging Europeanism as a form of pan-nationalism logically presupposes that the same political and economic reasons lying at the basis of the nationalist ideology also play a fundamental role in Euronationalism. In other words, the answers to the questions 'why the nation?' and 'why Europe?' should be somehow connected.

In Chapter 1, where the reasons for nation building were discussed, reference has been made to the Gellnerian idea that along with political reasons, economic circumstances were especially important in the process of the formation of nation-states. According to this perspective, which is partially contested by ethno-symbolists who prefer to underline the irrational character of the national sentiment that existed *ab aeterno* but arose at a random moment in history for unclear reasons, the process of nationalisation would have been more or less intentionally steered by economic, political and intellectual elites, occasionally with the support of parts of the populations. In this perspective, the national sentiments of all the

[12] H Mikkeli, *Europe as an Idea and an Identity* (n 5), 62.

[13] Ibid, 80.

[14] G Delanty, *Inventing Europe* (n 4), 71, 80 and 104–5.

[15] Cited by T Szamueli, *The Russian Tradition* (London, Fontana, 1998) 136 and G Delanty, *Inventing Europe* (n 4), 76.

[16] For this reason, a distinction between Europeanism as a civic phenomenon and Euronationalism as an ethno-cultural one—proposed for instance by T Risse, *A Community of Europeans? Transnational Identities and Public Spheres* (New York, Cornell University Press, 2010)—cannot be fully accepted in this place, since it assumes nationalism as a chiefly ethno-cultural phenomenon, forgetting its civic variations which can, on the contrary, be conceptualised in terms of civic Euronationalism.

artists, poets and intellectuals who spread the national idea were surely genuine rather than the result of opportunistic calculations, but those pleas would have remained unheard by history if the new kind of modern society had not needed nationalism.[17] This process took place only in a recent era for the reason that, according to Gellner, the political organisation of the nation-state was the most convenient one to fit the needs of industrialising societies. This new kind of society asked for worker mobility which, in turn, required some kind of egalitarianism: 'Nationalism is rooted in a *certain kind* of division of labour, one which is complex and persistently, cumulatively changing'.[18] In particular, only a unified space with no borders any more would have allowed for the necessary circulation of workers, while the national ideal, instilling in people the idea of a common belonging which replaced the stronger ties of the community of origin, facilitating people's mobility and representing—it is opportune to repeat these words—a 'substitute for factors of integration in a disintegrating society'.[19]

If these reasons justified eighteenth- and nineteenth-century nationalism in the first place, it is easy to see that they are also of paramount importance to the European economic project. Such a shift from the nation-state to the supranational dimension is explainable since, while the framework of the nation-state represented an enlarged territorial and economic unit that could foster the economic development in the eighteenth and nineteenth centuries, facilitating the convergence of supply and demand on a larger scale, in the twentieth century the process of economic globalisation made national borders often appear as a limitation or at least an alteration of the normal dynamics of the markets, rather than that protected environment necessary to cultivate the economy and make transactions possible.[20] Marxist authors could expect that the normal outcome of this economic development would be colonialism, which was indeed hypocritically pursued by several European states exactly in the years in which the national principle affirmed itself in Europe, sometimes itself appearing as a form of internal colonialism. Nonetheless, after the horrific events of the world wars the

[17] E Gellner, *Nations and Nationalism* (Oxford, Blackwell, 1983) 61.

[18] Ibid, 24.

[19] M Hroch, *Nationale Bewegungen früher und heute. Ein europäischer Vergleich*, 14, quoted by EJ Hobsbawm, *Nations and Nationalism since 1780. Programme, Myth, Reality* (Cambridge, Cambridge University Press, 1990), 173.

[20] 'For example the German-French-Swiss valley of the upper Rhine is more likely to form a coherent market for many products than the national area of any one of the three States. It is due to the nationalization of economic thought in the nineteenth century and to the intervention of the nation State by trade law and other regulations that economic data were distorted, that homogeneous transboundary markets were divided into their national components and that these components were apportioned to the respective national markets. As a result, products of the same kind whether toothpaste or mineral water, pocket knives or instant coffee, still differ considerably in Basle, Freiburg and Colmar'. In this context, private law rules represent the framework that allow the functioning of the market, and some of its basic principles are even the 'prerequisite' of it, so that it would be erroneous to think that the simple elimination of state interventions could open up the market enabling the circulation of goods among countries, J Basedow, 'A Common Contract Law for the Common Market' (1996) 33 *Common Market Law Review* 1169–95, 1179–81.

conventional road of military colonialism was at least partially abandoned as history took a different course. In this context, the development of the European communities seems to respond at a higher level to the same needs to which nationalism could give an answer only some centuries ago: 'Taking Gellner's [...] argument that nationalism came into being to serve society in the process of industrialisation with a culturally uniform mode of communication, it could be argued that the idea of Europe is today fulfilling this role'.[21]

The economic perspective cannot, however, aim at explaining everything on its own. In the experience of the post-war European integration process (which includes but does not limit itself to the European communities) there is also a fundamental quest for international peace that was more accentuated than in the nationalist movements of the eighteenth and nineteenth centuries. At any rate, the two dimensions—political and economic—have always been strongly intertwined. In this regard, it must be noticed that since its first conception while Europe was still facing self-destruction during the Second World War, the European integration project was already thought of as a way to achieve a Kantian perpetual peace exactly by means of a limitation of national sovereignty and by combating economic protectionism.[22] Some years later, after the experiences of the European Coal and Steel Community and the EURATOM, the Treaty of Rome aimed at establishing a common market on the basis of the free movement of goods, capital, services, and persons—mainly workers—within the whole European territory. That mobility of workers which, in a modernist perspective is the reason behind the development of nationalism, was elevated in the European context to a fundamental freedom. Following a similar line of reasoning, the pivotal argument employed today by the Commission and many advocates of legal harmonisation in Europe is that legal diversity represents a hindrance in the exercise of those fundamental freedoms of circulation. In other words, even the creation of a European system of private law would be necessary to enable the mobility of businesses and consumers within the European territory. Considering these elements, if one accepts the modernist interpretation, it becomes apparent that the same reasons lie behind both nationalism and Europeanism, and the whole discourse about harmonisation of private law in Europe ultimately rests on a possibly Euronationalist assumption.

4.3 THE EUROPEAN IDENTITY

In the Europeanist view and independently from the political consequences to be drawn, Europe is characterised by a set of common traits which make it something more than a mere—actually quite questionable—geographical concept. In

[21] G Delanty, *Inventing Europe* (n 4), 8.

[22] *See* J Monnet, 'Algiers Memorandum' of 5 August 1943, now in T Salmon and W Nicoll (eds), *Building European Union. A Documentary History and Analysis* (New York, Palgrave, 1997) 21.

other words, there would be something which makes institutions and people in Europe at least more similar to one another than to institutions and people in other parts of the world. These traits are what concur to define the so-called European identity. Despite the different traditions of the various nationalities in Europe, several intellectuals have nonetheless argued that those differences seem secondary if compared with the deeper elements that keep Europeans together. This would concern not just political institutions but even cultural identities: 'The souls of the French and English and Spanish are, and will be, as different as you like, but they possess the same psychological architecture' and

> [i]f we were to take an inventory of our mental stocks today—opinions, standards, desires, assumptions—we should discover that the greater part of it does not come to the Frenchman from France, nor to the Spaniard from Spain, but from the common European stock. Today, in fact, we are more influenced by what is European in us than by what is special to us as Frenchmen, Spaniards and so on.[23]

This view was already denounced by Rousseau, who, in quite strongly critical terms—and exhorting the Polish people not to give in to the temptation of imitating different nations—affirmed that there were no longer Frenchmen, Germans, Spaniards or Englishmen, but only Europeans with the same tastes, passions and customs, since none of them had been shaped along national lines by national institutions.[24]

He recognised in any case that Europe was more than just a geographical qualification and it constituted a community held together by the same religion, traditions and even laws, which could have served as basis for a future political common organisation which still respected national spirits.[25] The idea that Europe is characterised by a distinctive set of political principles which are not to be found elsewhere appears as a historical leitmotif so that, similar to national identities, also the more abstract European identity has mostly been construed in contrast to other civilisations. For a large part of history, in particular the association Europe/freedom and non-Europe/despotism has been repeated,[26] and that idea still influences even contemporary legal thought, as will be shown.

But even Euro-friendly enthusiasms could easily become an instrument for concealed national egoism and interests[27] or, in another sense, be a simple and

[23] J Ortega y Gasset, *The Revolt of the Masses* (New York, Mentor, 1950) 133–34.

[24] J-J Rousseau, *Considérations sur le gouvernement de Pologne, et sur sa réformation projetée* (Londres, 1782) 17.

[25] J-J Rousseau, *Extrait du projet de paix perpétuelle de Monsieur l'abbé de Saint-Pierre* (Paris, 1761).

[26] F Chabod, *Storia dell'idea d'Europa* [1961] (Roma, Laterza, 2010).

[27] Inasmuch as private law is concerned, the impression is that a strategy of hegemonic domination employed by national actors 'is to play up the idea of a European legal tradition in order to constitute a transnational space within which, working as cosmopolitans, they have a chance of exercising more influence than would be possible in a world of dispersed national systems with strong German and French blocs', D Kennedy, 'Thoughts on Coherence, Social Values and National Tradition in Private Law', in MW Hesselink (ed), *The Politics of a European Civil Code* (The Hague, Kluwer, 2006) 30.

rather irritating expression of the gusto of multilingual travelling elites, hardly representative of the experience of most people induced to migrate primarily for basic economic reasons.[28] If what Herder thought of the nation cannot be taken as evidence for the thoughts of a Westphalian peasant,[29] it could also be said that neither can Rousseau's idea of Europe be considered representative of the thoughts of the already legendary 'Polish plumber'.

These common aspects are, to be sure, still largely insufficient to make a 'nation' out of Europe, and the very idea of a nationalism which strives for the political recognition of a hypothetical European nation sounds odd. Even acknowledging the elusiveness of the idea of nation, even the most audacious Europeanist these days would still have many difficulties in defending the view that Europe is already a nation. In this sense, the European Union could at the most evolve into some kind of multi-national superstate, very different from the nineteenth century idea of state. In this light, the most fundamental claim of nationalism cannot be achieved, since even if a superstate were to be created, this political unit could never coincide with the national one. For those liberal nationalists who consider that the nation-state is still the only viable mechanism to implement democracy, this circumstance would signify the impossibility for the European Union to move in a more federalist direction. But in this sense, the lack of a European nation could quite easily become the questionable justification for why a further democratisation of European institutions should not be pursued. This point is crucial for the institutional development of Europe, so that at least some remarks need to be made in this regard.

The idea of something like a European nation that evolves into a supranational state necessarily conflicts with the nationalist principle for those who adopt mainly primordialist positions or at least acknowledge ethnic factors a pivotal role in the process of the creation of nations. To them, it is clear that the diversity existing on the continent cannot be reduced under the idea of a European nation.[30] National identifications are vivid, popularised and established, unlike the European identity.[31] In this sense, the decisive element is not much the fact that Europeans do not share the same blood, but rather that they very often do not even share the same historical memories and myths.[32] In contrast, nationalists in past centuries could appeal to a very different set of common beliefs and traditional popular myths to highlight the particularity of specific national groups;

[28] L Passerini, 'Introduzione. Dalle ironie dell'identità alle identità dell'ironia', in L Passerini (ed), *Identità culturale europea. Idee, sentimenti, relazioni* (Firenze, La Nuova Italia, 1998) 8.

[29] EJ Hobsbawm, *Nations and Nationalism since 1780* (n 19), 48.

[30] AD Smith, 'A Europe of Nations. Or the Nation of Europe?' (1993) 30 *Journal of Peace Research* 129–35, 134.

[31] AD Smith, 'National Identity and the Idea of European Unity' (n 3), 62.

[32] A short outline of Smith's argument can be found in H Mikkeli, *Europe as an Idea and an Identity* (n 5), 217–19.

these were myths punctually rediscovered[33] or even plainly invented.[34] But while these differences are hardly deniable, for those who adopt a modernist view, these divergences are still insufficient in order to think of Europe and nation as two irreconcilable concepts. In the modernist perspective, no actual nation existed naturally before it was built at a certain moment in history, building upon a series of pre-national allegiances among people in certain geographical areas. In this sense, the idea of making Europe a nation is definitely not much more foolish than was the idea of bringing together Catalans and Basques under the Spanish kingdom, Berliners and Bavarians under the German empire or Sardinians and Neapolitans under the Italian state in the first place. In this sense, it is interesting to note that the same words used by Bismarck to express doubts concerning the political idea of Europe—'geographical expression'—had been also employed by Metternich with regard to the Italian peninsula, just before Italy was eventually unified, actually in quite an anomalous way, in 1861. In conclusion, 'Europe does not exist any more naturally than do nations'.[35] Even more stimulatingly, the idea of Europe, although in a very different form, historically precedes the idea of many European nations.

An aprioristic rhetoric on the imagined nature of nations should nonetheless be avoided, as in reality the development and functioning of nation-states is a much more intricate process than disquisitions on the artificiality of nations may suggest. Rather, taking a modernist approach, one should not be much interested in verifying whether something as a European nation exists and has good reasons to strive for political unity, but rather verify whether strategies are in place to 'build' it. In other words, the European idea should be considered as a normative concept subject to critical reflection.[36] In this light, one could think whether some of the nation-building strategies that have been more or less usefully employed in the past for nation-states are being employed at the supranational level to lend a kind of 'national' legitimacy to the European political model, regardless of the tedious question as to whether Europe would be reduced to a unity called 'nation': that question is redundant and would inevitably lead to the frustrating compromise conclusion—typical of discussants tired of arguing and in search of an easy settlement—that basically any view is right as long as we recognise that we are presupposing different definitions.

The main point that has to be addressed is therefore whether the process of Europeanisation presents similar characteristics to a process of nationalisation and whether—and which—'nation-building' techniques are being used and to

[33] A-M Thiesse, *La création des identités nationales: Europe XVIIIe-XXe siècle* (Paris, Éditions du Seuil, 1999) 107.

[34] EJ Hobsbawm, 'Introduction: Inventing Traditions', in EJ Hobsbawm and T Ranger (eds), *The Invention of Tradition* (Cambridge, Cambridge University Press, 1983) 1.

[35] G Delanty, *Inventing Europe* (n 4), 3.

[36] Ibid, 2.

what purpose. These points lead us to face a tricky problem political scientists have been dealing with for years: the definition of a 'European identity'.

4.3.1 Does a European Identity Exist?

Despite the political importance it could have, European identity remains an extremely vague idea, and the problem of identifying what such an identity is concretely based on remains open. The definition of European identity is in the end analogous to the nationalist individuation of the criteria on which belonging to the nation could be based. Not by coincidence, a political scientist considered in the end the whole idea of a European identity as a pan-nationalist programme.[37] The question as to what is European identity echoes undeniably the most fundamental dilemma of every nation, and could be rephrased in *qu'est-ce que l'Europe?* Similarly and even more than national identity, also the European identity appears to be an elusive and blurry concept which needs to be constructed rather than discovered.

According to one perspective, an authentic and comprehensive cultural unity in Europe has probably never existed, and has been invented only retrospectively.[38] While an 'idea of Europe' has somehow been a constant in history—though filled with very different contents and used with diverse goals, as has already been shown—it is rather unclear what the criteria of identification are which define the 'European' enough to make him or her different from an American, an Egyptian or a Chinese person. Given all the contradictory answers that can be given to this fundamental question, we might just throw in the towel, admitting that a European identity simply does not exist[39] or that this could at most be represented by its plurality and incoherence. The quest for a European identity would, therefore, be a merely rhetorical discourse brought about with the intention of culturally legitimising political constructions.[40] In an analytical perspective, of course, plurality as the defining feature of identity is a contradiction in terms; identity is etymologically and by definition 'the same' and can hardly accept plurality *within* itself. But politics is not the same as logics, and in political terms, such a new pluralist understanding of identity marks a considerable difference from the politics of identity traditionally promoted by nationalism.

However, as appealing as a radical conclusion can be, the fact that the discourse on a European identity appears as a rhetorical and instrumental exercise does not

[37] *See* N Wilterdink (1993), 'The European Ideal: An Examination of European and National Identity', 34 *European Journal of Sociology* 119–36.

[38] G Delanty, *Inventing Europe* (n 4), 80.

[39] S Papcke 'Who Needs European Identity and What Could It Be?', in B Nelson, D Roberts and W Veit (eds), *The Idea of Europe. Problems of National and Transnational Identity* (New York, Berg, 1992) 61–74.

[40] *See* G Delanty, *Inventing Europe* (n 4), 143.

necessarily imply that, at least in the eyes of people, there is no common identity.[41] Even empirical studies reveal that only a very small minority of Europeans do not think that such a thing as a European identity exists, even if their opinions subsequently diverge as to 'what' this is.[42] Thus, advocates for Europe have a case in sustaining that there is something which makes people in Europe somehow similar, even if Europeans are often not aware of it, embedded as they are in the 'banal nationalism' of the countries in which they live, and that make them 'subconsciously think and act much alike', while 'the coincidence of their opinions is not limited or restricted by national or state line'.[43]

4.3.2 Political Meaning of a European Identity

The expression 'European identity' has become common not only for popular use but also in political discourse. The attempt to find out the nature and contents of this concept appears particularly interesting from an institutional perspective too, since also '[t]he European Union as a political entity struggles to achieve a common identity for its citizens'.[44] The reason is that finding a European identity has a political importance within the legal architecture of the European Union, where it could serve as a form of civic legitimation for the whole supranational structure. If something like a European 'people' or 'nation' were to be 'imagined' on the basis of that shared identity, a new social subject would be created, which would reasonably demand representation in a European rather than in a national dimension. All in all, even the European citizenship was brought about in 1992 'by a deep sense of malaise and public disaffection with the European construct which threatened to undermine its political legitimacy'.[45] This point is relevant also for the politics of private law; for instance, critics of Europeanisation point out that only national legislators are in the ideal position to assess what the interests and preferences of their own co-nationals are[46] but if one sees a unity of interests and preferences among the citizens of Europe, then the reason why the national legislator should be preferred in a multi-level governance system becomes theoretically questionable.

At the present day, however, the existence of such a European subject is dubious.[47] Since the existence of a strong European identity has been denied by several

[41] M Barberis, *Europa del diritto* (Bologna, il Mulino, 2008) 61.

[42] More precisely, 3% of the respondents to Special Eurobarometer 346 Wave 73.3, April 2011, 95.

[43] J McCormick, *Europeanism* (Oxford, Oxford University Press, 2010) 220–21.

[44] F van Schendel and I Aronstein, 'Introduction: Euroscepticism and Multiculturalism' (2010) 6 *Utrecht Law Review* 1–7, 1.

[45] JHH Weiler, 'To Be a European Citizen: Eros and Civilization', in JHH Weiler, *The Constitution of Europe. "Do the New Clothes Have an Emperor?" and Other Essays on European Integration* (Cambridge, Cambridge University Press, 1999) 329.

[46] *See* Chapter 3, 3.1.1: 'The Ideal Locus of Private Law in the European Context'.

[47] E-W Böckenförde, *Welchen Weg geht Europa?* (München, Friedrich von Siemens Stiftung, 1997) 39–40.

commentators,[48] the lack of a European *demos* would make the entire idea of a European *demo*cracy hardly imaginable within a supranational framework. This point has not remained solely within the realm of pure academic interest. In one of its most important judgments—the famous *Maastricht-Urteil* of 1993—the German *Bundesverfassungsgericht* has denied that a European people actually exists. The legal consequences of this sociological premise, maintained constant through the years and confirmed in the later *Lissabon-Urteil* of 2009,[49] coherently follow: the democratic legitimacy of the European institutions necessarily involves national institutions, in the first place the parliaments, which remain the only bodies legitimated to represent national peoples, the only ones actually 'existing' and to which sovereignty belongs as expressly stated by national constitutions. On the contrary, the European Union must be defined as a mere '*Staatenverbund zur Verwirklichung einer immer engeren Union der—staatlich organisierten—Völker Europas (Art. A EUV), keinen sich auf ein europäisches Staatsvolk stützenden Staat*' ('*Staatenverbund* for the realisation of an ever closer union among peoples of Europe organised in states, and not a state based upon a European people').[50] On the basis of this argument, the German Constitutional Court stressed—until most recently in the decision concerning the constitutionality of the ESM Treaty and the Fiscal Compact[51]—that the participation of national parliaments in the administration of the European Union is a condition of legitimacy for German participation in that supranational organisation. The nation-state is indeed still the most important context in which democracy can be exercised and the political form of organisation for the national *Volk*, while any theoretical discussion as to possible transnational identities and redefinitions of the concept of people cannot so simply overlook the question as to the institutional framework demanded by democracy.

4.3.3 Constitutional Europatriotism

If the post-modernist view that a European identity is necessarily incoherent and in the end not a real 'identity' may appear unsatisfactory, it can be expected that more suitable results can be obtained by referring to a theory elaborated by one of the best-known advocates of modernity. The European identity could be built upon a theory of constitutional patriotism. The idea, developed in particular by Habermas, seems to be particularly useful for developing criteria of identification within Europe which are civic enough to make up, on the one hand, for the lack of any ethnic or cultural similarity between the Europeans and on the other hand, to

[48] M Kumm, 'Why Europeans Will Not Embrace Constitutional Patriotism' (2008) 6 *International Journal of Constitutional Law* 117–36, 118.

[49] German Constitutional Court, *Lissabon* [2009] BVerfGE 123, 267.

[50] German Constitutional Court, *Maastricht* [1993] BVerfGE 89, 155.

[51] German Constitutional Court [2012] BVerfGE, 2 BvR 1390/12.

avoid dangerous involutions in intolerance which characterised several nationalist projects in the past.

According to this view, as known, citizenship should be founded on a series of shared liberal values—often of a more procedural than substantive nature—while respect for these values represents the only condition of admission to the community. What would keep Europeans together is therefore the commitment to a set of shared values. In this sense, even the criticism that there is no such thing as a European *demos* can be dismissed inasmuch as it conceives of nations in purely ethnic terms as a community of descent, while a civic understanding of nations would allow us to move from the plurality of national ethnic *demoi* to the unity of a European civic *demos*.[52] In this sense, Europeans are not such because they share the same ethnic origin, religion or language, but rather because they all adhere to the same civic manifesto of liberal values. Adhering to a civic understanding of the nation, it becomes easier to imagine a European unity in that sense: already Renan thought that '*Les nations ne sont pas quelque chose d'éternel. Elles ont commencé, elles finiront. La confédération européenne, probablement, les remplacera*' ('Nations are not something eternal. They have begun, they will end. They will be replaced, in all probability, by a European confederation').[53] In this understanding, the dimension of European political ideology becomes fundamental.

This interpretation also has its drawbacks and has been criticised in particular for assuming that abstract legal principles can be used to develop a strong collective identity: a European identity would be excessively 'thin'. However, this criticism overlooks that '[a]bstract principles may be thin, but identities focused on them are not',[54] which is even more important considering that 'the common core of a European identity is the character of the painful learning process it has gone through, as much as its results'.[55] Commentators have nonetheless also expressed the concern that it is unlikely that European citizens will develop a common identity, given the actual institutional scenario (with regard in particular to electoral politics and accountability of the institutions) which does not favour the emergence of that 'public sphere', the existence of which is fundamental for the development of a common identity. If this is true, therefore, it can be concluded that citizens' attitudes towards the EU will 'continue wavering between fickle support and a lack of interest in European political life, on the one hand, and a stubborn nationalism, on the other'.[56] However, it cannot be overlooked that more recently

[52] J Habermas 'Why Europe Needs a Constitution' 11 *New Left Review* 5–26, 15–16. *See* also A Pizzorusso, *Il patrimonio costituzionale europeo* (Bologna, il Mulino, 2002) 176–79.

[53] E Renan, *Qu'est-ce qu'une nation?: Conférence faite en Sorbonne, le 11 mars 1882* (Paris, Calmann Lévy, 1882) 28.

[54] M Kumm, 'Why Europeans Will Not Embrace Constitutional Patriotism' (n 48), 123.

[55] J Habermas, 'Why Europe Needs a Constitution' (n 51), 21.

[56] M Kumm, 'Why Europeans Will Not Embrace Constitutional Patriotism' (n 48), 127 ff. In a similar sense, A Glencross, 'A Post-National EU? The Problem of Legitimising the EU Without the Nation and National Representation' (2010) 59 *Political Studies* 1–20, where particular emphasis is put on the role of the nation-state as mechanism of democracy.

certain topics related also to private and economic law have generated debates and even demonstrations across the whole of Europe, as has been notably the case with the Anti-Counterfeiting Trade Agreement (ACTA), eventually abandoned by the European Parliament also under the pressure of those protests. Whereas it might still be insufficient to speak of a common European public sphere, it is nonetheless an important sign that something like that could very easily develop out of spontaneous popular initiative in spite of academic scepticism.

As has been previously highlighted, although constitutional patriotism rejects ethnic nationalism, it shows continuity with at least the idea (not necessarily the practice) of civic nationalism. A Euronationalism which is in the first place inspired by constitutional patriotism can qualify as a manifestation of *civic* nationalism, different from the kind of Euronationalism based on ethnic or religious criteria which is also rapidly re-emerging. In any case, if we imagine the European identity as a construction based on the civic and voluntaristic criteria of the acceptance of a set of constitutional values, the question crops up consequently as to what are those constitutional values that have to be agreed upon by all Europeans and that concur to shape a European identity.

4.3.4 What Are the European Values?

In a way, the success of given political structures that have arisen in the Old World and later exported to the New World is so remarkable that these elements alone have become insufficient to be considered as characteristically European features rather than those of some kind of 'Western' civilisation. So for example, while Europe has always been associated with freedom in opposition to Asia which was associated with despotism—and even recently the legal philosopher Bobbio could spot a European 'ideology' based on (or at least rhetorically self-represented as based on) the rule of freedom[57]—it is self-evident that freedom cannot be considered a European prerogative any more, as it also represents a fundamental element, for instance, of the American or Japanese form of government. Europe could then at most be considered to be the historical cradle of the liberal values of a general Western tradition, but still not the only representative of those values in the present. In this sense, that contrast between the self and the other which makes possible the definition of identity becomes more complicated. The definition of European characteristic features presumes a logical operation against which the same criticisms that have been made of the systematizations of national cultures could be directed and that does not seem sufficient to embrace European diversity anyway.

[57] N Bobbio, 'Grandezza e decadenza dell'ideologia europea' (1986) 3 *Lettera internazionale*, 1–5.

The preambles of treaties and constitutions are always useful—though also easily misleading[58]—documents to get a grasp of the political dimension of the legal rules contained there and can offer some guidance to identifying a set of common political values. In the case of the European treaties, these already entail a list of fundamental principles that are—and shall be—shared by all European states. The need for a strong collective identity supporting the European project became more considerable along with the extension of competences of the European communities themselves, as a sign of the necessary interrelation between political power and civic legitimacy based on identity. While the Treaty of Rome, 1957, could only maintain a low profile, though already generically referring to values as solidarity between the peoples of Europe (and overseas) as well as peace and liberty, some decades later, the Treaty of Maastricht, 1992, could go into more detail, and the contracting parties confirmed 'their attachment to the principles of liberty, democracy and respect for human rights and fundamental freedoms and of the rule of law'. These principles are not purely rhetoric formulae, but rather conditions of adhesion to and permanence within the European Union, as the lack of respect for one of these principles can lead to the exclusion of a Member State from the Union. Even the treaties, in other terms, focus on a commonality of political values as elements that bind together European states. At the latest stage in this evolution, the new article 2 of the Treaty on the European Union now reads that:

> The Union is founded on the values of respect for human dignity, freedom, democracy, equality, the rule of law and respect for human rights, including the rights of persons belonging to minorities. These values are common to the Member States in a society in which pluralism, non-discrimination, tolerance, justice, solidarity and equality between women and men prevail.

To some extent, these values are laid down in the legal rules of several European states. Following the traditions of intellectuals who assumed that Europe shares certain political principles, constitutionalists pointed out that there is a set of basic values that bind all Member States and can lead to the notion of a European constitutional heritage, with respect for human rights assuming pivotal importance in this context.[59] If there is something that characterises the (self-representation of) European political identity, this seems to be its mixture of democracy and rights, liberalism and constitutionalism.[60] In this light, a sensitivity for fundamental rights manifested by the European institutions—notably including the Court of Justice that tied the activities of the other institutions to the respect of those values considered as an integral part of the EU legal system even before this

[58] This holds true for many constitutional provisions too and, in this sense, 'Most constitutions guaranteeing free speech and elections are as informative about the societies they allegedly define as a man saying "Good morning" is about the weather', E Gellner, *Nations and Nationalism* (n 17), 28.

[59] A Pizzorusso, *Il patrimonio costituzionale europeo* (n 52).

[60] M Barberis, *Europa del diritto* (n 41), 58.

principle was explicitly laid down in the provisions of the treaties,[61] but that only more recently made a stronger use of those principles—also serve the function of shaping a common political identity.

These elements, nonetheless, only concur to define the political values that are shared by the national systems but do not offer any guarantee that these values will be shared by citizens as well. Political principles, in other words, could define the identity of Europe but not of the Europeans. Nonetheless, empirical research shows that respect for human rights, peace, democracy and rule of law are perceived as the values that represent the European Union even by most European citizens.[62] While it would admittedly be difficult to turn against these values, it is remarkable that people *imagine* the European identity as based exactly on those ideals.

While the treaties necessarily adopt quite generic terms, moreover, it seems possible to identify further characteristics typical of Europe. Habermas and Derrida in particular singled out six characteristics that would distinguish Europe from other world powers, writing during historical events that dramatically divided a considerable portion of European public opinion from the government of the United States in particular. The two philosophers identified several features of Europe's political profile, among which the *privatisation of faith*, a particular conception of *politics and market* characterised by distrust in the market's ability to correct its own failures, *the struggle for 'more social justice'*, *sensitivity to injuries to personal and bodily integrity* which translates into the rejection of capital punishment, and the idea of the *mutual limitation of sovereignty*.[63] In the end, according to Habermas, the common core of European identity 'is the lasting memory of a nationalist excess and moral abyss'.[64] The predisposition towards a supranationality that goes beyond nationalism seems according to this view even inherent in the European identity, and also later commentators have highlighted that the 'levels of nationalism' in the European states are remarkably low if compared to

[61] ECJ 29/69 (1969) Stauder; ECJ 11/70 (1970) Internationale Handelsgesellschaft; ECJ 4/73 (1974) Nold.

[62] Eurobarometer 69, November 2008, cited in J McCormick, *Europeanism* (n 43), 63. However, a more recent survey by the Eurobarometer (Special Eurobarometer 346, Wave 73.3, April 2011, 95) asked this question: 'In your opinion, which of the following are the most important elements that go to make up a European identity?'. The answers were: the single currency, the euro (36%), democratic values (32%), geography (22%), common culture (22%), common history (17%), a high level of social protection (13%), symbols, flag, hymn and motto (11%), common religious heritage (5%), other (1%). There is no European identity (spontaneous, 3%), don't know (6%). Furthermore, more than 53% declared to feel attached to the European Union. The leading position is taken by 'the single currency', which represents a new option if compared with previous analogous surveys. In this sense, the introduction of this new option sent 'democratic values' at the second place of the ranking. The highly educated respondents, however, still place democratic values at the first position (97).

[63] J Habermas and J Derrida, 'February 15, or What Binds Europeans Together: A Plea for a Common Foreign Policy, Beginning in the Core of Europe' (2003) 10 *Constellations* 291–97, 295–97.

[64] J Habermas, *The Inclusion of the Other: Studies in Political Theory* (Cambridge MA, MIT Press, 1998) 28.

those of various non-European countries.[65] Political scientists have built upon these foundations, more specifically identifying some characteristics that seem to be typical of European societies in contrast to others even within the general category of the 'West'.[66]

Habermas and Derrida put emphasis on aspects of the European identity as the focus for fundamental rights (including bodily integrity) as well as social rights. In this light, the promotion of citizens' welfare is an expression of the social nature of Europe, particularly developed in an era in which Europe had to define its identity as a third way between the opposite economic and political models embodied by the United States and the Soviet Union. In this regard, a non-European observer can perceive that 'in Europe today it seems as though every country except Britain claims that one of the things that is distinctive about its national tradition is its highly social character'.[67]

4.4 LAW AS A EUROPE-BUILDING TOOL

Legal rules can also serve to promote a collective identity in Europe in the same way in which they can be (and have been) used as an instrument for nation building. While historically such a function of law has been undertaken for the consolidation of nations organised both on a civic and an ethno-cultural basis, if one accepts constitutional patriotism as the parameter for the construction of a collective identity, the function of legal rules becomes even more important: in this case, indeed, the object of identification of the citizens would plainly be law itself, as long as law is able to reflect faithfully the liberal values shared by citizens. In this light, the attempts that have been made in recent years to bring to fruition a Constitution for Europe assume a particular social importance and it is understandable why the idea of a European Constitution was sustained by Habermas in particular.[68]

4.4.1 Public Law

As the events surrounding the 'rise and fall' of the European Constitution are well known, it suffices to say that the proposed treaty adopted the rhetoric and symbolic function of national constitutionalism rather than its substance: while the denomination 'Constitution' appeared to be quite improper for a treaty of that kind, the classic symbolism which is usually associated with constitutional

[65] J McCormick, *Europeanism* (n 43), 71 ff.

[66] *See* ibid.

[67] D Kennedy, 'Thoughts on Coherence, Social Values and National Tradition in Private Law', in MW Hesselink (ed), *The Politics of a European Civil Code*, 29.

[68] J Habermas, 'Why Europe Needs a Constitution' (n 52), 5–26.

charters in Member States was present in that project as well. The bashful use of the term 'Constitution' in the ambiguous official denomination of the Treaty establishing a Constitution for Europe, as well as the reference to concepts like a flag, an anthem and a day of celebration confirmed the undisguised intention of competing with the Member States in nation-building practices, through the employment of classical instruments of—according to Billig's terminology—'banal nationalism'.[69] In other terms, 'in attempting to move beyond nationalism, the European Community attempted to fashion a European identity using the very tools of nationalism'.[70] This seems to confirm the idea that the European institutions embarked upon a Euronationalist project,[71] the outcome of which has been quite unsuccessful thus far.

This attempt, which may have been perceived as an undue interference in matters belonging to the historical consciousness of nation-states, may contribute to explain part of the firm political resistance encountered by that treaty and its definitive rejection following the famous French and Dutch referendums of 2005, furthermore preceded by inflamed debates in nationalist terms in those countries.[72] No wonder, then, that in order to overcome such resistance, the treaty projects had to renounce eventually not only the denomination of constitution and all references in the text of the treaty to flag and anthem—which will, however, continue to be employed as symbols of the Union by several Member States, with the telling exception of France and the Netherlands[73]—but even to a comprehensive form that included all different treaties, including notably the Charter of Fundamental Rights, in a single text that could resemble a national constitutional charter. With a brilliant expression that alludes to the official denomination of the abandoned treaty, the new treaty has been defined by a commentator as the treaty which does *not* establish a Constitution for Europe.[74] The European institutions have therefore initially embraced nation-building techniques, abandoning them—to the regret in particular of the European Parliament[75]—after the resistance of nations

[69] M Billig, *Banal Nationalism* (London, Sage, 1995).

[70] G Delanty, *Inventing Europe* (n 4), 128.

[71] 'Today such an "invented tradition" is clearly in the process of invention with the proliferation of a paraphernalia of emblems and slogans of the new official culture', ibid, 128.

[72] As to the Dutch experience, J Leerssen, *National Thought in Europe: A Cultural History* (Amsterdam, Amsterdam University Press, 2006) 243, highlights the role played in the results of a Eurosceptic twist in the political campaigns of most political parties for the elections in 2004. *See* also LFM Besselink, 'National and Constitutional Identity before and after Lisbon' (2010) 6 *Utrecht Law Review* 36–49, 43.

[73] Declaration 52 annexed to the Treaty of Lisbon: 'Belgium, Bulgaria, Germany, Greece, Spain, Italy, Cyprus, Lithuania, Luxemburg, Hungary, Malta, Austria, Portugal, Romania, Slovenia and the Slovak Republic declare that the flag with a circle of twelve golden stars on a blue background, the anthem based on the 'Ode to Joy' from the Ninth Symphony by Ludwig van Beethoven, the motto 'United in diversity', the euro as the currency of the European Union and Europe Day on 9 May will for them continue as symbols to express the sense of community of the people in the European Union and their allegiance to it'.

[74] J Ziller, *Il nuovo Trattato europeo* (Bologna, il Mulino, 2007) 115.

[75] *See* ibid, 25.

perceived as determined by nationalist concerns. Nonetheless, this is only part of the story, as the motivations that led to the rejection of the 'constitutional' treaty appear to be more intricate and are still passionately debated.[76]

4.4.2 Private Law

While the notion of constitutional patriotism refers firstly to the acceptance by citizens of a series of fundamental rules of a public nature, it is definitely not only public law that has an importance in the process of building a collective identity. As an instrument that governs the reciprocal relations between citizens, private law can also be used for constructivist purposes. Such a particular community-building aspect has been a constant factor in legal history since the emergence of the modern idea of a code, and it is likely to gain a new meaning in the era of the constitutionalisation of private law. In this sense, the creation of a European identity can benefit from the creation of a system of private law for all European states. Such a constructivist purpose is explicitly envisaged by a group of European private law scholars, who point out that:

> A common system of European contract law signifies an aspiration towards a shared European identity. It marks a commitment to an ever-closer union of peoples, of cultures, and of values. It is designed to bind citizens of Europe to a shared identity. The harmonisation of contract law represents a significant step towards the construction of such an identity.[77]

The view that the establishment of a common market with common rules may foster the natural development of a sentiment of belonging and identity is criticised nowadays by authors who study the dynamics leading to the construction of collective identities.[78] Nonetheless, it has established itself as part of the argumentation (or rhetoric) of the European institutions; in one famous and divisive directive, it is stated that '[t]he elimination of barriers to the development of service activities between Member States is essential in order to strengthen the integration of the peoples of Europe'.[79]

4.4.2.1 Promoting Unity Through Civil Codifications

Ever since the *Code Napoléon*, civil codifications have been seen as the founding manifestos for a new society and have represented important instruments of nation building, unifying the legislation on the territory, promoting national

[76] *See* for example, Eurobarometer, Flash EB172, June 2005 on 'The European Constitution: Post-referendum Survey in The Netherlands', 28.

[77] Study Group on Social Justice in European Private Law, 'Social Justice in European Contract Law: A Manifesto' (2004) 10 *European Law Journal* 653–74, 656.

[78] A-M Thiesse, *La création des identités nationales* (n 33) 16.

[79] Directive on services in the internal market, 2006/123/EC (1).

cohesion by trying to instill the values considered significant for the definition of the national identity in the population. The role that the code has played in the construction of the nation-states in past centuries has therefore been pivotal.[80] Legislators were well aware of this particular political function, and sometimes explicitly presented their creation as one of the 'supreme factors of unity' for their own country.[81] Accordingly, codifications prove to be instruments historically and conceptually linked to nationalism, through which rising nation-states have been able to destroy the legal particularism which threatened the unity of the nation,[82] or, more recently, give a new ideological connotation to an already unified nation. Rather than merely technical tools, codifications have been political instruments of internal colonisation.[83] In this sense, while it is common knowledge that a unique legislation presupposes the existence of a political institution, it should be clarified that a civil codification is—usually but not necessarily and particularly so in a modernist perspective—a consequence of the unity of the *state* but it can precede and contribute to the unity of the *nation*; although this view is generally objected to exactly by those who portray the code as a symbol of national unity.[84]

Furthermore, legal scholars have been aware of this political function of the code. Firstly, it was already Thibaut's belief that a codification on the model of the French one would have contributed to national unity bringing about a sentiment of brotherhood among the Germans, since the application of the same laws '*hat immer zauberischen Einfluß auf Völkerliebe und Völkertreue gehabt*'('has always had magical influence on people's love and loyalty').[85] In this sense a code does not require the actual existence of a community that recognises itself as a nation, but rather this would follow as a consequence of the application of the same legal rules. Portalis adopted a similar perspective, sustaining that to maintain different laws for people living under the same government with a plethora of economic and personal relations with one another would have only led to confusion and trouble,[86] thus jeopardising the national social unity that would have come into existence as a result of civil codification: once the code is in place, so Portalis,

[80] S Rodotà, 'Il codice civile e il processo costituente europeo' (2005) 23 *Rivista critica del diritto privato* 21–33, 24.

[81] G Vacca, *Relazione ministeriale al Re sul codice civile del Regno d'Italia* (Torino, Stamperia Reale, 1866) XIII.

[82] F Wieacker, *Industriegesellschaft und Privatrechtsordnung* (Frankfurt am Main, Athenäum-Fischer-Taschenbuch-Verlag, 1974) 89.

[83] P Cappellini, 'Il codice eterno. La forma-codice e i suoi destinatari. Morfologie e metamorfosi di un paradigma della modernità', in P Cappellini and B Sordi (eds), *Codici. Una riflessione di fine millennio* (Milano, Giuffrè, 2002) 19.

[84] 'La nation doit précéder le Code et non l'inverse', R Cabrillac, 'L'avenir du Code civil' (2004) 13 *La semaine juridique* 547–51, 548–49 ; Y Lequette, 'Le Code européen est de retour' (2011) 3 *Revue des contrats* 1028–44.

[85] See Chapter 2, 2.1.2: 'Civic'.

[86] J-É-M Portalis, 'Exposé des Motifs de la Loi relative à la Réunion des Lois civiles en un seul corps, sous le tire de Code civil des Français' in *Recueil complet des discours prononcés lors de la présentation du code civil, par les divers orateurs du conseil d'état et du tribunat, et discussion particulière de ces deux*

'[*n*]*ous ne serons plus Provençaux, Bretons, Alsaciens, mais Français*' ('we will no longer be Provençal, Bretons, Alsatians, but French').[87]

Can the ongoing discussion on the possibility of enacting a civil code for Europe be considered a part of that Euronationalist project which already became visible in the case of the European Constitution? In this perspective, the idea of a European civil code would perform the same function of building a collective identity that Thibaut already referred to. Traces of Thibaut's line of reasoning can be found in various projects of European codifications and compilations of rules. For instance, the academic project of a European Code of Contracts, a spontaneous academic project that aims nonetheless at founding the basis for a future body of European rules on contracts, identifies its *raison d'être* in the need for ensuring the good functioning of the common market as well as in the necessity of establishing a common European consciousness. In 2004, the authors noticed, also quoting the preamble of the Single European Act, that:

> Si quinze pays ont d'ores et déjà décidé de confluer dans l'Union Européenne, le droit qui y est en vigueur deviendrait un fait anachronique et risquerait inefficacement fragmenté, continuant de cette manière à diviser, voire même à opposer, ces citoyens qui ont au contraire fermement choisi de vivre dans l'unité, de 'parler davantage d'une seule voix et d'agir avec cohésion et solidarité afin de défendre plus efficacement leurs intérêts communs'.[88]

While that effort has remained a purely academic one—despite its declared intention to create the basis for a binding statute—the possibility of adopting a single civil codification for the continent has not remained a theoretical perspective or an academic exercise but had also become a concrete possibility after its appearance on the political agenda of the European Union. As it has already been mentioned,[89] the European Parliament in particular has been the most outspoken advocate of this solution and in this regard the resolutions of 1989[90] and later again of 1994[91] should be mentioned. As the subject of a European codification became of particular interest in the academic world, the idea was once again proposed as a political option and presented as a possible means of improving the coherency of European private law by the European Commission

corps avant la rédaction définitive de chaque projet de loi. Tome I. Discours (Paris, Firmin Didot Frères, 1838) 797.

[87] Ibid, 797.

[88] G Gandolfi, 'Introduction' in *Accademia dei Giusprivatisti Europei: Code Européen des contrats* (Milano, Giuffrè, 2004) at LII, 'If fifteen countries have already decided to converge as the European Union, the law in force would become anachronistic and possibly inefficiently fragmented, continuing to separate or even oppose citizens who on the contrary have firmly chosen to live in unity, aiming "to speak ever increasingly with one voice and to act with consistency and solidarity in order more effectively to protect its common interests"'.

[89] *See* 'Introduction', I.2.2: 'Plans for Further Europeanisation'.

[90] A2-157/89 (1989).

[91] A3-0329/94 (1994).

in 2001.[92] After the consultation started that year, the option gained little support from stakeholders,[93] unlike the ideas of compilation of principles that may serve as a toolbox for legislators or even an optional instrument that could be chosen by private parties. The Commission therefore explicitly rejected the idea of a European code meant to replace national private law legislations, stating that this option was not on the agenda but efforts to improve the coherence of European private law should nonetheless be made.[94] It is against this background that the Draft Common Frame of Reference—'a European Civil Code in disguise'[95]—was created by a network of private lawyers representing the entire European area. Regardless of official terminology, furthermore, even an optional instrument as envisaged by the Commission would not be much different from a European code in addition to the ones of the Member States.[96]

Taking the historical link between code and nation-state into consideration, the employment at the supranational level of such an instrument can be interpreted in two ways. Firstly, as an indirect confirmation of the suggestion that in modern (or rather post-modern) societies the idea of code has finally severed ties with nationalism and become a purely technical category.[97] The political value of the code would have disappeared, lost in a historical phase which is now gone forever, and its success would now reside in its purely technical characteristics such as its systematic coherence—by the way, already jeopardised by the advent of the age of decodification and the increasingly regulatory function of private law. Nevertheless, in the new historical context characterised by a renewed nationalism it could be premature to diagnose the end of the political nature of the code, as the experience of recodification in Central and Eastern European countries shows particularly clearly. As a matter of fact, the prediction of the irreversibility of the decodification processes has been proven wrong by the increase in the number of codifications in the world that rather suggest the beginning of an era of recodification.

In another sense, the use of the category of code at a supranational level could on the other hand be seen as evidence of the more or less explicit willingness to replicate typically nationalist categories. The fact that the legal instrument that put an end to the European legal cultural unity is now invoked to promote a European identity therefore appears as something more than just an irony of history. Already Koschaker, in the opening of his celebrated work on Europe and Roman law, indeed noted how European the character of private law had been

[92] COM(2001) 398 final.

[93] COM(2003) 68 final.

[94] COM(2004) 651 final.

[95] H-W Micklitz, 'Failure or Ideological Preconceptions—Thoughts on Two Grand Projects: The European Constitution and the European Civil Code' (2010) *EUI Working Paper* 2010/4 1–25, 12.

[96] B Heiderhoff, *Gemeinschaftsprivatrecht* (München, Sellier, 2007) 250.

[97] N Irti, *Codice civile e società politica* (Roma, Laterza, 2004) 49; *see* also N Irti, *L'età della decodificazione* (Milano, Giuffrè, 1979).

ever since the establishment of the University of Bologna,[98] while it was only the emergence of the national thought and the civil codification on the continent that altered that unity.[99] Nonetheless, since events cannot repeat themselves in the same way, a perfect imitation of nation-building strategies at the European level does not seem likely in the present day, so that the traditional idea of code assumes new nuances in the modern European context.

The creation of a code that replaces all national codifications is not on the political agenda any more, probably reflecting a lesson learned from the history of the European constitution.

> It is hardly the time to be seen to be moving towards anything that remotely resembles a European Civil Code; if the voters of Europe did not want a constitution it is hardly the moment to force a civil code, even just a contract code on them.[100]

Code and Constitution have shared the same failure, also due to insufficiently transparent drafting processes,[101] and in a broader sense, to the lack of a European 'public sphere'. But in this perspective, the preference for a form that clearly resembles—besides the reticence of using this term and the intention of camouflaging it with other words—a code appears as an expression of an unconscious methodological nationalism of those scholars called to draw projects of these instruments.[102] Such a form could be better explained on the basis of symbolic arguments,[103] which becomes even clearer if one considers that even the structure and the contents of codification projects appear to follow those of national codifications, which might nonetheless be slightly outdated, inasmuch as they focus on certain fields only, overlooking other areas which are on the contrary particularly relevant in today's society and economy. On the other hand, even the criticisms mounted against, in particular, the DCFR project, seem to underline that this instrument has the nature of a code, for example, attacking the excess of powers it acknowledges to judges, a criticism which is particularly robust if it pertains to a code that has to be applied by judges, but which seems less persuasive if moved to a simple toolbox primarily thought to be for legislators.[104]

[98] P Koschaker, *Europa und das römische Recht* (München, Biederstein Verlag, 1947), 1.

[99] *See* also Study Group on Social Justice in European Private Law, 'Social Justice in European Contract Law: A Manifesto', 654.

[100] D Wallis, 'European Contract Law—The Way Forward: Political Context, Parliament's Preoccupations and Process' (2006) 6 *ERA-Forum Special Issue on European Contract Law—Developing the Principles for a 'Common Frame of Reference' for European Contract Law* 8–11, 8.

[101] H-W Micklitz, 'Failure or Ideological Preconceptions' (n 95), 3.

[102] JM Smits, 'The Draft Common Frame of Reference, Methodological Nationalism and the Way Forward' (2008) 4 *European Review of Contract Law* 270–80.

[103] L Antoniolli and F Fiorentini (eds), *A Factual Assessment of the Draft Common Frame of Reference* (Munich, Sellier, 2011) 34–39.

[104] MW Hesselink, 'If You Don't Like our Principles We Have Others. On Core Values and Underlying Principles in European Private Law: A Critical Discussion of the New "Principles" Section in the Draft Common Frame of Reference', in R Brownsword, H-W Micklitz, L Niglia and S Weatherill (eds), *The Foundations of European Private Law* (Oxford, Hart Publishing, 2011) 69.

In this sense, the impression that there is a political agenda to promote a European identity behind the intention to codify European private law is shared by several legal authors.[105] More generally, the importance of the code would therefore mainly reside in its symbolic significance for the close connection between European states.[106] Alpa notes that, besides all other advantages of a possible European codification:

> Unitary codification re-enforces unity and is proactive for political unity. But if it is true that the legal component—that is the entire organisation of law in a community—constitutes an essential characteristic of that community the drafting of a unitary code at a European dimension will become one of the aggregate factors in cementing that same European Community, and a factor in defining the collective European identity.[107]

Although it is debatable whether a code could play a significant role as a symbol for all citizens, according to one view it could at least perform this function in the more restricted area of professional interest of legal scholars and practitioners that in this sense could develop the consciousness of belonging to the same pan-European category.[108]

4.4.2.2 Promoting Values and Culture Through Material Private Law

Civil codifications can certainly exert a particular symbolic importance on those who are used to working with them, but it is more debatable whether they will have the same effect on the general population, normally unaware of the characteristics of the legal system under which they live. If this is true, the symbolic value of the code is probably perceived by legal scholars to be more important than it actually is for society as a whole. Its impact is stronger on the 'internal' legal culture than on the 'external' legal culture.[109] In this sense, a European civil codification could still advance the cause of European identity at least among legal scholars, without jeopardising the cultural identities of the citizens of the Member States.[110]

However, the role of codifications within nation-building endeavours cannot be exclusively a symbolic one: codifications perform functions which make them something more significant than mere forms of 'banal nationalism' like anthems

[105] H Collins, 'European Private Law and the Cultural Identity of the States' (1995) 3 *European Review of Private Law* 353–65, 365; N Jansen, Binnenmarkt, *Privatrecht und europäische Identität* (Tübingen, Mohr Siebeck, 2004) 90.

[106] B Heiderhoff, *Gemeinschaftsprivatrecht* (n 96), 248.

[107] G Alpa, 'European Community Resolutions and the Codification of "Private Law"' (2000) 2 *European Review of Private Law* 321–33, 333.

[108] J Basedow, 'A Common Contract Law for the Common Market' (n 20), 1183.

[109] LM Friedman, *The Legal System. A Social Science Perspective* (New York, Russell Sage Foundation, 1975) 223.

[110] J Basedow, 'Codification of Private Law in the European Union: The Making of a Hybrid' (2001) 9 *European Review of Private Law* 35–49; J Basedow, 'A Common Contract Law for the Common Market' (n 20), 1182.

or flags. Unlike flags, legal rules steer people's behaviour. The significance of this aspect in a nation-building perspective becomes clear, looking again at legal history, since a direct link between the principles laid down in the code and the political values proposed by the state can be found in several past experiences. In this sense, the French codification embodies part of the revolutionary principles of equality (though weakened after the Napoleonic experience) which characterised the foundation of the French civic nation as opposed to the king, who epitomised the very notion of state and nation; the draft of a Nazi *Volksgesetzbuch*, at the other extreme, employed a racist criterion to attribute legal subjectivity and in several provisions aimed at instilling militaristic values in the citizens according to the predominant militaristic and racist connotation of the regime, which based itself on an ethnic conception of the nation. Rapidly setting aside the project of Franco–Italian codification, the Italian fascist experience gave birth to a code that through its clause of good faith interpreted in a cooperative manner, aimed at leading subjects to act 'as a people' according to the corporativist organisation of the state,[111] while provisions on corporate and labour law organised even private enterprises according to fascist principles of hierarchy. More recently, after socialist codes had required privates to act in the interest of the socialist state, new codifications in post-socialist countries embraced marked liberalism with the intent of rapidly freeing themselves from their past, looking at other Western codifications and aiming to promote a new open society. Many other examples could be cited. All these are cases in which law has been used to shape society possibly leading to changes in people's attitudes, but that can also be easily interpreted by sociologists interested in the systematization of cultures as evidence of the 'spirit' of that nation glossing over the nation-building function of law. In this sense, it is private law as such, rather than the mere form of the codification, which plays a role among the different nation-building strategies.

Is it then conceivable that private law can in the same way play a role in the construction of a European identity? This cannot be excluded; indeed, despite the oft-alleged technical nature of private law, 'the construction of European contract law involves an identification process for the citizens of Europe'.[112] But in order to foster such an identification process it is first necessary to individuate what the values to be fostered are, that is: what the European values are. This inevitably leads us back to the previous question as to the constitutive values of the European identity.

On the one hand, if one accepts the post-modernist view that a European identity does not exist and can only be represented by its incoherence and plurality, one should conclude that a Euronationalist private law representing that

[111] A Somma, 'Buona fede contrattuale e gestione del conflitto sociale', in A D'Angelo, PG Monateri and A Somma, *Buona fede e giustizia contrattuale: modelli cooperativi e modelli conflittuali a confronto* (Torino, Giappichelli, 2005) 85 ff.

[112] R Sefton-Green, 'Social Justice and European Identity in European Contract Law' (2006) 2 *European Review of Contract Law* 275–86, 284.

fragmented identity could only be a non-unified one in which nation-states remain completely free to regulate their own private law, since plurality and diversity are characteristic features of the European identity: to be European, one should be national. Peculiar as this might sound, this is already the mechanism at the basis of several legal concepts in Europe, with the most famous and revealing case being European citizenship, automatically obtained by all those who are citizens of one of the Member States and no-one else, while the EU explicitly renounces its interference in the considerations behind the citizenship policies of the Member States.[113] Such a postmodernist approach is compatible with ethno-cultural visions of the nation, but it can easily lead to nihilistic results, dooming Europe to remain a purely cultural notion rather than an authentic political category.

In a civic or constitutional-patriotic perspective, on the other hand, one can identify more concrete values that are interpreted as constitutive of the European identity and later promote them through private law instruments. In particular the academic project of the Common Frame of Reference explicitly refers to the values that—as has been clarified earlier—had already been individuated as characterising the political ideology of Europe. Its first outline edition, in particular, individuated a set of 11 'core aims of European private law' that immediately resemble the catalogue of values laid down in the treaties on which the EU is based and that are said to be shared by all European countries.[114] That edition more specifically mentioned the values of justice, freedom, protection of human rights, economic welfare, solidarity and social responsibility, promotion of the internal market, preservation of cultural and linguistic plurality, rationality, legal certainty, predictability and efficiency in its introduction.[115] In other words, aside from more typically economic–legal principles such as efficiency and predictability, the list put particular emphasis on the subjects of fundamental rights, justice and welfare, interestingly enough resembling the 'catalogue' of Habermas and Derrida.

In this sense, there was something more than a mere allusion to the symbolism of national codification—furthermore already strongly challenged by terminological reticence and political uncertainties—but rather the intention to promote European values in the relations between private citizens. Facing criticisms and counter-proposals from legal scholars in Germany and France, the drafters of the DCFR later reduced the list of such core aims, only speaking of four underlying

[113] *See Declaration of Nationality of a Member State* adopted with the Treaty of Maastricht, 'The Conference declares that, wherever in the Treaty establishing the European Community reference is made to nationals of the Member States, the question whether an individual possesses the nationality of a Member State shall be settled solely by reference to the national law of the Member State concerned'.

[114] MW Hesselink, 'If You Don't Like Our Principles We Have Others' (n 104), 70–71.

[115] C von Bar, E Clive, H Schulte-Nölke and H Beale, J Herre, J Huet, P Schlechtriem, M Storme, S Wann, P Varul, A Veneziano, F Zoll (eds), *Principles, Definitions and Model Rules of European Private Law. Interim Outline Edition* (Munich, Sellier, 2008) 13.

principles: justice, freedom, security and efficiency.[116] In this sense, the resistance coming from the Member States may have limited the Euronationalist potential of those projects. The introduction to the latest published version of the DCFR clarifies the relationship between the different underlying principles, also including a short but telling reference to their political and historical background:

> At one level, freedom, security, and justice are ends in themselves. People have fought and died for them. Efficiency is less dramatic. In the context of private law, however, these values are best regarded not as ends in themselves but as means to other ends—the promotion of welfare, the empowering of people to pursue their legitimate aims and fulfil their potential.[117]

It would nonetheless be wrong to look only at the projects that more clearly resemble codification and conclude that only those replicate nationalist tools at a new level. It is, rather, necessary to consider the role of the EU as a regulator of the market, looking also at the intersection of private law and regulation in those areas that are traditionally left outside the code. There too, we could find clear instances of rules, occasionally significantly encroaching on the private autonomy of individuals, which may also serve community-building purposes.

This is manifestly the case of the directives meant to create an internal market for broadcasters. The Audiovisual Services Directive of 2010,[118] which repealed the Television Without Borders Directive[119] of 1989, requires Member States to ensure, where practicable and by appropriate means, that broadcasters reserve the majority of their transmission time for European works. The role of 'print-capitalism' as a pivotal element in the nationalist development has been highlighted and, again, the different dimensions of media, culture and market appear as interrelated and barely separable aspects of the same community building endeavours even today at the European level, but with some relevant differences. European identity does not attempt to replace national ones: European works are still works originating from the single Member States, so that the directive, underlining their role in promoting media pluralism and that national regulators remain free to determine the contents of their programming, stresses that 'The independence of cultural developments in the Member States and the preservation of cultural diversity in the Union therefore remain unaffected'.[120]

[116] MW Hesselink, 'If You Don't Like Our Principles We Have Others' (n 104), 70–71.

[117] C von Bar, E Clive, H Schulte-Nölke et al (eds), *Principles, Definitions and Model Rules of European Private Law: Draft Common Frame of Reference (DCFR)*, vol 1 (Munich, Sellier, 2009) 37.

[118] Directive on the coordination of certain provisions laid down by law, regulation or administrative action in Member States concerning the provision of audiovisual media services, 2010/13/EU, Art 16(1).

[119] Directive on on the coordination of certain provisions laid down by Law, Regulation or Administrative Action in Member States concerning the pursuit of television broadcasting activities, 89/552/EEC, Art 4(1).

[120] 2010/13/EU (19); 89/552/EEC.

4.4.2.3 Fundamental Rights and Social Justice

Regardless of the fate of the European codification proposals, it is evident, therefore, that the constitutive values of European identity as identified by political theorists do not need explicit recognition in the form of something analogous to a civil code, and can rather be already present in the contents of European private law. In this context a particular role is played by the respect for fundamental rights (freedom of information and media pluralism as mentioned above are among them) and justice.

Fundamental rights are distinctively an important element in the legal architecture of Europe. The necessity for the protection of these rights is sanctioned at several levels: in national constitutions, in the jurisprudence of the Court of Justice of the European Union but also in various international treaties that bind Member States. The reference to the Charter of Fundamental Rights in the Treaty of Lisbon is in this sense only the latest step in a process that started a longer time ago. It can also be noticed that the respect for fundamental rights is such a fundamental element of the legal architecture of Europe that it even allows the Union to derogate from the obligations stemming from the Charter of the United Nations. As decided in the famous *Kadi* case,[121] indeed, not even respect for a resolution of the Security Council of the UN can deprive a citizen of fundamental rights recognised in Europe. In doing so, the European Court judged not dissimilarly from a national constitutional court, adhering to a 'constitutionalist' vision of public international law.[122]

The respect for fundamental rights as a defining aspect of European identity, however, also plays a primary role in private law. It is now commonly spoken of a constitutionalisation of private law, in the sense of a growing influence of constitutional provisions in the regulation of relationships between citizens, and judges throughout Europe show a tendency to employ categories such as fundamental rights in private law.[123] In a nation-building perspective, the connection between private and constitutional law provisions allows for the distinctive values of a constitutional–patriotic legal order to find direct or indirect application in the private relations between citizens. What is more, if all European judges employ these categories, which are basically identical in all Member States and are now part of the constitutional law of the Union,[124] it could be expected that a new

[121] Court of Justice, *Kadi*, joined cases C-402/05 and C-415/05.

[122] M Kumm 'How Does European Union Law Fit into the World of Public Law? Costa, Kadi and Three Conceptions of Public Law' (2011) *New York University Public Law and Legal Theory Working Papers. Paper 262* 1–37, 29.

[123] *See* C Mak, *Fundamental Rights in European Contract Law. A Comparison of the Impact of Fundamental Rights on Contractual Relationships in Germany, the Netherlands, Italy and England* (Alphen aan den Rijn, Kluwer Law International, 2008).

[124] G Alpa, 'European Community Resolutions and the Codification of "Private Law"' (n 107), 328.

bottom-up convergence will occur, which will, in turn, help the development of a common private law for Europe.[125]

The definition of a scheme of social justice for private law, too, becomes of pivotal importance for the definition of a common European identity in which justice is considered a fundamental value:

> To say that a future European contract law [...] needs a scheme of social justice with all its economic, political and cultural dimensions, is to say that we have to look for a common understanding between the Member States on what type of social justice best fits the perception of our identity as Europeans.[126]

Already, the Treaty on the European Union, at Art 3, stated that the European Union 'shall promote economic, social and territorial cohesion, and solidarity among Member States'. This intention represents, at least theoretically, the overcoming of the traditional nationalist view according to which, given that justice is a concept depending on national cultures, systems of justice can efficiently work only within nation-states. But it is exactly 'solidarity' the notion that becomes politically more divisive and practically unviable as soon as crises make national divisions and interests re-emerge. The nationalist interpretation of social justice also lies, as already seen, at the basis of several objections to the possibility of developing uniform rules of contract law promoting solidarity; it is nonetheless not the only interpretation imaginable, and a 'European civil code' that 'would help to establish solidarity without forcing societies and peoples of Europe to adopt uniform cultural practices'—for example in the form of a code of principles—could also be conceived.[127]

Quite interestingly, the possibility of elaborating a shared scheme of social justice for European contract law has not been excluded by the Court of Justice of the EU. While it has shown to be particularly deferential to the localist interpretation of clauses like public policy—as became clear particularly in the *Omega* case—the Court has proved to be more 'Europeanist'—at least in theory—when confronted with issues of contract law in a strict sense. In this sense, mention has to be made of the *Freiburger Kommunalbauten* case: in that case which concerned a preliminary ruling for interpretation of the unfair terms directive, the European Court stated that it is up to national judges to verify whether a given term can be considered as unfair under the provisions of the directive. Although not only the practical significance of the decision but also its reasoning could seem consistent with the approach in the *Omega* decision, this is because the fairness of a given

[125] C Mak, 'Harmonising Effects of Fundamental Rights in European Contract Law' (2006) 1 *Erasmus Law Review* 59–79. For the objections to this interpretation, *see* Chapter 3: 33.2 'The Social Argument'.

[126] B Lurger, 'The Common Frame of Reference/Optional Code and the Various Understandings of Social Justice in Europe', in T Wilhelmsson, E Paunio and A Pohjolainen (eds), *Private Law and the Many Cultures of Europe* (Alphen aan den Rijn, Kluwer Law International, 2007) 192.

[127] H Collins, *The European Civil Code. The Way Forward* (Cambridge, Cambridge University Press, 2008) 130.

contractual term has to be assessed concretely by referring 'to all the circumstances attending the conclusion of the contract',[128] so that, in the words of the European judges, the European Court should not rule on the application of 'general criteria to a particular term, which must be considered in the light of the particular circumstances of the case in question'.[129] However, 'in the context of its jurisdiction [...] to interpret Community law, the Court may interpret general criteria used by the Community legislature in order to define the concept of unfair terms.'[130] In this sense, it would be technically possible to elaborate a European notion of (un) fairness that national judges then would have to apply, taking into account the specific circumstances of the case, so that the nationalist perspective which confines the notion of justice within the borders of the nation appears to have been superseded.[131] More precisely, the European general notion of fairness could then have to be applied in concrete taking into consideration also national particularities, which could reconcile the opposite European and national perspectives. In that specific case, nevertheless, the European Court rejected its own competence on the basis of disputable arguments (not completely coherent with the previous case-law) that in the end appear to be detrimental to the coherence of the system of European private law.[132]

4.5 EUROPEAN CULTURE

In several places in this book it has been pointed out that theories of nationalism acknowledge a particular importance to the notion of culture. Culture is more important according to some conceptions—ethno-cultural nationalism in particular—than to other views—civic nationalism—but it is still present in all of them. Culture is described as being typical of a particular group—the nation—and justifies the need for an overlap of political and national unit. In this sense, also Euro-nationalism, similarly to other types of nationalism, cannot leave the cultural dimension aside. While opponents of Europeanisation like to put emphasis on the irreconcilable diversity of all the cultures and legal cultures that exist within Europe, advocates of Europeanisation tend to insist on the unity of the cultural dimension in Europe. This holds true for both general culture and legal culture.

[128] 93/13/EEC, Art 4(1).

[129] Court of Justice, *Freiburger Kommunalbauten*, C-237/02, para. 22.

[130] Court of Justice, *Freiburger Kommunalbauten*, C-237/02, para. 22.

[131] For the opposing argument, see R Sefton-Green, 'Multiculturalism, Europhilia and Harmonization: Harmony or Disharmony?' (2010) 6 *Utrecht Law Review* 50–67, 55, according to whom the decision of the Court 'may have been due to the fact that it was aware that good faith is a culturally-sensitive concept'.

[132] MW Hesselink, 'Case Note to ECJ—Freiburger Kommunalbauten v Hofstetter' (2006) 3 *European Review of Contract Law* 366–75.

As to the former, several political theorists point out an underlying cultural unity in Europe which is strong enough to bridge political distinctions; so, for example, the existence of the Iron Curtain was considered not significant from a cultural perspective, since the inhabitants of cities such as Prague, Budapest or Warsaw always thought of themselves as being Europeans,[133] also to mark a difference from the Soviet power. In this perspective, all people belonging to the European cultural tradition share some cultural characteristics[134] even if living in very different political systems, so that in the end it seems that '[e]conomics and politics may divide, but culture can unite'.[135] Similarly from a nationalist perspective, political and ideological distinctions would be overshadowed by the fundamental unity of culture. What about the culture of law?

While opponents of Europeanisation can easily point at the diversity of the legal traditions of the countries that make up Europe, the unity of European legal culture may seem to be more difficult to state than the unity or at least similarity of general culture. The era of nationalism had indeed brought about a state of affairs in which each nation-state has developed a model of its own, occasionally 'exporting' it to other countries. In this way, different legal families have been fashioned, the existence of which still seems to be perceivable in a set of elements that have garnered new interest in recent years, in particular after a few influential studies have—very debatably—claimed to be able to link indexes of economic development to the 'legal origin' of a given system.[136] Nonetheless, even if it is true that legal traditions practically diverge in different countries as a result of different historical developments and political choices, some scholars affirm that, again, all European countries share certain characteristic cultural traits that concur to define a European legal culture. This proposition does not appear, moreover, as the mere propaganda of the institutions of the European Union, as opponents of harmonisation occasionally like to suggest, as it was already clear to those who, looking at the material contents of norms[137] while the Second World War was still going on, noticed that '[*n*]*ach ihrem Sinn und Inhalt stimmen wesentliche Begriffe und Institutionen der europäischen Völker in auffälliger Weise überein. Hier gibt es eine sehr starke Gemeinschaft europäischen Rechts*' ('the meaning and content of essential concepts and institutions of the European peoples are surprisingly similar. In this regard, there is a very strong European legal community'),[138] while the

[133] R Hoggart and D Johnson, 'Ideas About an "Idea of Europe"', in C Joyce (ed), *Questions of Identity: A Selection from the Pages of New European* (London, IB Tauris & Co, 1988) 98–99.

[134] Ibid, 98–99.

[135] Ibid, 99.

[136] R La Porta, F Lopez-de-Silanes, A Shleifer and RW Vishny, 'Legal Determinants of External Finance' (1997) 52 *Journal of Finance* 1131–50. Critically on this approach, M Siems, 'Statistische Rechtsvergleichung' (2008) 72 *Rabels Zeitschrift für ausländisches und internationales Privatrecht* 354–90.

[137] C Schmitt, *Die Lage der europäischen Rechtswissenschaft* (Tübingen, Internationaler Universitäts-Verlag, 1950) 8.

[138] Ibid, 9, English translation by GL Ulmen (1990) 23 *Telos. A Quarterly Journal of Critical Thought* 37.

law of such a '*europäische Gemeinschaft*' still shows traces of 'common law' which remain manifest regardless of the differentiation of the various legal families.

In this sense, the element of culture represents one of those aspects as to which a convergence of values already exists in Europe and on which Europeanisation can be based rather than a hindrance to Europeanisation,[139] considering that national rules are 'embedded in an already partly common legal culture'.[140] By categorising culture as European rather than national, as it is often done, the cultural argument moves in favour of Europeanisation, rather than standing against it.[141] Once again, thus, the notion of culture—the pivotal element around which modern theories of nationalism revolve—can be employed to legitimise political projects, emphasising the homogeneity of given groups in opposition to others. Nonetheless, the definition of a set of cultural traits of the European legal experience is particularly complicated, since on the one hand, laws are already sufficiently differentiated within Europe and, on the other hand, the legal doctrines that were elaborated in that region later developed and were somehow 'exported' to other countries, so that it is now challenging to identify the peculiarity of a European legal culture within a broader category such as what is commonly defined as the Western legal tradition.

According to Berman's classic study, the macro legal tradition developing from Roman and Canon law spread from the lecture rooms of the University of Bologna to the rest of the continent was characterised by certain elements: a 'relatively sharp' distinction between legal and other types of institutions, the fact that legal institutions are administrated by 'a special corps of people', the fact that lawyers and jurists are specially trained for their profession, the pivotal role of legal scholarship for the legal system itself, the fact that law is intended as a coherent and integrated system, the capacity of this system to grow over centuries and organically change with an internal logic, and the fact that the 'historicity of law is linked with the concept of its supremacy over the political authorities'.[142]

This new category was capable of superseding the traditional distinction between common and civil law systems made by comparative lawyers opposing them to, among others, socialist systems. But in a period in which the socialist legal family dissolved and most countries that were previously expressions of it have become part of a Europe that strives to develop an identity of its own, new systematisations are needed to go beyond Berman's position and single out characteristics that outline only the European legal culture. A European legal culture,

[139] On this function of legal culture in a European sense, R Cotterrell, 'Comparative Law and Legal Culture', in M Reimann and R Zimmermann (eds), *The Oxford Handbook of Comparative Law* (Oxford, Oxford University Press, 2006) 713 ff.

[140] JM Smits, *The Making of European Private Law: Toward a Ius Commune Europaeum as a Mixed Legal System* (Antwerp, Intersentia, 2002) 271.

[141] J Basedow, 'Rechtskultur—zwischen nationalem Mythos und europäischem Ideal' (1996) 3 *Zeitschrift für Europäisches Privatrecht* 379–81, 381.

[142] HJ Berman, *Law and Revolution. The Formation of the Western Legal Tradition* (Cambridge MA, Harvard University Press, 1983) 7–12.

in other words, should be able to collocate itself in a middle position between the Western legal tradition and the classic legal families including, of course, the divide between civil and common law.

The legal culture of Europe has in this perspective to be compared and contrasted with legal culture in other Western countries. In this sense, it has already been compared and contrasted to American common law, from which it seems distinguishable in particular because of its more evident positivistic character that, even if in slightly different terms, seems to be present even in the common law of England.[143] In this light, English law appears to belong to the European family more than to the common law tradition,[144] and historical analyses underlying the basic unity of the medieval *ius commune* experience and the influence of Roman law in Britain offer support to the theory of the explicitly European character of that legal system too. In this sense, a link is created between the historical *ius commune* and the idea of a modern *ius commune* of Europe, even if in this way the *ius commune* loses its historical dimension, becoming mere legitimation for modern political constructions, at the risk of embracing retrospective and misleading interpretations of history. Political scientists have already warned that 'we should not overstate the political or cultural unity of the Middle Ages', for such unity is mostly a 'myth'.[145]

Abandoning a purely historical perspective fixated on the unity of the *ius commune*, the characteristics of what could be called a *new* European legal culture have been also sketched out.[146] The main aspect of this new culture seems to be a shift from formalism to pragmatism and interdisciplinary approaches. To a certain extent, this development brings Europe closer to the American legal experience, which has been strongly marked by legal realism (paradoxically imported into the New World by European jurists),[147] pointing again in the direction of a Western legal tradition which is notwithstanding less and less similar to the one initially described by Berman. More generally, it has been concluded that there is a set of values which are common to the Western legal orders aimed at bringing together private subjects' interest to each other and to the interests of the community and that among others include the principle of protection of individuals and their fundamental freedoms, equality in difference, the importance of private property with its contextual limitation in the general interest, the protection of the worker, the economic freedoms and so on.[148]

Considering these elements, legal culture does not necessarily appear as the great opponent of forms of forced harmonisation or unification of European contract law, as this is not exclusively national but possibly even European. In this

[143] MW Hesselink, *The New European Legal Culture* (Deventer, Kluwer, 2001) 21.

[144] R Zimmermann, '"Common law" und "civil law", Amerika und Europa', in R Zimmermann (ed), *Amerikanische Rechtskultur und europäisches Privatrecht* (Tübingen, Mohr Siebeck, 1995) 9.

[145] G Delanty, *Inventing Europe* (n 4), 41.

[146] MW Hesselink, *The New European Legal Culture* (n 143).

[147] Ibid, 72–74.

[148] G Alpa and M Andenas, *Fondamenti del diritto privato europeo* (Milano, Giuffrè, 2005) 44 ff.

light, the fundamental nationalist claim that cultural similarity underlying the members of a nation requires a political organisation in the form of the nation-state can be employed to affirm, beyond nationalism, the desirability of supranational and multi-level political organisations which are representative of that cultural homogeneity; this operation, however, can only be made at the cost of putting emphasis on unity and downplaying diversity, through ideological readings of history, which always bear a concrete risk of falsification.

4.6 PERSPECTIVES OF NATION AND EUROPE-BUILDING

Even the project of the Europeanisation of private law advocated by several European(ist) scholars and proposed intermittently by the European institutions can be interpreted as the repetition of older mechanisms of nation-building at a new supranational governance level, aimed at the creation of a European identity which can provide the political construction with civic legitimacy, even if this does not imply institutional unification, as has been the case with modern nation-states. The recognition of the conceptual link between Europeanisation and nation-building processes urges us also to give serious consideration to the possible risks connected to a Euronationalist endeavour, keeping in mind the too often forgotten high costs that even unification of nation-states demanded when it took place in various countries. Historically, those costs did not consist in a simple 'vanishing of local identities', as a naïve and superficial rhetoric often likes to suggest, but more concretely entailed dramatic changes in economic and social structures. On the other hand, this operation, potentially like any nation-building process, is not something negative per se that has to be rejected because of its artificiality—in particular if one considers that the form of identification proposed by this Euronationalism seems mainly based on the acceptance of a set of liberal and social values, as advocated in particular by the idea of constitutional patriotism.

Constitutional patriotism offers indeed a chance, that is to confer the European construction—both in its current *sui generis* structure and in possible evolutions—a liberal, democratic and modern rather than post-modern character, in which diversity is acknowledged but not sanctified, without giving in to nihilism and in which identity is intended as an overarching category that allows the coexistence of different national and local characters. In this light, a European identity would not be imposed as a substitute for traditional national cultures and therefore would not easily lead, as it has been feared in the opposite case,[149] to 'alienation and rejection' from the nation-states. One could question that, beyond the beautiful declarations of intents, European and national identities can really coexist. In any case, such a concern seems to take for granted a mutual exclusivity

[149] R Sefton-Green, 'Social Justice and European Identity in European Contract Law' (n 112), 285.

of identities, hardly justifiable if one adheres to the view that identities are plural (though occasionally conflicting). Moreover, as one author has suggested, the European identity emerges from national allegiances just like the national identities emerged from older ethnic ones, so that it would be a mistake to consider a new European identity as a radical break from national identities.[150] This holds particularly true if such an identity is based on constitutional patriotism, for this does not require the suppression of local identities but rather enables the institutional framework through which these can coexist.[151]

Undeniably, law is already a fundamental factor in this process, since it has been the main instrument through which the European Union itself has been constructed.[152] What is more, law can translate the values that lie at the basis of a constitutional-patriotic society in the reality of daily relations between citizens. If one accepts this point, it will be easy to conclude that the elaboration of a private law which is more focused on the respect for those collective values, first and foremost fundamental rights and justice, will be one of the elements that can promote a European identity that does not necessarily contradict national allegiances. The importance of private law in this light consists in its ability to give a concrete and tangible shape to abstract values and rights, whose constructivist function would otherwise remain in a raw rhetorical dimension.[153] A possible way forward for European legal integration which seems inspired by constitutional patriotism inasmuch as it envisages a transnational civil society kept together by the respect for certain principles including private law[154] has indeed been proposed in the form of a code or a statute that, 'unlike the nationalist civil codes of the nineteenth century', is structured as 'a code of principles' representing 'an agreement on principles as a symbol of solidarity between the peoples of Europe, as a shared commitment to shared values, much like the European Convention for the Protection of Human Rights and Fundamental Freedoms'.[155]

Does this mean that the elaboration of a European civil code is required for the promotion of a collective identity in Europe? Again, a distinction should be made between private law as such and civil codification. To speak of the symbolic function of a European civil code can be quite misleading, and produce new unnecessary tensions between the two sides of the 'Legal' English Channel. It is in fact very questionable that people will identify with a civil code and feel part of a community only because a unitary code is in place.[156] More likely, the codification is perceived to be an important part of national identity only by

[150] G Delanty, 'L'identità europea come costruzione sociale', in L Passerini (ed), *Identità culturale europea. Idee, sentimenti, relazioni* (Firenze, La Nuova Italia, 1998) 47–66, 61.

[151] J Habermas, *Die postnationale* Konstellation. *Politische Essays* (Berlin, Suhrkamp, 1998) 150.

[152] G Alpa and M Andenas, *Fondamenti del diritto privato europeo* (n 148), 31.

[153] Giving human rights a horizontal effect was already suggested as a means of enhancing transnational democracy by JHH Weiler, 'To Be a European Citizen' (n 45), 355–56.

[154] H Collins, *The European Civil Code* (n 127), 22.

[155] Ibid, 136.

[156] G Alpa and M Andenas, *Fondamenti del diritto privato europeo* (n 148), 31.

lawyers themselves, while realistically speaking, it is not seen as such by ordinary citizens.[157] Was Thibaut thus wrong when he affirmed that a civil code would have led to a spirit of brotherhood?

Simply, the historical context has dramatically changed since the time when Thibaut proposed a codification for a united Germany, and it is more uncertain nowadays that a European codification can have the same political meaning that it had in the past for nation-states. In the period in which the nation-state arose overshadowing legal particularism, the code represented the best employable instrument to promote a shared national identity, inasmuch as it could also perform a 'constitutional function': codifications represented the civic manifesto of the new bourgeois societies and often included constitutional as well as criminal and procedural provisions. In performing a constitutional function, codifications were therefore more effective than the constitutions of the nineteenth century.[158] However, the constitutional function of the code that accompanied the rise of the nation-state faded away when new national constitutions appeared after the Second World War.[159] Provisions of a constitutional nature can still be found in codifications immediately preceding the end of the war, exemplified by the 1942 Italian *Codice civile*, but already after the end of that military event, it is the constitution that has started playing the most important function in the dynamics of construction of collective identities. This particular meaning of the constitution becomes clear if one looks beyond Europe and considers the political experience of the United States. In that context, 'without a common ethnic, racial, or religious heritage, American identity is peculiarly dependent on the idea of law'[160] and of the Constitution in particular. The idea that the Constitution is, more particularly, 'a product of reason, deliberation, and political science remains a vital part of [the American] political self-understanding'.[161]

Considering these important changes in the political scenario of Europe, it is judicious to affirm that civil codifications may still play a role in the construction of a European legal culture of the lawyers, which might interest legal scholars and practitioners but leaves citizens relatively uninterested. Unlike civil codes, constitutions and the declarations of rights post the Second World War period were capable of appealing to the deepest sentiments of the nation's citizenry.[162] If this is true, insisting on the function of construction of the collective identity of the codification appears anachronistic. As a form, it is unable to work properly as a

[157] G Alpa, 'European Community Resolutions and the Codification of "Private Law"' (n 107), 330.

[158] A Pizzorusso, *Il patrimonio costituzionale europeo* (n 52), 38.

[159] L Mengoni, *L'Europa dei codici o un codice per l'Europa?* (Roma, Centro di studi e ricerche di diritto comparato e straniero: saggi, conferenze e seminari, 1992) 1–2.

[160] PW Kahn, *The Cultural Study of Law. Reconstructing Legal Scholarship* (Chicago, University of Chicago Press, 1999) 9.

[161] Ibid, 10.

[162] S Rodotà, 'Un Codice per l'Europa? Diritti nazionali, diritto europeo, diritto globale', in P Cappellini and B Sordi (eds), *Codici. Una riflessione di fine millennio* (Milano, Giuffrè, 2002) 541.

'banally nationalist' symbol and could even be counterproductive, particularly in a context characterised by rising nationalism in the Member States. The symbolic added value of the code should be reconsidered, and this holds true for both the European project and established national codifications. As underlined before, it is true that codifications are still very popular political instruments and even within Europe there are cases in which new codes have entered into force following important political and social transformation. However, in those cases it was rather the content of private law that was completely changed and new values—corresponding to those laid down also in the new constitutions—introduced to organise the economic and social relations between citizens.

In this sense, it is not the form of the code that is important as such, while it is the role of private law that has to be acknowledged as a persisting element in nation building. It has been previously noticed, for instance, that potentially significant rules in a Europe-building perspective can already be found in directives with a more clearly regulatory function in economic law. On the contrary, it does not seem plausible that a European civil code would play any significant role in the construction of a European identity per se outside the limited circle of legal scholars and, as an instrument which is historically linked to the nationalist experience, the political advisability of transferring such a code at the European level could even be doubtful. Nevertheless, a substantive European private law that promotes constitutional-patriotic values regardless of its form, bringing about that adaptation of the black letter rule of the codes to the new constitutional values called for by certain authors,[163] may advance even the cause of European identity.

[163] S Rodotà, 'Il codice civile e il processo costituente europeo' (n 80), 25.

Conclusion

THIS BOOK HAS attempted to highlight the conceptual and historical links between private law and the ideology of nationalism, to investigate the role of the latter as a significant factor in the evolution of contemporary jurisdictions and to verify whether it still plays a role in today's processes of Europeanisation of private law. It is now clear that the answer to the fundamental question as to whether nationalism has exercised and still exercises an influence on private law in Europe cannot be satisfyingly answered as a simple yes–no question. The subject is much more multifaceted and it requires several remarks.

If one only considered theory, the direct impact of the nationalist political principle on private law should be excluded at first sight. Nationalism—as the ideology maintaining the coincidence of the national and the political unit—has indeed revealed to be a 'poor' philosophy, which prescribes a particular kind of state organisation but fails to suggest which ideals are appropriate to structure the reciprocal relations between citizens—something that makes it compatible with numerous and diverse ideologies but at the same time makes it seemingly neutral to private law, which is on the contrary concerned exactly with the regulation of those relations. However, it is not necessarily the most elaborated political doctrines that exercise the weightiest influence in historical development, and this holds particularly true for nationalism, which has become a fundamental conceptual category for reading many of the historical and political events that took place in recent centuries and which still occasionally re-emerges in unexpected ways in only seemingly internationalised societies.

Regardless of its theoretical foundations, nationalism's practical significance in history has been such that soon after its emergence, the traits of private law in Europe were completely altered. Still today, traditional private law basically maintains much of those traits while processes such as Europeanisation appear as processes of denationalisation. What is more, much of the rhetoric that was associated with private law in the period in which it became nationalised—and directly drew from nationalist thought—still seems to survive in the legal studies and conditions to different extents contemporary processes of denationalisation. In this context, even the methodology adopted by lawyers, mostly centred on national law, necessarily leads to forms of methodological nationalism, detectable even when legal analyses concern non-national law. This state of affairs results nonetheless in a paradox, since while legal education and doctrine is still primarily focused on traditional and national private law, new regulations highly invasive to private relations are being created at the transnational and supranational level. Legal categories often appear inadequate to properly conceptualise those phenomena that appear (sometimes even misleadingly) to be detached from the national level. The product of that mismatch is often tension and resistance.

To take note of these aspects, it has been necessary first to look back in history, most particularly to that specific era in which nationalism clearly manifested itself and according to several historians, modern nations took form. As already known, during a considerable part of European history, private law maintained a mixed universal–localist dimension—as a result of the intersection of local customs, jurisprudence based on Roman law, commercial practices and natural law—and started undergoing a process of national definition only in more recent times. This is not just linked to the appearance of the modern state, but more deeply to the emergence of national thought during the eighteenth and nineteenth centuries. Logically, before that moment, private law could not have been national for the very simple reason that nation states did not exist. This is indeed not to say that the state did not exist either: rather, it was the idea of a state that embraces a nation—as a community of people sharing some characteristics and conscious of their common identity and diversity from other groups—that was still lacking. Even today, private laws are more likely to diverge among *nations* rather than among *states*, considering in particular those countries in which the coincidence of nation and state appears to be less perfectly accomplished than in archetypal nation-states.

It is in particular a merit of recent studies on nationalism—usually labelled as 'modernist' in opposition to the 'primordialist' approach—to have exposed much of the rhetorical character of the views of nineteenth-century nationalists who adhered to an organicist vision of the nation considered as something natural with its own history and traits—a sort of enlarged family—and that still seems to influence the popular understanding of nations. In this new analytical perspective, nations are rather communities that have often been conceived—building upon pre-existing group allegiances often of an ethnic, linguistic or religious nature—by political and cultural groups for specific reasons. According to a strongly materialistic but still quite insightful view, the success of nationalism in that period had to be linked to the needs of modern capitalism and industrialisation, which asked for the establishment of a new territorial and political unit in which commerce could be protected and fostered and in which workers could move with more ease. In this light, nationalisation of law was an aspect of crucial importance.

But the possibility of speaking of a general theory of nationalism is made complicated by the diversity of particular expressions of that ideology. It is in particular the difficulty—or even impossibility—of defining the nation in clear and universal terms that let different nationalist manifestations arise. In particular in France, nationalism had the main function of challenging the king's pretence to embody the state—*l'État, c'est moi*—and hand over that power to a new historical subject. Such a significant institutional change could be brought about only by means of a revolution and in that context nationalism—of an enlightened inspiration—took primarily a civic and egalitarian, though not necessarily democratic, connotation (which it was by the way not able to uphold for a considerable length of time); the nation coincided with the citizens in opposition to the king and the *ancien régime*. Following the momentous events that led to the rise of Napoleon, the French private law system finally became stable in the structure of the civil code, which still shows traces of that civic nationalist view, as revealed by the establishment of a unified legal treatment for all legal subjects—which translated the revolutionary idea of equality. The very ideology of the code, that managed to nationalise law in France giving a new competence to the elected parliament, is a manifestation of that understanding of the nationalistic principle, which still seems to persist in the present-day imagery of the *Code civil*.

The development had been more multifaceted in Germany, where due to political fragmentation, civic forms of nationalism—represented in the legal discourse by advocates of codification such as Thibaut—did not meet with particular success and were soon overshadowed by ethno-cultural understandings of the nation. Nationalism studies have often pointed out the diversity (at least theoretically and for a short period of time) between the French and the German nationalist experiences, and legal history can reveal how that opposition is also reflected in the legal development of those countries. A cultural understanding of the nation had been advocated in particular by Herder, whose work had been highly influential in that period of patriotic fervour representing an important source of inspiration for lawyers, most notably those belonging to the Historical School of Law. It is in this period that concepts like the *Volksgeist*—in reality a not particularly innovative idea—were mostly developed in the legal discourse and characterised with a nationalist undertone: every nation has a 'spirit' and law, similarly to language, is a natural expression of that spirit. A few years earlier, Montesquieu had already spoken of the spirit of the nation and its influence of the laws of a country, but that spirit was influenced in turn by several elements—first and foremost meteorological conditions—including law itself, which could still be modified by the legislator. Within the context of German nationalism with a poetic inspiration drawn from Romanticism, the emphasis was now put on the strict bond between law and the cultural roots of the nation, linked closely enough to make the idea of a legislator who intervenes on private law untenable. This view was revealed to be a particularly valuable one for a country such as Germany that—unlike France—was not unified yet and needed to base the unity of its people on shared folk elements. For the same reason, the ideas of the Historical School of Law met with success in other countries (some more than others) that were embracing nation-building practices in that pivotal period of their history.

Here, nationalism studies should help us draw distinctions between civic, cultural and ethnic understandings of the nation. In particular the conception of Savigny was predominantly cultural—he even identified the traditional law of Germany with Roman law and constantly wavered between the two only seemingly paradoxically intertwined dimensions of cultural nationalism and legal Europeanism. In legal historiography, this ambivalence has made possible various and opposite interpretations of the Savignyian thought. Moved by the comprehensible intention of distancing itself from the disastrous experience of *ethnic* nationalism and to emphasise on the other hand the European inspiration of German scholarship in that historical period, contemporary scholarship occasionally emphasises predominantly the European elements of the Historical School of Law (which, by the way, could be detected even in the thought of philosophers whose name is otherwise habitually associated to nationalism), downplaying its continuity with the intellectual context of *cultural* nationalism.

That cultural vision of the nation, however, was soon overwhelmed by ethnic and later racist variations of nationalism. The common element that served to keep the nation together was now identified with race. In the twentieth century, the attempts of the Nazi and the Italian fascist regimes to 'ethnicise' private law were gloomy signs of this tendency. Historians still discuss whether these latter manifestations can be considered a direct and logical evolution from previous nationalist forms; the law scholar can just detect a slow and increasingly worrying shift from cultural to ethnic understanding of the nation in the legal studies of that period, but at the same time he recognises the evident contrasts concerning several other aspects between the legal thought of the nineteenth century legal scholars and the legal theory promoted by the fascist experiences.

While nowadays nationalism is usually associated with those dramatic historical events, in and of itself, nationalism has been freed from fascist and racist connotations. In particular, modern advocates of nationalism in political theory highlight that imperialistic fascist experiences even represented the contradiction of the nationalist principle aimed at giving each nation a state. After that concept had become almost a political taboo, a number of contemporary political theorists have legitimised the idea of nationalism in more recent years, making it acceptable by showing its compatibility with liberal principles as well as its persisting usefulness in the contemporary world. Nonetheless, while the idea that any nation should have the right to establish a state of its own became a guiding principle in the first decades of the twentieth century, the historical events of the Second World War led people to accept the view that nationalism was to be blamed for those tragedies and the only way to reduce the possibility of such conflicts in the future was to put constraints on national sovereignty. In this context, a fundamental paradox arose, resulting in an unending tension between opposite forces. On the one hand, the world order is basically organised along national lines according to the nationalist principle; on the other hand, nationalism in itself is looked down on as something dangerous. In the aftermath of the Second World War, the process of denationalisation was accelerated by the creation of several international organisations, while the creation and later institutional evolution of the European Communities is a famous example thereof.

The impact of these events on private law in Europe is self-evident and could be synthesised in one expression: European private law. From the perspective of the legal scholar, it is nonetheless clear that there is strong tension between the trends of denationalisation and the status quo dating back to the era of the nationalisation of law. Such tension gives rise to several episodes of resistance to Europeanisation that are detectable even inasmuch as private law is concerned.

In the first place, the elaboration of European private law rules can be jeopardised by the attempts of the Member States to steer the drafting process in a direction that serves best the interests—material or symbolic—of the nation-state. This should not surprise, since political scientists have already pointed out that Europe can easily represent the institutional framework in which nation-states pursue their own particular interest, trying to influence the elaboration of common rules. In the second place, since European private law is usually issued in the form of directives in need of implementation by the Member States, national resistance can also emerge at another level, inspired by the need for Member States to safeguard particularly relevant national interests or the systematic coherence of their private law system. While these practices do not necessarily stand in contrast with the purposes of European integration—that in the area of private law has implied a mere harmonisation by means of directives rather than unification—they can occasionally lead to a contrast between European and national interests—especially when it comes to particularly important areas or even symbols of the nation-state—that frustrate the aims of integration and ultimately reveal the continuing importance of the order attained in the era of the nationalisation of law. In this sense European private law becomes 'renationalised', even if such renationalisation is often brought about at the expense of the uniformity of European law. Even the judiciary, structurally thought to give application to national law, can easily contribute to this process of renationalisation of law, which in the end does not appear as a deliberate nationalist agenda but rather as the coherent and path-dependent continuation of practices that preserve a nationalistic state of affairs.

To grasp more clearly the importance of the national dimension in the private law discourse and its theoretical implications, it is particularly helpful to turn our attention to the reflections of the legal scholars who have over the years—also explicitly stirred by the European institutions—engaged in an extensive, multidisciplinary, as well as highly normatively oriented, debate on the advantages and disadvantages of a European private law. In this debate not only the legal but also the economic, political and, in a broader sense, cultural implications of the process of Europeanisation have been analysed and the reasons justifying 'resistance' as well as the defence of the national state of affairs of private law are systematically presented and discussed. According to the most recurring arguments employed in that context and taken into consideration in this book—most notably the economic, social and cultural arguments—Europeanisation would be unfeasible or undesirable for the reason that it would lead to results that are economically inefficient or even unjust, and would in any case disrespect cultural diversities whose safeguard should fall within the scope of the European treaties. These arguments are based on the underlying assumption that different Member States have different understandings as to particular policy choices, social values or cultures, so that in the end the idea of unification or harmonisation extended to particularly sensitive issues appears as unattainable. The cultural argument assumes a particular importance in this sense, and even the other arguments ultimately appear to rest upon the cultural one. In other words, cultural pluralism would require legal pluralism, since law and culture are tied to one another and cannot be dissociated. It should not surprise now that the defence of nation rests upon a defence of culture since, as we have seen, culture has become the predominant criterion to identify a nation.

On a closer look, therefore, the assumption upon which those arguments rest appears to be inherently nationalistically biased, and shows in particular links to the cultural understanding of nation, which has become the most widespread one after the historical failure of ethnic nationalisms; cultures are considered different among nations and not also across or within nations. Actually, advocates of national cultural pluralism do not deny the existence of different levels of culture , but coherent policy implications do not follow from the recognition of the existence of transnational or subnational cultural segments. Such an idea that culture basically corresponds to the nation is widespread in legal discourse, where scholars resort to studies that claim to have discovered and systematised cultural variations among nations in order to prove the necessary link between law and culture. Nevertheless, on closer analysis, these studies appear to lean toward nationalist methodologies and assumptions themselves. Critics testify that distinctions of cultures based on national categories are still questionable instruments to be employed to investigate the specificities of legal institutions. In fact, while it cannot be proved that 'dimensions of national culture', as they are called, are false per se, these can at most describe—accepting the unavoidable imprecision of otherwise necessary generalisations—but hardly explain or even less *predict* variations in legal rules and institutions. Their employment in comparative law with the aim of *explaining* differences in law and institutions or *predicting* how legal transplants would be accepted in culturally different contexts—normally coinciding with the jurisdiction of the nation-state—should therefore be measured particularly carefully, while the level of care should increase as the degree of statistical accuracy of the generalisation decreases.

In a broader perspective, while the existence of a blurry concept such as national culture—which can reveal itself in a series of easily detectable behavioural habits—can hardly be empirically disproved (the very observation of the existence of cultural pluralism in the world and to a lesser extent in Europe would otherwise be a mere hallucination), the suggestion that the criterion for identifying nationality is exactly culture remains a fundamental assumption that even anthropologists see with some suspicion and only nationalists have repeatedly advanced, occasionally linking culture with race. The link between culture and nation was indeed highlighted in clear terms during the period of German cultural nationalism, in particular by Herder—whose view spread into legal studies thanks to the idea of *Volksgeist* that still emerges in some incarnation in the contemporary debate—while more recently political theorists adhering to the idea of liberal nationalism have deepened and strengthened the relation between culture and nationality.

Starting from the idea that nationality and culture are synonymous, liberal nationalist authors have drawn normative implications, explaining why the political and the national unit should coincide. Only this condition would guarantee democracy, efficiency, justice and respect for culture within the state. Besides, for a functional similarity, certain arguments widespread in the European private law discourse even show a structural resemblance to liberal nationalist views. But while the ideological underpinning of those arguments need to be considered more attentively, the existence of those conceptual links should not be taken to mean the fallacy of those positions, since liberal nationalism has to be viewed too as a legitimate political principle which can contribute to a better understanding of world politics and even offer—at least partially—a counterweight to otherwise uncontrollable globalising trends in a world order which desperately strives for a difficult balance between opposite exigencies with a strong tendency to degenerate. Provided that the pursuit of the national interest can never legitimise internationally illegal acts, therefore, liberal nationalism appears still to be able to offer at least a certain number of arguments suitable to the theoretical and political elaboration of even post-national institutions.

Interestingly enough, in this light, underlying nationalist assumptions seem to inspire not only opposition to the denationalisation of law, but even the process of Europeanisation itself—something which has been termed 'Euronationalism' in a purposely open-ended fashion in this book. During several centuries of nation building, strategies have been employed to spread national consciousness and establish the nation-state. Civil codifications in continental Europe can be seen as one of those instruments too, whose political, rather than just legal, function is widely recognised by historians. Those same nation-building strategies could now likely be repeated at the European level to foster the development of a shared collective identity for European citizens, that is the famous and highly discussed idea of a 'European identity'. Not only the instruments of 'banal nationalism' on which much of the discussion in the political debate and media has been (sometimes naïvely) focusing—flags, anthems and so on—can serve the cause of European identity, but more substantially and importantly, law itself can be a factor in this context. In this light, the attempts to elaborate not only something similar to a constitutional charter but also a civil codification—in the form of a mandatory code or even a less pretentious optional instrument—can be seen as an attempt to define the values that should be accepted and represent the object of identification for people according to a model of constitutional patriotism, which appears as the most viable solution to fostering social and political integration in a context, such as the European, which is characterised by an apparent lack of homogeneity between citizens, be it of an ethnic, linguistic or cultural nature. Much of the discussion as to European plans for instruments that resemble the form and content of a codification is conditioned by the awareness of a nationalistic added value of the code. Nevertheless, while that added value has reasonably faded away over the years, not resisting to tendencies of decodification and, more importantly, the emergence of modern constitutions with an important nation-building function after the Second World War, private law as such and independently of its form can still play a sociologically important role in the creation of collective identities. It is already possible to identify certain substantive rules in European law which can perform that function.

The concept of European identity has been discussed extensively in political science, but any attempt to define it unambiguously, singling out the element that makes a person 'European' regardless of national identity, has admittedly not led to appreciable results as of yet. Even the legal concept of European citizenship is a derivative one and follows from traditional national citizenship. Ultimately, to analyse it from the perspective of the nationalism studies, the question of European identity does not seem much dissimilar from the one '*qu'est-ce qu'une nation?*'. From this perspective, the main difference between the traditional construction of national identity and the attempt to establish a European identity—even one which is respectful of other identities and cultures—could even simply seem that national identities have already been constructed. In this sense, even the opposition between primordialist and modernist conceptions of nationalism—which is already less radical than it might seem—loses importance outside a purely historiographical perspective. One may consider national identities as natural evidence or imagined artefacts but it is hardly deniable that, even like self-fulfilling prophecies, they already 'exist' in the acceptance of people, while the role of nation-states (or at least, of some of them) in international politics remain visibly preponderant despite an often tedious rhetoric on the fading away of the nation in the globalised world. Already the fact that nations can be conceived of as *imagined* communities—and not *imaginary*, as it is often said, misquoting a famous expression—gives a hint in this sense. On the contrary, European identity remains in a less developed phase, apparently deprived of that set of components and imagery on which national movements have based their claims for centuries.

Against this background, it becomes easy to become distrustful and to return to the safe haven of our national identities, laws and concepts, admitting that the only thing that Europeans share, beside a rather limited geographical area on the world map, is the fact that they have been fighting each other for the past few thousand years, and certainly not common laws. This conclusion, nonetheless, would be hardly justifiable. Exactly for that reason, and mindful of the fact that historically most collective identities—including those that we take for granted and at times mythicise—have been built by the occasionally contemptible means of homogenisation and repression of differences, the development of a new shared identity for Europe, while respecting diversity and preventing the economic and social wrongs that even unification processes can produce, appears as a stimulating challenge from a theoretical, an historical and even a legal point of view. Private law could be, again, an important factor in this challenge.

Bibliography

Abu-Lughod, J, 'Writing against Culture', in RG Fox (ed), *Recapturing Anthropology. Working in the Present* (Santa Fe, School of American Research Press, 1991) 137–62

Acton, JEED, 'Nationality', in JEED Acton, *Essays on Freedom and Power* (New York, Meridian Books, 1955) 141–70

Albi, A, *EU Enlargement and the Constitutions of Central and Eastern Europe* (Cambridge, Cambridge University Press, 2005)

Alpa, G, *L'arte di giudicare* (Roma, Laterza, 1996)

—— ,'European Community Resolutions and the Codification of "Private Law"' (2000) 2 *European Review of Private Law* 321–33

——, 'La competizione tra ordinamenti: un approccio realistico', in A Zoppini (ed), *La concorrenza tra ordinamenti giuridici* (Roma, Laterza, 2004) 43–57

Alpa, G, and Andenas, M, *Fondamenti del diritto privato europeo* (Milano, Giuffrè, 2005)

Alter, KJ, *The European Court's Political Power. Selected Essays* (Oxford, Oxford University Press, 2010)

Amato, C, 'Case Note. Article 1469-*sexies* of the Italian Civil Code: A Tale of National Resistance' (2005) 1 *European Review of Contract Law* 240–45

Amodio, C, 'Nell'occhio del ciclone. La Francia alla prova dei processi di denazionalizzazione del diritto' (2009) 40 *Politica del diritto* 605–38

Anderson, B, *Imagined Communities: Reflection on the Origin and Spread of Nationalism* [1983] (London, Verso, 2006)

Antokolskaia, M, 'The Harmonisation of Family Law: Old and New Dilemmas' (2003) 1 *European Review of Private Law* 28–49

Antoniolli, J, and Fiorentini, F (eds), *A Factual Assessment of the Draft Common Frame of Reference* (Munich, Sellier, 2011)

Aristotle, *Politics* [350 BCE] English translation (Mineola, NY, Dover, 2000)

Arts, W, Hagenaars, J, and Halman, J, 'The Cultural Diversity of European Unity: An Introduction', in W Arts, J Hagenaars and J Halman (eds), *The Cultural Diversity of European Unity. Findings, Explanations and Reflections from the European Values Study* (Leiden, Brill, 2003) 1–12

Badosa Coll, F, '"… Quae ad ius Cathalanicum pertinet": The Civil Law of Catalonia, *ius commune* and the Legal Tradition', in HL MacQueen, A Vaquer and S Espiau Espiau (eds), *Regional Private Laws and Codification in Europe* (Cambridge, Cambridge University Press 2003) 172–98

Balibar, ER, and Wallerstein, IM, *Race, Nation, Class: Ambiguous Identities* (London, Verso, 1991)

Bamforth, N, Malik, M, O'Cinneide, C, *Discrimination Law: Theory and Context* (London, Sweet & Maxwell, 2008)

Bar, C von, Clive, E, Schulte-Nölke, H and Beale, H, Herre, J, Huet, J, Schlechtriem, P, Storme, M, Wann, S, Varul, P, Veneziano, A, Zoll, F (eds), *Principles, Definitions and Model Rules of European Private Law. Draft Common Frame of Reference (DCFR). Interim Outline Edition* (Munich, Sellier, 2008)

——, *Principles, Definitions and Model Rules of European Private Law. Draft Common Frame of Reference (DCFR). Outline Edition* (Munich, Sellier, 2009)

——, *Principles, Definitions and Model Rules of European Private Law. Draft Common Frame of Reference (DCFR)* Vol 1 (Munich, Sellier, 2009)

Barberis, M, *Europa del diritto* (Bologna, il Mulino, 2008)

Barbero, D, 'Negazione della legge ingiusta come valore giuridico e resistenza' (1949) *Iustitia* 25 ff

Barcellona, M, 'Per un codice civile europeo', in M Meli and MR Maugeri (eds), *L'armonizzazione del diritto privato europeo. Il piano d'azione 2003* (Milano, Giuffrè, 2004) 175–97

Barry, B, 'Statism and Nationalism: A Cosmopolitan Critique', in I Shapiro and L Brilmayer (eds), *Global Justice* (New York, New York University Press, 1999) 12–66

Basedow, J, 'A Common Contract Law for the Common Market' (1996) 33 *Common Market Law Review* 1169–95

——, 'Rechtskultur—zwischen nationalem Mythos und europäischem Ideal' (1996) 3 *Zeitschrift für Europäisches Privatrecht* 379–81

——, 'Codification of Private Law in the European Union: The Making of a Hybrid' (2001) 9 *European Review of Private Law* 35–49

——, 'The Case for a European Contract Law', in S Grundmann and J Stuyk (eds) *An Academic Green Paper on European Contract Law* (The Hague, Kluwer Law International, 2002) 147–57

Beck, U, *Der kosmopolitische Blick. Oder: Krieg ist Frieden* (Frankfurt am Main, Suhrkamp, 2004)

——, *Das Deutsche Europa. Neue Machtlandschaften im Zeichen der Krise* (Berlin, Suhrkamp, 2012)

Beiser, F, *Hegel* (New York, Routledge, 2005)

Beitz C, 'Rawls's Law of Peoples' (2000) 110 *Ethics* 669–96

Benes, T, 'From Indo-Germans to Aryans. Philology and the Racialization of Salvationist National Rhetoric, 1806–30', in S Eigen and M Larrimore (eds), *The German Invention of the Race* (Albany NY, State University of New York Press, 2006) 167–81

Berg, PAJ van den, *The Politics of European Codification. A History of the Unification of Law in France, Prussia, the Austrian Monarchy and the Netherlands* (Groningen, Europa Law Publishing, 2007)

Bergh, R van den, 'Forced Harmonisation of Contract Law in Europe: Not To Be Continued', in S Grundmann and J Stuyk (eds) *An Academic Green Paper on European Contract Law* (The Hague, Kluwer Law International, 2002) 249–68

——, 'Private Law in a Globalizing World: Economic Criteria for Choosing the Optimal Regulatory Level in a Multi-Level Government System', in MG Faure and A van der Welt (eds), *Globalization and Private Law. The Way Forward* (Cheltenham, Edward Elgar Publishing, 2010) 57–96

Berlin, I, 'Nationalism: Past Neglected and Present Power', in I Berlin, *Against the Current. Essays in the History of Ideas* (London, Hogarth Press, 1979) 141–70

Berman, HJ, *Law and Revolution. The Formation of the Western Legal Tradition* (Cambridge MA, Harvard University Press, 1983)

Berman, N, '"But the Alternative is Despair": European Nationalism and the Modernist Renewal of International Law' (1993) 106 *Harvard Law Review* 1792–903

Besley, T and Coate, S, 'Centralized versus Decentralized Provision of Local Public Goods: A Political Economy Approach' (2003) 87 *Journal of Public Economics* 2611–37

Besselink, LFM, 'National and Constitutional Identity Before and After Lisbon' (2010) 6 *Utrecht Law Review* 36–49

Bile, F, 'La Corte di cassazione di fronte al diritto comunitario', in N Lipari (ed), *Diritto privato europeo e categorie civilistiche* (Napoli, Edizioni Scientifiche Italiane, 1998) 201–17

Billig, M, *Banal Nationalism* (London, Sage, 1995)

Bin, R and Caretti, R, *Profili costituzionali dell'Unione Europea* (Bologna, il Mulino, 2009)

Birch, AH, 'Another Liberal Theory of Secession' (1984) 32 *Political Studies* 596–602

Bleckmann, A, *Allgemeine Grundrechtslehren* (Köln, Heymann, 1979)

Bloch, M, *Feudal Society* vol 2 (Chicago, Chicago University Press, 1964)

Bobbio, N, 'Grandezza e decadenza dell'ideologia europea' (1986) 3 *Lettera internazionale* 1–5

Böckenförde, E-W, 'Die Historische Rechtsschule und das Problem der Geschichtlichkeit des Rechts', in E-M Böckenförde, *Recht, Staat, Freiheit* (Frankfurt am Main, Suhrkamp, 1991) 9–41

——, *Welchen Weg geht Europa?* (München, Friedrich von Siemens Stiftung, 1997)

Boele-Woelki, K, 'The Road Towards a European Family Law' (1997) 1 *Electronic Journal of Comparative Law*

Bogdandy, A von, 'Hegel und der Nationalstaat' (1991) 30 *Der Staat* 513–35

Bonell, MJ, 'Comparazione giuridica e unificazione del diritto', in G Alpa, MJ Bonell, D Corapi, L Moccia, V Zeno-Zencovich and A Zoppini, *Diritto privato comparato. Istituti e problemi* (Roma, Laterza, 2004) 3–33

Booker, C and North, R, *The Castle of Lies. Why Britain Must Get Out of Europe* (London, Duckworth, 1996)

Bovenberg, L, 'Unity Produces Diversity: The Economics of Europe's Social Capital', in W Arts, J Hagenaars and J Halman (eds), *The Cultural Diversity of European Unity. Findings, Explanations and Reflections from the European Values Study* (Leiden, Brill, 2003) 403–19

Bretone, M, *Diritto e tempo nella tradizione europea* (Bari, Laterza, 2004)

Breuilly, J, *Nationalism and the State* (Manchester, Manchester University Press, 1985)

Broberg, MP and Fenger, N, *Preliminary References to the European Court of Justice* (Oxford, Oxford, University Press, 2010)

Brubaker, R, *Ethnicity without Groups* (Cambridge MA, Harvard University Press, 2004)

Bryde, B-O, in I von Munch and P Kunig, *Grundgesetz-Kommentar. Band 1. Präambel bis Art. 19* (München, Beck, 2000)

Burke, P, *What is Cultural History?* (Cambridge, Polity Press, 2008)

Busse, C, *Die völkerrechtliche Einordnung der Europäischen Union* (Köln, Heymann, 1999)

Buthman, WC, *The Rise of Integral Nationalism in France: With Special Reference to the Ideas and Activities of Charles Maurras* (New York, Columbia University Press, 1939)

Cabrillac, R, 'L'avenir du Code civil' (2004) 13 *La semaine juridique* 547–51

Caenegem, RC van, *Judges, Legislators & Professors: Chapters in European Legal History* (New York, Cambridge University Press, 1987)

——, *European Law in the Past and the Future. Unity and Diversity over Two Millennia* (Cambridge, Cambridge University Press, 2002)

Caney, S, 'Liberalism and Communitarianism: A Misconceived Debate' (1992) 40 *Political Studies* 273–89

Cannata, CA, *Lineamenti di storia della giurisprudenza europea. II. Dal medioevo all'epoca contemporanea* (Torino, Giappichelli, 1976)

Canovan, M, *Nationhood and Political Theory* (Cheltenham, Edward Elgar Publishing, 1996)

Canovan, M, 'Patriotism Is Not Enough' (2000) 30 *British Journal of Political Science* 413–32

Capitant, H, *Introduction à l'étude du droit civil* (Paris, A Pedone Editeur, 1929)

Cappellini, P, 'Il codice eterno. La forma-codice e i suoi destinatari. Morfologie e metamorfosi di un paradigma della modernità', in P Cappellini and B Sordi (eds), *Codici. Una riflessione di fine millennio* (Milano, Giuffrè, 2002) 11–68

Caroni, P, 'Savigny und die Kodifikation. Verusch einer Neudeutung des "Berufes"' (1969) 86 *Zeitschrift der Savigny-Stiftung für Rechtsgeschichte. Germanistische Abteilung* 97–176

——, 'La cifra codificatoria nell'opera di Savigny' (1980) 9 *Quaderni fiorentini per la storia del pensiero giuridico moderno* 69–111

Carter, JC, *The Proposed Codification of Our Common Law* (New York, *Evening Post* Job Printing Office, 1884)

Caruso, D, 'The Missing View of the Cathedral: The Private Law Paradigm of European Legal Integration' (1997) 3 *European Law Journal* 3–32

Castellino, G, *International Law and Self-determination* (The Hague, Kluwer Law International, 2000)

Chabert, G, *L'idée européenne. Entre guerres et culture: de la confrontation à l'union* (Bruxelles, Peter Lang, 2007)

Chabod, F, *Storia dell'idea d'Europa* [1961] (Roma, Laterza, 2010)

Cicero, *De Legibus* [52 BCE]

Cliteur, P, *Natuurrecht, cultuurrecht, conservatisme. Grondslag van de democratische rechtsstaat* (Leeuwarden, Universitaire Pers Fryslân, 2005)

Coing, H, 'Savignys rechtspolitische und methodische Anschauungen in ihrer Bedeutung für die gegenwärtige deutsche Rechtswissenschaft', in H Coing, *Gesammelte Aufsätze zu Rechtsgeschichte, Rechtsphilosophie und Zivilrecht*, vol 1 (Frankfurt am Main, Vittorio Klostermann, 1982) 178–90

——, *Europäisches Privatrecht. Bd. II 19. Jahrhundert: Überblick über die Entwicklung des Privatrechts in den ehemals gemeinrechtlichen Ländern* (München, Beck'sche Verlagsbuchhandlung, 1989)

Cole, GDH, *Social Theory* (London, Methuen & Co, 1920)

Collins, H, 'European Private Law and the Cultural Identity of the States' (1995) 3 *European Review of Private Law* 353–65

——, 'Does Social Justice Require the Preservation of Diversity in the Private Laws of Member States of Europe?', in T Wilhelmsson, E Paunio and A Pohjolainen (eds) *Private Law and the Many Cultures of Europe* (Alphen aan den Rijn, Kluwer Law International, 2007) 155–76

——, 'La giustizia contrattuale in Europa', in A Somma (ed), *Giustizia sociale e mercato nel diritto europeo dei contratti* (Torino, Giappichelli, 2007) 83–105

——, *The European Civil Code. The Way Forward* (Cambridge, Cambridge University Press, 2008)

Colombi Ciacchi, A, 'The Constitutionalization of European Contract Law: Judicial Convergence and Social Justice' (2006) 2 *European Review of Contract Law* 167–80

Comparato, G, 'Behind Judicial Resistance to European Private Law' in H-W Micklitz and Y Svetiev (eds) *A Self-Sufficient European Private Law—A Viable Concept? EUI Working Paper 2012/31* 97–113

Connor, W, 'Nation-building or Nation-destroying?' (1972) 24 *World Politics* 319–55
——, *Ethnonationalism. The Quest for Understanding* (Princeton, Princeton University Press, 1994)
Costamagna, C, 'Il diritto internazionale nell'ordine nuovo' (1941) *Lo Stato* 401–20
Constantinesco, LJ, *Das Recht der Europäischen Gemeinschaften I. Das institutionelle Recht* (Baden-Baden, Nomos, 1977)
Cotterrell, R, *The Sociology of Law. An Introduction* (London, Butterworths, 1992)
——, *Law's Community* (Oxford, Clarendon Press, 1995)
——, 'Comparative Law and Legal Culture', in M Reimann and R Zimmermann (eds), *The Oxford Handbook of Comparative Law* (Oxford, Oxford University Press, 2006) 709–37
Cronaca degli avvenimenti di Sicilia da aprile 1860 a marzo 1861: estratta da documenti (Italy, 1863)
D'Holbach, P-HT, *Système social. Principes naturels de la morale et de la politique avec un examen de l'influence du gouvernement sur les moeurs* (Paris, Chez Niogret Libraire-Éditeur, 1882)
Dahl, RA, *Democracy and Its Critics* (New Haven, Yale University Press, 1989)
Dahrendorf, R, *Perché l'Europa? Riflessioni di un europeista scettico* (Roma, Laterza, 1997)
——, *Why Europe? On the Purposes of the EU after Enlargement* (Maastricht, Universiteit Maastricht, 2004)
——, *The Modern Social Conflict. The Politics of Liberty* (New Brunswick, Transaction Publishers, 2008)
Dam, C van, 'European Tort Law and the Many Cultures of Europe', in T Wilhelmsson, E Paunio and A Pohjolainen (eds) *Private Law and the Many Cultures of Europe* (Alphen aan den Rijn, Kluwer Law International, 2007) 57–80
——, 'Who is Afraid of Diversity? Cultural Diversity, European Co-operation, and European Tort Law' (2009) 20 *King's Law Journal* 281–308
Dann, O, 'Der moderne Nationalismus als Problem historischer Entwicklungsforschung', in O Dann (ed), *Nationalismus und sozialer Wandel* (Hamburg, Hoffmann und Campe, 1978) 9–21
——, 'Funktionen des Nationalismus in modernen Gesellschaften', in O Dann (ed), *Nationalismus und sozialer Wandel* (Hamburg, Hoffmann und Campe, 1978) 209–22
David, R, *The International Unification of Private Law. International Encyclopedia of Law*, vol II chapter 5 (Tubingen, Mohr, 1969)
Dawson, JP, *Oracles of the Law* (Westport, Greenwood Press, 1978)
De Felice, R, *Autobiografia del fascismo. Antologia di testi fascisti 1919–1945* (Torino, Einaudi, 2004)
De Gispert I Català, N, 'The Codification of Catalan Civil Law', in HL MacQueen, A Vaquer and S Espiau Espiau (eds), *Regional Private Laws and Codification in Europe* (Cambridge, Cambridge University Press, 2003) 164–71
De Vries, MS, 'The Rise and Fall of Decentralization: A Comparative Analysis of Arguments and Practices in European Countries' (2000) 38 *European Journal of Political Research* 193–224
De Witte, B, 'The Past and Future of the European Court of Justice in the Protection of Human Rights', in P Alston, *The EU and Human Rights* (Oxford, Oxford University Press, 1999) 859–85
Delanty, G, *Inventing Europe. Idea, Identity, Reality* (Basingstoke, Macmillan, 1995)
——, 'L'identità europea come costruzione sociale', in L Passerini (ed), *Identità culturale europea. Idee, sentimenti, relazioni* (Firenze, La Nuova Italia, 1998) 47–66

Deveaux, M, *Cultural Pluralism and Dilemmas of Justice* (Ithaca, Cornell University Press, 2000)

Domarus, M, *Hitler. Reden und Proklamationen 1932–1945*, vol 1 (Wiesbaden, Löwit, 1973)

Drobnig, U, 'Abschied vom BGB? ' (2007) 85 *Deutsche Richterzeitung* 257–61

Dukas, H and Hoffman, B, *Albert Einstein: The Human Side* (Princeton, Princeton University Press, 1979)

Ehrmann, HW, *Comparative Legal Cultures* (London, Prentice-Hall, 1976)

Eidenmüller, H, Faust, F, Grigoleit, HC, Jansen, N, Wagner, G and Zimmermann, R, 'Der Gemeinsame Referenzrahmen für das Europäische Privatrecht. Wertungsfragen und Kodifikationsprobleme' (2008) 11 *JuristenZeitung* 529–84

Eisenhardt, U, *Deutsche Rechtsgeschichte* (Munich, Beck, 2008)

Ergang, RR, *Herder and the Foundations of German Nationalism* (New York, Columbia University Press, 1931)

Eriksen, TH, *Ethnicity and Nationalism. Anthropological Perspectives* (London, Pluto Press, 2002)

Faure, MG, 'Towards a Harmonized Tort Law in Europe? An Economic Perspective' (2001) 8 *Maastricht Journal of European and Comparative Law* 339–50

——, 'How Law and Economics May Contribute to the Harmonisation of Tort Law in Europe', in R Zimmermann (ed), *Grundstrukturen des europäischen Deliktsrechts* (Baden-Baden, Nomos, 2003) 31–82

——, 'Economic Analysis of Tort Law and the European Civil Code', in A Hartkamp, MW Hesselink, EW Hondius, C Mak and E du Perron (eds), *Towards a European Civil Code. Fourth and Expanded Edition* (The Hague, Kluwer Law International, 2011) 977–1000

——, 'Globalization and Multi-level Governance of Environmental Harm', in MG Faure and A van der Walt, *Globalization and Private Law. The Way Forward* (Cheltenham, Edward Elgar Publishing, 2010) 383–425

Faure, MG and Hartlief, T, 'Naar een harmonisatie van aansprakelijkheidsrecht in Europa? Een kritisch rechtseconomisch perspectief' (2003) *Nederlands Juristenblad* 170–77

Faure, MG, Smits, JM and Schneider, H (eds) *Towards a European Ius Commune in Legal Education and Research: Proceedings of the Conference Held at the Occasion of the 20th Anniversary of the Maastricht Faculty of Law* (Antwerp, Intersentia, 2002)

Fauvarque-Cosson, B and Mazeaud, D (eds) *European Contract Law. Materials for a Common Frame of Reference: Terminology, Guiding Principles, Model Rules/Produced by Association Henri Capitant des Amis de la Culture Juridique Française and Société de Législation Comparée* (Munich, Sellier, 2008)

Fehr, H, *Schweizerischer und deutscher Volksgeist in der Rechtsentwicklung* (Frauenfeld, Von Huber, 1926)

Feldman, N, 'When Judges Make Foreign Policy' *The New York Times*, 25 September 2008

Fichte, JG, *Nachgelassene Werke*, vol 3 (Bonn, A Marcus, 1835)

——, *Werke*, vol 5 (Leipzig, Meiner 1910)

Figueras Pàmies, M, *La Escuela Jurídica catalana frente a la Codificación española. Durán y Bas: su pensamiento jurídico-filosófico* (Barcelona, Bosch, 1987)

Flessner, A, 'Rechtsvereinheitlichung durch Rechtswissenschaft und Juristenausbildung' (1992) 56 *Rabels Zeitschrift für ausländisches und internationales Privatrecht* 243–60

Fontanelli, F and Martinico, G, 'Between Procedural Impermeability and Constitutional Openness: The Italian Constitutional Court and Preliminary References to the European Court of Justice' (2010) 16 *European Law Journal* 345–64

Forsyth, MG (ed), *Federalism and Nationalism* (Leicester, Leicester University Press, 1985)
Frank, H, 'Die Zeit des Rechts' (1936) *Deutsches Recht* 1 ff
Friedman, LM, 'Legal Culture and Social Development' (1969) 4 *Law and Society Review* 29–44
——, *A History of American Law* (New York, Simon & Schuster, 1973)
——, *The Legal System. A Social Science Perspective* (New York, Russell Sage Foundation, 1975)
Gandolfi, G, 'Introduction', in *Accademia dei Giusprivatisti Europei: Code Européen des contrats* (Milano, Giuffrè, 2004) LI–LVIII
Gans, C, *The Limits of Nationalism* (Cambridge, Cambridge University Press, 2003)
Gellner, E, *Thought and Change* (London, Weidenfeld & Nicolson, 1964)
——, *Nations and Nationalism* (Oxford, Blackwell, 1983)
——, *Nationalism* (London, Weidenfeld & Nicolson, 1997)
Ghisalberti, C, *La codificazione del diritto in Italia. 1865–1942* (Roma, Laterza, 1985)
Giaro, T, 'Diritto romano attuale. Mappe mentali e strumenti concettuali', in PG Monateri, T Giaro and A Somma, *Le radici comuni del diritto europeo. Un cambiamento di prospettiva* (Roma, Carocci, 2005) 77–168
Giddens, A, *The Nation State and Violence* (Cambridge, Polity Press, 1985)
Gilbert, P, *The Philosophy of Nationalism* (Boulder Colorado, Westview Press, 1998)
Gilbin, R, *Global Political Economy. Understanding the International Economic Order* (Princeton, Princeton University Press, 2001)
Glencross, A, 'A Post-National EU? The Problem of Legitimising the EU without the Nation and National Representation' (2010) 59 *Political Studies* 1–20
Glenn, HP, 'The Nationalist Heritage', in P Legrand and R Munday (eds), *Comparative Legal Studies: Traditions and Transitions* (Cambridge, Cambridge University Press, 2003) 76–99
Goldmann, K, *Transforming the European Nation State: Dynamics of Internationalization* (London, Sage, 2001)
Goldsmith, J and Posner, E, 'Does Europe Believe in International Law?' *The Wall Street Journal*, 25 November 2008
Gönczi, K, 'Die deutsch–ungarischen Rechtsverbindungen von der Frühen Neuzeit bis in die Gegenwart: Wissenstransfer, Kodifikationen und *liaisonmen*' (2000) 46 *Osteuropa-Recht* 215–29
Goode, R, 'Contract and Commercial Law: The Logic and Limits of Harmonisation' (2003) 7(4) *Electronic Journal of Comparative Law*
——, 'The Harmonization of Dispositive Contract and Commercial Law—Should the European Community Be Involved?', in EM Kieninger (ed), *Denationalisierung des Privatrechts? Symposium anlässlich des 70. Geburtstages von Karl Kreuzer* (Tübingen, Mohr Siebeck, 2005) 1–32
Goodin, RE, 'What is So Special about our Fellow Countrymen?' (1988) 98 *Ethics* 663–86
——, 'Conventions and Conversions, or, Why Is Nationalism Sometimes so Nasty?', in R McKim and J McMahan (eds), *The Morality of Nationalism* (Oxford, Oxford University Press, 1997) 88–104
Goodman, J, *Nationalism and Transnationalism. The National Conflict in Ireland and European Union Integration* (Aldershot, Avebury Press, 1996)
Grandi, D, *Tradizione e Rivoluzione nei Codici Mussoliniani* (Roma, Tipografia delle Mantellate, 1940)
——, 'Diritto romano-fascista e germanico-nazista di fronte alla rivoluzione del secolo XX' (Roma, Tipografia della Camera dei fasci e delle corporazioni, 1940)

Grimm, D, *Deutsche Verfassungsgeschichte, 1776–1866: Vom Beginn des modernen Verfassungsstaats bis zur Auflösung des Deutschen Bundes* (Frankfurt am Main, Suhrkamp, 1988)
Grossi, P, *L'ordine giuridico medievale* (Roma, Laterza, 2006)
——, *L'Europa del diritto* (Roma, Laterza, 2007)
——, *Mitologie giuridiche della modernità* (Milano, Giuffrè, 2007)
Grundmann, S and Kerber, W, 'European System of Contract Laws—A Map for Combining the Advantages of Centralised and Decentralised Rule-making', in S Grundmann and J Stuyck (eds), *An Academic Green Paper on European Contract Law* (The Hague, Kluwer Law International, 2002) 295–342
Grundmann, S and Stuyck, J (eds) *An Academic Green Paper on European Contract Law* (The Hague, Kluwer Law International, 2002)
Haas, EB, 'What is Nationalism and Why Should We Study It?' (1986) 40 *International Organization* 707–44
Habermas, J, 'Historical Consciousness and Post-Traditional Identity', in J Habermas, *The New Conservatism: Cultural Criticism and the Historians' Debate* (Cambridge, Polity Press, 1989) 249–67
——, 'Staatsbürgerschaft und nationale Identität' [1990], in J Habermas, *Faktizität und Geltung: Beiträge zur Diskurstheorie des Rechts und des demokratischen Rechtsstaats* (Frankfurt, Suhrkamp, 1994) 632–60
——, 'Struggle for Recognition in the Democratic Constitutional State', in C Taylor and A Gutmann (eds), *Multiculturalism: Examining the Politics of Recognition* (Princeton, Princeton University Press, 1994) 107–49
——, 'Über den internen Zusammenhang von Rechtsstaat und Demokratie', in UK Preuss (ed), *Zum Begriff der Verfassung, die Ordnung des Politischen* (Frankfurt am Main, Fischer, 1994) 83–94
——, *The Inclusion of the Other: Studies in Political Theory* (Cambridge MA, The MIT Press, 1998)
——, *Die postnationale Konstellation. Politische Essays* (Berlin, Suhrkamp, 1998)
——, 'Why Europe Needs a Constitution' (2001) 11 *New Left Review* 5–26
——, 'The European Nation State and the Pressures of Globalization', in P De Greiff and C Cronin (eds), *Global Justice and Transnational Politics* (Cambridge MA, The MIT Press, 2002) 217–34
——, *Zur Verfassung Europas. Ein Essay* (Berlin, Suhrkamp, 2011)
Habermas, J, and Derrida, J, 'February 15, or What Binds Europeans Together: A Plea for a Common Foreign Policy, Beginning in the Core of Europe' (2003) 10 *Constellations* 291–97
Hall, JA, 'Nationalisms: Classified and Explained', in S Periwa (ed), *Notions of Nationalism* (Oxford, Oxford University Press, 1995) 8–33
Halpérin, J-H, *L'impossible Code civil* (Paris, PUF, 1992)
——, *Entre nationalisme juridique et communauté de droit* (Paris, Presses Universitaires de France, 1999)
Halsted, JB, *Romanticism* (New York, Harper & Row, 1969)
Hamerow, T, *The Social Foundations of German Unification, 1858–1871* (Princeton, Princeton University Press, 1972)
Hannerz, U, *Transnational Connections. Culture, People, Places* (London, Routledge, 1996)
Hansen, L, 'Sustaining Sovereignty. The Danish Approach to Europe', in L Hansen and O Wæver (eds), *European Integration and National Identity. The Challenge of the Nordic States* (New York, Routledge, 2002) 50–87

Happacher, E, 'Der italienische Verfassungsgerichtshof und das Vorabentschei dungsverfahren gemäß Art. 234 EGV: neue Entwicklungen' (2009) 22 *Jahrbuch für Italienisches Recht* 149–62
Harmathy, A, 'A Survey of the History of Civil and Commercial Law', in A Harmathy (ed), *Introduction to Hungarian Law* (The Hague, Kluwer, 1998) 11–21
Hartkamp, A, Hesselink, MW, Hondius, EW, Mak, C and du Perron, E (eds), *Towards a European Civil Code. Fourth and Expanded Edition* (The Hague, Kluwer Law International, 2011)
Hayek, FA von, 'The Use of Knowledge in Society' (1945) 35 *American Economic Review* 519–30
——, *Law, Legislation and Liberty. Vol 2. The Mirage of Social Justice* (London, Routledge & Kegan Paul, 1976)
——, *Law, Legislation and Liberty. Vol 3. The Political Order of a Free People* (London, Routledge & Kegan Paul, 1979)
——, *The Road to Serfdom* (London, Routledge, 2007)
——, *The Constitution of Liberty* (London and New York, Routledge, 2009)
Hayes, CJH, *Essays on Nationalism* (New York, Reiss, 1966)
Hart, HLA, *The Concept of Law* (Oxford, Clarendon Press, 1961)
——, 'Bentham and the Demystification of the Law' (1973) 36 *The Modern Law Review* 2–17
Hattenhauer, H, *Thibaut und Savigny: Ihre programmatischen Schriften* (Munich, Vahlen, 1973)
Hearn, J, *Rethinking Nationalism. A Critical Introduction* (London, Palgrave Macmillan, 2006)
Hedemann, J, Lehmann, H and Siebert, W, *Volksgesetzbuch: Grundregeln und Buch I: Entwurf und Erläuterungen* (München, Beck, 1942)
Hegel, GWF, *Elements of the Philosophy of Right* [1820] English translation, edited by A Wood and HB Nisbet (Cambridge, Cambridge University Press, 1991)
——, *Vorlesungen über die Philosophie der Geschichte* [1837] vol 12 (Frankfurt am Main, Suhrkamp, 1970)
Heidemann, M, 'International Commercial Harmonisation and National Resistance. The Development and Reform of Transnational Commercial Law and its Application within National Legal Culture' (2010) 21 *European Business Law Review* 227–44
Heiderhoff, B, *Gemeinschaftsprivatrecht* (München, Sellier, 2007)
Heine, H, *Sämmtliche Werke*, vol 5 (Hamburg, Hoffmann und Campe, 1867)
Herr, F, *Der Glaube des Adolf Hitler. Anatomie einer politischen Religiosität*, (München, Bechtle, 1968)
Hespanha, AM, *Introduzione alla storia del diritto europeo* (Bologna, il Mulino, 2003)
Hesselink, MW, *The New European Legal Culture* (Deventer, Kluwer, 2001)
——, *Contractenrecht in perspectief* (The Hague, Boom Juridische uitgevers, 2004)
——, 'The Politics of a European Civil Code' (2004) 10 *European Law Journal* 675–97
——, 'Case Note to ECJ—Freiburger Kommunalbauten v Hofstetter' (2006) 3 *European Review of Contract Law* 366–75
——, 'The Ideal of Codification and the Dynamics of Europeanisation: The Dutch Experience' (2006) 12 *European Law Journal* 279–305
——, *CFR & Social Justice. A short study for the European Parliament on the values underlying the draft Common Frame of Reference for European private law: what roles for fairness and social justice?* (Munich, Sellier, 2008)

——, 'A Spontaneous Order for Europe? Why Hayek's Libertarianism Is Not the Right Way Forward for European Private Law', in H-W Micklitz and F Cafaggi (eds), *European Private Law after the Common Frame of Reference* (Cheltenham, Edward Elgar Publishing, 2010) 123–46

——, 'If You Don't Like our Principles We Have Others. On Core Values and Underlying Principles in European Private Law: A Critical Discussion of the New "Principles" Section in the Draft Common Frame of Reference', in R Brownsword, H-W Micklitz, L Niglia and S Weatherill (eds), *The Foundations of European Private Law* (Oxford, Hart Publishing, 2011) 59–71

——, 'The New European Legal Culture—Ten Years On' (2011) *Centre for the Study of European Contract Law Working Paper* 1–6

——, 'An Optional Instrument on EU Contract Law: Can it Increase Legal Certainty and Foster Cross-border Trade?', in MW Hesselink, A van Hoek, M Loos and A Salomons (eds), *Groenboek Europees contractenrecht: naar een optioneel instrument?* (Den Haag, Boom, 2011) 9–23

——, 'The Case for a Common European Sales Law in an Age of Rising Nationalism' (2012) 8 *European Review of Contract Law* 342–66

Hobsbawm, EJ, *The Age of Capital. 1848–1875* (London, Weidenfeld and Nicolson, 1975)

——, 'Introduction: Inventing Traditions', in EJ Hobsbawm and Ranger, T (eds), *The Invention of Tradition* (Cambridge, Cambridge University Press, 1983) 3–14

——, *Nations and Nationalism since 1780. Programme, Myth, Reality* (Cambridge, Cambridge University Press 1990)

Hobsbawm, EJ and Ranger, T (eds), *The Invention of Tradition* (Cambridge, Cambridge University Press, 1983)

Hofstede, G, *Culture's Consequences: International Differences in Work-Related Values* (London, Sage, 1980)

——, 'Commentaar naar aanleiding van JTh Leerssen, "Over nationale identiteit"' (1989) 16 *Theoretische geschiedenis* 360–65

——, 'Dimensions Do Not Exist: A Reply to Brendan McSweeney' (2002) 55 *Human Relations* 1355–61

——, *Culture's Consequences: Comparing Values, Behaviors, Institutions, and Organizations Across Nations* (London, Sage, 2003)

Hofstede, G and Hofstede, GJ, *Cultures and Organizations. Software of the Mind* (New York, McGraw-Hill, 2005)

Hoggart, R and Johnson, D, 'Ideas About an "Idea of Europe"', in C Joyce (ed), *Questions of Identity: A Selection from the Pages of* New European (London, IB Tauris & Co, 1988) 93–100

Holmes, S and Sunstein, CR, *The Cost of Rights. Why Liberty Depends on Taxes* (New York, Norton, 1999)

Horstmann, R-P, 'Hegels Theorie der bürgerlichen Gesellschaft', in L Siep (ed), *GWF Hegel. Grundlinien der Philosophie des Rechts* (Berlin, Akademie Verlag, 2005) 193–216

Hroch, M, 'From National Movement to the Fully-formed Nation' (1993) 198 *New Left Review* 3–20

——, *Das Europa der Nationen. Die moderne Nationsbildung im europäischen Vergleich* (Göttingen, Vandenhoeck & Ruprecht, 2005)

Hublet, C, 'The Scope of Article 12 of the Treaty of the European Communities *vis-à-vis* Third-Country Nationals: Evolution at Last?' (2009) 15 *European Law Journal* 757–74

Hume, D, *An Enquiry Concerning the Principles of Morals* [1751] (La Salle, Open Court, 1966)

Huntington, SP, *The Clash of Civilizations and the Remaking of World Order* (New York, Simon & Schuster, 1996)
——, 'Foreword. Cultures Count', in LE Harrison and SP Huntington (eds), *Culture Matters. How Values Shape Human Progress* (New York, Basic Books, 2000) XIII–XVI
Hurka, T, 'The Justification of National Partiality', in R McKim and J McMahan (eds), *The Morality of Nationalism* (Oxford, Oxford University Press, 1997)
Ignatieff, M, *Blood and Belonging: Journeys into the New Nationalism* (London, Vintage, 1994)
Ilumoka, AO, 'Legal Imperialism and Chauvinism: Lessons from Africa', in *Impérialisme et chauvinisme juridiques/Imperialism and Chauvinism in the Law* (Geneve, Schulthesse, 2004) 39–54
Ingersoll, HH, 'Some Anomalies of Practice' (1892) 1 *The Yale Law Journal* 89–94
Inglehart, R and Baker, WE, 'Modernization, Cultural Change, and the Persistence of Traditional Values' (2000) 65 *American Sociological Revue* 19–51
Irti, N, *L'età della decodificazione* (Milano, Giuffrè, 1979)
——, *Codice civile e società politica* (Roma, Laterza, 2004)
Jachtenfuchs, M, *Die Konstruktion Europas. Verfassungsideen und institutionelle Entwicklung* (Baden-Baden, Nomos-Verlag, 2002)
Jakobs, HH, 'Karl Larenz und der Nationalsozialismus' (1993) 17 *Juristen Zeitung* 805–15
James Gregor, A, *Mussolini's Intellectuals. Fascist Social and Political Thought* (Princeton, Princeton University Press, 2005)
Jansen, N, *Binnenmarkt, Privatrecht und europäische Identität* (Tübingen, Mohr Siebeck, 2004)
——, 'Das gelehrte Recht und der Staat', in R Zimmermann (ed), *Globalisierung und Entstaatlichung des Rechts. Teilband II. Nichtstaatliches Privatrecht: Geltung und Genese* (Tübingen, Mohr Siebeck, 2008) 159–86
Jayme, E, *Pasquale Stanislao Mancini. Internationales Privatrecht zwischen Risorgimento und praktischer Jurisprudenz* (Ebelsbach, Verlag Rolf Gremer, 1980)
Jennings, WI, *The Approach to Self-Government* (Cambridge, Cambridge University Press, 1956)
Jhering, R von, *Geist des römischen Rechts auf den verschiedenen Stufen seiner Entwicklung* [1852] (Leipzig, Breitkopf & Härtel, 1907)
Joerges, C and Singh, N (eds), *Darker Legacies of Law in Europe. The Shadow of National Socialism and Fascism over Europe and its Legal Traditions* (Oxford, Hart Publishing, 2003)
Joerges, C and Schmid, C, 'Towards Proceduralization of Private Law in the European Multi-Level System', in A Hartkamp, MW Hesselink, EW Hondius, C Mak and E du Perron (eds), *Towards a European Civil Code. Fourth and Expanded Edition* (The Hague, Kluwer Law International, 2011) 277–309
Kahn, PW, *The Cultural Study of Law. Reconstructing Legal Scholarship* (Chicago, University of Chicago Press, 1999)
Kapferer, B, *Legends of People, Myths of State: Violence, Intolerance, and Political in Sri Lanka and Australia* (Washington, Smithsonian, 1998)
Katz, J, *From Prejudice to Destruction: Anti-Semitism, 1700–1933* (Cambridge MA, Harvard University Press 1980)
Kautsky, K, 'Nationality and Internationality' (2009) 37 *Critique. Journal of Socialist Theory* 371–89
Kedourie, E, *Nationalism* (New York, Frederick A Praeger Publisher, 1962)
Keitner, CI, *The Paradoxes of Nationalism. The French Revolution and Its Meaning for Contemporary Nation Building* (Albany, University of New York Press, 2007)

Kennedy, D, 'Thoughts on Coherence, Social Values and National Tradition in Private Law', in MW Hesselink (ed), *The Politics of a European Civil Code* (The Hague, Kluwer, 2006) 9–31

Keohane, RO, 'Ironies of Sovereignty: The European Union and the United States', in JHH Weiler, I Begg and J Peterson (eds), *Integration in an Expanding European Union. Reassessing the Fundamentals* (Oxford, Blackwell, 2003) 308–29

Kilbride, JE and Yarczower, M, 'Ethnic Bias in the Recognition of Facial Expressions: A Cross-cultural Comparison Between Zambia and the United States' (1983) 8 *Journal of Nonverbal Behavior* 27–41

Kilpatrick, C, 'Community or Community of Courts in European Integration? Sex Equality Dialogues between UK Courts and the ECJ' (1998) 4 *European Law Journal* 121–47

Kimminich, O, *Deutsche Verfassungsgeschichte* (Baden-Baden, Nomos, 1987)

Kochenov, D, 'Mevrouw De Jong Gaat Eten: EU Citizenship and the Culture of Prejudice' (2011) *EUI Robert Schuman Centre for Advanced Studies Working Paper No. 2011/06* 1–21

Kohn, H, *Nationalism: Its Meaning and History* (Princeton, Van Nostrand, 1965)

——, *The Idea of Nationalism: A Study in its Origins and Background* (New York, Macmillan, 1967)

Kokott, J, 'Report on Germany', in A-M Slaughter, A Stone Sweet and JHH Weiler (eds), *The European Courts and National Courts—Doctrine and Jurisprudence. Legal Change in its Social Context* (Oxford, Hart Publishing, 1998) 77–131

Koschaker, P, *Europa und das römische Recht* (München, Biederstein Verlag, 1947)

Kötz, H, 'Rechtsvereinheitlichung—Nutzen, Kosten, Methoden, Ziele' (1986) 50 *Rabels Zeitschrift für ausländisches und internationales Privatrecht* 1–7

——, 'The Jurisdiction of Choice: England and Wales or Germany?' (2010) 6 *European Review of Private Law* 1243–57

Kramer, EA, *Europäische Privatrechtsvereinheitlichung. Institutionen, Methoden, Perspektiven* (Saarbrücken, Europa-Institut der Universität des Saarlandes, 1988)

Kumm, M, 'Why Europeans Will Not Embrace Constitutional Patriotism' (2008) 6 *International Journal of Constitutional Law* 117–36

——, 'How Does European Union Law Fit into the World of Public Law? Costa, Kadi and Three Conceptions of Public Law' (2011) *New York University Public Law and Legal Theory Working Papers. Paper 262* 1–37

Kymlicka, W, 'Misunderstanding Nationalism', in R Beiner (ed), *Theorizing Nationalism* (Albany NY, State University of New York Press, 1999) 131–40

——, *Contemporary Political Philosophy. An Introduction* (Oxford, Oxford University Press, 2002)

Lando, O, 'The Principles of European Contract Law and the Lex Mercatoria', in J Basedow (ed), *Private Law in the International Arena/Privatrecht in der internationalen Arena. Liber Amicorum Kurt Siehr* (The Hague, TMC Asser Press, 2000) 391–404

——, 'Can Europe Build Unity of Civil Law whilst Respecting Diversity?' (2006) *Europa & diritto privato* 1–18

Lando, O and Beale, H, *Principles of European Contract Law. Pt I and II. Combined and Revised* (The Hague, Kluwer Law International, 2000)

——, *Principles of European Contract Law. Pt III* (The Hague, Kluwer Law International, 2003)

La Porta, R, Lopez-de-Silanes, F, Shleifer, A and Vishny, RW, 'Legal Determinants of External Finance' (1997) 52 *Journal of Finance* 1131–50

Larenz, K, *Deutsche Rechtserneuerung und Rechtsphilosophie* (Tübingen, Mohr, 1934)

——, 'Rechtsperson und subjektives Recht', in G Dahm, ER Huber and K Larenz, *Grundfragen der neuen Rechtswissenschaft* (Berlin, Junker und Dünnhaupt, 1935) 225–60

Laski, HJ, *Studies in the Problem of Sovereignty* (New Haven, Yale University Press, 1917)

Legrand, P, 'European Legal Systems Are Not Converging' (1996) 45 *International and Comparative Law Quarterly* 52–81

——, 'Against a European Civil Code' (1997) 60 *The Modern Law Review* 44–63

——, 'The Impossibility of Legal Transplants' (1997) 4 *Maastricht Journal of European and Comparative Law* 111–24

——, 'On the Unbearable Localness of the Law: Academic Fallacies and Unseasonable Observations' (2002) 1 *European Review of Private Law* 61–76

——, 'The Same and the Different', in P Legrand and R Munday (eds), *Comparative Legal Studies: Traditions and Transitions* (Cambridge, Cambridge University Press, 2003) 240–311

——, 'A Diabolical Idea', in A Hartkamp, MW Hesselink, E Hondius, C Joustra, E du Perron and M Veldman (eds), *Towards a European Civil Code. Third Fully Revised and Expanded Edition* (The Hague, Kluwer Law International, 2004) 245–72

——, 'Antivonbar' (2005) 1 *Journal of Comparative Law* 13–40

Leerssen, J, 'Over nationale identiteit' (1988) 15 *Theoretische geschiedenis* 417–29

——, 'Culturele verschillen en nationale ideologieën: een naschrift' (1989) 16 *Theoretische geschiedenis* 361–65

——, 'The Rhetoric of National Character: A Programmatic Survey' (2000) 21 *Poetics Today* 267–92

——, *National Thought in Europe. A Cultural History* (Amsterdam, Amsterdam University Press, 2006)

——, 'Imagology: History and Method', in M Beller and J Leerssen (eds), *Imagology. The Cultural Construction and Literary Representation of National Characters. A Critical Survey* (Amsterdam, Rodopi, 2007) 17–32

——, 'Feminien en klagen, dat is twee keer hetzelfde zeggen' *NRC Handelsblad/Opinie & Debate* 21 November 2009

Leible, S, 'Marktintegration und Privatrechtsvereinheitlichung. Notwendigkeit und Grenzen', in A Furrer (ed), *Europäisches Privatrecht im wissenschaftlichen Diskurs* (Bern, Stämpfli, 2006) 5–77

——, 'Non-Discrimination' (2006) 6 *ERA-Forum Special Issue on European Contract Law—Developing the Principles for a 'Common Frame of Reference' for European Contract Law* 76–89

Lenin, VI, *Imperialism, the Highest Stage of Capitalism: A Popular Outline* [1917] English translation (London, Lawrence & Wishart, 1948)

——, *Collected Works*, vol 20 (Moscow, Progress Publishers, 1972)

Leoni, B, *Il problema della scienza giuridica* (Torino, Giappichelli, 1940)

Lequette, Y, 'Le Code européen est de retour' (2011) 3 *Revue des contrats* 1028–44

Lokin, JHA and Zwalve, WJ, *Hoofdstukken uit de Europese codificatiegeschiedenis* (The Hague, Boom, 2006) 271–310

Łopatka, A, 'Cultural Diversity and Cultural Human Rights', in G Doeker-Mach and KA Ziegert (eds), *Law and Legal Culture in Comparative Perspective* (Stuttgart, Franz Steiner Verlag, 2004) 216–21

Low, G, 'The (Ir)Relevance of Harmonization and Legal Diversity to European Contract Law: A Perspective from Psychology' (2010) 18 *European Review of Private Law* 285–307

Lurger, B, 'The "Social" Side of Contract Law and the New Principle of Regard and Fairness', in A Hartkamp, MW Hesselink, EW Hondius, C Mak and E du Perron (eds), *Towards a European Civil Code. Fourth and Expanded Edition* (The Hague, Kluwer Law International, 2011) 353–86

——, 'The Common Frame of Reference/Optional Code and the Various Understandings of Social Justice in Europe', in T Wilhelmsson, E Paunio and A Pohjolainen (eds), *Private Law and the Many Cultures of Europe* (Alphen aan den Rijn, Kluwer Law International, 2007) 177–99

MacIntyre, A, *After Virtue: A Study in Moral Philosophy* (Notre Dame, University of Notre Dame Press, 1981)

——, *Is Patriotism a Virtue?* (Lawrence, University Press of Kansas, 1984)

Mährlein, C, *Volksgeist und Recht. Hegels Philosophie der Einheit und ihre Bedeutung in der Rechtswissenschaft* (Würzburg, Königshausen und Neumann, 2000)

Maine, HS, *Ancient Law: Its Connection with the Early History of Society, and its Relation to Modern Ideas* (New York, Charles Scribner & Co, 1867)

Mak, C, 'Harmonising Effects of Fundamental Rights in European Contract Law' (2006) 1 *Erasmus Law Review* 59–79

——, *Fundamental Rights in European Contract Law. A Comparison of the Impact of Fundamental Rights on Contractual Relationships in Germany, the Netherlands, Italy and England* (Alphen aan den Rijn, Kluwer Law International, 2008)

——, 'The Constitutional Momentum of European Contract Law. On the Interpretation of the DCFR in Light of Fundamental Rights' (2009) 17 *European Review of Private Law* 513–30

Mancini, PS, *Della nazionalità come fondamento del diritto delle genti* [1851] (Torino, Giappichelli, 1994)

——, *Diritto internazionale. Prelezioni con un saggio sul Machiavelli* (Napoli, Marghieri, 1873)

Markesinis, BS, 'Why a Code is Not the Best Way to Advance the Cause of European Legal Unity' (1997) 5 *European Review of Private Law* 519–24

Markham, R and Wang, L, 'Recognition of Emotion by Chinese and Australian Children' (1996) 27 *Journal of Cross-Cultural Psychology* 616–43

Martin, K, *French Liberal Thought in the Eighteenth Century* (London, Phoenix House, 1962)

Marx, AW, *Faith in Nation: Exclusionary Origins of Nationalism* (Oxford, Oxford University Press, 2003)

Marx, K and Engels, F, *Werke*. Vol 13 (Berlin, Karl Dietz Verlag, 1971)

——, *Werke*. Vol 1 (Berlin, Karl Dietz Verlag, 1988)

Masferrer, A, 'Defense of the Common Law against Postbellum American Codification: Reasonable and Fallacious Argumentation' (2008–10) 50 *The American Journal of Legal History* 355–431

Mäsh, G, 'Le droit communautaire des contrats et son influence sur le droit national des Etats membres', in G Mäsh, D Mazeaud and R Schulze (eds), *Nouveaux défis du droit des contrats en France et en Europe* (Munich, Sellier, 2009) 17–28

Mattei, U, 'Why the Wind Changed. Intellectual Leadership in Western Law' (1995) 42 *American Journal of Comparative Law* 195–218

——, 'Hard Minimal Code Now: A Critique of "Softness" and a Plea for Responsibility in the European Debate over Codification', in S Grundmann and J Stuyck (eds), *An Academic Green Paper on European Contract Law* (The Hague, Kluwer Law International, 2002) 215–34

——, 'The Comparative Law and Economics Approach to the European Civil Code. An Introduction', in U Mattei, *The European Codification Process. Cut and Paste* (The Hague, Kluwer Law International, 2003) 1–28

——, 'The Professional Project. Scholars', in U Mattei, *The European Codification Process. Cut and Paste* (The Hague, Kluwer Law International, 2003) 29–66

——, 'Perché il piano d'azione privilegia i poteri forti. Critica della retorica *soft*', in M Meli and MR Maugeri (eds), *L'armonizzazione del diritto privato europeo. Il piano d'azione 2003* (Milano, Giuffrè, 2004) 3–22

Mattei, U and Di Robilant, A, 'The Art and Science of Critical Scholarship. Post-modernism and International Style in the Legal Architecture of Europe' (2002) 10 *European Review of Private Law* 29–59

Mayall, J, *Nationalism and International Society* (Cambridge, Cambridge University Press, 1990)

McCormick, J, *Europeanism* (Oxford, Oxford University Press, 2010)

McCorquodale, R, 'Self-Determination: A Human Rights Approach' (1994) 43 *International and Comparative Law Quarterly* 857–85

McKay, D, *Federalism and the European Union* (Oxford, Oxford University Press, 1999)

McKendrick, E, *The Creation of a European Law of Contracts. The Role of Standard Form Contracts and Principles of Interpretation* (Deventer, Kluwer, 2004)

McMahan, J, 'The Limits of National Partiality', in R McKim and J McMahan (eds), *The Morality of Nationalism* (Oxford, Oxford University Press, 1997) 107–38

McSweeney, B, 'Hofstede's Model of National Cultural Differences and Their Consequences: A Triumph of Faith—A Failure of Analysis' (2002) 55 *Human Relations* 89–118

——, 'The Essentials of Scholarship: A Reply to Geert Hofstede' (2002) 55 *Human Relations* 1363–72

McWhinney, E, 'Re-thinking Federal Constitutional Law Theory: The Contemporary Limits of Classical, Juridical Federalism' in *Toward Comparative Law in the 21st Century. The 50th Anniversary of the Institute of Comparative Law in Japan* (Tokyo, Chuo University Press, 1998) 487–97

Melucci, A and Diani, M, Nazioni senza stato. I movimenti etnico-nazionali in Occidente (Milan, Feltrinelli, 1992)

Mengoni, L, *L'Europa dei codici o un codice per l'Europa?* (Roma, Centro di studi e ricerche di diritto comparato e straniero: saggi, conferenze e seminari, 1992)

Michaels, R, 'Rechtskultur', in J Basedow, K Hopt and R Zimmermann (eds), *Handwörterbuch des Europäischen Privatrechts. Band II* (Tübingen, Mohr/Siebeck, 2009) 1255–59

——, 'Code vs Code. Nationalist and Internationalist Images of the Code Civil in the French Resistance to a European Codification' (2012) 8 *European Review of Contract Law* 277–95

Michelmann, F, 'Morality, Identity and "Constitutional Patriotism"' (2001) 14 *Ratio Juris* 253–71

Micklitz, H-W, 'The Visible Hand of European Regulatory Private Law. The Transformation of European Private Law from Autonomy to Functionalism in Competition and Regulation' (2009) 28 *Yearbook of European Law* 3–60

——, 'Failure or Ideological Preconceptions—Thoughts on Two Grand Projects: The European Constitution and the European Civil Code' (2010) *EUI Working Paper* 2010/4 1–25

——, 'Introduction. Social Justice and Access Justice in Private Law', in H-W Micklitz (ed), *The Many Concepts of Social Justice in European Private Law* (Northampton MA, Edward Elgar Publishing, 2011) 3–57

——, (ed), *The Many Concepts of Social Justice in European Private Law* (Northampton MA, Edward Elgar Publishing, 2011)

Mikkeli, H, *Europe as an Idea and an Identity* (Basingstoke, Palgrave, 1998)

Miklós, A, 'Nationalist Criticisms of Cosmopolitan Justice' (2009) 1 *Public Reason* 105–24

Milhaupt, CJ, 'Beyond Legal Origin: Rethinking Law's Relationship to the Economy: Implications for Policy' (2009) 57 *American Journal of Comparative Law* 831–45

Mill, JS, *Considerations on Representative Government* [1861] (New York, Harper & Brothers Publishers, 1867)

Miller, D, *On Nationality* (Oxford, Clarendon Press, 1995)

——, *Citizenship and National Identity* (Cambridge, Polity Press, 2000)

——, *Principles of Social Justice* (Cambridge MA, Harvard University Press, 2003)

——, *National Responsibility and Global Justice* (Oxford, Oxford University Press, 2007)

Molengraaff, WLPA, 'De dageraad van het wereldrecht' (1899) 63 *De Gids* 89–113

Monateri, PG, 'Black Gaius: A Quest for the Multicultural Origins of the "Western Legal Tradition"' (2000) 51 *Hastings Law Journal* 479–564

Montesquieu, C-L de, *De l'esprit des loix*, vol 2 [1748] (London, 1777)

Montmorency, JEG de, 'Savigny', in J MacDonell and E Manson (eds), *Great Jurists of the World* (London, John Murray, 1913)

Moreau, JN, *Exposition et défense de notre constitution monarchique française*, vol 2 (Paris, Moutard, 1789)

Morrison, M, Tay, L and Diener, E, 'Subjective Well-Being and National Satisfaction: Findings From a Worldwide Survey' (2011) 22 *Pyschological Science* 166–71

Muir Watt, H, 'Private International Law Beyond the Schism' (2011) 2 *Transnational Legal Theory* 347–427

Mulhall S and Swift, A, *Liberals and Communitarians* (Malden, Blackwell Publishing, 2007)

Müller, J, 'A General Theory of Constitutional Patriotism' (2008) 6 *International Journal of Constitutional Law* 72–95

Müller-Graff, P, 'Common Private Law in the European Community', in B de Witte and C Forder (eds), *The Common Law of Europe and the Future of Legal Education* (Deventer, Kluwer, 1992) 239–54

Nairn, T, *The Break-up of Britain* (London, Verso, 1981)

——, *Forces of Nationalism: Janus Revisited* (London, Verso, 1997)

Nelken, D, 'Towards a Sociology of Legal Adaption', in D Nelken and J Feest (eds), *Adapting Legal Cultures* (Oxford, Hart Publishing, 2001) 7–54

——, 'Legal Culture', in JM Smits (ed), *Elgar Encyclopedia of Comparative Law* (Cheltenham, Edward Elgar Publishing, 2006) 372–381

Neves, M, *Transconstitutionalism* (Oxford, Hart Publishing, 2013)

Niglia, L, 'The Non-Europeanisation of Private Law' (2001) 4 *European Review of Private Law* 575–99

Nussbaum, M, 'Patriotism and Cosmopolitanism', in J Cohen (ed), *For Love of Country: Debating the Limits of Patriotism* (Boston, Beacon Press, 1996) 3–17

——, *Women and Human Development. The Capabilities Approach* (Cambridge, Cambridge University Press, 2000)

Oates, WE, *Fiscal Federalism* (New York, Harcourt Bruce Jovanovich, 1972)

——, 'An Essay on Fiscal Federalism' (1999) 37 *The Journal of Economic Literature* 1120–49

Ogus, A, 'Competition between National Legal Systems: A Contribution of Economic Analysis of Comparative Law' (1999) 48 *International and Comparative Law Quarterly* 405–18

——, 'The Contribution of Economic Analysis of Law to Legal Transplants', in JM Smits (ed), *The Contribution of Mixed Legal Systems to European Private Law* (Antwerp, Intersentia, 2001) 27–38

Orgad, L, '"Cultural Defense" of Nations: Cultural Citizenship in France, Germany and the Netherlands' (2009) 15 *European Law Journal* 719–37

Ortega y Gasset, J, *The Revolt of the Masses* (New York, Mentor, 1950)

Ousselin, E, 'Victor Hugo's European Utopia' (2006) 34 *Nineteenth-Century French Studies* 32–43

Özkırımlı, U, *Theories of Nationalism. A Critical Introduction* (New York, Saint Martin's Press, 2000)

Pagano, U, 'Can Economics Explain Nationalism?', in A Breton, G Galeotti and R Wintrobe (eds), *Nationalism and Rationality* (Cambridge, Cambridge University Press, 1995) 173–203

Panebianco, M, 'La recente giurisprudenza comunitaria della Corte costituzionale', in *Studi in Onore di Modestino Acone*, vol I (Napoli, Jovene, 2010) 137–68

Papcke, S, 'Who Needs European Identity and What Could It Be?' in B Nelson, D Roberts and W Veit (eds), *The Idea of Europe. Problems of National and Transnational Identity* (New York, Berg, 1992) 61–74

Parekh, B, *A New Politics of Identity. Political Principles for an Interdependent World* (Basingstoke, Palgrave Macmillan, 2008)

Passerini, L, 'Introduzione. Dalle ironie dell'identità alle identità dell'ironia', in L Passerini (ed), *Identità culturale europea. Idee, sentimenti, relazioni* (Firenze, La Nuova Italia, 1998) 1–25

Pawlik, M, 'Hegels Kritik an der politischen Philosophie Jean-Jacques Rousseaus' (1999) 38 *Der Staat* 21–40

Pizzorusso, A, *Il patrimonio costituzionale europeo* (Bologna, il Mulino, 2002)

Plamenatz, J, 'Two Types of Nationalism', in E Kamenka (ed), *Nationalism: The Nature and Evolution of an Idea* (Canberra, Australian National University Press, 1976) 22–36

Planert, U, 'Wann beginnt der "modern" deutsche Nationalismus?' in J Echternkamp and SO Müller (eds), *Die Politik der Nation. Deutscher Nationalismus in Krieg und Krisen 1790 bis 1960* (München, Oldenbourg, 2002) 25–59

Pogge, TW, 'Priorities of Global Justice', in TW Pogge (ed), *Global Justice* (Oxford, Blackwell, 2001) 6–23

——, '"Assisting" the Global Poor', in DK Chatterjee (ed), *The Ethics of Assistance. Morality and the Distant Needy* (Cambridge, Cambridge University Press, 2004) 260–88

Polenz, P von, *Geschichte der deutschen Sprache* (Berlin, Walter de Gruyter, 2009)

Portalis, J-É-M, *Discours préliminaire du premier projet de code civil. Motifs et discours prononcés lors de la publication du code civil* [1801] (Bordeaux, Éditions Confluences, 2004)

——, 'Exposé des Motifs de la Loi relative à la Réunion des Lois civiles en un seul corps, sous le tire de *Code civil des Français*', in *Recueil complet des discours prononcés lors de la présentation du code civil, par les divers orateurs du conseil d'état et du tribunat, et discussion particulière de ces deux corps avant la rédaction définitive de chaque projet de loi. Tome I. Discours* [1804] (Paris, Firmin Didot Frères, 1838) 793–97

Proudhon, P-J, *Oeuvres Choisies* (Paris, Gallimard, 1967)

Puchta, GF, *Das Gewohnheitsrecht*, vol 1 (Erlangen, Palm, 1828)

——, *Cursus der Institutionen* [1841] (Leipzig, Breitkopf und Härtel, 1875)

Purnhagen, KP, 'The Architecture of Post-National European Contract Law from a Phenomenological Perspective—A Question of Institutions' (2011) *CSECL Working Paper 25* 1–19

Rachlinski, JJ, 'The Psychology of Conflict of Laws', in JM Smits (ed), *The Need for a European Contract Law. Empirical and Legal Perspectives* (Groningen, Europa Law Publishing, 2005) 96–120

Radbruch, G, 'Five Minutes of Legal Philosophy (1945)' English translation (2006) 26 *Oxford Journal of Legal Studies* 13–15

——, *Rechtsphilosophie* (Stuttgart, Koehler, 1973)

Raimondi, L, 'Cittadini dell'Unione europea in cerca di lavoro e principio di non discriminazione: osservazioni in margine alla sentenza *Vatsouras*' (2010) 2 *Il Diritto dell'Unione Europea* 443–62

Rawls, J, *Theory of Justice* (Cambridge MA, Harvard University Press, 1971)

——, *Political Liberalism* (New York, Columbia University Press, 1993)

——, *The Law of Peoples* (Cambridge MA, Harvard University Press, 1999)

Reding, V, 'Warum Europa ein optionales europäisches Vertragsrecht benötigt' (2011) 19 *Zeitschrift für Europäisches Privatrecht* 1–6

Reimann, M, 'The Historical School against Codification: Savigny, Carter, and the Defeat of the New York Civil Code' (1989) 37 *The American Journal of Comparative Law* 95–119

Renan, E, *Qu'est-ce qu'une nation?: Conférence faite en Sorbonne, le 11 mars 1882* (Paris, Calmann Lévy, 1882)

Rigaux, F, 'Nations et nationalismes au cours des deux derniers siècles', in H-P Mansel, T Pfeiffer, H Kronke, C Kohler and R Hausmann (eds), *Festschrift für Erik Jayme*, vol 2 (München, Sellier, 2004) 1201–15

Riker, WH, 'Federalism', in FI Greenstein and NW Polsby (eds), *The Handbook of Political Science. Vol V. Government Institution and Processes* (Reading MA, Addison-Wesley, 1975) 93–106

Risse, T, 'Sovereignty Puzzles: A Comment on Keohane', in JHH Weiler, I Begg and J Peterson (eds), *Integration in an Expanding European Union. Reassessing the Fundamentals* (Oxford, Blackwell, 2003) 335–39

——, *A Community of Europeans? Transnational Identities and Public Spheres* (New York, Cornell University Press, 2010)

Roberti, M, *Svolgimento storico del diritto privato in Italia*, vol 1 (Padova, Antonio Milani, 1935)

Robertson, R, 'After Nostalgia? Willful Nostalgia and the Phases of Globalization', in BS Turner (ed), *Theories of Modernity and Postmodernity* (London, Sage, 1990) 45–61

Rodotà, S, 'Un Codice per l'Europa? Diritti nazionali, diritto europeo, diritto globale', in P Cappellini and B Sordi (eds), *Codici. Una riflessione di fine millennio* (Milano, Giuffrè, 2002) 541–78

——, 'Il codice civile e il processo costituente europeo' (2005) 23 *Rivista critica del diritto privato* 21–33

Rösler, H, 'Schutz des Schwächeren im Europäischen Vertragsrecht. Typisierte und individuelle Unterlegenheit im Mehrebenenprivatrecht' (2009) 73 *Rabels Zeitschrift für ausländisches und internationales Privatrecht* 889–911

Roth, WH, 'Transposing "Pointilist" EC Guidelines into Systematic National Codes—Problems and Consequences' (2002) 6 *European Review of Private Law* 761–76

Rousseau, J-J, *Extrait du projet de paix perpétuelle de M. l'abbé de Saint-Pierre* (Paris, 1761)

——, *Considérations sur le gouvernement de Pologne, et sur sa réformation projetée* (Londres, 1782)

——, 'Discours sur l'économie politique' [1755] in *Œuvres de JJ Rousseau. Ouvrages de politique. Partie I* (Lyon, 1796) 261–343

——, *Du Contrat Social ou Principes du Droit politique* [1762] (Paris, Ernest Flammarion éditeur, 1910)

Russell, B, *Freedom and Organisation 1814–1914* (London, Allen & Unwin, 1934)

Rutgers, JW, 'The Draft Common Frame of Reference, Public Policy, Mandatory Rules and the Welfare State', in A Somma (ed), *The Politics of the Draft Common Frame of Reference* (Alphen aan den Rijn, Kluwer Law International, 2009) 115–28

——, 'Het (a)sociale gezicht van Europa: kanttekeningen bij het optioneel instrument', in MW Hesselink, A van Hoek, M Loos and A Salomons (eds), *Het Groenboek Europees contractenrecht: naar een optioneel instrument?* (The Hague, Boom, 2011) 125–32

Sacco, R, 'Formante', in *Digesto italiano. Discipline privatistiche. Sez. civ*, vol VIII (Torino, UTET, 1992) 438–42

——, *Sistemi giuridici comparati* (Torino, Giappichelli, 2002)

Salmon, T and Nicoll, W (eds), *Building European Union. A Documentary History and Analysis* (New York, Palgrave, 1997)

Sánchez Lorenzo, S, 'What Do We Mean When We Say "Folklore"? Cultural and Axiological Diversity as a Limit for a European Private Law' (2006) 2 *European Review of Private Law* 197–219

Sandel, MJ, *Liberalism and the Limits of Justice* (Cambridge, Cambridge University Press, 1982)

Savigny, FC von, *Vom Beruf unsrer Zeit für Gesetzgebung und Rechtswissenschaft* (Heidelberg, Mohr und Zimmer, 1814)

——, 'Über den Zweck dieser Zeitschrift' (1815) 1 *Zeitschrift für geschichtliche Rechtswissenschaft* 1–17

——, Of the Vocation of Our Age for Legislation and Jurisprudence (A Hayward trans London 1831 & Arno Press reprint 1975)

Schauer, F, *Profiles, Probabilities, and Stereotypes* (Cambridge MA, Harvard University Press, 2003)

Schendel, F van and Aronstein, I, 'Introduction: Euroscepticism and Multiculturalism' (2010) 6 *Utrecht Law Review* 1–7

Schermaier, MJ, 'Una superficiale e arbitraria modifica del BGB? Perché la riforma dello *Schuldrecht* si è rivelata un insuccesso' (2005) 9 *Contratto e impresa/Europa* 898–919

Schieder, T, *Staatensystem als Vormacht der Welt. 1848–1918* (Frankfurt am Main, Propyläen, 1977)

Schiek, D, Waddington, L and Bell, M, *Cases, Materials and Text on National, Supranational and International Non-Discrimination Law* (Oxford, Hart Publishing, 2007)

Schmitt, C, *Der Begriff des Politischen* [1932] (Berlin, Duncker & Humboldt, 2009)

——, *Die Lage der europäischen Rechtswissenschaft* (Tübingen, Internationaler Universitäts-Verlag, 1950)

Schnack, I and Schoof, W (eds), *Briefe der Brüder Grimm an Savigny aus dem Savignyschen Nachlaß* (Berlin, Erich Schmidt, 1953)

Schröder, J, 'Zur Vorgeschichte der Volksgeistlehre. Gesetzgebungs-und Rechtsquellentheorie im 17. und 18. Jahrhundert' (1992) 109 *Zeitschrift der Savigny-Stiftung für Rechtsgeschichte. Germanistische Abteilung* 1–47

Schroeder, K-P, *Vom Sachenspiegel zum Grundgesetz. Eine deutsche Rechtsgeschichte in Lebensbildern* (München, Beck, 2001)

Schubert, W, 'Das französische Recht in Deutschland zu Beginn der Restaurationszeit (1814–1820)' (1977) 94 *Zeitschrift der Savigny-Stiftung für Rechtsgeschichte. Germanistische Abteilung* 129–84

Schulte-Nölke, H, Twigg-Flesner, C and Ebbers, M, *EC Consumer Law Compendium. The Consumer* Acquis *and its Transposition in the Member States* (Munich, Sellier, 2008)

Schwarz, J, *Der Aufbau Europas. Pläne und Dokumente 1945–1980* (Bonn, Osang, 1980)

Schwarzmantel, J, *Socialism and the Idea of the Nation* (New York, Harvester Wheatsheaf, 1991)

Schwerin, C von, *Grundzüge der deutschen Rechtsgeschichte* (München-Leipzig, Duncker & Humblot, 1934)

Seers, D, *The Political Economy of Nationalism* (Oxford, Oxford University Press, 1983)

Sefton-Green, R, 'Social Justice and European Identity in European Contract Law' (2006) 2 *European Review of Contract Law* 275–86

——, 'Cultural Diversity and the Idea of a European Civil Code', in MW Hesselink, *The Politics of a European Civil Code* (The Hague, Kluwer Law International, 2006) 71–88

——, 'The European Union, Law and Society: Making the Societal–Cultural Difference', in T Wilhelmsson, E Paunio and A Pohjolainen (eds), *Private Law and the Many Cultures of Europe* (Alphen aan den Rijn, Kluwer Law International, 2007) 37–55

——, 'DCFR, the *Avant-projet* Catala and French Legal Scholars: A Story of Cat and Mouse?' (2008) 12 *Edinburgh Law Review* 351–73

——, 'Multiculturalism, Europhilia and Harmonization: Harmony or Disharmony?' (2010) 6 *Utrecht Law Review* 50–67

——, 'French and English Crypto-nationalism and European Private Law. An Exercise in Sentiment and Reason' (2012) 8 *European Review of Contract Law* 260–76

Sen, A, 'Justice across Borders', in P De Greiff and C Cronin (eds), *Global Justice and Transnational Politics* (Cambridge MA, The MIT Press, 2002) 37–51

——, *Identity and Violence. The Illusion of Destiny* (New York, Norton, 2006)

Seton-Watson, H, *Nations and States* (London, Methuen, 1977)

Shafer, BC, *Faces of Nationalism. New Realities and Old Myths* (New York, Harcourt Brace Jovanovich, 1972)

Siems, M, 'Statistische Rechtsvergleichung' (2008) 72 *Rabels Zeitschrift für ausländisches und internationales Privatrecht* 354–90

Silverman, M, *Deconstructing the Nation: Immigration, Racism and Citizenship in Modern France* (London, Routledge, 1992)

Smith, AD, *Nationalism in the Twentieth Century* (New York, University Press, 1979)
——, *Theories of Nationalism* (London, Duckworth, 1983)
——, *National Identity* (London, Penguin, 1991)
——, 'National Identity and the Idea of European Unity' (1992) 68 *International Affairs* 55–76
——, 'A Europe of Nations. Or the Nation of Europe?' (1993) 30 *Journal of Peace Research* 129–35
——, *Nations and Nationalism in a Global Era* (Cambridge, Polity Press, 1995)
——, *Nationalism and Modernism* (London, Routledge, 1998)
——, *Nationalism: Theory, Ideology, History* (Cambridge, Polity Press, 2001)
——, 'The Poverty of Anti-nationalist Modernism' (2003) 9 *Nations and Nationalism* 357–70
Smits, JM, *The Good Samaritan in European Private Law: On the Perils of Principles Without a Programme and a Programme for the Future* (Deventer, Kluwer, 2000)
——, 'Multiculturalisme en Europees privaatrecht: een pleidooi' (2000) 17 *Nederlands Tijdscrhift voor Burgerlijk Recht* 289–92
——, 'Towards a Multi-Layered Contract Law for Europe', in S Grundmann and J Stuyk (eds), *An Academic Green Paper on European Contract Law* (The Hague, Kluwer Law International, 2002) 387–98
——, *The Making of European Private Law: Toward a Ius Commune Europaeum as a Mixed Legal System* (Antwerp, Intersentia, 2002)
——,*The Need for a European Contract Law. Empirical and Legal Perspectives* (ed), (Groningen, Europa Law Publishing, 2005)
——, 'Legal Culture as Mental Software, or: How to Overcome National Legal Culture?', in T Wilhelmsson, E Paunio and A Pohjolainen (eds), *Private Law and the Many Cultures of Europe* (Alphen aan den Rijn, Kluwer Law International, 2007) 141–51
——, 'The Draft Common Frame of Reference, Methodological Nationalism and the Way Forward' (2008) 4 *European Review of Contract Law* 270–80
——, 'Human Dignity and Uniform Law: An Unhappy Relationship' (2008) *TICOM Working Paper 2008/2* 2–10
——, 'Beyond Euroscepticism: On the Choice of Legal Regimes as Empowerment of Citizens' (2010) 6 *Utrecht Law Review* 68–74
——, 'Democracy and (European) Private Law: A Functional Approach', in MG Faure and A van der Welt (eds), *Globalization and Private Law. The Way Forward* (Cheltenham, Edward Elgar Publishing, 2010) 15–31
Snijders, W, 'Building a European Contract Law: Five Fallacies and Two Castles in Spain' (2003) 7(4) *Electronic Journal of Comparative Law*
Snyder, LL, *The New Nationalism* (Ithaca NW, Cornell University Press, 1968)
Solari, G, *Socialismo e diritto privato. Influenza delle odierne dottrine socialiste sul diritto privato* [1906] (Milano, Giuffrè, 1980)
Somma, A, *Diritto comunitario vs. diritto comune europeo* (Torino, Giappichelli, 2003)
——, 'Buona fede contrattuale e gestione del conflitto sociale', in A D'Angelo, PG Monateri, and A Somma, *Buona fede e giustizia contrattuale: modelli cooperativi e modelli conflittuali a confronto* (Torino, Giappichelli, 2005) 75–121
——, *I giuristi e l'Asse culturale Roma-Berlino* (Frankfurt am Main, Klostermann, 2005)
——, 'Da Roma a Washington', in PG Monateri, T Giaro and A Somma, *Le radici comuni del diritto europeo. Un cambiamento di prospettiva* (Roma, Carocci, 2005) 169–239
Spencer, P and Wollman, H, *Nationalism: A Critical Introduction* (London, Sage, 2002)

Sperl, H, *Nationalismus, Internationalismus und Rechtsordnung* (Wien, Hölder, 1924)

Springer, R, *The National Problem* (Moscow, Obshchestvennaya Polza Publishing House, 1909)

Stalin, JV, *Marxism and the National Question* [1913] (Moscow, Foreign Languages Publishing House, 1947)

Sternberger, R, *Verfassungspatriotismus* (Hannover, Niedersächische Landeszentrale für politische Bildung, 1982)

Steunenberg, B and Voermans, WJM, *The Transposition of EC Directives: A Comparative Study of Instruments, Techniques and Processes in Six EU Member States* (Leiden University, Leiden/Research and Documentation Centre of the Ministry of Justice Paper, 2006)

Stoll, A, *Friedrich Karl von Savigny: Ein Bild seines Lebens mit einer Sammlung seiner Briefe. Bd 2: Professorenjahre in Berlin 1810–1842* (Köln, Heymann, 1929)

Stolleis, M, '"Fortschritte" der Rechtsgeschichte in der Zeit des Nationalsozialismus', in M Stolleis and D Simon (eds), *Rechtsgeschichte im Nationalsozialismus* (Tübingen, Mohr, 1989) 178–97

——, 'Vormodernes und postmodernes Recht' (2008) 37 *Quaderni fiorentini per la storia del pensiero giuridico moderno* 543–51

Stromberg, RN, *European Intellectual History since 1789* (Englewood Cliffs, Prentice Hall, 1981)

Study Group on Social Justice in European Private Law 'Social Justice in European Contract Law: A Manifesto' (2004) 10 *European Law Journal* 653–74

Szamueli, T, *The Russian Tradition* (London, Fontana, 1998)

Tamanaha, BZ, 'Understanding Legal Pluralism: Past to Present, Local to Global' (2008) 30 *Sydney Law Review* 375–411

Tamir, Y, *Liberal Nationalism* (Princeton, Princeton University Press, 1993)

Tan, K-C, 'Liberal Nationalism and Cosmopolitan Justice' (2002) 5 *Ethical Theory and Moral Practice* 431–61

Telders, BM, 'Nationalisme en internationalisme', in BM Telders, *Verzamelde geschriften* V ('s-Gravenhage, Nijhoff, 1949) 68–81

Templeton, AR, 'Human Races: A Genetic and Evolutionary Perspective' (1999) 100 *American Anthropologist* 632–50

Teresi, F, 'Finalmente inizia il dialogo tra la Corte costituzionale e la Corte europea [Nota a C. Cost. 15 aprile 2008, n. 102; ord. C. Cost. 15 aprile 2008, n. 103]' (2008) 17 *Nuove Autonomie* 129–33

Teubner, G, 'Legal Irritants: Good Faith in British Law or How Unifying Law Ends up in New Divergences' (1998) 61 *The Modern Law Review* 11–32

Thatcher M, 'The European Family of Nations' [1988] in M Holmes (ed), *The Eurosceptical Reader* (New York, Saint Martin's Press, 1996) 88–96

Thibaut, AFJ, *Über die Nothwendigkeit eines allgemeinen bürgerlichen Rechts für Deutschland* (Heidelberg, Mohr und Zimmer, 1814)

Thiesse, A-M, *La création des identités nationales: Europe XVIIIe-XXe siècle* (Paris, Éditions du Seuil, 1999)

Tiebout, C, 'A Pure Theory of Local Expenditures' (1956) 64 *Journal of Political Economy* 416–24

Torres Pérez, A, *Conflicts of Rights in the European Union. A Theory of Supranational Adjudication* (Oxford, Oxford University Press, 2009)

Trujillo, I, *Giustizia globale. Le nuove frontiere dell'eguaglianza* (Bologna, Il Mulino, 2007)

Ulmen, GL, 'The Plight of European Jurisprudence' (1990) 23 *Telos. A Quarterly Journal of Critical Thought* 35–70

Vacca, G, *Relazione ministeriale al Re sul codice civile del Regno d'Italia* (Torino, Stamperia Reale, 1866)

Vacca, L, 'Cultura giuridica e armonizzazione del diritto europeo', in O, Troiano, G Rizzielli and MN Miletti (eds), *Harmonisation Involves History? Il diritto privato europeo al vaglio della comparazione e della storia* (Milan, Giuffrè, 2004) 37–51

Varga, C, *Codification as a Socio-Historical Phenomenon* (Budapest, Akadémiai Kiadó, 1991)

Varul, P, 'The Creation of New Estonian Private Law' (2008) 1 *European Review of Private Law* 95–109

Vincent, A, 'Liberal Nationalism: An Irresponsible Compound?' (1997) 45 *Political Studies* 275–95

Vink, MP and de Groot, G-R, 'Birthright Citizenship. Trends and Regulations in Europe' (2010) *EUDO Citizenship Observatory* 1–36

Vogenauer, S, 'An Empire of Light? Learning and Lawmaking in the History of German Law' (2005) 64 *Cambridge Law Journal* 481–500

——, 'An Empire of Light? II Learning and Lawmaking in Germany Today' (2006) 26 *Oxford Journal of Legal Studies* 627–63

Wagner, G, 'The Economics of Harmonization: The Case of Contract Law' (2002) 39 *Common Market Law Review* 995–1023

——, 'The Virtues of Diversity in European Private Law', in JM Smits (ed), *The Need for a European Contract Law. Empirical and Legal Perspectives* (Groningen, Europa Law Publishing, 2005) 3–24

——, 'Economic Analysis of Cross-Border Legal Uncertainty. The Example of the European Union', in JM Smits (ed), *The Need for a European Contract Law. Empirical and Legal Perspectives* (Groningen, Europa Law Publishing, 2005) 27–51

Walicki, A, *The Enlightenment and the Birth of Modern Nationhood: Polish Political Thought from Noble Republicanism to Tadeusz Kosciuszko* (Notre Dame, University of Notre Dame Press, 1989)

Wallis, D, 'European Contract Law—The Way Forward: Political Context, Parliament's Preoccupations and Process' (2006) 6 *ERA-Forum Special Issue on European Contract Law—Developing the Principles for a 'Common Frame of Reference' for European Contract Law* 8–11

Walzer, M, *Spheres of Justice* (Oxford, Basic Books, 1983)

Watson, A, *Legal Transplants. An Approach to Comparative Law* (Edinburgh, Scottish Academic Press, 1974)

——, 'Legal Transplants and Law Reform' (1976) 92 *Law Quarterly Review* 79–84

——, 'Legal Transplants and European Private Law', in JM Smits (ed), *The Contribution of Mixed Legal Systems to European Private Law* (Antwerp, Intersentia, 2001) 15–26

Watts, RL, *New Federations: Experiments in the Commonwealth* (Oxford, Oxford University Press, 1966)

Weatherill, S, 'Why Object to the Harmonization of Private Law by the EC?' (2004) 5 *European Review of Private Law* 633–60

Weber, M, 'Politik als Beruf', in *Wissenschaft als Beruf, 1917/1919; Politik als Beruf, 1919* (Tübingen, Mohr Siebeck, 1994) 35–88

Wehler, H-U, *Nationalismus. Geschichte, Formen, Folgen* (München, Beck, 2001)
Weiler, JHH, 'The Transformation of Europe' (1991) 100 *The Yale Law Journal* 2403–83
——, 'To Be a European Citizen: Eros and Civilization', in JHH Weiler, *The Constitution of Europe. 'Do the New Clothes Have an Emperor?' and Other Essays on European Integration* (Cambridge, Cambridge University Press, 1999) 324–57
——, 'A Constitution for Europe? Some Hard Choices' (2004) 40 *Journal of Common Market Studies* 563–80
Weinreich, M, 'Der YIVO un di problemen fun undzer tsayt' (1945) 25 *YIVO Bletter* 3–18
Wieacker, F, *Privatrechtsgeschichte der Neuzeit unter besonderer Berücksichtigung der deutschen Entwicklung* (Göttingen, Vandenhoek & Ruprecht, 1952)
——, *Industriegesellschaft und Privatrechtsordnung* (Frankfurt am Main, Athenäum-Fischer-Taschenbuch-Verlag, 1974)
——, *A History of Private Law in Europe: With Particular Reference to Germany*, English translation (Oxford, Clarendon Press, 1995)
Wieland, CM, *Sämmtliche Werken*, vol 31 (Leipzig, Göschen, 1858)
Wilhelmsson, T, *Social Contract Law and European Integration* (Aldershot, Dartmouth, 1995)
——, 'Private Law in the EU: Harmonized or Fragmented Europeanisation?' (2002) 10 *European Review of Private Law* 77–94
——, 'Varieties of Welfarism in European Contract Law' (2004) 10 *European Law Journal* 712–33
——, 'Introduction: Harmonization and National Cultures', in T Wilhelmsson, E Paunio and A Pohjolainen (eds), *Private Law and the Many Cultures of Europe* (Alphen aan den Rijn, Kluwer Law International, 2007) 3–20
——, 'The Average Consumer: A Legal Fiction?', in T Wilhelmsson, E Paunio and A Pohjolainen (eds), *Private Law and the Many Cultures of Europe* (Alphen aan den Rijn, Kluwer Law International, 2007) 243–68
Williamson, D, 'Forward from a Critique of Hofstede's Model of National Culture' (2002) 55 *Human Relations* 1373–95
Wilterdink, N, 'The European Ideal: An Examination of European and National Identity' (1993) 34 *European Journal of Sociology* 119–36.
Wolf, E, *Grosse Rechtsdenker der deutschen Geistesgeschichte* (Tübingen, Mohr, 1963)
Wood, S, *Germany, Europe and the Persistence of Nations. Transformation, Interests and Identity, 1989–1996* (Aldershot, Ashgate, 1998)
Würtenberg, T, *Zeitgeist und Recht* (Tübingen, Mohr, 1987)
Xiaojing Xu, Xiangyu Zuo, Xiaoying Wang and Shihui Han, 'Do You Feel My Pain? Racial Group Membership Modulates Empathic Neural Responses' (2009) 29 *The Journal of Neuroscience* 8525–29
Yunus, M and Jolis, A, *Banker to the Poor: The Autobiography of Muhammad Yunus, Founder of the Grameen Bank* (London, Autum, 1998)
Zajtay, I, *Introduction à l'étude du droit hongrois. La formation historique du droit civil* (Paris, Libraire du Recueil Sirey, 1953)
Zelst, B van, *The Politics of European Sales Law. A Legal–Political Inquiry into the Drafting of the Uniform Commercial Code, the Vienna Sales Convention, the Dutch Civil Code and the European Consumer Sales Directive in the Context of the Europeanisation of Contract Law* (Alphen aan den Rijn, Kluwer Law International, 2008)
Ziller, J, *Il nuovo trattato europeo* (Bologna, il Mulino, 2007)

Zimmermann, R, '"Common law" und "civil law", Amerika und Europa', in R Zimmermann (ed), *Amerikanische Rechtskultur und europäisches Privatrecht* (Tübingen, Mohr Siebeck, 1995) 1–10

——, *The Law of Obligations. Roman Foundations of the Civilian Tradition* (Oxford, Clarendon Press, 1996)

——, 'Roman Law and the Harmonisation of Private Law in Europe', in A Hartkamp, MW Hesselink, EW Hondius, C Mak and E du Perron (eds), *Towards a European Civil Code. Fourth and Expanded Edition* (The Hague, Kluwer Law International, 2011) 27–54

——, '*Ius Commune* and the Principles of European Contract Law: Contemporary Renewal of an Old Idea', in HL MacQueen and R Zimmermann (eds), *European Contract Law: Scots and South African Perspectives* (Edinburgh, Edinburgh University Press, 2006) 1–42

Zitelmann, VE, *Die Möglichkeit eines Weltrechts* (München-Leipzig, Duncker & Humblot, 1916)

Zoppini, A, 'La concorrenza tra gli ordinamenti giuridici' in A Zoppini (ed), *La concorrenza tra ordinamenti giuridici* (Roma, Laterza, 2004) 5–40

Zweigert, K and Kötz, H, *Einführung in die Rechtsvergleichung auf dem Gebiete des Privatrechts* (Tübingen, Mohr, 1996)

Index

www.ingramcontent.com/pod-product-compliance
Lightning Source LLC
LaVergne TN
LVHW052247200926
848481LV00002B/303
* 9 7 8 1 5 0 9 9 0 7 4 1 0 *